W9-CEY-118

FEB 2001

LEGAL INFORMATION ONLINE ANYTIME

24 hours a day

www.nolo.com

AT THE NOLO.COM SELF-HELP LAW CENTER, YOU'LL FIND

- Nolo's comprehensive Legal Encyclopedia filled with plain-English information on a variety of legal topics
- Nolo's Law Dictionary—legal terms <u>without</u> the legalese
- Auntie Nolo—if you've got questions, Auntie's got answers
- The Law Store—over 250 self-help legal products including: Downloadable Software, Books, Form Kits and eGuides
- Legal and product updates
- Frequently Asked Questions
- NoloBriefs, our free monthly email newsletter
- Legal Research Center, for access to state and federal statutes
- Our ever-popular lawyer jokes

Quality LAW BOOKS & SOFTWARE FOR EVERYONE

Nolo's user-friendly products are consistently first-rate. Here's why:

- A dozen in-house legal editors, working with highly skilled authors, ensure that our products are accurate, up-to-date and easy to use
- We continually update every book and software program to keep up with changes in the law
- Our commitment to a more democratic legal system informs all of our work
- We appreciate & listen to your feedback. Please fill out and return the card at the back of this book.

OUR "NO-HASSLE" GUARANTEE

Return anything you buy directly from Nolo for any reason and we'll cheerfully re-fund your purchase price. No ifs, ands or buts.

An Important Message to Our Readers

This product provides information and general advice about the law. But laws and procedures change frequently, and they can be interpreted differently by different people. For
specific advice geared to your specific situation, consult an expert. No book, software or
other published material is a substitute for personalized advice from a knowledgeable
lawyer licensed to practice law in your state.

4th edition

Patent, Copyright & Trademark

By Attorney's Stephen Elias and Richard Stim

Edited by Beth McKenna

NOLO

Keeping Up to Date

To keep its books up-to-date, Nolo issues new printings and new editions periodically. New printings reflect minor legal changes and technical corrections. New editions contain major legal changes, major text additions or major reorganizations. To find out if a later printing or edition of any Nolo book is available, call Nolo at 510-549-1976 or check our website at www.nolo.com.

To stay current, follow the "Update" service at our website at www.nolo.com. In another effort to help you use Nolo's latest materials, we offer a 35% discount off the purchase of the new edition of your Nolo book when you turn in the cover of an earlier edition. (See the "Special Upgrade Offer" in the back of the book.)

This book was last revised in: JANUARY 2001.

FOURTH EDITION	JANUARY 2001
Editor	BETH MCKENNA
Illustrations	LINDA ALLISON & MARI STEIN
Book & Cover Design	TERRI HEARSH
Proofreading	KRISTIN BARENDSEN
Printing	BERTELSMAN SERVICES, INC.

Elias, Stephen.
   Patent, copyright & trademark / by Stephen Elias and Richard Stim. -- 4th ed.
     p. cm.
   Includes index.
   ISBN 0-87337-601-3
   1. Intellectual property--United States--Popular works. I. Title: Patent, copyright, and trademark. II. Stim, Richard III. Title.
KF2980.E44 2000
346.7304'8--dc21   00-040215

For information on bulk purchases or corporate premium sales, please contact the Special Sales Department. For academic sales or textbook adoptions, ask for Academic Sales. Call 800-955-4775 or write to Nolo.com, 950 Parker Street, Berkeley, CA 94710.

Acknowledgments

I dedicate this book to my uncle Paul and aunt Laverne, who taught me that curiosity is the best policy.

I wish to express my deepest gratitude to the following people:

Lisa Goldoftas and Ralph Warner, editors extraordinaire.

Terri Hearsh, who put the book together and made it beautiful.

Stephanie Harolde and Ling Yu, both of whom made sure the book works.

Steve Fishman, Kate McGrath and David Pressman, whose works and ideas are an integral part of the book in ways too diverse and numerous to mention.

All the wonderful folks at Nolo who contribute in so many ways to making a Nolo book all that it can be.

Catherine Jermany Elias, who is always there for me.

—S.E.

Table of Contents

Introduction

In simple terms, intellectual property is a product of the human intellect that has commercial value. Intellectual property encompasses a wide range of creations—from fiction, poetry, songs, designs and artwork to ads, product names, mechanical inventions, processes, chemical formulas, machines and software.

The commercial value of intellectual property comes from the ability of its owner to control its use. If the owner could not legally require payment in exchange for use, ownership of the intellectual property would have intellectual worth but no commercial value.

> **EXAMPLE 1:** Jayna writes a novel about romance in cyberspace. As the author/ owner, she has the legal right to prevent others from reprinting the book, making a movie or creating a television miniseries based on the novel. It is this right that can produce revenue for Jayna: she can sell publishing rights to a publisher, movie rights to a movie producer and television rights to a net- work in exchange for royalties based on book, movie and TV proceeds.

> **EXAMPLE 2:** Todd invents a process for inserting modified genes into cancer cells. He applies for and receives a patent, a monopoly awarded by the federal government that allows Todd to require anyone who wants to use the process to pay him a negotiated license fee. If no one wants to use the process, Todd won't make any money off it (unless he uses it in his own gene therapy clinic).

A. How Intellectual Property Law Works

Intellectual property law is an umbrella term for all the statutes, government regu- lations and court decisions that together determine who owns intellectual property and what rights go along with that ownership. In addition, intellectual property law specifies:

- the conditions under which intellectual property rights may be sold or loaned (licensed) to others for specific purposes
- how to settle contract disputes that arise from marketing intellectual property, and
- how to take advantage of government procedures and programs that establish or enhance protection of intellectual property rights.

Intellectual property law primarily offers protection to the owner of intellectual property by giving the owner the right to file a lawsuit asking a court to enforce whatever rights are being transgressed. As a result, some experts describe intellectual property laws as "affirmative rights" rather than as "protection." Noted patent attorney and author David Pressman suggests thinking of intellectual property laws as tools that can be used when needed, but not as any kind of defensive shield. In other words, intellectual property laws won't prevent someone from stepping on the owner's rights. But the laws do give an owner the ammunition to take a trespasser to court. For example, upon request of the copyright owner, a court will halt unauthorized copying of material protected by the copyright. But if the copyright owner does not sue the copier, no action will be taken and the copier will get away with this illegal behavior.

1. Types of intellectual property laws

Intellectual property law consists of several discrete legal categories. Although these categories can overlap with respect to a particular intellectual property, they each have their own characteristics and terminology.

- **Trade secret law** affords the owner of commercial information that provides a competitive edge the right to keep others from using such information if the information was improperly disclosed to or acquired by a competitor and the owner of the information took reasonable precautions to keep it secret.

- **Copyright law** protects all types of original creative expression, such as that produced by authors, composers, artists, designers, programmers and Web page designers. However, copyright law does not protect the ideas and concepts underlying an expressive work; it only protects the literal form the expressive work takes. For example, copyright protects the actual words used to write a novel about life on a submarine where the crew faces almost certain death because of damaged engines. But copyright won't prevent other writers from either writing novels about submarine life or using the same basic plot, as long as they don't copy the first novelist's literal expression. Copyright protection lasts a long time, often 100 years or more.

- **Trademark laws** protect the distinctive (unique, creative or well-known through use) names, designs, logos, slogans, symbols, colors, packaging, containers and any other devices that are used by businesses to identify the source of their goods and services, and distinguish them in the marketplace. This protection can last indefinitely.

- **Patent law** gives the inventor of a new and nonobvious invention the right to exclusive use of that invention for a limited term. How long the inventor retains the exclusive right depends on the kind of patent. A utility patent (the most common type of patent) goes into effect when issued by the U.S. Patent and Trademark Office and expires 20 years after the application for the patent was filed. A design patent (for an inventive but nonfunctional design) lasts 14 years after the date the patent issues. A plant patent expires 20 years from the date the patent was filed.

2. Unfair competition laws

Courts are frequently asked to intervene when one business uses unfair tactics to compete with another business. Among the unfair tactics the courts have condemned is a business trying to lure customers away from a competing business by confusing customers as to which business or products they are dealing with. The most common way to confuse customers is for a second business to market its goods or services under a name or other mark that is confusingly similar to that used by the first business on its goods or services.

Although courts originally decided these types of disputes without the benefit of a legislative enactment, Congress and most state legislatures have now legislated the basic principles developed by the courts to deal with unfair business practices. All together, these court decisions and statutes are termed unfair competition law. And under this body of law, a business may obtain a court order preventing a competitor from engaging in unfair business practices.

Unfair competition is not usually considered a separate branch of intellectual property law, as it targets general business practices rather than intellectual property as such. However, because the use of misleading names and marks to improperly lure customers away from another business is also very much what trademark law is concerned with, the two types of law often overlap.

> **EXAMPLE:** The name used by Joe's Pizza is very ordinary and not distinctive enough to be considered a trademark. If, however, another business opens up down the street under a "Joes's Pizza" sign, the courts may use unfair competition laws to force the second user to modify the name to distinguish it from the first.

3. International laws

Under a variety of treaties, most countries in the world offer protection to U.S. intellectual property used abroad. And under these same treaties, the U.S. protects intellectual property created in these other countries. Several major international treaties—the Berne Convention is the most important—govern rights in copyrights in most countries. International patent rights are broadly recognized under the Paris Convention and the Patent Cooperation Treaty. Trademark owners also have some international rights under the Paris Convention. And trade secrets receive international protection under GATT (General Agreement on Tariffs and Trade).

Legal Basis of Intellectual Property Laws

The sources of intellectual property laws vary according to the subject matter. Trade secret law derives both from federal and state legislation, and from court cases that have developed their own set of principles used to decide new trade secret cases that come before them (termed the "common law"). Trademark and unfair competition laws originate primarily in both federal and state statutes, but also, especially in the area of unfair competition, come from court decisions that apply principles developed by earlier courts as part of the common law. Copyright and patent laws originate in the U.S. Constitution and are specifically and exclusively implemented by federal statutes. In all these intellectual property areas, court decisions interpreting and enforcing applicable statutes also provide an important source of intellectual property law.

4. Intersection of intellectual property laws

Although each category of intellectual property law is aimed at a particular type of intellectual property, trade secret, copyright, patent and trademark laws occasionally intersect with each other with respect to a particular intellectual property item. Some common examples of this are as follows:

- **Trade secret and copyright.** It is possible to maintain a work of expression as a trade secret and still have it protected by copyright up until the time that it is published—that is, distributed to the public on an unrestricted basis. This is because the nature of trade secret law arises from the actions taken by the owner of the work to keep the work secret for the purpose of getting a jump on competitors, while copyright law automatically applies to any work of expression the instant it becomes fixed in a tangible form. The best example of an intellectual property item that is usually protected by both copyright and trade secret law is the written code underlying most computer software (called source code).

- **Trade secret and patent.** It is possible to pursue a patent application while simultaneously maintaining the invention as a trade secret, at least for the first 18 months of the U.S. patent application process. The U.S. Patent and Trademark Office (PTO) treats applications as confidential until they are published. If the applicant intends to file a patent application abroad, the PTO will publish the application within 18 months of the filing date. This publication effectively ends trade secret protection. If the applicant will not be filing abroad, the trade secret information in the patent application is kept confidential and is only published if the PTO grants the patent. At that point, the applicant gives up trade secret rights in order to obtain patent rights. If the applicant is not filing abroad and the patent application is rejected, the trade secret will remain intact and the competition will not know about the invention.

- **Copyright and trademark.** These laws may apply to the same item. For instance, the expressive artwork in a package design may be protected by copyright while the overall look and feel of the package may be protected as trade dress (a form of trademark). Likewise, an advertisement may include some material covered by copyright (for example, a jingle) and other material covered by trademark (the product or company name). The difference here is that copyright protects the literal expression while trademark protects whatever is used to designate the source of a product or service being offered in the marketplace.

- **Patent, copyright and trademark.** Patent law can intersect with copyright and trademark law in the area of product configuration. In short, when it comes to a product design—say, jewelry or a toy—the creator may, at least theoretically, be able to invoke any or all of these three approaches to intellectual property protection. (The reason we use the word "theoretically" is that courts always are trying to distinguish between the different forms of intellectual property and are prone to restrict the contexts in which they overlap.)

EXAMPLE: A design patent can issue on the new, unobvious, nonfunctional design of an article of manufacture—for example, stylistic ornamentation added to a pair of eyeglasses. Trademark law may be used to protect the appearance of the ornamentation if it is intended to be—and is—used to distinguish the particular brand of eyeglasses in the marketplace. And copyright law may also be used to protect certain expressive aspects of the design.

B. How to Use This Book

This book contains short explanations of the key terms and concepts used in intellectual property law. It is separated into four self-contained parts, each of which is targeted to one of the main intellectual property law categories. The four parts are:

    Part 1: Trade Secret Law

    Part 2: Copyright Law

    Part 3: Patent Law, and

    Part 4: Trademark Law.

You'll find a short overview of the category at the beginning of each part, followed by an alphabetical list of terms defined in that part. We also provide a number of useful lists and charts of additional information, as well as some samples of official forms that apply to each topic.

1. What legal rights apply to your creative work?

If you are concerned with a creation of your own, you'll first need to know what form (or forms) of intellectual property applies to it in order to get to the right part of this book. These basic rules should point you in the right direction:

- **Trade secrets** consist of designs, devices, processes, compositions, techniques, formulas, information or recipes that are kept secret by their owner and which give their owner a competitive business advantage. (See Part 1: Trade Secret Law.)
- **Copyrights** protect original and tangible forms of expressing creative ideas, but not the ideas themselves. A creative nonfunctional design may be copyrightable. (See Part 2: Copyright Law.)
- **Utility patents** apply to new processes, machines, manufactures, compositions of matter, or new uses of any of the above if they are novel, nonobvious and useful. (See Part 3: Patent Law.)
- **Design patents** apply to unique and ornamental shapes or designs that are also nonfunctional. (See Part 3: Patent Law.)
- **Plant patents** may be issued for any asexually or sexually reproducible plants (such as flowers) that are both novel and unobvious. (See Part 3: Patent Law.)
- **Trademarks** apply to marketing devices: the name of a product or service or the symbols, logos, shapes, designs, sounds or smells used to identify them. They must be distinctive or have become well-known through long use or advertising. (See Part 4: Trademark Law.)
- **Unfair competition** is a legal theory that extends protection to certain kinds of intellectual property when trademark, copyright and patent law don't apply. It applies when one business represents its products or services in a way that confuses customers and stops them from buying from another business. (See Part 4: Trademark Law.)

2. Use of intellectual property laws chart

Below, we've provided a detailed chart to further help you identify the applicable law. The chart lists categories of creations, followed by indications of what sorts of intellectual property laws generally apply.

Guide to Use of Intellectual Property Protections

CREATIVE WORK	APPLICABLE LEGAL RIGHTS					
	Trade Secret	Copyright	Patent	Trademark	Unfair Competition	No Rights
advertisement (billboard, card, flyer, sign)		■		■		
advertising copy		■				
architectural drawings, renderings		■				
arrangement of facts		■				
artwork (see specific entries)		■		■		
biography		■				
biological inventions	■		■			
blueprints		■				
book design				■		■
book titles						■
carpet design			■	■		
cartoons		■		■		
characters—animated		■		■		
characters—books						■
characters—comic strips		■		■		
characters—TV or movies						■
charts		■				
chemical inventions	■		■			
choreographed works		■				
clothing accessories and designs (belt, hats, scarves, suspenders)			■			
comic strips		■		■		
commercial names				■	■	
computers	■		■			
containers			■	■		
cosmetics	■		■			
databases		■				
decorative hardware			■	■		
design (see specific entries)		■	■	■		
drawings		■				
electrical inventions	■		■			
electronic inventions	■		■			
engineering plans		■				
etchings		■				
fabric	■		■			
fabric design		■	■	■		
facts						■
flowcharts	■	■				
food inventions	■		■			
forms		■				
formulas—chemical	■		■			

CREATIVE WORK	APPLICABLE LEGAL RIGHTS					
	Trade Secret	Copyright	Patent	Trademark	Unfair Competition	No Rights
formulas—cosmetic	■		■			
formulas—food	■		■			
furniture design			■	■		
games—board, box and instructions		■	■	■		
hardware			■	■		
housewares			■	■		
ideas by themselves	■					
interior design		■		■		
Internet domain names				■		
jewelry		■	■	■		
labels				■		
landscape designs		■	■			
laser light show	■	■				
law of nature						■
lectures		■				
lithographs		■				
logos				■	■	
machines	■		■			
machines—internal parts	■		■			
magazines		■		■		
magic tricks or techniques	■		■			
manufacturing process			■			
maps		■				
mathematical algorithms	■					
mechanical inventions	■		■			
medical accessories, devices (splints, braces, supports)		■	■			
method of doing business			■			
movie—film or video		■				
movie—plot (not written)	■					
movie—script	■	■				
movie—treatment	■	■				
murals		■				
musical composition		■				
musical instrument		■	■			
names—business				■	■	
names—entertainer/celebrity				■	■	
names—famous animals				■		
names—product or service				■	■	
odors—new use/process	■		■			
odors—used in marketing				■		
packaging			■	■		
paintings		■				
pamphlets		■				

CREATIVE WORK	APPLICABLE LEGAL RIGHTS					
	Trade Secret	Copyright	Patent	Trademark	Unfair Competition	No Rights
periodicals		■		■		
photographic processes	■		■			
photographs		■				
plants and plant inventions	■		■			
plays—written or performances		■				
pottery		■		■		
prints		■				
project designs	■	■				
radio programs		■		■		
record books		■				
recreational gear			■	■		
reproductions		■				
schedules		■				
scientific treatises		■	■			
sculpture		■				
shapes			■	■		
shoes			■	■		
signs		■		■	■	
slogans				■	■	
software	■	■	■			
software titles				■		
songs—jingles for marketing		■		■	■	
songs—not written or recorded	■					
songs—recorded or written		■				
sounds—new ways to make	■		■			
sounds—original sequence		■				
sounds—used in marketing				■	■	
sporting goods—designs		■	■	■		
sporting goods—equipment			■			
stained glass		■				
structural plans		■				
symbols				■	■	
titles—books, plays					■	
titles—magazines				■	■	
titles—movies, songs, TV shows					■	
toys		■	■	■		
translations		■				
videotape		■				
wallpaper design		■				
weavings		■		■		
Web pages		■		■	■	
words by themselves						■
writing—articles, essays, poems, novels, short stories, nonfiction books		■				

C. More Self-Help Intellectual Property Resources

Although this desk reference provides a great deal of information about the language and law associated with intellectual property, it cannot possibly provide step-by-step instructions for following various government procedures and programs to protect works of intellectual property.

Fortunately, there are a number of excellent self-help resources if you're interested in intellectual property—whether you're using a lawyer or doing research on your own. At the risk of being accused of shameless marketing, we provide below brief descriptions of resources published by Nolo that provide just this sort of detailed guidance. (Order information is at the back of this book, or visit our website at http://www.nolo.com.)

- *The Copyright Handbook*, by Stephen Fishman. Official copyright forms and step-by-step instructions take the reader through the process of protecting all kinds of written expression under U.S. and international copyright laws. It provides detailed information on topics such as transfer of copyright ownership, works for hire, fair use and infringement.
- *The Public Domain: How to Find and Use Copyright-Free Writings, Music, Art & More* by Stephen Fishman is an authoritative book devoted to what is and is not protected by copyright law. This book is an essential roadmap for determining whether music, writing, artwork and movies are free to use.
- *Copyright Your Software* by Stephen Fishman. Software developers, programmers, publishers and authors will all benefit from reading this book. It explains everything they need to know about software copyright protection, and provides official copyright forms along with step-by-step instructions.
- *Software Development: A Legal Guide*, by Stephen Fishman. This book covers essential information for anyone in the software industry. Topics include software development and intellectual property laws, legalities of working with independent contractors and employees, publishing agreements and multimedia development. Ready-to-use contracts and agreements are provided on a PC disk.
- *Nolo's Patents for Beginners*, by David Pressman and Richard Stim. This quick and easy guide to patent law sets out the basics for protecting, searching, documenting and registering patentable inventions.
- *Patent It Yourself*, by David Pressman. This definitive guide is highly recommended by patent attorneys, inventors, librarians, journalists and the U.S. Patent and Trademark Office. Patent attorney and former patent

examiner David Pressman takes inventors through the entire process—from conducting a patent search to filing a successful application. The book provides all the forms necessary to patent an invention, along with step-by-step instructions.

- *The Patent Drawing Book,* by Jack Lo and David Pressman. This book teaches how to use pen and ink, computerized drawing programs and photography to prepare patent drawings that conform to PTO rules.

- *The Inventor's Notebook* by Fred Grissom and David Pressman is an annotated book that can be used by inventors to document their inventions in case they later have to prove that they deserve the patent as the first true inventors. *The Inventor's Notebook* also contains a number of forms and charts from *Patent It Yourself* and information on how to do market research for an invention.

- *License Your Invention* by Richard Stim guides the reader through the important process of giving others permission to use, develop and market an invention.

- *Patent Searching Made Easy* by David Hitchcock shows how to use the Internet and other free resources to search the U.S. patent database (all patents issued since the beginning of the country). This book is especially intended for creative people who want to quickly find out whether someone has already obtained a patent on their bright idea, and who want to search patents for a particular type of invention to get ideas for possible improvements.

- *Patent It Yourself,* by David Pressman (software). The bestselling book *Patent It Yourself* is also available in software for Windows users. The program includes all forms to document and file a patent.

- *Trademark: Legal Care for Your Business and Product Name*, by Kate McGrath and Stephen Elias. This book shows owners of trademarks and service marks how to choose a distinctive name, conduct a trademark search, register a mark with the U.S. Patent and Trademark Office and protect the mark once it's in use. This book also helps the reader sort out the legalities of trademark conflicts. Step-by-step instructions and official trademark forms are included.

- *The Trademark Registration Kit* by Patricia Gima and Stephen Elias provides all the forms and instructions you need to file a trademark application with the U.S. Patent and Trademark Office and take the necessary steps to deal with trademark examiners.

- *Getting Permission: How to License and Clear Copyrighted Materials Online and Off* by Richard Stim spells out how to obtain permission to use art, music, writing or other copyrighted works. It explains who to ask for permission and how much to expect to pay, and includes a wide variety of permission and licensing agreements.

●

Part 1

Trade Secret Law

The most important point to understand about trade secrets is that there is no crisp, clear definition of what they are. Rather, the context in which a dispute over ownership of information arises will determine whether a court will treat the information as a trade secret. As a general rule, information that has commercial value and that has been scrupulously kept confidential will be considered a trade secret; the owner of the information will be entitled to court relief against those who have stolen or divulged it in violation of a duty of trust or a written nondisclosure agreement.

1. What kind of information qualifies as a trade secret?

A trade secret may consist of any formula, pattern, physical device, idea, process, compilation of information or other information that both:

- provides the owner of the information with a competitive advantage in the marketplace, and
- is treated in a way that can reasonably be expected to prevent the public or competitors from learning about it, absent improper acquisition or theft.

Trade secrets often comprise customer lists and other sensitive marketing information. Other specific items that may be trade secrets include:

- biological inventions (unpatented)
- chemical inventions (unpatented)
- computer hardware
- computer software
- cosmetics
- electrical inventions (unpatented)
- electronic inventions (unpatented)
- fabric
- food inventions
- formulas—chemical
- formulas—cosmetic
- formulas—food
- machines
- machines—internal parts
- magic tricks or techniques
- manufacturing processes
- mechanical inventions
- medical devices—mechanical
- movie plots (not written)

Overview

- movies—script
- movies—treatment
- musical composition
- odors/processes
- photographic processes, and
- project designs.

The one element that these items of information have in common is that they have the potential to make money for their owners if they are kept secret from would-be competitors and are used to make money in the marketplace.

Related terms: business information as trade secret; customer lists; databases as trade secrets; formulas as trade secrets; GATT (General Agreement on Tariffs and Trade); ideas as trade secrets; industrial know-how as trade secrets; industrial secret; methods and techniques as trade secrets; patterns and designs as trade secrets; processes as trade secrets; software and trade secrets.

2. What makes something a trade secret?

As mentioned, a trade secret is any information that both benefits a business commercially and is kept a secret. More specifically, when deciding whether something qualifies as a trade secret, courts will typically consider the following factors:

- the extent to which the information is known outside of the particular business entity
- the extent to which the information is known by employees and others involved in the business
- the extent to which measures have been taken to guard the secrecy of the information
- the value of the information to the business, and

- the difficulty with which the information could be properly acquired or independently duplicated by others.

Related terms: competitive advantage; compilation of information as a trade secret; copyright and trade secret law compatibility; head start rule; in-house trade secrets; notice to employees of trade secret; novelty and trade secrets; parallel research; patent application, effect on trade secrets; physical devices, ability to maintain as trade secrets; read-only memories (ROMs) and trade secrets; reasonably precautionary measures to protect trade secrets; source code as trade secret; trade secret, defined; trade secret owner; Uniform Trade Secret Protection Act.

3. How are trade secrets lost or stolen?

Information that qualifies as a trade secret is subject to legal protection (against theft and misappropriation) as a form of valuable property—but only if the owner has taken the necessary steps to preserve its secrecy. If the owner has not diligently tried to keep the information secret, courts will usually refuse to extend any help to the trade secret owner if others learn of the information.

Some activities that the courts will commonly treat as trade secret theft—which means the owner will be afforded some judicial relief, such as damages or an order preventing use of the stolen information—are:

- disclosures by key employees (current and former managers, scientists and others occupying positions of trust) in violation of their duty of trust toward their employer
- disclosures by employees (current and former) in violation of a confidentiality agreement entered into with their employer
- disclosures by suppliers, consultants, financial advisors or others who signed nondisclosure agreements with the trade secret owner, promising not to disclose the information
- industrial espionage, and
- disclosures by any person owing an implied duty to the employer not to make such disclosure, such as directors, corporate offices and other high-level salaried employees.

When a disclosure is considered wrongful, the courts may also consider use of the information wrongful and issue an order (injunction) preventing its use for a particular period of time.

Related terms: accidental disclosure of trade secrets; antitrust law and trade secrets; beta testing and trade secrets; confidential employment relationship; confidentiality agreements; covenant not to compete by employee; disclosure of confidential information; duty of trust; exit interview; Freedom of Information Act, exemption of trade secrets; illegal restraint of trade; improper acquisition of trade secrets; improper disclosure of trade secrets; industrial espionage; infringement of trade secret; loss of trade secrets; maintained as a trade secret; nondisclosure agreement; notice to former employee's new employer; piracy; public domain and trade secrets; public records and trade secrets; reverse engineering and trade secrets; theft of trade secrets; unsolicited idea disclosure.

4. May trade secrets be sold?

As with other types of property—such as goods, accounts receivable, patents and trademarks—trade secrets may be sold by one business to another. Most trade secret sales occur as part of the sale of the business owning the trade secret, but that is not mandatory.

Related terms: covenant not to compete by owners of a sold business; licensing of trade secrets; specific performance of covenant not to compete.

5. How is trade secret protection enforced?

If the court finds that trade secret theft has occurred, it may issue an order (injunction) requiring all those wrongfully in possession of the information to refrain from using it or disclosing it to others. The court may also award the trade secret owner money damages to compensate for any monetary loss suffered as a result of the theft. In cases involving willful or deliberate theft, the court may also award punitive damages to punish the wrongdoer. Finally, in clear-cut cases, federal and state criminal antitheft laws may be invoked and the trade secret thief subjected to criminal prosecution.

Related terms: damages in trade secret infringement actions; federal trade secret statute; independent conception, defense to trade secret claim; injunctions in trade secret cases; predetermination of rights in technical data; temporary restraining order; territorial restriction agreements—trade secrets; trade secret infringement action; tying arrangements; unjust enrichment and trade secrets; World Intellectual Property Organization (WIPO).

6. Trade secret resources

If you're interested in preparing your own trade secret protection contracts for software, you may want to consult *Software Development: A Legal Guide*, by Stephen Fishman (Nolo).

If you have access to the World Wide Web you can find valuable information about trade secrets by using the Trade Secret Home Page at http://www.execpc. com/~mhallign. This site provides discussions of recent developments and general background information on trade secrets. Also visit Findlaw at http://www.findlaw. com, a general purpose legal search engine. Click on intellectual property in the topics section of the home page and then click on the trade secret subcategory when the intellectual property page appears. From there you can find appropriate statutes and discussions of trade secret principles.

Overview

Definitions

Trade Secret Law

Below are concise definitions of the major concepts and terminology associated with explaining, protecting and enforcing trade secrets.

accidental disclosure of trade secrets

Valuable business information that is inadvertently disclosed to the public usually doesn't qualify as a trade secret, so the courts won't protect it as such. This means that the disclosed information can be used by competitors without fear of a lawsuit by the information's original owner.

> **EXAMPLE:** Independent Robotics conducts a guided tour of its plant. One of the company's engineers accidentally leaves a top secret diagram of a new robot in full view, where it is seen by a competitor on the tour. This diagram (and the information contained in it) has lost its trade secret status due to the fact that it was discovered accidentally, without any intentional wrongdoing by the employee or the competitor.

Related terms: loss of trade secrets; reasonably precautionary measures to protect trade secrets.

advantage over competitors

See competitive advantage.

anti-competition agreements

See covenant not to compete by employee; covenant not to compete by owners of a sold business.

antitrust law and trade secrets

The primary purpose of antitrust law is to preserve a free, competitive marketplace by preventing companies from engaging in behavior that unduly dominates the marketplace or restricts free trade. Antitrust law consists of treaties, federal and state statutes and court opinions that:

- restrict businesses from engaging in practices with the intent to create a dominant or monopolistic market position, and
- prohibit businesses from making agreements with other businesses or individuals that impose significant restrictions or restraints on trade, such as price fixing, territorial restriction agreements, bid rigging and tying arrangements.

In some circumstances, trade secret owners may violate the antitrust laws by using their trade secrets to unfairly discriminate against other companies. For example, if a clothing manufacturing company that has discovered a new method for protecting cotton from shrinkage shares this secret with one competitor for the purpose of driving a third competitor out of business, the antitrust laws may have been violated (conspiracy in restraint of trade and monopolistic practices). In general, deciding whether a particular activity violates the antitrust laws involves such variables as the intent of the actors, the degree of harm done to other companies and the level of commerce that is affected (local, state, national or international).

Related terms: illegal restraint of trade; licensing of trade secrets; territorial restriction agreements—trade secrets; tying arrangements.

beta-testing and trade secrets

After new products and services are developed, but before being released to the public, they are often tested exhaustively under real-life conditions to make sure that they work properly. Called beta-testing, this reality check is especially important in the case of computer software, which is usually so complex that its performance in disparate real-life situations cannot accurately be predicted on the basis of the written code. To identify any potential problems and mistakes (bugs) in the software, the software developer will commonly allow a number of people free use of the software in exchange for keeping track of any problems they encounter. To preserve the software as a trade secret during the beta-test phase, the developer customarily requires beta-testers to sign nondisclosure agreements containing a promise to not talk about the software with anyone, unless authorized by the developer.

Related terms: nondisclosure agreement; software and trade secrets.

business information as trade secret

A business's internal information can qualify as a trade secret if its disclosure would negatively affect that business's competitiveness. For example, the following types of information commonly are considered to be trade secrets because they provide a business with a competitive edge:

- information concerning the characteristics of customers
- information relevant to the cost and pricing of goods
- sources of supply, especially if disclosure would divulge the nature of a secret ingredient
- books and records of the business
- mailing lists and other sales information
- customer lists
- information regarding new business opportunities (such as the price and physical characteristics of real estate), and
- information regarding the effectiveness and performance of personnel, distributors and suppliers.
- methods of doing business

On the other hand, business information is not protectable as a trade secret if it can be independently developed with little difficulty. Information that might not generally qualify as a trade secret includes general employee handbooks and personnel policies that discuss the rights and responsibilities of workers based on applicable federal and state law.

Related terms: competitive advantage; compilation of information as a trade secret; customer lists; databases as trade secrets; industrial know-how as trade secrets; industrial secret.

commercial piracy

See piracy.

competition by former employees

See confidential employment relationship; covenant not to compete by employee.

competitive advantage

A competitive advantage may be gained from any confidential information, idea, item or state of events that can potentially be exploited to enhance the income or assets of a business. If the owner of information cannot derive economic benefit from the information, there is no trade secret. Conversely, if keeping the information secret will give its owner a competitive advantage, the item may qualify as a trade secret, assuming that secrecy is, in fact, maintained.

EXAMPLE: Universal Programming, Inc., develops and distributes business software. One of its employees creates an outline permitting user interface screens to be quickly and efficiently edited while programming is in process. If other software companies have developed equally quick and efficient screen editors, Universal's program does not provide a competitive advantage and, although the program uses an innovative approach, it probably will not qualify as a protectable trade secret. On the other hand, if Universal's innovative new screen editor works faster than others in general use throughout the industry or offers unique features, this would give Universal a competitive advantage because it may produce software faster or better than its competitors. In this situation, the screen editor program would qualify for trade secret status as long as Universal treats the program as confidential and other companies do not independently create the same innovations.

Related terms: trade secret, defined.

compilation of information as a trade secret

Trade secrets are often thought to involve a new approach, formula, device or method for accomplishing a given end. However, a genuinely innovative structuring or reorganization of otherwise public information that creates a competitive advantage can also qualify as a trade secret if it is maintained as one.

Much existing information is now being reorganized so that it can be more easily stored in and retrieved from computer databases. Often referred to as "knowledge engineering," these new machine-searchable formats themselves may qualify as innovative compilations. They deserve treatment as trade secrets if maintained as such, because they enable a business to analyze old information in new ways that can lead to a competitive edge.

EXAMPLE: A hearing aid manufacturer designs an innovative way to create a specialized mailing list of deaf Americans from available census data. Although the census data is certainly not a trade secret, the mailing list would qualify as a trade secret in that it is not available to anyone else, and would provide the manufacturer with a competitive advantage.

Related terms: business information as trade secret; customer lists; databases as trade secrets.

computer programs and trade secrets

See software and trade secrets.

confidential employment relationship

Much of trade secret law is concerned with how employees may act with respect to an employer's trade secrets during and after the period of their employment, even if these matters are not set out in a written agreement.

Certain management and high-level employees who come in contact with trade secrets during the course of their work legally have an inherent duty to treat them as confidential—that is, preserve them as trade secrets. This duty is said to create a confidential employment relationship between the employee and the business. The higher the level of expertise or responsibility possessed by the employee, the more likely this confidential employment relationship exists. For instance, an engineer, scientist or corporate executive will usually be deemed to be subject to a high duty of trust (or confidential employment relationship), while a receptionist, office clerk or janitor will not. However, no employee is legally permitted to intentionally set out to steal a firm's trade secrets.

It is common practice for firms possessing trade secrets to require employees with access to them to sign confidentiality agreements, promising not to utilize or disclose any of the firm's trade secrets during future employment. Whether or not such an agreement is signed, however, if an employee or former employee uses information obtained in the course of a confidential employment relationship for personal gain or to benefit a competitor, courts will usually impose a damage award against the employee.

Related terms: confidentiality agreements; duty of trust; exit interview.

confidentiality agreements

Contracts between employees and employers, in which the employee agrees to treat as confidential all trade secrets he or she learns about in the course of employment, are referred to as confidentiality agreements. If the employer later tries to prevent an employee from using infor-mation considered to be a trade secret, a confidentiality agreement can establish that the employee recognized a duty to cooperate in this endeavor. Competitors who learn of trade secrets through an employee's violation of a confidentiality agreement with a former employer may also be prevented from com-mercially using the information, even if they didn't know the employee had breached a confidentiality agreement.

A confidentiality agreement can also help establish that a business treated particular information as a trade secret—a necessary

Definitions

element to claiming legal protection. If, however, a court determines that a confidential employment relationship or duty of trust existed between the employer and employee, it is usually not necessary to show the existence of a written confidentiality agreement.

The term "nondisclosure agreement" is used interchangeably with "confidentiality agreement." However, a "nondisclosure agreement" more properly describes an agreement between trade secret owners and others in a non-employment setting. (A sample confidentiality agreement is provided below.)

Related terms: confidential employment relationship; duty of trust; nondisclosure agreement; reasonably precautionary measures to protect trade secrets.

copyright and trade secret law compatibility

A copyright consists of the exclusive right to reproduce, display, perform, distribute and make alterations to an original work of expression. Simply put, copyright law protects the original expressions of ideas, but not the ideas themselves.

Copyright and trade secret laws sometimes protect the same kinds of information and sometimes are mutually exclusive of each other. Here are the salient points of how trade secret and copyright legal protections can work together under the Copyright Act of 1976:

- Trade secret and copyright protection are both available for unpublished works as long as the idea (or ideas) in the work are sufficiently innovative to qualify as a trade secret (any confidential information that provides a business with a competitive advantage), and the information is kept confidential.
- Trade secret and copyright protection may both be available for works that are distributed on a limited and restricted basis under a copyright licensing arrangement requiring the licensee (user) to recognize and maintain the trade secret aspects of the work. This dual protection is especially pertinent for the computer software business.
- Trade secret protection is generally not available for software if the source code is made available to the public on an unrestricted basis through such means as listing it in a computer magazine or on a medium of distribution (for instance, a floppy disk).
- Works that are widely distributed without specific licensing agreements will generally lose their trade secret status but may be entitled to copyright protection.
- The deposit of a physical copy of the work that is being registered with the U.S. Copyright Office operates to disclose any trade secrets in the work

Sample

> ### CONFIDENTIALITY AGREEMENT
>
> 1. I understand and acknowledge that during my employment with Mystery Software, Inc. (the "Company") I have received or been exposed to trade secrets of the Company including, but not limited to those listed on Exhibit A to this Agreement.
>
> 2. I acknowledge that I have read, signed and been furnished with a copy of my Employment Agreement with the Company. I certify that I have complied with and will continue to comply with all of the provisions of the Employment Agreement, including my obligation to preserve as confidential all of the Company's trade secrets.
>
> 3. I certify that I do not have in my possession, I have not retained copies of, nor have I failed to return: any system documentation, user manuals, modification reports, training instructions, formulas, compilers, data structures, algorithms, computer source code, notebooks, notes, drawings, proposals or other documents or materials (or extracts thereof), or equipment or other property belonging to the Company.
>
> 4. During my employment I contributed to the development of the Company's trade secrets. I acknowledge that, as provided in my Employment Agreement, all right, title and interest in and to any programming conceived or developed by me, whether in whole or in part, during the course of my employment by the Company belongs to the Company.
>
> _____
> Employee's typed or printed name
>
> _____
> Employee's signature
>
> _____
> Date

Definitions

Reprinted with permission from *Software Development: A Legal Guide* by Stephen Fishman (Nolo).

unless the deposit in some way masks the material that comprises the trade secret. For instance, it is possible to deposit samples of source code with major portions blacked out so that the parts of the code being maintained as a trade secret are not disclosed. There are several other methods for simultaneously registering a computer program and maintaining trade secrets. One common way is to withhold the source code altogether and deposit object code—which is impossible to understand when read in the U.S. Copyright Office.

Related terms: ideas as trade secrets; reasonably precautionary measures to protect trade secrets; software and trade secrets.
See also Part 2 (Copyright Law): Copyright Act of 1976.

covenant not to compete by employee

This is legalese for a written promise by an employee not to compete with his or her employer, or take employment with a competing business, for a specified length of time after the employer-employee relationship ends. Usually, a covenant not to compete is part of a more comprehensive employment agreement signed by the employee.

By delaying former employees from going to work for competitors or starting their own competing businesses, covenants not to compete minimize the risk that trade secrets will be disclosed or used to compete with the former employer.

Agreements restricting the right of employees to compete have often proved difficult to enforce in court, as courts tend to dislike contracts that restrict a worker's rights to earn a living. Employees with high levels of responsibility are more likely to be held to their promise, while those with less important responsibilities may be able to escape from the restriction on the premise that they would not be in a position to harm the employer's interest, and it would more severely affect their ability to support themselves.

Covenants not to compete are banned in some countries, and banned or greatly restricted in a few states, including California. Most state courts will, however, enforce covenants not to compete if they are seen as necessary to protect trade secrets and they are drafted to minimize the restriction of the employee's right to work and/or engage in commerce.

EXAMPLE: Peter Erickson is hired as a high-level laser specialist by Laser Fair Corp., a company engaged in making holographs for amusement parks. As a condition of employment, Peter is required to sign a covenant not to compete in work specifically involving amusement park holographs for a one-year period. This narrower covenant would likely be enforceable in most states. If, however, Peter signed a covenant not to engage in any holography or related laser work for a five-year period after leaving the company, most courts would refuse to uphold it. Given the fast-changing nature of the field, such an agreement is both broader in scope and longer in duration than is needed to protect Laser Fair's competitive interest in trade secrets acquired by Peter.

A court is more likely to shorten the time periods for restrictive covenants when the employee works in an area of developing technology such as software or the Internet. For example, one court ruled that an Internet employee's one-year restriction on working for a competitor was too long "given the dynamic nature of this [Internet] industry, its lack of geographical borders, and the employee's former cutting-edge position." (*EarthWeb, Inc. v. Schlack*, 71 F. Supp.2d 299, 313 (S.D. N.Y. 1999).) Another court limited an Internet employee's non-compete restriction to six months. (*DoubleClick, Inc. v. Henderson*, 1997 LEXIS 577, (Sup. Ct. N.Y. Co. 1997).)

Related terms: confidentiality agreements; reasonably precautionary measures to protect trade secrets.

covenant not to compete by owners of a sold business

As a condition of the sale of an existing business, its owners, officers or directors are commonly required to promise in writing not to compete with the purchased business for a specific time period. These promises (or covenants) constitute recognition that part of the value of the purchased business consists of trade secrets. If former owners, officers or directors were permitted to utilize this information in competing businesses, the purchasers of the existing business would not be getting their money's worth. For this reason, courts are usually willing to enforce these covenants.

criminal prosecution for trade secret theft

See theft of trade secrets.

customer lists

A list of a business's customers may qualify as a trade secret if the list contributes to the business's competitive advantage and is kept secret. In trade secret law, there are essentially three types of customer lists:

- customer lists maintained by retail concerns
- lists of clients maintained by professionals, and

Definitions

- lists of retail concerns maintained by wholesalers.

Lists of customers maintained by retail concerns and lists of clients maintained by professionals most easily qualify as trade secrets for two reasons:

- the individual names on the list have usually been obtained as a direct result of efforts by the retail concern or professional to establish good will, and
- a list of retail customers or clients gives its possessor a significant competitive advantage over other retail concerns or professionals.

Lists of retailers a wholesaler sells to are often not protectable as trade secrets. Because retailers are usually easy to identify through trade directories and other sources, a list of them ordinarily would not confer a competitive advantage on its possessor. But there are exceptions—for instance, a list of bookstores that order certain types of technical books and pay their bills promptly may be very valuable to a wholesale book distributor.

Related terms: business information as trade secret; databases as trade secrets.

damages in trade secret infringement actions

If a trade secret owner suffered monetary loss as a result of a trade secret theft, the owner may be able to get a court to award either:

- money damages measured by the profits earned by the competitor as a result of the use of the trade secret, or
- money damages measured by the loss of profits by the trade secret owner, due to the improper trade secret leak.

Further, if the theft was intentional, courts in many states may impose punitive damages (damages awarded to the plaintiff for the purpose of punishing the wrongdoer and providing an example to other would-be trade secret thieves). By contrast, in other states, treble damages (three times the amount of proven actual damages) is the most that can be awarded in a trade secret case. For example, in a state that allows punitive damages, a court might award the plaintiff $1,000,000, even if the trade secret owner only proves $10,000 worth of actual damages. But in states where punitive damages are defined as treble damages, the court could only award $30,000 in the same case.

Related terms: injunctions in trade secret cases; trade secret infringement action.

databases as trade secrets

A database is information of any type organized in a manner to facilitate its retrieval. An encyclopedia, for example, is a database that is organized alphabetically and contains information that can be retrieved by subject.

The term "database" currently is understood as referring to computer databases. Computer databases usually consist of information linked in a way to allow its quick retrieval, either by specific item or in combination with other items.

Databases may be protected as trade secrets. For instance, a database that allows a book publisher to identify people who purchased certain categories of books in the previous year would qualify as a trade secret if it were kept confidential.

A database often contains component materials that are protected by copyright. Sometimes this copyrighted material is owned by someone other than the database owner, as in the case of a database of archived newspaper articles where the copyright in the articles is owned by their original authors or publishers. Even so, this type of database can still be a trade secret because the way the materials are organized is at least as valuable as the materials themselves.

EXAMPLE: Windtronics Inc. creates a database consisting of all articles published on wind power. The database structure allows retrieval by key word and/or by any of 200 key wind-power concepts. Windtronics then establishes a thriving consulting business, based on its ability to retrieve information quickly from its database. Windtronics must obtain permission to copy the articles from their authors (or other current owners), since the creation of the database necessarily involves copying the articles into electronic form. Nevertheless, the database itself can be a trade secret if it is maintained as one and gives Windtronics a competitive advantage.

Related terms: competitive advantage; compilation of information as trade secret; copyright and trade secret law compatibility; customer lists.

disclosure of confidential information

See confidentiality agreements; Internet and trade secrets; nondisclosure agreement.

disclosure of confidential information during lawsuit

See litigation and disclosure of trade secrets.

duty of trust

Over the years, the courts have recognized that certain business relationships require a higher than normal degree of trust between the parties. These relationships are often referred to as "fiduciary relationships," and people or businesses in these relationships are said to owe a duty of trust to each other. Those with a duty of trust have an obligation to take the interests of another person or a business into account when engaging in commercial activity potentially affecting that person or business. For instance, an employer and a high-level employee or provider of a service (expert consultant, lawyer, accountant) have a duty of trust to deal fairly with each other under all circumstances.

If a person violates (breaches) a duty of trust, the courts are usually willing to grant whatever remedy is necessary to undo the harm caused by the breach. For example, if a high-level executive breaches a duty owed to his or her employer by disclosing trade secrets to a competitor, the employer may go to court to prevent further breaches, to receive an award of damages from the employee and to prevent the competitor from using the disclosed trade secrets.

Criminal prosecutions seldom are brought in breach of trust cases, which are almost always viewed as civil matters.

Related terms: confidential employment relationship; trade secret infringement action.

Economic Espionage Act of 1996

See Federal Trade Secret Act.

email and confidentiality

See Internet and trade secrets.

employees, covenant not to compete

See covenant not to compete by employee.

employees, notice of trade secrets

See notice to employees of trade secrets.

employees' rights and duties towards trade secrets

See confidential employment relationship.

employment contracts and trade secrets

See confidentiality agreements; covenant not to compete by employee.

exit interview

An employer may conduct an interview with a departing employee, in which the employee is reminded of the trade secrets he or she has knowledge of and warned that his or her unauthorized disclosure of these trade secrets may result in being held personally liable for damages.

Related terms: duty of trust; notice to employees of trade secrets.

Federal Trade Secret Statute

The Economic Espionage Act of 1996 makes the theft of trade secrets a federal crime. The Act prohibits the theft of a trade secret by a person intending or knowing that the offense will injure a trade secret owner. The Act also makes it a federal crime to receive, buy or possess trade secret information knowing it to have been stolen. The Act's definition of "trade secret" is similar to that of the Uniform Trade Secrets Act. The penalties for a violation of this new statute include a potential prison term of 15 years and fines up to five million dollars, depending on whether the defendant is an individual or a corporation. The Act is set out in full in the statutes following this part of the book.

fiduciary duty and trade secrets

See duty of trust.

formulas as trade secrets

Product formulas that both are kept confidential and add to a business's competitive advantage may qualify as trade secrets. A formula can consist of any combination of ingredients that results in a particular product. Examples of the many formulas that have been granted trade secret status are those for soft drinks, butter flavoring, industrial solvents, floor wax and rat poison.

Freedom of Information Act, exemption of trade secrets

In its regulatory capacity, the federal government often requires businesses to submit information that the businesses consider to be trade secrets, such as the precise formula used in a drug for which FDA approval is being sought. The Freedom of Information Act (FOIA), located in 5 United States Code, Section 552, ordinarily provides the public with broad access to documents possessed by the executive branch of the federal government. However, to encourage businesses to file the appropriate records, trade secrets are exempt from the disclosure requirement otherwise imposed on the government by the FOIA. This means that businesses are able to comply with government regulations without necessarily giving up their secrets.

However, although the government is not required to disclose trade secrets under the FOIA, it is often difficult, if not impossible, for an agency official to tell from the information itself whether or not it is considered a trade secret by the company that submitted it. So, to protect their trade secrets, companies submitting trade secret information should clearly label the material as such. If the agency receives a request for the information, the agency is then supposed to contact the company and give it a chance to argue why the information should not be disclosed. If, however, the agency chooses to release the information in question against the company's wishes, there is little that can be done about it. The courts have prohibited affected businesses from filing lawsuits against the agencies involved (called "reverse FOIA suits").

Definitions

freedom of speech and trade secrets

The First Amendment to the U.S. Constitution prohibits the government from placing restrictions on a person's freedom of speech. One exception to this "prior restraint" rule is that a court may prohibit the publication of trade secrets that have been obtained in violation of an employment agreement. Courts weigh several factors when making a prior restraint determination, including the commercial interest in the trade secrets, the individual's right to speak freely and the illegal behavior used to acquire the trade secrets. Prohibiting publication is less likely if the trade secrets are obtained by legitimate means.

EXAMPLE: An attorney accidentally attaches trade secret information to a publicly filed court document. A reporter uncovers this inadvertent disclosure and arranges to publish the information in a newspaper. A court is unlikely to restrain this publication since the information was obtained legally.

Keep in mind that some trade secret information, for example a business plan, may be protected under copyright law. In that case, the owner of the trade secret can sue claiming copyright infringement as a result of the unauthorized publication, regardless of whether the information was obtained legally.

Related terms: injunctions in trade secret cases; temporary restraining order; protective order; copyright and trade secret compatibility.

GATT (General Agreement on Tariffs and Trade)

The General Agreement on Tariffs and Trade (GATT) is a treaty among most of the world's industrialized nations that addresses a number of factors affecting international trade, including how each signing country treats trade secrets belonging to businesses in the other signing countries. Under GATT, most industrial countries have pledged themselves to provide protection to trade secrets owned by residents of all signatory nations.

geographical licenses

See territorial restriction agreements—trade secrets; licensing of trade secrets.

head start rule

When a court finds that a business improperly possesses trade secrets belonging to another business, it sometimes orders that the non-owning business cannot use the trade secrets for a period of time. How long a business is restricted from using another business's trade secrets depends on the length of time it would have taken the offending business to independently develop the information that constitutes the secret. In other words, the rightful trade secret owner is provided with a commercial "head start" in the information's use. This head start remedy recognizes that the essential value of a trade secret is the competitive advantage it affords its owner.

Related terms: injunctions in trade secret cases; trade secret infringement action.

hiring employees from competitors to obtain trade secrets

See improper acquisition of trade secrets.

ideas as trade secrets

Ideas alone can be protected as trade secrets only if they are generally unknown in the business community, offer a competitive advantage and are treated confidentially. The real value of any idea will ultimately depend on its commercial success. An idea that offers the possibility of helping a business compete should be maintained as a trade secret until such time as it appears to lack feasibility or others independently think of it. Otherwise, a golden opportunity for obtaining an advantage over potential competitors may be lost.

Trade secret protection is also available for ideas that later become an invention, up to the time that a patent covering the invention issues. Once a patent issues, the underlying ideas become part of the patent, which information is available to the public, and are no longer considered trade secrets.

Trade secret protection for ideas should be contrasted with copyright protection, which only protects the actual expression of the idea and not the idea itself. Because of this difference, trade secret law can often best protect the conception and development stages of a work before it is finally fixed in a tangible medium and published, at which point copyright protection takes over.

Related terms: copyright and trade secret law compatibility; patent application, effect on trade secrets.

illegal restraint of trade

Commercial activity by one business showing a strong tendency to restrict or curtail the free flow of commerce is considered an illegal restraint of trade. Examples of illegal restraints are tying arrangements (requiring the purchase of one product as a prerequisite to buying another), price setting agreements (two or more businesses agree to set prices at a particular level), and territorial restriction agreements (private agreements to restrict the use of a trade secret to certain geographical areas).

Related terms: antitrust law and trade secrets; licensing of trade secrets; territorial restriction agreements—trade secrets.

implied duty not to disclose trade secrets

See duty of trust.

Definitions

improper acquisition of trade secrets

This phrase describes the situation where a business obtained a trade secret through means that the law considers impermissible, such as:

- deliberate theft through misrepresentation, burglary or industrial espionage, or
- knowingly obtaining or using trade secrets that have been obtained by theft or improperly disclosed by a person who breached a nondisclosure agreement, confidentiality agreement, implied duty not to disclose trade secrets or duty of trust.

Under these circumstances, an injured trade secret owner can file a trade secret infringement lawsuit to stop the other company from using the information, and perhaps to recover money damages and punitive damages.

EXAMPLE: The Bayside Graphics company develops and tries to keep secret a program that greatly improves the graphics capability of a popular business-forecasting package. If a competitor discovers the information by illegally spying on Bayside—for instance, the competitor steals Bayside's trash during a five-minute period when it is left unprotected and thereby discovers the trade secret—improper acquisition has occurred and court relief can be obtained.

The U.S. government may also file criminal charges against the trade secret thief under the federal trade secret statute.

Related terms: damages in trade secret infringement actions; federal trade secret statute; industrial espionage; theft of trade secrets; trade secret infringement action.

improper disclosure of trade secrets

When someone communicates trade secrets to others in violation of a confidentiality agreement, nondisclosure agreement, duty of trust or confidential employment relationship, it is known as an improper disclosure of trade secrets. Those who improperly disclose trade secrets may be held liable for all resulting harm to the trade secret owner's economic interests.

Related terms: damages in trade secret infringement actions; improper acquisition of trade secrets; nondisclosure agreement; trade secret infringement action.

independent conception, defense to trade secret claim

For a trade secret owner to obtain court-ordered relief against a competitor who is using the trade secret, there must be a showing that the competitor improperly acquired it. A trade secret is not improperly acquired if it is independently conceived of, or is discovered by a competitor through parallel research.

To preserve their ability to raise independent conception as a defense to a trade secret infringement action, most large companies will not:

- sign a nondisclosure agreement tendered by an outsider who wants to sell something to the company, or
- examine any work developed by an outsider unless the outsider signs a written statement giving up the right to treat the work as a trade secret.

Related terms: improper acquisition of trade secrets; parallel research; trade secret infringement action; unsolicited idea disclosure.

independently developed

See independent conception, defense to trade secret claim.

industrial espionage

In the trade secret context, industrial espionage consists of any activity directed toward discovering a company's trade secrets by such underhanded or illegal means as:

- electronic surveillance
- bribery of employees to disclose confidential information
- placing of a spy among the company's employees
- tapping of a company's phones, computers or e-mail, or
- theft of documents containing confidential information.

In the U.S., an owner of trade secrets obtained by an outsider as a result of industrial espionage may recover large damages if the secrets are subsequently used by the guilty party and the thief is subject to criminal persecution under the federal trade secret statute. In some countries, however, trade secret theft through industrial espionage is tolerated as a normal part of doing business.

Related terms: improper acquisition of trade secrets.

industrial innovations as trade secrets

See competitive advantage; trade secret, defined.

industrial know-how as trade secrets

An organization called the International Chamber of Commerce defines industrial know-how to include applied technical knowledge, methods and data that are necessary for realizing or carrying out techniques that serve industrial purposes. Industrial know-how differs from business know-how, which normally involves white collar managerial and marketing techniques.

The kind of information encompassed by the term "industrial know-how" will qualify as a trade secret if it is specialized, not generally known in the relevant business community, provides a company with a competitive advantage, and is maintained as a trade secret.

In France, Germany, Japan, the U.S., and many other countries, industrial know-how can constitute a trade secret even when the general process or method to which it relates is patented or otherwise publicly available. For example, sword making methods are widely known in Japan, but such factors as ceramic techniques, temperature of the fire and temperature of the water often determine whether the sword is a masterpiece or a failure. Because the industrial know-how associated with any of these factors can provide a competitive advantage, it can qualify as a trade secret.

Related terms: industrial secret; methods and techniques as trade secrets.

industrial secret

Industrial secrets are trade secrets of a technical, technological, scientific or mechanical nature. Secret processes, formulas, unregistered industrial designs, manufacturing techniques and methods, secret machinery, devices, and the like are all examples.

The laws of some countries, such as Japan, distinguish between industrial secrets and commercial secrets. In the U.S., however, courts generally treat all trade secrets alike, regardless of their type. In other words, whether or not a trade secret is business information, industrial know-how or an industrial secret has no legal consequence in the U.S.

Related terms: industrial know-how as trade secrets; trade secret, defined.

inevitable disclosure rule (also known as the inevitability doctrine)

This rule—that trade secret disclosure is unavoidable in certain situations—was popularized by a 1995 case in which Pepsico successfully argued that a former executive could not help but rely on Pepsico's company secrets at his new job with a rival. (*Pepsico Inc. v. Redmond,* 54 F.3d 1262 (7th Cir. 1995).) Not all courts have accepted the inevitable disclosure rule and the doctrine is more likely to be applied if there is an additional showing of bad faith, underhanded dealing, or employment by a competitor lacking comparable technology.

infringement of trade secret

When a business makes commercial use of a trade secret that was improperly disclosed or improperly acquired from another business, infringement is said to have occurred.

Related terms: improper acquisition of trade secrets; trade secret infringement action.

in-house trade secrets

A trade secret may still legally exist—and be entitled to protection—even though many people know about it, as long as the knowledge is kept within the business that owns it. For example, in large corporations, trade secrets may be known by hundreds or even thousands of people on a "need to know" basis. As long as the business takes adequate measures to prevent the secrets from being disclosed to the public or to other businesses, the trade secret status of the information is maintained.

Related terms: notice to employees of trade secrets; reasonably precautionary measures to protect trade secrets.

injunctions in trade secret cases

A court order directed at persons or businesses who have either improperly acquired trade secrets, or who threaten to improperly disclose them, is known as an injunction. Typically, an injunction is sought as part of a trade secret infringement action, to prohibit a defendant from using a trade secret belonging to the plaintiff (the party bringing the action) or from disclosing it to others. This type of judicial relief is common in trade secret litigation, since one of the trade secret owner's primary goals is to stop any further erosion of the competitive advantage gained by keeping the information secret.

Courts are authorized to issue emergency injunctions, called temporary restraining orders (or TROs), when a trade secret owner shows that a trade secret is at risk of being lost as a result of the defendant's behavior. The court must then schedule a hearing at which all sides may be heard. If, after this hearing, the court still believes that a trade secret is at stake and that the trade secret owner will probably win at trial, it can issue a provisional or "preliminary" injunction. This order will continue to prevent the defendant from using or disclosing the trade secret pending a final decision in the case. As a practical matter, once a preliminary injunction is granted, the parties will often settle, rather than fight the case through to trial and beyond.

EXAMPLE: Space Age Robotics International (SARI) is a small business with five employees. It has developed a computer security system that visually recognizes people and responds to their voice commands. SARI plans to make a product announcement in about a month. In the meantime, Fred Gregory, SARI's chief engineer, suddenly quits and joins Universal Systems Inc., a competitor. A week later, SARI learns from the grapevine that Fred is working around the clock to build a similar visual recognition system for Universal.

Claiming trade secret infringement, SARI immediately files an action against Fred and Universal, and asks the court to first grant a temporary restraining order (TRO), and then a preliminary injunction, preventing Fred from making any further disclosures to Universal and Universal from disclosing anything they have already learned from Fred. The basis for this request (motion) is that if it is not granted, SARI will suffer irreparable injury because its valuable trade secrets will be lost. The court issues a TRO and schedules a hearing 14 days later, at which time SARI's motion for a preliminary injunction is considered. At this hearing, both SARI and Universal present oral arguments regarding the applicable law as well as written statements of their respective legal positions (called "points and authorities"). Both sides also submit written statements under oath (affidavits or declarations) describing the facts in the case as they see them. Although witnesses occasionally appear in preliminary injunction hearings, that is somewhat exceptional.

The judge determines that a preliminary injunction is necessary to preserve SARI's trade secrets and that, when the case is finally tried, SARI will probably win. Accordingly, a preliminary injunction is issued to remain in effect pending the trial of the case. Because the trial will not occur for at least a year, and because both SARI and Universal need to get on with their respective businesses, they agree to settle the dispute. Universal agrees to scrap its budding vision project, Fred agrees to keep his knowledge to himself, and SARI agrees to drop its infringement action and request for damages in exchange for reimbursement of its legal costs.

Related terms: improper acquisition of trade secrets; improper disclosure of trade secrets; trade secret infringement action.

Internet and trade secrets

The publication of confidential information on the Internet will almost always cause the loss of trade secret rights regardless of whether it was done inadvertently or maliciously. The result of such a posting is that competitors who obtain the information legally, that is, those who did not violate trade secret laws to get the information, are entitled to use it.

There are many ways a trade secret is disclosed in cyberspace. Sometimes the disclosure is the result of revenge by an angry employee or contractor, sometimes it occurs because a hacker has uncovered information without permission of the website owner, and sometimes it is the result of carelessness—often by employees of the business who may discuss secrets in online chats.

There are exceptions to the "posting equals disclosure" rule. One court ruled that posting on the Web does not automatically cause the loss of trade secret status because the posting may not result in the secret being "generally known." The court required a review of the circumstances surrounding the posting and consideration of the interests of the trade secret owner, the policies favoring competition, and the interests—including First Amendment rights—of innocent third parties who acquire information on the Internet. (*Religious Tech. Ctr. v. Netcom On-Line Comm. Servs. Inc.*, 923 F. Supp. 1231 (N.D. Cal. 1995).) In addition to violations of trade secret law, the improper disclosure of trade secrets on the Internet may lead to claims of copyright infringement.

How risky is it to send trade secrets by email? There's much less risk in the transmission of email than in its storage. The transmission of email usually doesn't jeopardize confidentiality because each email message is broken into packets of information and reassembled at the delivery point making it difficult to intercept. Also, the nature of email requires that the address is typed exactly and if it is not, it almost always bounces back to the sender.

The danger from loss of confidentiality occurs when email is stored either on the sender's computer, a host computer (for example, an Internet service provider like America Online) or at the recipient's computer. These stored files can be acquired legally by employers, lawyers or the police, or they can be acquired illegally by hackers. Email transmissions also pose a threat to confidentiality when the information is subsequently posted on a bulletin board or in a chat group. For this reason, businesses generally institute trade secret procedures on company computers, including password protection and encryption of messages— a process that uses sophisticated software to garble the sender's words and then

Definitions

allows the recipient to unscramble and read them. In addition, companies prevent outsiders from penetrating the office network by the use of firewalls, protective computer hardware or software systems.

Related terms: software and trade secrets; improper disclosure of trade secrets; copyright and trade secret compatibility.

know-how

See industrial know-how as trade secrets; methods and techniques as trade secrets.

licensing of trade secrets

A trade secret owner may license a trade secret by permitting others to use the trade secret in exchange for an agreement to treat it as confidential. Licenses commonly are limited to specific time periods, types or fields of commerce and specific purposes. There are no government agencies that oversee trade secret licenses, but trade secret licenses are subject to applicable antitrust prohibitions against monopolistic or restraint of trade activities.

Under a trade secret license, ownership of the trade secret remains with the original owner, while the licensee has the right to use the trade secret as long as it complies with the specific terms and time limits of the license. The license agreement should always include a clause stating that the trade secret in question is confidential information and must be maintained properly as a trade secret by the licensee.

One common type of license provides the owner with a royalty based on a percentage of the retail or wholesale price of each item sold that takes advantage of the trade secret. Many other compensation arrangements are possible. For example, the license may provide for a flat fee for each separate use of the secret, a monthly or annual fee, the reciprocal use of information belonging to the licensee or some combination of all of these arrangements.

Related terms: antitrust law and trade secrets; trade secret owner.

litigation and disclosure of trade secrets

State and federal laws establish rules regarding the use and disclosure of trade secrets during litigation. If one party requests trade secret information from another, a court will balance the interests of the litigants. If the failure to disclose would cause injustice or conceal a fraud, the owner of the trade secret will be required to disclose it. In order to preserve secrecy, the court will issue a protective order that requires that all participants in the lawsuit—the litigants, attorneys, independent contractors—maintain confidentiality. Protective orders can be made by order of the court, or the parties may agree to the protection of confidential information.

Related terms: injunctions in trade secret cases; protective order; temporary restraining order.

loss of trade secrets

Trade secrets, and the judicial protection their status confers, may be lost by any conduct that:

- releases the trade secret into the public domain, and
- does not constitute wrongful conduct such as theft, violation of a nondisclosure agreement or breach of a duty of trust.

EXAMPLE: Sonoma Foods Inc. (SFI) conceives of a new way to lengthen the shelf life of jams and jellies. Initially, SFI takes careful steps to preserve its invention as a trade secret. However, over a few drinks at a trade show, SFI's chief executive officer tells an employee from another food company about the invention without first asking for a nondisclosure agreement. Such behavior might result in the loss of the idea as a trade secret, especially if the other company proceeds to implement the idea or tell others about it. Should SFI bring an infringement suit against the other company, the SFI officer's disclosure would definitely constitute a defense. Even though the trade secret was lost, however, it might still be possible for SFI to apply for and obtain a patent on its new process.

Related terms: accidental disclosure of trade secrets; patent application, effect on trade secrets; public domain and trade secrets; public records and trade secrets; reasonably precautionary measures to protect trade secrets.

maintained as a trade secret

Information will not be treated as a trade secret by the courts unless it has been maintained as such. This consists of taking all reasonable measures to preserve the secrecy of information considered to be a company trade secret.

Related terms: reasonably precautionary measures to protect trade secrets.

methods and techniques as trade secrets

Specialized business knowledge related to a specific process or method, commonly known as business know-how, can qualify as a trade secret in many countries if it is so treated. Examples of such know-how include specialized barbecue methods of cooking (including the use of special cuts of meat and secret sauces) and methods and techniques for running group sessions of a how-to-quit-smoking organization.

Definitions

On the other hand, general business knowledge or expertise not related to a specific process or method is usually not protectable as a trade secret. The courts rarely protect information that is generally known to, or available to, the business community and thus is not secret.

Related terms: industrial know-how as trade secrets; processes as trade secrets; trade secret, defined.

misappropriation of trade secrets

See theft of trade secrets.

money damages

See damages in trade secret infringement actions.

non-competition clauses in employment contracts

See covenant not to compete by employee.

nondisclosure agreement

A nondisclosure agreement is a legally binding contract in which a person or business promises to treat specific information as a trade secret and not to disclose the information to others without proper authorization. If the trade secret is disclosed in violation of the nondisclosure agreement, the trade secret owner can file a trade secret infringement action, obtain an injunction to stop further use of the trade secret, recover money damages, and possibly recover punitive or treble damages. (A sample nondisclosure agreement is provided below.)

Trade secret nondisclosure agreements should be used whenever it is necessary to disclose a trade secret to another person or business for such purposes as development, marketing, evaluation or fiscal backing. Through the conscientious use of nondisclosure agreements, trade secrets can be distributed to a relatively large number of people without destroying their protected status.

Although nondisclosure agreements are usually in the form of written contracts, they may also be implied if the context of a business relationship suggests that such agreement was intended by the parties. For instance, a business that conducts patent searches for inventors is expected to keep the information about the invention secret, even if no written nondisclosure agreement is signed, since the nature of the business is to deal in confidential information.

Related terms: beta-testing and trade secrets; confidentiality agreements; trade secret infringement action.

notice to employees of trade secrets

For information to qualify as a trade secret, employers must insure that it is treated as confidential. All employees (and anyone else who may come in

Sample

NONDISCLOSURE AGREEMENT

This is an agreement, effective June 11, 200X, between The Accountant's Own Software Company (the "Discloser") and Sandra Miller (the "Recipient"), in which Discloser agrees to disclose, and Recipient agrees to receive, certain trade secrets of Discloser on the following terms and conditions:

1. **Trade Secrets:** Recipient understands and acknowledges that Discloser's trade secrets consist of information and materials that are valuable and not generally known by Discloser's competitors. Discloser's trade secrets include:

   (a) Any and all information concerning Discloser's current, future or proposed products, including, but not limited to, unpublished computer code (both source code and object code), drawings, specifications, notebook entries, technical notes and graphs, computer printouts, technical memoranda and correspondence, product development agreements and related agreements.

   (b) Information and materials relating to Discloser's purchasing, accounting and marketing, including, but not limited to, marketing plans, sales data, unpublished promotional material, cost and pricing information and customer lists.

   (c) Information of the type described above which Discloser obtained from another party and which Discloser treats as confidential, whether or not owned or developed by Discloser.

2. **Purpose of Disclosure:** Recipient shall make use of Discloser's trade secrets only for the purpose of evaluating Discloser's software for use in Recipient's business.

3. **Nondisclosure:** In consideration of Discloser's disclosure of its trade secrets to Recipient, Recipient agrees that it will treat Discloser's trade secrets with the same degree of care and safeguards that it takes with its own trade secrets, but in no event less than a reasonable degree of care. Recipient agrees that, without Discloser's prior written consent, Recipient will not:

   (a) disclose Discloser's trade secrets to any third party;

   (b) make or permit to be made copies or other reproductions of Discloser's trade secrets; or

Reprinted with permission from *Software Development: A Legal Guide* by Stephen Fishman (Nolo).

Definitions

(c) make any commercial use of the trade secrets.

Recipient will not disclose Discloser's trade secrets to Recipient's employees, agents and consultants unless: (1) they have a need to know the information in connection with their employment or consultant duties; and (2) they personally agree in writing to be bound by the terms of this Agreement.

4. **Return of Materials:** Upon Discloser's request, Recipient shall promptly (within 30 days) return all original materials provided by Discloser and any copies, notes or other documents in Recipient's possession pertaining to Discloser's trade secrets.

5. **Exclusions:** This agreement does not apply to any information which:

    (a) was in Recipient's possession or was known to Recipient, without an obligation to keep it confidential, before such information was disclosed to Recipient by Discloser;

    (b) is or becomes public knowledge through a source other than Recipient and through no fault of Recipient;

    (c) is independently developed by or for Recipient;

    (d) is or becomes lawfully available to Recipient from a source other than Discloser; or

    (e) is disclosed by Recipient with Discloser's prior written approval.

6. **Term of Agreement:** This Agreement and Recipient's duty to hold Discloser's trade secrets in confidence shall remain in effect until the above-described trade secrets are no longer trade secrets or until Discloser sends Recipient written notice releasing Recipient from this Agreement, whichever occurs first.

7. **No Rights Granted:** Recipient understands and agrees that this Agreement does not constitute a grant or an intention or commitment to grant any right, title or interest in Discloser's trade secrets to Recipient.

8. **Warranty:** Discloser warrants that it has the right to make the disclosures under this Agreement. **NO OTHER WARRANTIES ARE MADE BY DISCLOSER UNDER THIS AGREEMENT. ANY INFORMATION DISCLOSED UNDER THIS AGREEMENT IS PROVIDED "AS IS."**

9. **Injunctive Relief:** Recipient recognizes and acknowledges that any breach or threatened breach of this Agreement by Recipient may cause Discloser irreparable harm for which monetary damages may be inadequate. Recipient agrees, therefore, that Discloser shall be entitled to an injunction to restrain

Definitions

Recipient from such breach or threatened breach. Nothing in this Agreement shall be construed as preventing Discloser from pursuing any remedy at law or in equity for any breach or threatened breach of this Agreement.

10. **Attorney Fees:** If any legal action arises relating to this Agreement, the prevailing party shall be entitled to recover all court costs, expenses and reasonable attorney fees.

11. **Modifications:** All additions or modifications to this Agreement must be made in writing and must be signed by both parties to be effective.

12. **No Agency:** This Agreement does not create any agency or partnership relationship between the parties.

13. **Applicable Law:** This Agreement is made under, and shall be construed according to, the laws of the State of Nevada.

Discloser: The Accountant's Own Software Company

By: _____
                    (signature)

_____
                (typed or printed name)

Title: _____

Date: _____

Recipient: Sandra Miller

By: _____
                    (signature)

_____
                (typed or printed name)

Title: _____

Date: _____

Definitions

contact with the information), must know in no uncertain terms that the information is confidential, and that they have an obligation not to disclose it.

The best way to give this notice is to require all employees coming in contact with the secret to sign confidentiality agreements. However, an express written notice to employees regarding the status of the information and their obligation of confidentiality will also usually provide a basis for judicially protecting the information in the event of a later threatened or actual disclosure.

Companies often put employees on notice of trade secret status by using:

- signs on walk-in areas where trade secrets are being stored or used
- confidentiality labels on documents
- initial employment interviews in which the business's trade secrets are discussed and the need to keep them confidential is stressed, and
- exit interviews where departing employees are cautioned against disclosing the company's trade secrets in their new employment.

Related terms: confidential employment relationship; confidentiality agreements; reasonably precautionary measures to protect trade secrets.

notice to former employee's new employer

When an employee with knowledge of his or her employer's trade secrets takes a new job with a competing company, the first employer will often send the new employer a letter. The first employer will emphasize that the former employee is legally bound not to disclose any trade secrets and that, if he or she does, any such disclosure may not be used by the new employer. If the new employer then makes use of the trade secrets, the first employer may obtain greater damages and other enhanced judicial relief.

Related terms: improper disclosure of trade secrets; trade secret infringement action.

novelty and trade secrets

For information to qualify as a trade secret, it must generally not be known or used in the relevant industry. Strictly speaking, information constituting a trade secret need not be novel in the sense of "new" or "innovative." It simply must provide its owner with a competitive advantage.

> **EXAMPLE:** Robotics World rediscovers a principle of movement first pioneered by the nineteenth-century European moving doll industry. If this particular principle has been lost to the modern world, it can qualify as a trade secret, even though it is in no way novel. As long as the principle of movement provides its owner with a competitive advantage, it is legally identical to trade secrets that are independently conceived.

Related terms: competitive advantage; parallel research; trade secret, defined.

obligation of confidentiality

See duty of trust.

ownership of trade secret rights

See trade secret owner.

parallel research

Parallel research refers to situations where similar information or ideas are developed by two or more companies through their independent efforts. Especially where cutting edge technologies are involved, many companies are likely to be engaged in similar research and development activity, which can be expected to produce trade secrets. This means that the same basic information may be properly viewed as a trade secret by many different companies.

> **EXAMPLE:** A new cola company inadvertently creates the exact cola formula used by an existing company. Both the new and old companies are entitled to protect their formulas as trade secrets, even though the second formula is not novel.

Related terms: head start rule; independent conception, defense to trade secret claim; unsolicited idea disclosure.

patent application, effect on trade secrets

To obtain a patent on an invention, the inventor must fully describe the invention in the patent application. The U.S. Patent and Trademark Office (PTO) treats patent applications as confidential, making it possible to apply for a patent and still maintain the underlying information as a trade secret, at least for the first 18 months of the application period. Effective December 2000, the PTO will publish a patent application 18 months after the filing date but only if the applicant intends also to file abroad. (The 18-month publication statute was enacted in order to make U.S. patent laws more like those of foreign countries.) Because an application is published by the PTO after 18 months, all of the secret information becomes public and the trade secret status of the application is lost.

However, if an applicant states at the time of filing that the application will not be filed abroad, the information in the patent application will become publicly available only if and when a patent is granted. If the applicant is not filing abroad and the patent is rejected, confidentiality is preserved because the PTO does not publish rejected applications. If the PTO approves the patent application, it will be published in the Official Gazette. Inventors are willing to accept this trade-off—loss of trade secrecy for patent rights—because the patent can be used to prevent anyone else from exploiting the underlying information.

Publication after 18 months does provide one advantage for a patent applicant. If a patent later issues, the patent owner can later recover damages from infringers from the date of publication provided that the infringer had notice of the publication.

Related terms: loss of trade secrets; reverse engineering and trade secrets.

patterns and designs as trade secrets

Patterns and designs may qualify as trade secrets if they create a competitive advantage and are kept secret. Examples of patterns and designs that have been protected as trade secrets are advanced design plans for a new minicomputer, designs for electronic circuitry and schematic plans for an innovative metal door frame.

Related terms: industrial secret; trade secret, defined.

physical devices, ability to maintain as trade secrets

Physical devices—for example, tools, products and components—can qualify as trade secrets if they provide their owner with a competitive advantage and are kept secret. Such devices can easily be protected when they are used solely in the trade secret owner's manufacturing or production process. In addition, if distribution is limited and the devices are licensed rather than sold, the trade secret protection may be preserved if the license prohibits reverse engineering. However, the more the world shrinks and the faster information moves, the harder it will be to preserve trade secrecy by licensing restrictions.

Once products are widely distributed, trade secret status is usually impossible to maintain. Anyone may examine these products and figure out how they work —that is, reverse engineer them. When reverse engineering is accomplished, the trade secret enters the public domain.

EXAMPLE: Jason invents, manufactures and distributes a device that allows people to use their microcomputers to preprogram their VCRs to reject certain kinds of ads. He calls it AdOut. Physically, AdOut consists of an integrated circuit board inside a black box and ports to interface it with a VCR and computer. Jason has designed the box so that it can be opened to replace the circuit board if that component fails. If Caryl Curious were to open the box, examine the board, figure out how AdOut works, and start manufacturing her own device called AdScreen, Jason would have no grounds for relief against Caryl under trade secret laws. Why not? Because Caryl lawfully obtained the necessary information through reverse engineering. If, however, Jason either owns a patent or copyright on some aspect of the AdOut hardware or software that was copied by Caryl, Jason can obtain court relief on those grounds.

Related terms: licensing of trade secrets; reasonably precautionary measures to protect trade secrets; reverse engineering and trade secrets; trade secret, defined.

piracy

A colloquial term, "piracy" refers to any activity directed toward the improper acquisition of a trade secret or other forms of intellectual property that belong to another. The word has no legal significance.

Related terms: improper acquisition of trade secrets; industrial espionage; theft of trade secrets.

predetermination of rights in technical data

Before hiring a business or consulting firm for research and development projects likely to produce patentable inventions and trade secrets, the government routinely requires a contract that contains clauses predetermining who will own the rights to the patents and secrets in question. Predetermination of rights provisions are also typically found in agreements between universities and corporations, and corporations and independent contractors.

EXAMPLE: The federal government contracts with a biotech firm to "manufacture" a new life form that will survive on the Moon. Because such a project is likely to result in a number of extremely valuable discoveries, the contract between the biotech firm and the government should address in advance who will own intellectual property rights in the new life forms and the discoveries associated with their development.

Although ownership of intellectual property rights can be a subject for negotiation, the government will typically demand ownership of all rights in the main product being developed, but will allow the private party to own the rights to any "side-products," including information that can qualify as trade secrets.

Related terms: trade secret owner.

preliminary injunctions in trade secret infringement actions

See injunctions in trade secret cases.

premature disclosure

See loss of trade secrets.

price setting

See illegal restraint of trade.

processes as trade secrets

A "process" consists of a series of steps that lead to a particular result. Any process may qualify for trade secret status if it is generally not known in the industry, adds to a business's competitive advantage and is maintained as a trade secret. Among the processes that have been afforded protection as a trade secret in the past are those involving photographic development, silk screening, centrifugal processing for blood plasma fractionation and the manufacture of chocolate powder and tobacco flavoring.

Related terms: industrial know-how as trade secrets; methods and techniques as trade secrets; trade secret, defined.

protective order

In the event a trade secret is disclosed as part of a lawsuit, the trade secrecy can be preserved by a protective order. This order prohibits the participants in the lawsuit from disclosing the secret and it "seals" the court record pertaining to the trade secret, making it unavailable as a public document. Protective orders can be made by order of the court or the parties may agree (or stipulate) to the protection of confidential information. Protective orders are authorized under Section 5 of the Uniform Trade Secrets Act and under Federal Rule of Civil Procedure 26(c)(7).

Related terms: litigation and trade secrets; injunctions in trade secret cases; temporary restraining order.

professional client lists

See customer lists.

protecting a trade secret

See reasonably precautionary measures to protect trade secrets.

provisional relief in a trade secret infringement action

See injunctions in trade secret cases.

public domain and trade secrets

Trade secrets are considered to be in the public domain—situations where their owners have no legal recourse under trade secret law against disclosure and use by others—when the owner of the trade secret:

- is negligent or impermissibly sloppy in keeping it confidential
- fails to seek relief quickly in court if the trade secret becomes known to others through wrongful behavior (for instance, in violation of a nondisclosure agreement or through industrial espionage), or
- loses the rights to court protection of the trade secret by doing something forbidden under the law (for instance, using the trade secret in violation of the antitrust laws).

EXAMPLE: Microwave Systems wants to raise some venture capital to fund the promotion of its new mini satellite dish system, which it plans to sell to consumers for an affordable price. To accomplish this goal, it prepares a magazine article describing its revolutionary system, without intending to disclose its trade secrets. However, Manfred Manufacturer reads this article and learns enough details to start his own dish business. Microwave would not be able to claim an infringement of trade secret, since its ideas became a matter of public knowledge through its own disclosure.

Even if the secret becomes public because of someone's improper actions, such as the breaking of a nondisclosure agreement or industrial espionage, it will still be in the public domain if the information becomes well known. In short, once the trade secret cat is out of the owner's bag, the trade secret is gone unless the cat stays very close to home and the owner quickly retrieves it.

EXAMPLE: Using the same mini satellite dish business, suppose that no article appeared, and Manfred Manufacturer learns of the details of Microwave System's dish through the breach of a nondisclosure agreement by one of Microwave's employees. If only Manfred and a few of his associates know about the information, it may still qualify for trade secret status. If, on the other hand, the employee published the information in a major magazine, the trade secret is lost, regardless of the initial wrongfulness of the employee's action.

Of course, Microwave would be able to sue the offending employee for the loss.

It is possible for information to be in the public domain for the purpose of trade secret law, but still subject to restrictions under another set of laws. For instance, certain trade secrets in a computer program might pass into the public domain under trade secret law but still be entitled to a patent. If a patent is obtained, no one can use the invention comprising the former trade secret without the patent owner's permission. Similarly, an author may treat his or her novel as a trade secret while it is being written. Once the novel is published, the trade secret aspect of the novel falls into the public domain, but the novel itself will continue to be protected by copyright.

Related terms: loss of trade secrets; trade secret infringement action; trade secret owner.

public records and trade secrets

Any information contained in a public record (a document, tape, disk or other medium that is open to inspection by the public) cannot qualify as a trade secret, since by definition it is not confidential. However, because companies are often required by state and federal governments to file documents that, of necessity, contain trade secrets, there are usually laws that allow the withholding of the precise data that make up the trade secrets, even if the rest of the document is released for inspection.

Related terms: Freedom of Information Act, exemption of trade secrets; litigation and disclosure of trade secrets; protective order.

read-only memories (ROMs) and trade secrets

Internal operating instructions and other programs that are a physical part of the computer (for instance, read-only memories or ROMs) do not usually qualify for protection as a trade secret once the computer is marketed. This is because it is usually possible to figure out the design and logic of the ROM through reverse engineering, and any trade secrets that can become known in this manner are considered to be in the public domain.

Related terms: public domain and trade secrets; reverse engineering and trade secrets; software and trade secrets.

reasonably precautionary measures to protect trade secrets

Information will only qualify as a trade secret if its owner takes appropriate measures to keep it secret. What constitutes reasonably precautionary measures depends on the type of secret and the industry involved. This issue usually arises when a trade secret infringement action is filed, and the defendant claims that the information should not be considered as a trade secret because appropriate precautionary measures were not taken. If a court determines that the business claiming infringement has in fact taken appropriate measures to maintain the confidentiality of the information, it will be protected. If not, judicial relief will be denied and the information will no longer be considered a trade secret. Clearly, a certain amount of judicial discretion is involved in these decisions.

Measures typically considered to be reasonable precautions include:

- requiring employees to sign confidentiality agreements
- requiring all outside persons with whom the information is shared to sign nondisclosure agreements
- restricting physical access to areas where trade secrets are located
- consistently enforcing specific rules formulated by the company regarding confidentiality of the information and physical access to it
- using encryption or other code-like devices to make sure that trade secret information cannot easily be understood, even if read by an unauthorized person
- giving notice to all persons coming in contact with the information that it is considered a trade secret
- posting warnings on the wall of areas where trade secrets are kept or used reminding employees about company rules regarding trade secrets
- conducting exit interviews with employees, specifically warning them against improper disclosure of trade secrets
- adequately protecting against unauthorized intrusion into computer databases that contain trade secrets
- shredding sensitive documents prior to disposing of them, and
- if the scope of the operation and the value of the secrets warrants it, taking such physical security measures as posting guards, maintaining tight control over keys (including keys to the photocopy machine) and requiring visitors to wear badges.

Not all of these measures are necessary in every context, although the more of them that are employed, the better position the company will be in to claim that reasonable precautionary measures to protect the trade secrets have been taken. Just what measures are considered to be reasonably precautionary in a given case will depend on the size of the company, the value of the trade secrets and the nature of the technology involved.

Related terms: notice to employees of trade secrets; trade secret infringement action.

retail customer lists

See customer lists.

reverse engineering and trade secrets

The act of examining a product or device and figuring out the ideas and methods involved in its creation and structure is referred to as reverse engineering. Normally we think of engineering as the intellectual means by which something is built, or an idea is transformed into practice. In this context, "reverse engineering" consists of taking apart and reducing a product or device into its constituent parts and concepts.

The idea of reverse engineering is of crucial importance to trade secret law. This is because of the rule that any information learned about an item through the process of legitimate reverse engineering is considered to be in the public domain for trade secret purposes and therefore no longer protectable as a trade secret. However, the fact that a particular invention or technology can be figured out through reverse engineering has no effect on whether it is entitled to protection under the patent laws.

EXAMPLE: Ivan creates a machine capable of producing holographic games (games consisting of pictures projected onto three-dimensional space so that the images and characters appear realistic). Ivan treats the details of production as a trade secret. Once the machine is marketed, however, it will probably be possible to figure out through reverse engineering how it is constructed. If this is done, the machine can be freely manufactured and sold by the party doing the reverse engineering without Ivan being entitled to any court relief on trade secret grounds. However, Ivan would be entitled to protection under the patent laws if he has sought and obtained a patent on his invention.

Related terms: physical devices, ability to maintain as trade secrets; source code as trade secret.

sale of business, covenant not to compete

See covenant not to compete by owners of a sold business.

screening incoming information for unsolicited disclosures

See unsolicited idea disclosure.

software and trade secrets

An innovative computer program will often qualify for trade secret status at least during its development and testing stage. From a program's first conception, information and ideas about it often give an owner a competitive edge as long as they are kept secret. Once a program is fixed in a tangible medium of expression (that is, put down on tape, disk or paper in tangible form), it may still remain a trade secret. In addition, its expression (not the ideas behind that expression) is also protected under the copyright laws.

When a program is distributed, dual copyright and trade secret protections can continue if certain precautions are taken. For instance, if all "purchasers" of the program are required to sign a license forbidding disclosure of trade secrets, both trade secret and copyright protection may be available for distributed copies (the more limited the distribution is, the more likely the trade secret protection will exist). Or, if the owner of the program only distributes object code (usually the case except for programs written in BASIC) and keeps the source code locked in a secure place, it is similarly possible to maintain both trade secret and copyright protection for the program.

If the software owner registers the program with the U.S. Copyright Office, a printout of portions of the object code—or portions of the source code with critical parts blacked out—can be deposited as part of the registration. This will permit the trade secret to be maintained along with the registered copyright.

EXAMPLE: Harry Hildebrand conceives of a utility that will analyze a computer user's daily use of the computer and produce a report showing which programs were used, for how long and the overall pattern of usage. Because such a utility would have commercial value, the basic ideas behind it will qualify as a trade secret as long as Harry treats them that way. Suppose that Harry decides to press ahead with his idea. All the information produced by the development process, including the first flow charts, the written code (the source code) and the instructions to the computer produced by the compiler (the object code) separately and together, can properly qualify as trade secrets if they are treated as such.

Once the program is "up and running" on the computer, Harry has others test the program to see if it actually works, and whether programming "bugs" need to be corrected. Because Harry still considers the program to be a trade secret, he has the testers sign nondisclosure agreements in which they agree to keep the program confidential and preserve its trade secret status. In addition, because the program is now fixed in tangible form, it is protected under copyright law without losing trade secret status. When Harry registers the program with the U.S. Copyright Office, he deposits the object code.

Related terms: beta-testing and trade secrets; copyright and trade secret law compatibility; reverse engineering and trade secrets; source code as trade secret.

Definitions

source code as trade secret

The specific instructions written by a programmer to tell a computer what to do are referred to as the source code. The language used to write the source code cannot usually be read directly by the computer and must be translated by a compiler into language the computer can understand, which is called object code.

When software is sold to the public, it is in object code form—that is, it is already compiled. Because object code is mostly a series of ones and zeros, it cannot readily be figured out through reverse engineering (called "decompiling" in this instance). The source code, on the other hand, can be figured out, and any trade secrets that the software owner wishes to maintain in the code can be easily obtained. For that reason, source code is usually kept secret, locked in the owner's vault.

Related terms: reverse engineering and trade secrets.

specific performance of covenant not to compete

If a former employee or owner of a business threatens to violate a contract (covenant) not to compete with the business, a court may order the owner or employee to comply with the agreement. Whether a court will issue this type of order depends on a number of "fairness" or equity factors, such as:

- the length of time competition is prohibited
- in the case of employees, the effect of the agreement on the employee's ability to make a living, and
- whether the court concludes that the original covenant not to compete agreement was unnecessarily broad.

Generally, non-competition agreements that are limited in terms of time and scope have a better chance of being enforced than those that are open-ended. And a few states, including Texas and California, severely restrict the ability of an employer to enforce a non-competition agreement against a former employee.

Related terms: covenant not to compete by employee; covenant not to compete by owners of a sold business; injunctions in trade secret cases.

temporary restraining order

A court order that can be immediately obtained by a plaintiff in an intellectual property infringement lawsuit case with little or no advance notice to the defendant is a temporary restraining order (TRO). TROs place events in a holding pattern ("maintain the status quo") until the court can more fully determine what kind of protection is required, if any. Typically, TROs only last for a few days, or at most, two to three weeks. While the TRO is still in effect, a court will hear the argument of all sides to the dispute and more thoroughly consider the underlying issues.

Related terms: injunctions in trade secret cases; trade secret infringement action.

territorial restriction agreements—trade secrets

Trade secret licenses commonly are granted separately to different countries or groups of countries. They also are sometimes used to restrict an operation to a particular region of the U.S. Such restrictions allow a trade secret owner to distribute information or products through a number of different publishing, marketing or manufacturing enterprises that are regionally strong, rather than through just one national or international operation.

> EXAMPLE: The owner of a secret ingredient for a fried chicken batter issues 50 licenses, each one restricted to a particular state. The owner then might issue foreign licenses to individual nations or groups of nations, such as the European Economic Community (EEC, or Common Market).

Territorial restrictions in trade secret licenses are also designed to allow the owner of a trade secret to limit the use of the information to areas other than those in which the owner's business is located. In this way, the owner hopes to escape competition while still receiving the maximum benefit from the trade secret.

> EXAMPLE: A New York law book publisher develops a computerized "expert system" for helping people prepare their own divorce cases. If the publisher is only interested in marketing the system in New York state, it might well license the basic program, with its attendant trade secrets, for use in all other states.

Related terms: licensing of trade secrets; World Intellectual Property Organization (WIPO).

theft of trade secrets

Because trade secrets are a type of property, criminal prosecution is available in most states for their theft. A prosecution may also be brought by the federal government under the federal Industrial Espionage Act.

Although state criminal laws affecting trade secrets differ from state to state, the typical law applies to anybody who intentionally:

- physically takes records or articles reflecting the trade secret
- copies or photographs such records or articles

Definitions

- assists in either of these acts, or
- discloses the trade secret to another after having received knowledge of the secret in the course of a confidential employment relationship.

EXAMPLE: Alice Engineer is hired by LaserDisk, Inc., to design a home laser disk unit. Alice is informed of certain LaserDisk trade secrets relevant to her design work. About a year later, Alice becomes unhappy with her employment and takes a better job at a competing company. She discloses LaserDisk's trade secrets to the new company. Because Alice learned of the trade secrets in the course of a trust relationship at LaserDisk (a relationship usually considered to exist between highly skilled employees and their employer), she is subject to criminal prosecution if the state in question has a trade secret theft law. In every state, Alice could be sued in civil court in a trade secret infringement action.

Related terms: improper acquisition of trade secrets; improper disclosure of trade secrets; trade secret infringement action.

tools as trade secrets

See physical devices, ability to maintain as trade secrets.

trade secret, defined

In most states, a trade secret may consist of any formula, pattern, physical device, idea, process, compilation of information or other information that both:
- provides a business with a competitive advantage, and
- is treated in a way that can reasonably be expected to prevent the public or competitors from learning about it, absent improper acquisition or theft.

When deciding whether information qualifies as a trade secret under this definition, courts will typically consider the following factors:
- the extent to which the information is known outside of the particular business entity
- the extent to which the information is known by employees and others involved in the business
- the extent to which measures have been taken to guard the secrecy of the information
- the value of the information to the business, and
- the difficulty with which the information could be properly acquired or independently duplicated by others.

There is no crisp definition of what constitutes a trade secret. A trade secret is created and defined solely by reference to how certain information is handled, and to the value inherent in keeping it secret. Even if an item or piece of information otherwise qualifies as a trade secret, its moment-to-moment status will depend on how it is treated by its owners.

Related terms: ideas as trade secrets; reasonably precautionary measures to protect trade secrets; software and trade secrets; trade secret infringement action.

trade secret infringement action

The owner of a trade secret may bring a lawsuit, known as a trade secret infringement action, for the purpose of:

- preventing another person or business from using the trade secret without proper authorization, and
- collecting money damages for economic injury suffered as a result of the improper acquisition and use of the trade secret.

All persons and businesses responsible for the improper acquisition, and all those who have benefited from such acquisition, are typically named as defendants in infringement actions.

Among the most common situations that give rise to infringement actions are:

- Trade secrets are stolen through industrial espionage.
- An employee having knowledge of a trade secret changes jobs and discloses the secret to a new employer in violation of an express or implied confidentiality agreement with the first employer.
- Trade secrets are improperly disclosed in violation of a nondisclosure agreement.

To prevail in an infringement suit, the plaintiff (person bringing the suit) must be able to show that the information alleged to be a trade secret provides the plaintiff with a competitive advantage and has been continually treated by the plaintiff as a trade secret. In addition, the plaintiff must show that the defendant either improperly acquired the information (if accused of making commercial use of the secret) or improperly disclosed it (if accused of leaking the information).

The defendants in trade secret infringement cases commonly attempt to defend against the plaintiff's case by proving that:

- the information claimed to be a trade secret was known throughout the particular industry, and thus not a secret that should be subject to protection
- the information was lawfully disclosed by a person having knowledge of it
- the information was lawfully acquired through reverse engineering
- the information was the result of an independent conception, or
- the trade secret was being used by its owner in violation of the antitrust laws.

If the plaintiff can establish that a trade secret was, in fact, improperly used, disclosed or acquired by a defendant, the court can enjoin (stop) its further commercial use. Sometimes such injunctions are permanent—that is, they are final court orders in the case. More commonly, courts will employ the head start rule. This operates to give the rightful owner of the trade secret a "head start" in commercially exploiting it, by prohibiting its use by the competitor for such period of time as the court decides it would have taken the competitor to independently develop the information.

Because lawsuits tend to drag on for years, courts are authorized to issue preliminary injunctions prohibiting the competitor from using the secret in question pending a final determination in the case. These preliminary orders are often viewed by the parties as harbingers of how the case will finally turn out, and accordingly form the basis of a settlement (which precludes a full scale trial).

In addition to injunctive relief (both provisional and final), a court may award damages suffered by the original trade secret owner. These can consist of lost profits resulting from sales by the trade secret infringer, profits realized by the infringer from the wrongfully acquired trade secret and, occasionally, punitive or treble damages, depending on the state where the action is being tried.

Related terms: damages in trade secret infringement actions; independent conception, defense to trade secret claim; injunctions in trade secret cases; litigation and disclosure of trade secrets; reasonably precautionary measures to protect trade secrets; reverse engineering and trade secrets.

trade secret owner

The owner of a trade secret has a right to seek relief in court in the event someone else improperly acquires or improperly discloses the trade secret. The trade secret owner is also entitled to grant others a license to utilize the secret, or even to sell it outright.

Ownership of a trade secret is usually determined by the circumstances of its creation. In general, these ownership rules apply:

- trade secrets that arise from research and development activities conducted by manufacturing concerns belong to the company sponsoring the research and development
- retail customer lists belong to the business or individual who compiled the list
- trade secrets developed by an employee in the course of his or her employment belong to the employer, and
- trade secrets developed by an employee on his or her own time, and with personal equipment, usually belong to the employee.

EXAMPLE: A chef develops a special recipe and baking process for cheesecake during her off-work hours, and in her own kitchen. Even though she bakes the cheesecake for a restaurant, she would probably be entitled to preserve the recipe and process as her own trade secret. If, on the other hand, the recipe and process were developed at work with the restaurant facilities, the restaurant would own the trade secret.

Related terms: business information as trade secret; licensing of trade secrets.

trade secrets and antitrust laws

See antitrust law and trade secrets.

tying arrangements

When a business sells certain products on the condition that customers must purchase certain other products from the same business, it's referred to as a "tying arrangement." Tying arrangements usually occur when a seller has sufficient economic power, or a sufficiently unique and useful product, to enforce its conditions on the customers. Tying arrangements are sometimes considered a violation of antitrust law, as an impermissible "restraint on trade." However, no antitrust law is violated when a trade secret is involved and the "tying" is necessitated by an overriding business reason, rather than designed to secure a competitive advantage.

Definitions

EXAMPLE: Solely for the purpose of getting a leg up on its competitors, a computer manufacturer of both hardware and software requires customers to buy its hardware as a condition of purchasing its software. This would most likely be considered an illegal tying arrangement, since there was no issue of quality control or trade secret protection.

Related terms: antitrust law and trade secrets.

Uniform Trade Secret Protection Act

This model legislation was prepared for the ultimate purpose of creating the same trade secret laws in all 50 states. At present, only California and a few other states have adopted it. Overall, the provisions of the Uniform Trade Secret Protection Act are consistent with the general principles of trade secret law adopted by the courts under the common law (law established by court case decisions). (A copy of the Uniform Trade Secrets Act is set out in full at the end of this section.)

unique ideas as trade secrets

See ideas as trade secrets.

unjust enrichment and trade secrets

Some courts deciding cases involving the improper acquisition of a trade secret have ordered the guilty party to pay the trade secret owner all profits earned from the trade secret in question. The legal theory underlying this type of relief is that the wrongful possessor has been unjustly enriched by profiting from these trade secrets.

The unjust enrichment approach has also been used as a theoretical basis for providing judicial protection to trade secrets. Courts have long been willing to entertain disputes where one party was being unjustly enriched at the expense of another, so the improper acquisition of a trade secret is by nature the type of unjust enrichment that deserves judicial relief.

Related terms: damages in trade secret infringement actions; trade secret infringement action.

unsolicited idea disclosure

Although many people have creative brainstorms, they usually must share their ideas with others to enlist their help in commercially developing or promoting the idea. This process frequently involves approaching a well-known company to see if it is interested in the unsolicited idea.

Although a company may benefit from ideas generated by outside parties, it often will decline to be informed about such ideas. This is because the company may already be working on a similar idea, and wants to avoid later accusations of ripping off the outside party.

Companies tend to be particularly reluctant to consider ideas presented by outsiders when asked to sign a nondisclosure agreement, which treats the idea as a trade secret belonging to the outsider. In that situation, if the company rejects the idea but later markets a product or service that appears to incorporate the idea, the company may be vulnerable to charges of trade secret theft and forced into an expensive lawsuit.

Companies routinely require anyone presenting an unsolicited idea to sign a waiver agreement giving up the right to sue for trade secret infringement. If the "idea person" does not want to sign the agreement, the company will not examine the secret. Many companies go to great lengths to make sure ideas don't get past the front door absent the signing of such a waiver.

Probably the best way to get past a company's mechanisms for insulating itself from outside ideas is to trust the company. Very few companies are interested in ripping off creative people; most can be counted on to play straight. On the other hand, if trust does not seem an appropriate approach for one reason or another, companies are usually willing to examine an invention if either a regular patent application or a Provisional Patent Application has been filed on it (in either case the invention is said to have "patent pending" status).

Related entries: independent conception, defense to trade secret claim; trade secret infringement action.
See also Part 3 (Patent Law): Provisional Patent Application (PPA).

waiver agreement for unsolicited idea disclosure

See unsolicited idea disclosure.

wholesale customer lists

See customer lists.

World Intellectual Property Organization (WIPO)

This organization was formed to facilitate international agreements regulating intellectual property. WIPO is a policy-making body only, with no delegated authority to make binding decisions or impose sanctions. WIPO's membership consists of representatives from countries, and groups of countries, including:

- most European countries
- countries that are members of the United Nations body UNESCO
- Japan, and
- the United States.

Related terms: General Agreement on Tariffs and Trade (GATT).

Definitions

wrongfully disclosing trade secrets

See improper disclosure of trade secrets.

wrongfully obtaining trade secrets

See improper acquisition of trade secrets.

Definitions

Trade Secret Law

UNIFORM TRADE SECRETS ACT. This uniform act has been adopted—with minor variations—by every state except Massachusetts, Michigan, Missouri, New Jersey, New York, North Carolina, Ohio, Pennsylvania, Tennessee, Texas, Vermont and Wyoming. Following are relevant portions of the Act.

§ 1. Definitions

As used in this Act, unless the context requires otherwise:

(1) "Improper means" includes theft, bribery, misrepresentation, breach or inducement of a breach of a duty to maintain secrecy, or espionage through electronic or other means;

(2) "Misappropriation" means:

  (i) acquisition of a trade secret of another by a person who knows or has reason to know that the trade secret was acquired by improper means; or

  (ii) disclosure or use of a trade secret of another without express or implied consent by a person who

    (A) used improper means to acquire knowledge of the trade secret; or

    (B) at the time of disclosure or use, knew or had reason to know that his knowledge of the trade secret was

      (I) derived from or through a person who had utilized improper means to acquire it;

      (II) acquired under circumstances giving rise to a duty to maintain its secrecy or limit its use; or

      (III) derived from or through a person who owed a duty to the person seeking relief to maintain its secrecy or limit its use; or

    (C) before a material change of his position, knew or had reason to know that it was a trade secret and that knowledge of it had been acquired by accident or mistake.

(3) "Person" means a natural person, corporation, business trust, estate, trust, partnership, association, joint venture, government, governmental subdivision or agency, or any other legal or commercial entity.

(4) "Trade secret" means information, including a formula, pattern, compilation, program, device, method, technique, or process, that:
  (i) derives independent economic value, actual or potential, from not being generally known to, and not being readily ascertainable by proper means by, other persons who can obtain economic value from its disclosure or use, and
  (ii) is the subject of efforts that are reasonable under the circumstances to maintain its secrecy.

§ 2. Injunctive Relief

(a) Actual or threatened misappropriation may be enjoined. Upon application to the court, an injunction shall be terminated when the trade secret has ceased to exist, but the injunction may be continued for an additional reasonable period of time in order to eliminate commercial advantage that otherwise would be derived from the misappropriation.

(b) If the court determines that it would be unreasonable to prohibit future use, an injunction may condition future use upon payment of a reasonable royalty for no longer than the period of time the use could have been prohibited.

(c) In appropriate circumstances, affirmative acts to protect a trade secret may be compelled by court order.

§ 3. Damages

(a) In addition to or in lieu of injunctive relief, a complainant may recover damages for the actual loss caused by misappropriation. A complainant also may recover for the unjust enrichment caused by misappropriation that is not taken into account in computing damages for actual loss.

(b) If willful and malicious misappropriation exists, the court may award exemplary damages in an amount not exceeding twice any award made under subsection (a).

§ 4. Attorney's Fees

If (i) a claim of misappropriation is made in bad faith, (ii) a motion to terminate an injunction is made or resisted in bad faith, or (iii) willful and malicious misappropriation exists, the court may award reasonable attorney's fees to the prevailing party.

§ 5. Preservation of Secrecy

In an action under this Act, a court shall preserve the secrecy of an alleged trade secret by reasonable means, which may include granting protective orders in connection with discovery proceedings, holding in camera hearings, sealing the records of the action, and ordering any person involved in the litigation not to disclose an alleged trade secret without prior court approval.

§ 6. Statute of Limitations

An action for misappropriation must be brought within 3 years after the misappropriation is discovered or by the exercise of reasonable diligence should have been discovered. For the purposes of this section, a continuing misappropriation constitutes a single claim.

§ 7. Effect on Other Law

(a) This Act displaces conflicting tort, restitutionary, and other law of this State pertaining to civil liability for misappropriation of a trade secret.

(b) This Act does not affect:
  (1) contractual or other civil liability or relief that is not based upon misappropriation of a trade secret; or
  (2) criminal liability for misappropriation of a trade secret.

Statutes

§ 8. Uniformity of Application and Construction

This Act shall be applied and construed to effectuate its general purpose to make uniform the law with respect to the subject of this Act among states enacting it.

§ 9. Short Title

This Act may be cited as the Uniform Trade Secrets Act.

§ 10. Severability

If any provision of this Act or its application to any person or circumstances is held invalid, the invalidity does not affect other provisions or applications of the Act which can be given effect without the invalid provision or application, and to this end the provisions of this Act are severable.

§ 11. Time of Taking Effect

This Act takes effect on, and does not apply to misappropriation occurring prior to the effective date.

§ 12. Repeal

The following Acts and parts of Acts are repealed:
    (1)
    (2)
    (3)

THE ECONOMIC ESPIONAGE ACT OF 1996

§ 1. Short Title

This Act may be cited as the "Economic Espionage Act of 1996."

Title I.   Protection of Trade Secrets

§ 101.   Protection of Trade Secrets

§ 1831. Economic espionage

(a) In General - Whoever, intending or knowing that the offense will benefit any foreign government, foreign instrumentality, or foreign agent, knowingly
    (1) steals, or without authorization appropriates, takes, carries away, or conceals, or by fraud, artifice, or deception obtains a trade secret;
    (2) without authorization copies, duplicates, sketches, draws, photographs, downloads, uploads, alters, destroys, photocopies, replicates, transmits, delivers, sends, mails, communicates, or conveys a trade secret,
    (3) receives, buys, or possesses a trade secret, knowing the same to have been stolen or appropriated, obtained, or converted without authorization,
    (4) attempts to commit any offense described in any of paragraphs (1) through (3), or
    (5) conspires with one or more other persons to commit any offense described in any of paragraphs (1) through (3), and one or more of such persons do any act to effect the object of the conspiracy, shall, except as provided in subsection (b), be fined not more than $500,000 or imprisoned not more than 15 years, or both.
(b) Organizations - Any organization that commits any offense described in subsection (a) shall be fined not more than $ 10,000,000.

Statutes

§ 1832. Theft of trade secrets

(a) Whoever, with intent to convert a trade secret, that is related to or included in a product that is produced for or placed in interstate or foreign commerce, to the economic benefit of anyone other than the owner thereof, and intending or knowing that the offense will injure any owner of that trade secret, knowingly:

   (1) steals, or without authorization appropriates, takes, carries away, or conceals, or by fraud, artifice, or deception obtains such information;

   (2) without authorization copies, duplicates, sketches,. draws, photographs, downloads, uploads, alters, destroys, photocopies, replicates, transmits, delivers, sends, mails, communicates, or conveys such information;

   (3) receives, buys, or possesses such information, knowing the same to have been stolen or appropriated, obtained, or converted without authorization;

   (4) attempts to commit any offense described in paragraphs (1) through (3); or

   (5) conspires with one or more other persons to commit any offense described in paragraphs (1) through (3), and one or more of such persons do any act to effect the object of the conspiracy, shall, except as provided in subsection (b), be fined under this title or imprisoned not more than 10 years, or both.

(b) Any organization that commits any offense described in subsection (a) shall be fined not more than $5,000,000.

§ 1833. Exceptions to prohibitions

This chapter does not prohibit:

   (1) any otherwise lawful activity conducted by a governmental entity of the United States, a State, or a political subdivision of a State; or

   (2) the reporting of a suspected violation of law to any governmental entity of the United States, a State, or a political subdivision of a State, if such entity has lawful authority with respect to that violation.

§ 1834. Criminal forfeiture

(a) The court, in imposing sentence on a person for a violation of this chapter, shall order, in addition to any other sentence imposed, that the person forfeit to the United States -

   (1) any property constituting or derived from, any proceeds the person obtained, directly or indirectly, as the result of such violation; and

   (2) any of the person's or organization's property used, or intended to be used, in any manner or part, to commit or facilitate the commission of such violation, if the court in its discretion so determines, taking into consideration the nature, scope, and proportionality of the use of the property in the offense.

(b) Property subject to forfeiture under this section, any seizure and disposition thereof, and any administrative or judicial proceeding in relation thereto, shall be governed by section 413 of the Comprehensive Drug Abuse Prevention and Control Act of 1970 (21 U.S. C. 8 5 3), except for subsections (d) and 0) of such section, which shall not apply to forfeitures under this section.

§ 1835. Orders to preserve confidentiality

In any prosecution or other proceeding under this chapter, the court shall enter such orders and take such other action as may be necessary and appropriate to preserve the confidentiality of trade secrets, consistent with the requirements of the Federal Rules of Criminal and Civil Procedure, the Federal Rules of Evidence, and all other applicable laws. An interlocutory appeal by the United States shall lie from a decision or order of a district court authorizing or directing the disclosure of any trade secret.

§ 1836. Civil proceedings to enjoin violations

    (a) The Attorney General may, in a civil action, obtain appropriate injunctive relief against any violation of this section.

    (b) The district courts of the United States shall have exclusive original jurisdiction of civil actions under this subsection.

§ 1837. Applicability to conduct outside the United States

This chapter also applies to conduct occurring outside the United States if;

    (1) the offender is a natural person who is a citizen or permanent resident alien of the United States, or an organization organized under the laws of the United States or a State or political subdivision thereof, or

    (2) an act in furtherance of the offense was committed in the United States.

§ 1838. Construction with other laws

This chapter shall not be construed to preempt or displace any other remedies, whether civil or criminal, provided by United States Federal, State, commonwealth, possession, or territory law for the misappropriation of a trade secret, or to affect the otherwise lawful disclosure of information by any Government employees under section 552 of title 5 (commonly know as the Freedom of Information Act).

§ 1839. Definitions

As used in this chapter

    (1) the term 'foreign instrumentality' means any agency, bureau, ministry, component, institution, association, or any legal, commercial, or business organization, corporation, firm, or entity that is substantially owned, controlled, sponsored, commanded, managed, or dominated by a foreign government:

    (2) the term 'foreign agent' means any officer, employee, proxy, servant, delegate, or representative of a foreign government:

    (3) the term 'trade secret' means all forms and types of financial, business, scientific, technical, economic, or engineering information, including patterns, plans, compilations, program devices, formulas, designs, prototypes, methods, techniques, processes, procedures, programs, or codes, whether tangible or intangible, and whether or how stored, compiled, or memorialized physically, electronically, graphically, photographically, in writing if

        (A) the owner thereof has taken reasonable measures to keep such information secret; and

        (B) the information derives independent economic value, actual or potential, from not being general known to, and not being readily ascertainable through proper means by the public, and

    (4) the term 'owner', with respect to a trade secret, means the person or entity in whom or in which rightful legal or equitable title to or license in, the trade secret is reposed."

Part 2

Copyright Law

Overview   74

Definitions   83

Sample Forms   179

Statutes   187

Overview

P robably the best known of intellectual property categories, copyright automatically applies to all types of original expression, including art, sculpture, literature, music, songs, choreography, crafts, poetry, flow charts, software, photography, movies, CD-ROMs, video games, videos, websites and graphic designs. The automatic protection can be enhanced by registering the work with the U.S. Copyright Office for a nominal fee.

Copyright lasts for many years. Most often it lasts for the life of the work's creator (its author) plus 70 years. In cases where the creator is a business, the copyright lasts between 95 and 120 years. Although copyright protection is long-lived, it only applies to the literal expression, not to the ideas and concepts underlying that expression.

Most nations of the world offer copyright protection to works by U.S. citizens and nationals, and the U.S. offers its copyright protection to the citizens and nationals of these same nations.

1. What is a copyright?

A copyright gives the owner of a creative work the right to keep others from using the work without the owner's permission. The key to understanding copyright law is to understand the difference between an idea and the expression of the idea. Copyright applies only to a particular expression, not to the ideas or facts underlying the expression. For instance, copyright may protect a particular song, novel or computer game about a romance in space, but it cannot protect the underlying idea of having a love affair among the stars.

More specifically, a creative work (often referred to as a "work of authorship") must meet all of these three criteria to be protected by copyright:

- It must be original. In other words, the author must have created rather than copied it.
- It must be fixed in a tangible (concrete) medium of expression. For example, it might be expressed on paper, audio or video tape, computer disk, clay or canvas.
- It must have at least some creativity—that is, it must be produced by an exercise of human intellect. There is no hard and fast rule as to how much creativity is enough. To give an example, it must go beyond the creativity found in the telephone white pages, which involve a non-discretionary alphabetic listing of telephone numbers rather than a creative selection of listings.

Related terms: affirmative rights; *Apple Computer, Inc. v. Franklin; Apple Computer, Inc. v. Microsoft Corp.*; audiovisual works; collective work; compilations of original or unoriginal material; *Computer Associates Int'l v. Altai*; computer databases, copyright of; computer software, copyright of; copies, meaning under copyright law; copyright, explained; copyright and patent compared; copyrighted work; derivative work; display a work, defined; dramatic works, copyrights; exclusive copyright rights; factual works, defined; *Feist Publications Inc. v. Rural Telephone Service Co.*; first sale doctrine; ideas, not protected under copyright; indecent or immoral works, not protected; joint work; literary works, copyrights; merger doctrine; microcode and copyright; moral rights; motion pictures, copyrights; musical works and copyright protection; object code, copyrights; original work of authorship; output of computer, copyrightability of; pantomimes and choreographic works, copyrights; performing a work; phonorecords, defined; pictorial, graphic and sculptural works; printed forms, not copyrightable; public domain—copyright context; public performance of a work; recordings, copyright of; source code, copyrights; unpublished work, copyrightability of; work of the U.S. government, public domain; work of visual art.

2. How is a copyright created?

A creative work is protected by copyright the moment the work assumes a tangible form—which in copyright circles, is referred to as "fixed in a tangible medium of expression." Contrary to popular belief, providing a copyright notice and/or registering the work with the U.S. Copyright Office are not necessary to obtain basic copyright protection. But there are some steps that can be taken to enhance the creator's chances for success if he or she turns to the courts to enforce a copyright:

- *Place a copyright notice on a published work.* The copyright notice, or "copyright bug" as it is sometimes called, commonly appears in this form: "© (year of publication) (author or other basic copyright owner)." By placing this notice on a work that is published (distributed to the public

Overview

without restriction), the author prevents others from copying the work without permission and claiming that they did not know that the work was covered by copyright. This can be important if the author is forced to file a lawsuit to enforce the copyright, since it is much easier to recover significant money damages from a deliberate (as opposed to innocent) copyright infringer.

- *Register works with the U.S. Copyright Office.* Timely registration of the copyright with the U.S. Copyright Office—that is, registration within three months of the work's publication date, or before the infringement actually begins—makes it much easier to sue and recover from an infringer. Specifically, timely registration creates a legal presumption that the copyright is valid, and allows the copyright owner to recover up to $150,000 (and possibly attorney fees) without proving any actual monetary harm. Registration is accomplished by filing a simple form and depositing one or two samples of the work (depending on what it is) with the U.S. Copyright Office. The U.S. Copyright Office registration currently costs $30 for each work. (Sample registration forms are provided later in this part.)

Related terms: based on an earlier work; best edition of a work; certificate of registration; copyright claimant; copyright registration forms; creation of work, when protected by copyright; cyberspace, copyrights in; defective copyright notice; de minimis, defined; deposit with U.S. Copyright Office; failure to deposit work; false representation in copyright registration application; fixed in a tangible medium of expression; flow charts, registration of; Form CA, described; Form PA, described; Form RE, described; Form SE (short, regular and group), described; Form SR, described; Form TX, described; Form VA, described; identifying material, defined; Library of Congress, deposit requirement; notice of copyright; omission of copyright notice; published work, defined; Register of Copyrights; registration of copyright, defined; rule of doubt; single registration rule; special relief, defined; supplemental registration; timely registration, defined; U.S. Copyright Office.

3. Who owns a copyright?

With three important exceptions, copyrights are owned by the writers, poets, musicians, choreographers, composers, artists, software designers, sculptors, photographers, movie producers, craftspersons and other persons who create them. In the copyright world, these people are all called "authors."

Now for the exceptions:

- If a work is created by an employee in the course of his or her employment, the work is called a "work made for hire" and the copyright is owned by the employer.
- If the work is commissioned (created by an author working as an independent contractor), and the parties sign a written work made for hire agree-

ment, the copyright will be owned by the commissioning party as long as the work falls within one of the statutory categories of commissioned works that can qualify as works made for hire.

- If the author sells the copyright to someone else, the purchasing person or business owns the copyright.

Related terms: agency (for the purpose of determining works made for hire); author, defined; author as owner of copyright; coauthors; copyright owner, defined; work made for hire, defined.

4. Can copyrights be divided or transferred?

A copyright actually is a bundle of separate exclusive subrights, including the exclusive right to:

- reproduce the work
- display or perform the work
- distribute the work, and
- prepare adaptations of the work (derivative works).

When a copyright owner wishes to commercially exploit the work covered by the copyright, the owner typically transfers one or more of these rights to the publisher or other entity who will be responsible for getting the work to market. It is also common for the copyright owner to place some limitations on the exclusive rights being transferred. For example, the owner may limit the transfer to a specific period of time, allow the right to be exercised only in a specific part of the country or world, or require that the right be exercised only on certain computer platforms (those with UNIX operating systems, for example).

When all copyright rights are transferred unconditionally, it is generally termed an "assignment." When only some of the rights associated with the copyright are transferred, it is known as a "license." An exclusive license exists when the right being licensed can only be exercised by the licensee, and no one else. If the license allows others to exercise the same rights being transferred in the license, the license is said to be non-exclusive.

The U.S. Copyright Office allows buyers of exclusive and non-exclusive copyright rights to record the transfers in the U.S. Copyright Office. This helps to protect the buyers in case the original copyright owner later decides to transfer the same rights to another party.

Related terms: assignment of copyright; compulsory license; exclusive license, defined; grant of rights; licensing of copyrights; non-exclusive license; overlapping transfers of copyright; recordation of copyright transfers; revocation of license; shrink-wrap license; site license; termination of transfers; transfers of copyright ownership, generally.

Overview

5. How long does copyright protection last?

As a result of the Copyright Extension Act of 1998, most copyrights for works published after January 1, 1978 last for the life of the author plus 70 years. However, in the following circumstances, the copyright lasts between 95 and 120 years, depending on the date the work is published:

- the work belongs to the author's employer under the work made for hire law
- the work was commissioned under a work made for hire agreement (and fits within one of the categories of works that qualify for work made for hire treatment), or
- the author publishes and registers the work anonymously or under a pseudonym.

After a copyright expires, the work goes into the public domain, meaning it becomes available for anyone's use.

For works created before 1978, the duration times are different:

- If the work was published before 1923, it is in the public domain (available for use without permission).
- If the work was plublished between 1923 and 1963 and not renewed (see duration of copyright), it is in the public domain.
- If the work was published between 1923 and 1963 and it was renewed, the copyright lasts 95 years from the date of first publication.
- If the work was published between 1964 and 1977, the copyright lasts for 95 years from the date of publication.
- If the work was created but not published or registered before 1978, the copyright lasts at least until December 31, 2002 if the work remains unpublished, or until December 31, 2047 if the work is published before December 31, 2002.

Related terms: duration of copyrights; pseudonym, copyright under a; Sonny Bono Copyright Term Extension Act.

6. What happens if a copyright is infringed?

In the event someone infringes (violates) the exclusive rights of a copyright owner, the owner is entitled to file a lawsuit in federal court asking the court to:

- issue orders (restraining orders and injunctions) to prevent further violations
- award money damages if appropriate, and
- in some circumstances, award attorney fees.

Whether the lawsuit will be effective and whether damages will be awarded depends on whether the alleged infringer can raise one or more legal defenses to the charge. Common legal defenses to copyright infringement are:

- too much time has elapsed between the infringing act and the lawsuit (the statute of limitations defense)
- the infringement is allowed under the fair use defense
- the infringement was innocent (the infringer had no reason to know the work was protected by copyright)
- the infringing work was independently created (that is, it wasn't copied from the original), or
- the copyright owner authorized the use in a license.

Related terms: actual damages for copyright infringement; authorized use of copyrighted material; copyright infringement, defined; credit line; criminal copyright infringement; damages for copyright infringement; defenses to copyright infringement; expedited registration; importing of infringing works; independent creation, defense to infringement action; infringement action, explained; injunctions, copyright infringement; photocopies and copyright law; piracy, defined; plagiarism, defined; profits as damages; statute of limitations; temporary restraining order (TRO).

7. May a copyrighted work legally be used without an owner's permission?

Some uses of a copyrighted work are considered fair use—that is, the use may infringe but the infringement is excused because the work is being used for a transformative purpose such as research, scholarship, criticism or journalism. When determining whether an infringement should be excused on the basis of fair use, a court will use several factors including the purpose and character of the use, amount and substantiality of the portion borrowed, and effect of the use on the market for the copyrighted material.

It's important to understand that fair use is a defense rather than an affirmative right. This means that a particular use only gets established as a fair use if the copyright owner decides to file a lawsuit and the court upholds the fair use defense. There is, therefore, no way to find out in advance whether something will or won't be considered a fair use. Of course, if the copyright owner is willing to grant permission for the use, then the uncertainty surrounding the use goes away. For this reason, most people who propose to use a copyrighted work do what they can to obtain permission, and only rely on the fair use defense if permission is not granted or the copyright owner can't be located.

A person who infringes a copyright but has good reason to genuinely believe that the use is a fair use is known as an innocent infringer. Innocent infringers usu-

Overview

ally don't have to pay any damages to the copyright owner, but do have to cease the infringing activity or pay the owner for the reasonable commercial value of that use.

Related terms: archival copies; fair use, defined; innocent infringement of copyright.

8. What laws cover copyright protection in the U.S. and other countries?

In the U.S., copyright protection derives from the U.S. Constitution, which requires that original works of authorship be protected by copyright. The current (and exclusive) source of this protection is the federal Copyright Act of 1976, as amended. There are no state copyright laws.

Copyright protection rules are fairly similar worldwide, due to several international copyright treaties, the most important of which is the Berne Convention. Under this treaty, all member countries (in excess of 100 countries, including virtually all industrialized countries) must afford copyright protection to authors who are nationals of any member country. This protection must last for at least the life of the author plus 50 years, and must be automatic without the need for the author to take any legal steps to preserve the copyright.

In addition to the Berne Convention, the GATT (General Agreement on Tariffs and Trade) treaty contains a number of provisions that affect copyright protection in signatory countries. Together, the Berne Copyright Convention and the GATT treaty allow U.S. authors to enforce their copyrights in most industrialized nations, and allow the nationals of those nations to enforce their copyrights in the U.S.

Related terms: all rights reserved; Berne Convention; Buenos Aires Convention, defined; common law copyright laws; Copyright Act of 1909; Copyright Act of 1976; freedom of speech and copyrights or trademarks; GATT (General Agreement on Tariffs and Trade); international copyright protection; international rules on notice of copyright; manufacturing clause; national treatment; restored copyright under GATT; Semiconductor Chip Protection Act of 1984; simultaneous publication; Universal Copyright Convention (U.C.C.).

9. Copyright resources

If you're interested in hands-on, step-by-step instructions on obtaining copyright protection, you may want to consult *The Copyright Handbook,* by Stephen Fishman (Nolo). A detailed description is provided in the Introduction, Section C. (Order information is at the back of this book.)

If you have access to the World Wide Web you can find valuable information about copyright by using any of the following sites:

1. **http://www.nolo.com** Nolo Press offers self-help information about a wide variety of legal topics, including copyright law. (See the intellectual property topic in the Legal Encyclopedia, which incidentally includes selected entries from this part of the book.)

2. **http://www.nolo.com** This site offers regulations, guidelines, forms and links to other helpful copyright sites.

3. **Findlaw at http://www.findlaw.com.** This search engine offers a comprehensive list of copyright resources on the Web. Click "intellectual property" under the topic heading on the home page and click "copyright" from the subcategory list on the intellectual property page.

4. **The Copyright Website at http://www.benedict.com.** This site has articles, links and a slick design. Best of all, you can examine actual examples from real cases. Compare *2 Live Crew's* version of *Pretty Woman* to the original or view the allegedly pilfered images used in the movie *The Devil's Advocate*.

Copyright Law

In this section, we provide concise definitions of the words and phrases commonly used when dealing with copyrights.

abridgment of works

See derivative work.

access

In order to prove that a work was copied, sold or performed without authorization, the copyright owner must demonstrate that the person accused of infringement had a reasonable opportunity to view or hear the copyrighted work and that the two works—the infringer's and the copyright owner's—are substantially similar. The first requirement—the occasion to view or hear the copyrighted work—is referred to as access. If the infringement involves identical copies, such as photographs copied from a magazine, access may be presumed and does not need to be proved. That's because in cases of verbatim copying, it is virtually impossible that two works could have been independently created. For example, the makers of Beanie Babies successfully sued a company marketing a pig bean bag known as "Preston the Pig" that was identical to the Beanie Baby known as "Squealor." The similarity between the two was so close as to create a reasonable presumption of access. (*Ty Inc. v. GMA Accessories Inc.* 132 F.3d 1167 (7th Cir. 1997).)

When the copies are not identical, access can be proven in various ways. For example, in one case the owners of copyright in popular children's characters proved access because the representatives of a fast-food chain had visited their headquarters and discussed use of the characters in commercials. (*Sid & Marty Krofft Television Prods., Inc. v. McDonald's Corp.,* 562 F.2d 1157 (9th Cir. 1977).)

In another case, the owners of the song *He's So Fine* sued George Harrison alleging that Harrison's song *My Sweet Lord* infringed their copyright. It was determined that Harrison had access to *He's So Fine* since the song was on the British pop charts in 1963 during the same period when a song by the Beatles was also on the British charts. (*Abkco Music, Inc. v. Harrisongs Music, Ltd.*, 722 F.2d 988 (2d Cir. 1983).)

As a general rule, the more popular a work, the easier it is to prove access. Conversely, if a work was not published, the copyright owner has a harder time proving access.

Related terms: copyright infringement, defined; infringement action, explained.

actual damages for copyright infringement

A court may award a dollar amount in actual damages in an effort to approximate the real dollars a copyright owner lost as a result of the owner's copyrighted work being distributed, copied, displayed, performed or altered by someone else without proper authorization.

Related terms: copyright infringement, defined; damages for copyright infringement.

adaptations or alterations of original works

See derivative work.

affirmative rights

Many people use the term "protections" to refer to the benefits that go along with ownership of copyrights and other intellectual property such as trade secrets, patents and trademarks. For example, one might say, "My poem is protected by copyright." However, a number of commentators (among them David Pressman, well-known patent lawyer and author of *Patent It Yourself*), prefer to describe these legal protections as "affirmative rights" because owners must affirmatively exercise their rights if their copyright is infringed.

Affirmative rights include the owner's right to file a lawsuit, the right to recover damages and the right to obtain an injunction (a court order preventing the infringer from taking certain actions, such as using or selling the infringing material). Although observing this linguistic difference may lead to a better understanding of how intellectual property laws work, this book generally uses the more accepted and commonly used term "protection."

all rights reserved

This phrase was required as part of a copyright notice by the Buenos Aires Convention international treaty. Until recently, the term appeared in many copyright notices in an attempt to secure complete protection under that treaty. However, all signatory countries to the Buenos Aires Convention are now also members of other international agreements that don't require the "all rights reserved" phrase, so it no longer serves any useful purpose.

Related terms: international copyright protection; international rules on notice of copyright.

Altai case
See Computer Associates Int'l v. Altai.

anthologies, copyrightability of
See compilations of unoriginal or original material.

anonymous
An author's contribution to a work is anonymous if the author is not identified on the copies or phonorecords of the work. Copyright protection for anonymous and pseudonymous works is 95 years from the date of publication or 120 years from creation, whichever is shorter. However, if the name of the author is disclosed in the records of the Copyright Office, the work will be protected for the author's life plus 70 years.

> **EXAMPLE:** The 1995 bestseller *Primary Colors* was published anonymously. The media eventually determined that the book's author was Joe Klein, a writer for *Newsweek* magazine. If Mr. Klein died in 2030 without disclosing his name to the Copyright Office, the term of copyright for *Primary Colors* would end in 2090 (95 years from publication). If Mr. Klein disclosed his name, protection would extend until 2100 (70 years from his death.)

Related terms: author as owner of copyright, duration of copyright, pseudonym.

Apple Computer, Inc. v. Franklin
In this influential 1983 court decision, a federal Court of Appeals for the first time extended copyright protection to computer operating systems consisting of object code embedded in read-only memory chips, or ROMs. (*Apple Computer, Inc. v. Franklin Computer Corporation,* 714 F.2d 1240 (3rd Cir. 1983).)

The case arose when Franklin Computer Co. marketed an Apple compatible computer that used a ROM chip copied from the one Apple used for its Apple II line of computers. The result was that Franklin Computer owners could use software developed for Apple computers and thus Franklin could compete directly with Apple in the marketplace.

Apple sued Franklin, claiming that the operating system contained in the Apple ROM was protected by copyright. Franklin responded that neither object code nor operating systems were eligible for copyright protection because they were hardware, especially when embedded in a ROM, and thus were not within the reach of the copyright laws. The court disagreed with Franklin's position and decided that an operating system consisting of object code qualifies as "software" under the Copyright Act, whether it is embedded in a chip or simply maintained as code on a disk or tape. Today, experts mostly agree that in the U.S., object code is a work of expression protectable under the Copyright Act of 1976.

Related terms: computer software, copyright of.

Apple Computer, Inc. v. Microsoft Corp.

Apple Computer sued Microsoft, alleging that the Microsoft Windows operating system user interface infringed on Apple's copyright in the Macintosh user interface. The court ruled that the desktop metaphor employed by the Macintosh user interface was an unprotectable idea. The court also found that most of the individual elements that made up this desktop metaphor were not protected by copyright ideas, either because they were functional rather than original expression or because they were unprotectable ideas.

The court did leave open the possibility that a user interface as a whole might be protected against verbatim copying; but that was not the situation in this case, and therefore Microsoft did not infringe on Apple's copyright. *(Apple Computer, Inc. v. Microsoft Corp.*, 717 F. Supp. 1428 (N.D. Ca. 1989), 779 F. Supp. 133 (N.D. Ca. 1992).)

Related terms: computer software, copyright of.

architectural work

The design of a building is protected under copyright law. That is, the building, architectural plans, drawings or photographs cannot be reproduced without the consent of the owner of copyright in the architectural work—usually the architect or developer. There are some exceptions. For example, if the building is located in a place that is ordinarily visible to the public, photos or pictures of the building can be taken, distributed, or publicly displayed. Standard features such as common bathroom or kitchen design elements are not protected.

archival copies

The Computer Software Protection Act of 1980 defines archival copies as copies of software made by a software owner strictly for backup purposes—that is, to use if something happens to the original copy. The Act permits a computer program owner to make archival copies of the program as long as the owner retains the original copy of the program. But if the purchaser sells or gives away the original software to a new owner, all archival copies must either be included in the transfer or destroyed. The intention is to prevent two or more people from legally possessing copies of a program that has only been purchased from the copyright owner once.

> **EXAMPLE:** Ned Applequist pays $49.95 retail for WordScan, a spelling checker. As permitted under the Software Protection Act, Ned makes an archival copy as the legal owner of WordScan. If Ned later sells his original WordScan copy to Karen Goodperson for $20, he must either destroy his archival copy or give it to Karen as part of the sale.

arrangements, musical

See musical works and copyright protection.

assignment of copyright

The transfer of all or a portion of a copyright to a new owner is referred to as an assignment. Most commonly, an assignment involves the transfer of the entire copyright, as when a freelance writer assigns all copyright interests in a particular article to a magazine. But an assignment may also transfer less than the whole copyright. For example, an author might assign the right to promote, display, and distribute a novel to a publisher, while reserving the right to create derivative works (such as a screenplay) from that novel.

As a general rule, assignments are unconditional transfers of the rights in question, without limitations on how long the transfer lasts or the conditions under which the rights may be used. By contrast, licenses give permission for a party to use a copyright expression under certain specified conditions for a defined period of time.

Related terms: licensing of copyrights; transfers of copyright ownership, generally.

attorney fees in infringement actions

See infringement action, explained.

Audio Home Recording Act

During the 1980s, technology developed that allowed for digital reproduction of music by consumers. The recording industry was concerned that the consumer's ability to make near-perfect copies of recordings would result in uncontrolled infringement. The Audio Home Recording Act of 1992 (AHRA) was an attempt to balance the interests of the recording industry, manufacturers and consumers. The AHRA requires the manufacturers of certain digital devices to register with the Copyright Office and pay a statutory royalty on each device and piece of

Definitions

media sold. Manufacturers also have to use a copyright management system that permits only a copy to be made from an original (or first-generation copy). By following these rules, manufacturers are immune from lawsuits claiming copyright infringement. Consumers are also immune from claims of infringement when using devices covered by the AHRA so long as the copying is done for noncommercial use. The AHRA covers devices that are designed or marketed for the primary purpose of making digital musical recordings, such as DAT players and minidisc players. Computers or CD-writable drives are not covered by the AHRA, and therefore unauthorized copying on these devices is an infringement unless otherwise permitted under copyright law.

Related terms: MP3; cyberspace, copyrights in.

audiovisual works

This is one of the categories of expression that the Copyright Act of 1976 specifically protects. Movies, videotapes, videodisks, CD-ROM multimedia packages, training films and computer games are all examples of audiovisual works. The Copyright Act defines audiovisual works as ones consisting of "a series of related images intended to be shown on machines such as projectors, viewers or electronic equipment, with accompanying sounds, if any, whether the works are recorded on film, tape or other material." (17 United States Code, Section 101.)

Related terms: Copyright Act of 1976; Form PA, described.

author, defined

The "author" of a work of expression subject to copyright protection is one of the following:

- the person who creates the work
- the person or business that pays another to create the work in the employment context, or
- the person or business that commissions the work under a valid work made for hire contract.

For example, a songwriter may author a song, a movie producer may author a movie, a computer programmer may author a program and a toy designer may author a toy (unique toys with designs unrelated to their functions are protectable by copyright). In all these situations, however, if the creator does not work independently but creates the work in an employment relationship or under a valid work made for hire contract, the employer or person paying for the work is the author for copyright purposes.

Related terms: author as owner of copyright; copyright, explained; work made for hire.

author as owner of copyright

With two major exceptions, when a person first creates a work of expression, he or she is generally considered to be its author and, by virtue of that status, the owner of the copyright in the work. The exceptions are:

- When an author assigns all of his or her copyright ownership rights to another party before the work is created, that party becomes the author (and the owner of the copyright). This typically occurs when someone who is paid to create a work is required, as a condition of that payment, to assign all copyright rights in the future work to the paying party.
- When a work is created by an employee in the course of employment or as a commissioned work under a valid written work made for hire contract, the employer/commissioning party is considered the author (and owner of the copyright).

Because an author/owner of a copyright can always sell the copyright to someone else, it often is the case that a copyright in a work is eventually owned by someone other than its original author.

Related terms: assignment of copyright; transfers of copyright ownership, generally; work made for hire.

authorized use of copyrighted material

A person accused of infringing another's copyright may seek to prove as a defense that the use was authorized through a license or a transfer. Were such a case to go to court, the judge would seek to determine the conditions under which the license or transfer was granted, what was transferred, and to whom.

> **EXAMPLE:** Ethan, an author of virtual reality games, writes a freelance article for a new publication called *Virtually Yours*. The article is submitted under a license agreement giving *Virtually Yours* first serial rights to the article. Two years later, without Ethan's permission, *Virtually Yours* places the article on a popular electronic bulletin board and collects royalties each time the article is downloaded. Ethan sues *Virtually Yours* for copyright infringement, claiming his first serial rights license did not authorize electronic publication of the article. To decide whether *Virtually Yours* is guilty of infringement, the court will examine the factual context in which Ethan submitted the article, and the terms of the license.

Related terms: copyright infringement, defined; infringement action, explained; transfers of copyright ownership, generally.

automated databases

See computer databases.

Definitions

Definitions

backup copies of program

See archival copies.

based on an earlier work

When one original work of authorship has heavily relied upon an earlier one for its content and expression, it is said to be based on the earlier work and, under the Copyright Act of 1976, is considered to be a derivative work. The author of a derivative work must obtain permission from the owner of the copyright in the earlier work to copy, sell or distribute the derivative work. For example, a foreign language translation of a book is based on the book as it was originally written and is subject to the copyright in the original version; a movie that borrows the main characters, story line and some dialogue from a novel is based on that novel and is subject to that novel's copyright; and a song that has substantially the same melody as an earlier song is based on that song, even if the words are different, and is subject to the earlier song's copyright.

As a general rule, the more expression a subsequent work uses from an earlier work, the more likely it is to be considered a derivative work and therefore subject to the earlier work's copyright. However, assuming permission is obtained from the owner of the copyright in the earlier work, the derivative work is itself subject to copyright protection as an independent work.

Related terms: derivative work.

Berne Convention

Originally drafted in 1886, the Berne Convention is an international treaty that standardizes basic copyright protection among all of the countries signing it (currently over 100 member countries). For copyright purposes, a member country will afford the same treatment to an author from another country as it does to authors in its own country. In addition, each member country has agreed to protect what are called the author's moral rights in the work (generally, the right to proclaim or disclaim authorship and the right to protect the reputation of the work) and to extend copyright protection for at least the life of the author plus 50 years. No notice of copyright or other formality is required for basic copyright protection under the Berne Convention.

Under the General Agreement on Tariffs and Trade (GATT) treaty, enacted into U.S. law in December 1994, all signatories to GATT must also adhere to the Berne Convention if they don't already do so.

Related terms: GATT (General Agreement on Tariffs and Trade); international rules on notice of copyright; Universal Copyright Convention (U.C.C.).

best edition of a work

To register a work with the U.S. Copyright Office, the author must deposit the best edition of the work with the application. The "best edition of a work" is usually the best quality version of the work available at the time of registration or deposit. The U.S. Copyright Office has published a circular explaining the best version of a work for different types of deposits. Ask the U.S. Copyright Office for Circular R7b. You can also download this publication from the U.S. Copyright Office's website at http: www.loc.gov/copyright/circs. (The U.S. Copyright Office's phone number and address are listed under the "U.S. Copyright Office" entry.)

Related terms: deposit with U.S. Copyright Office; U.S. Copyright Office.

bootlegging

In 1994, as part of the implementation of the GATT Agreement, the United States passed legislation that allows a performer or record company to prevent the unauthorized recording of a live performance, even if the performer or record company does not own a copyright in any of the songs being performed. (17 United States Code, Section 1101.) A performer or record company can also prevent the "trafficking" in bootlegs from the live performance. "Trafficking" is the transportation or sale of unauthorized copies.

A record company has a right to sue bootleggers because the record company enters into recording agreements with each performer giving the company the exclusive right to release that performer's recordings. Under the new anti-bootlegging law, performers or record companies do not have to register with the Copyright Office in order to receive protection, and there is no time limit for how long the protection lasts. In other words, even though this law is part of the Copyright Act, it does not have the same formal requirements for copyright protection as other works for example, literary, musical or audiovisual works.

Buenos Aires Convention

The Buenos Aires Convention establishes copyright reciprocity between the U.S. and most Latin American nations. However, because all of these member nations are now also members of larger international treaties that supersede the Buenos Aires Convention, this treaty has little, if any, remaining significance.

When the Buenos Aires Convention had more importance, it guaranteed copyright protection in its member countries if the statement "all rights reserved" was placed on all expressions for which copyright protection was being claimed. This is why the "all rights reserved" phrase appears as a part of so many copy-

Definitions

right notices on published works, even if there is no longer any legal reason for it.

Related terms: international copyright protection; international rules on notice of copyright.

cease and desist letter

The opening salvo in any copyright dispute is usually a cease and desist letter from the copyright owner's attorney. This letter informs the alleged infringer of the validity and ownership of the copyrighted work, the nature of the infringement and the remedies that are available to the copyright holder unless the infringement is halted.

Related terms: copyright infringement, defined; damages for copyright infringement; infringement action, explained.

certificate of registration

When the U.S. Copyright Office approves a copyright application for registration, it mails the author (or other owner) a certificate of registration. This certificate consists of the copyright application stamped with a copyright registration number, the registration date and the U.S. Copyright Office seal at the top.

If the copyright owner sues another party for infringement, the certificate can be used as evidence that the copyright is valid. There is also a legal presumption that the certificate contains true statements—for example, the year the work was created, the fact of authorship and whether other works are incorporated in the work being copyrighted.

Related terms: copyright infringement, defined; infringement action, explained; supplemental registration.

charts, copyrightability of

See flow charts, registration of.

clearinghouses, copyright

Copyright clearinghouses organize and license works by their members. A person who wants to use one of these works contacts the clearinghouse and—depending on how the organization is structured—pays a fee and acquires a limited right to use the work for a specific purpose. Clearinghouses speed up the permissions process by providing a central source for a class or type of work. For example, Copyright Clearinghouse (http://www.copyright.com), Contentville (http://www.contentville.com) and icopyright (http://www.icopyright.com) provide permission for written materials. BMI (http://www.bmi.com) and ASCAP (http://www.ascap.com) provide permission for musical performances. Harry Fox Agency (http://www.hfa.com) provides permission to reproduce songs.

Corbis (http://www.corbis.com), Archive Photos (http://www.history.com) and Time, Inc. (http://www.thepicturecollection.com) are among several clearinghouses that grant permission to use photographs. Art Resource (http://www.artres.com) and the Visual Artists and Galleries Association (website under construction) grant permission for famous artwork. The Cartoonbank (http://www.cartoonbank.com) is one of several clearinghouses that licenses cartoons.

Related terms: permission, getting.

click-wrap agreement

See shrink-wrap and click-wrap agreements.

co-authors

Two or more people who have contributed significant creative input to a work of expression are legally considered co-authors. Co-authorship can take several forms. Probably the most common is a joint work, where the authors intend that their separate contributions be merged into a unified whole. Co-authors of a joint work share in the copyright of the whole work equally, unless they have signed a joint ownership agreement that provides differently. Absent an agreement to the contrary, any co-author may use the expression covered by the copyright without permission of other co-authors, but must account to the other co-authors and equally share with them any profits realized from the use.

Other forms of co-authorship appear in collective works and derivative works with more than one author, where each author owns only the copyright of the material he or she created:

- *Collective works.* Co-authors intend to keep their contributions separate—for instance, where one co-author is separately credited for chapters 1 through 10 and the other co-author is credited for chapters 11 through 20.

- *Coauthored derivative works.* Two or more authors create separate works and only later decide to combine them in one work.

Related terms: collective work; derivative work; joint work; collaboration agreement.

collaboration agreement

When co-authors want to specify their rights, obligations and percentage of copyright ownership and revenues, they enter into a collaboration agreement. Without a collaboration agreement, a court will presume that the co-authors share equally unless evidence to the contrary is introduced.

Related terms: co-authors; collective work, joint work.

collective work

A work such as a periodical, anthology or encyclopedia, in which a number of separate and independent works are assembled into one work, is referred to as a collective work. (17 United States Code, Section 101.) A collective work is a type of compilation, but unlike other compilations, such as a directory or book of quotes, the underlying elements assembled into a collective work can be separately protected; for example, a collection of short stories by John Updike or a collection of "greatest disco hits" recordings from the 1970s. Other examples of collective works would include a newspaper, a group of film clips or a poetry anthology. To create a collective work, either public domain materials must be used or the owners of the copyrights in the constituent parts must give their permissions. Assuming that these rules are followed, the creativity involved in organizing and selecting the constituent materials is itself subject to independent copyright protection.

> **EXAMPLE:** Phil prepares an anthology of what he considers to be the best American poems published in the years 1895 and 1995, calling this collective work *American Poetry—A Century of Difference.* Each 1995 poem is a separate and independent work protected by its own copyright. To use them, Phil must get the permission of each copyright owner. But because copyright protection has run out on the 1895 poems, they are now in the public domain and Phil can use them without obtaining anyone's permission. Once all needed permissions are assembled, Phil has created a new protectable collective work and owns a copyright in the overall work, but not in any specific poem.

Related terms: compilations of original or unoriginal material; original work of authorship.

commissioned work

See work made for hire.

common law copyright laws

The common law of copyrights is a set of legal principles applying to copyrights that U.S. courts developed from court decisions over a period of several hundred years prior to January 1, 1978 (at which time the 1976 Copyright Act took over and replaced whatever rules the courts had come up with). Primarily in cases of unpublished works, courts used these common law rules before 1978, as well as the rules set out in the Copyright Act of 1909, to determine whether a copyright existed, and the extent to which a work of authorship should receive legal protection.

Related terms: Copyright Act of 1909; Copyright Act of 1976.

compilations of original or unoriginal material

A compilation is a work formed by selecting, collecting and assembling preexisting materials or data in a novel way that forms an original work of authorship. Examples of compilations are databases (collections of information arranged in a way to facilitate updating and retrieval), anthologies and collective works. (17 United States Code, Section 101.)

The creative aspects of a compilation—such as the way it is organized and the selection of the materials to be included—are entitled to copyright protection whether or not the individual parts are in the public domain or are subject to another owner's copyright.

> **EXAMPLE:** Harry wants to assemble national anthems and feature them in a book of sheet music. The national anthems are all in the public domain due to their age. If Harry simply collected a group of national anthems and published them in alphabetical order without enhancing or organizing them in a special way or combining them with other materials, the collection would not be protected, because it is not considered to be creative. If, on the other hand, Harry compiled a selection of his favorite anthems (*Harry's Favorites*), the compilation (but not the music) is more likely to qualify for copyright protection, since the act of selecting the anthems involved some creative work on Harry's part.

Related terms: *Feist Publications Inc. v. Rural Telephone Service Co.*; original work of authorship.

compulsory license

Normally, in order for someone to reproduce, perform or distribute a copyrighted work, permission must be obtained from the copyright owner. However, in a few circumstances—known as compulsory licenses—a copyright owner's permission is not required.

Definitions

Definitions

The most common use of a compulsory license is in the music industry. Once a song has been recorded and distributed to the public on recordings, any person or group is entitled to record and distribute the song without obtaining the copyright owner's consent, provided they pay a fee and meet copyright law requirements.

In order to take advantage of this compulsory license, a notice must be sent to the copyright owner along with a fee set by the Copyright Office known as the statutory fee or statutory rate. As of August 2000, the fee is 7.55 cents per copy or 1.45 cents per minute of recording, whichever is greater. If a song is three minutes long and an artist makes 10,000 compact discs containing the song, the fee paid to the song's owner would be $755. A recording artist does not have to use the compulsory license and many recording artists seek permission directly from the song owner and negotiate for a lower rate.

> **EXAMPLE:** Lou writes the song "Up the Stars." Kate obtains permission from Lou to become the first artist to record the song. The song is released. Later, Barry and the Bushmen decide they want to record "Up the Stars." If Barry and the Bushmen are willing to pay the statutory fee, they do not need to ask Lou for permission but if they want to pay less per copy, they must obtain permission from Lou.

Keep in mind that the compulsory license for recording music only applies to nondramatic musical compositions and would not apply to dramatic music such an opera or an overture to a musical. The compulsory license only applies to phonorecords distributed to the public. Therefore it cannot be used to record a song for use on a television show's soundtrack. In that case, permission must be obtained from the copyright owner.

Under the terms of a compulsory license, the licensee is permitted to make a new arrangement of the composition as long as the basic melody or fundamental character of the work is not altered.

> **EXAMPLE:** Sammy composes a country ballad, "My Pickup Died," and licenses country singer Justine Carbo to be the first artist to record it. Later, Pauline and the Punkettes, a punk rap group, obtain a compulsory license and record Sammy's song but they change the words and eliminate the melody. Sammy can have Pauline's compulsory license revoked and prevent the recording from being distributed further or played.

In a different context, and without regard to the type of work involved, the concept of a compulsory license can arise in a copyright infringement action. A court has the power to order a copyright owner to grant a license to an innocent infringer instead of ordering the infringement stopped.

EXAMPLE: Willie innocently assumes a particular poem to be in the public domain, and uses it in his new novel. After the novel is published and selling well, Willie is sued by Carol, who claims copyright ownership in the poem. Even if the court finds that Carol does own the copyright in the poem, the court can require Carol to license Willie to use the poem in exchange for reasonable royalties. If, however, the court finds that Willie's use of the poem was a willful copyright violation, no such license may be ordered.

Finally, in countries that subscribe to the Universal Copyright Convention (U.C.C.), including the U.S., an author may be required to grant a compulsory license to a subscribing government to translate his or her work into that country's primary language if no translation has been published within seven years of the work's original date of publication. This rule precludes copyright owners in most countries from preventing the translation of works covered by their copyrights into different languages.

Related terms: derivative work; innocent infringement of copyright; musical works and copyright protection; mechanical right.

Computer Associates Int'l v. Altai

This federal appellate court case first applied a now commonly used technique called "filtration" to distinguish those aspects of software or software interfaces that are protected by copyright from those that are not. Filtration works by first eliminating from a software-related work such unprotectable elements as:

- ideas
- elements dictated by efficiency (that is, there is no other sensible way to write the code or handle the task)
- elements determined by external factors (such as the nature of the mechanical specifications of the computer on which the program is in-tended to run, compatibility requirements, manufacturers' design standards and the intended user base), and
- material taken from the public domain.

What's left of the work is then examined to see whether it qualifies for copy-right protection.

The *Altai* case itself dealt with whether a computer program interface was entitled to copyright protection. After the court applied the filtration process to the interface in question, nothing was left to protect, thus copyright protection was denied. *(Computer Associates Int'l v. Altai*, 982 F.2d 693 (2nd Cir. 1992).)

Related terms: computer software, copyright of.

computer databases, copyright of

A computer database, sometimes known as an automated database, is a collection of information or resources placed in a computer and organized to allow for rapid updating and retrieval. Examples of computer databases are:

- a mailing list organized so that mailings can be made according to certain criteria such as the residential area, average personal income or interests of the recipient
- a compilation of articles published on a particular subject (for example, female Parkinson's disease sufferers over 80), organized so that people can quickly retrieve and read the article dealing with their particular point of interest, and
- a listing of all items in a store's inventory arranged to permit an analysis by such variables as supplier, kind of product, price and length of time in stock.

Computer databases commonly consist both of materials protected by copyright and materials that are said to be in the public domain, either because their copyright has run out or because they consist of ideas and facts that themselves do not receive copyright protection.

Despite the fact that the database owner may not own any copyright interest in any of the material in the database, the structure and organization of the database itself can qualify as an original work of authorship, and thus be subject to copyright protection as a compilation.

EXAMPLE: Suppose Catherine Jermany gathers all articles in ten leading education journals since 1990, and indexes them, using several hundred subject-matter headings that she has developed. Then Jermany converts the full text of each article into computer-readable text and uses a database management program to build an index linked to each article and paragraph, with the result that a computer user can quickly locate the text of any paragraph of any relevant article. Jermany's database would qualify as an original work of authorship in terms of its structure and organization, and thus would be subject to copyright protection. However, as all of the constituent articles would already be subject to copyright protection by their authors (or the assignees or licensees of the authors), Jermany would have to obtain the authors' permission to reproduce the text of the articles for commercial purposes.

Although the original expression implicit in the structure and organization of a computer database is entitled to copyright protection, the labor and cost associated with building a database is not protected by copyright. For instance, the labor and cost associated with compiling an alphabetical telephone directory does not protect the information in the directory from being copied by others because there was no creativity exercised in building the database.

Computer databases can be registered with the U.S. Copyright Office using Form TX. The application must specify the parts of the database claimed as an original work of authorship by the database compiler, and must distinguish these from parts whose copyrights are owned by others.

Related terms: compilations of original or unoriginal material; *Feist Publications Inc. v. Rural Telephone Service Co.*; Form TX, described.

computer software, copyright of

A 1980 amendment to the Copyright Act of 1976 applies to all software, regardless of when it was first published. Under the 1980 amendment, computer software is protected in the same manner as other original works of authorship. Any computer program, defined as "a set of statements or instructions to be used directly or indirectly in a computer to bring about a certain result," can be protected by copyright if it constitutes an original work of authorship. The 1980 amendment also specifies the situations in which computer programs may be copied and altered without permission of the copyright owner.

The early 1980s saw a debate over whether some types of programs could be protected under the Copyright Act—especially those in object code form, those mechanically reproduced in a silicon chip as part of an integrated circuit (ROM chips), and templates (mask works) used in making ROM chips. The dispute centered on whether such programs were "hardware" (and therefore appropriately subject to patent rather than copyright protection) or "software" (and thus deserving of protection as a work of expression).

Most of these questions have been answered in favor of copyright protection for software regardless of its form (that is, whether it is source code or object code), and regardless of whether it is embedded in a chip or exists as an independent work on a computer disk. The lead case in this area is still *Apple Computer, Inc. v. Franklin Computer Corporation,* 714 F.2d 1240 (3rd Cir. 1983). Interestingly, under a different line of cases, software can now increasingly be protected by patent as well.

In the late 1980s and early 1990s, new questions arose about what aspects of software could receive copyright protection. Some of the burning issues have been:

- *Should copyright protection be limited to the literal code as written, or is the structure, sequence and organization of software code also entitled to copyright protection?* In *Whelan v. Jastrow,* 797 F.2d 1222 (3rd Cir. 1986), a federal circuit court of appeals held that protection for software code goes beyond the code's literal expression and extends to its structure, sequence and organization. Other courts have found this approach unworkable and have adopted the filtration approach taken in *Computer Associates Int'l. v. Altai,* 982 F.2d 693 (2nd Cir. 1992). That approach separates the code's ideas and other public domain elements from its expression and then extends protection only to the expression.

- *What aspects of computer screen displays and graphical user interfaces (GUIs) are entitled to copyright protection?* The filtration approach taken in the *Altai* case has been used by a number of courts to decide which aspects of a program interface are protected by copyright. The most prominent of these cases involved a suit by Apple against Microsoft, which claimed that the Microsoft Windows operating system violated a copyright owned by Apple in the Macintosh interface. *(Apple Computer, Inc. v. Microsoft Corp.,* 717 F. Supp 1428 (N.D. Ca. 1989), 779 F. Supp. 133 (N.D. Ca. 1992).)* Using the filtration approach, the court eliminated from copyright protection most individual elements of the Macintosh interface and refused to provide protection for the interface as a whole. In short, Microsoft won and Apple lost. The overall result of applying the filtration approach to computer user interfaces has been to afford computer user interfaces very little copyright protection.

- *How much originality must a factual database have to qualify for copyright protection?* In *Feist Publications Inc. v. Rural Telephone Service Co.,* 111 S.Ct. 1282 (1991), the U.S. Supreme Court ruled that an alphabetically arranged telephone directory involved insufficient creativity to qualify for copyright. As a result, the Copyright Act could not be used to compensate Feist Publications Inc. for the labor and expense involved in originally compiling the directory. The question remains, however, as to how much creativity is required to qualify a factual database for copyright. By its very nature, this issue can only be decided on a case-by-case basis.

The Software Publishers Association (SPA) has been the most active organization in ferreting out and suing copyright infringers, although some of the large software development companies are also active in enforcing the copyright laws.

Related terms: *Apple Computer, Inc. v. Franklin*; *Apple Computer, Inc. v. Microsoft Corp.*; copyright, explained; copyright infringement, defined; infringement action, explained.

Computer Software Protection Act of 1980

See archival copies; computer software, copyright of.

Computer Software Rental Amendments Act of 1990

See first sale doctrine.

copies, meaning under copyright law

For purposes of the copyright law, a copy is the physical form in which an expression is retained over time, no matter how brief. This includes such things as photocopies, tape recordings, photographs, carbon copies, manuscripts, printings, molds (for example, for plastic toy designs), computer disks and diskettes, videotapes, videodisks and ROMs. The placing of a program in dynamic computer memory (RAM) for a brief period of time has also been treated as copying which may constitute an infringement under the copyright act. (*Mai v. Peak,* 991 F.2d 511 (9th Cir. 1993).)

The Copyright Act defines copies as "material objects, other than phonorecords, in which a work is fixed by any method now known or later developed, and from which the work can be perceived, reproduced or otherwise communicated, either directly or with the aid of a machine or device." (17 United States Code, Section 101.)

The right to prepare copies of an original work of authorship—that is, put the work into some fixed form—is one of the primary rights protected by the overall copyright.

Related terms: copyright, explained; copyright infringement, defined; photocopies and copyright law.

Definitions

copyright, explained

Under the Copyright Act of 1976 (applicable to all works first published on or after January 1, 1978), a copyright consists of a bundle of rights held by the author or developer of an original work of authorship. The term "copyright" applies both to the entire bundle of rights and to any individual right or part of an individual right:

- the exclusive right to make copies
- the exclusive right to authorize others to make copies
- the exclusive right to make derivative works (that is, similar works based on the original, such as translations or updated versions)
- the exclusive right to sell (market) the work
- the exclusive right to display the work
- the exclusive right to perform the work (such as plays and musical compositions), and
- the exclusive right to obtain court relief in the event others infringe (violate) these rights.

Each of these exclusive rights can be sold separately through transfers of copyright ownership. For example, a transfer may give a party the exclusive right to make derivative works from an original work. In addition, each right may be divided, giving different parties exclusive rights during different periods of time or in different geographical areas.

Under the laws of most countries, any original work of authorship is considered the property of its owner; others are prevented from using this property without the owner's consent. The owner is usually the originator of the work—the actual author or somebody who paid for the work under an employment agreement or work made for hire contract. Sometimes, however, full ownership is transferred to somebody else before the work is finished. For instance, it is common for freelance software programmers to assign all of their copyright rights in the program to the publisher before programming begins, in exchange for advance royalties or payments to be received in phases as the project progresses. Usually termed a "grant of rights," this type of transfer shifts ownership of the copyright from the author to the publisher.

Among the categories of expressive works that are protected by copyright throughout the world are:

- literary works
- audiovisual works
- computer software

- graphic works
- musical arrangements, and
- sound recordings.

In short, practically any type of expression that can be fixed in a tangible medium of expression is eligible for copyright protection, assuming it is original and has at least some creativity. It is important to understand, however, that copyright law protects only the expression itself—not the underlying facts, ideas or concepts. This means it is often possible to legitimately produce an expression very similar to one that is already protected by copyright, as long as the original expression itself is not copied or used as a basis for the later work. The more factual in nature the original work, the more similar the second work can be without infringement occurring. Conversely, works of fiction are more susceptible to infringement claims, since they tend to involve far more original expression than do nonfiction works.

Although a copyright owner's permission must be obtained to make copies for commercial purposes, it is sometimes possible to copy without permission in situations collectively labeled as "fair use." These tend to be for educational and nonprofit purposes—situations where there is little or no commercial motive for using the material and the use of the material won't interfere with the natural market for the work being used.

Under the Copyright Act of 1976, an original work of authorship gains copyright protection the instant it becomes fixed in a tangible form. This means that such protection is available for both published and unpublished works. The protection lasts for:

- the life of the author plus 70 years, or
- 95 years from the date of publication or 120 years from the date of creation, whichever is shorter, if the author is an employer or commissioner of a work made for hire, or if the author uses a pseudonym or remains anonymous.

In addition to the automatic protection extended a copyright owner by the law, it is possible to gain crucially important protective benefits in the United States by placing a proper copyright notice on the work and registering it with the U.S. Copyright Office. Specifically, such registration is mandatory before a copyright infringement action can be filed in court. In addition, if the registration occurs in a timely manner (either within three months of publication or before the infringing activity begins) it is easier for the copyright owner to prevail in court and obtain effective relief against infringers.

Definitions

Definitions

Related terms: copyright infringement, defined; copyright owner, defined; duration of copyrights; fair use, defined; timely registration, defined; transfers of copyright ownership, generally.

Copyright Act of 1909

This federal statute governed copyrights in the U.S. between 1910 and 1978. Works first published prior to January 1, 1978, are still covered by the 1909 Act, unless the copyright has expired. The main practical differences between the 1909 Copyright Act and the 1976 Copyright Act (which replaced the 1909 Act) are:

- The 1909 Act granted protection only to published works. The 1976 Act extends its protection to both published and unpublished works.
- Protection under the 1909 Act could be permanently lost if even a single copy was distributed without the proper notice of copyright. The 1976 Act provided that the absence of a proper notice could be cured under certain circumstances. Moreover, since March 1989, there is no longer any requirement for a notice.

Note that GATT (General Agreement on Tariffs and Trade) has restored copyright protection for works of foreign authors that fell into the public domain in the U.S. prior to March 1989 because of faulty notice. These restored copyrights have the same duration as they would have had if they not been considered to be in the public domain.

Related terms: common law copyright laws; copyright, explained; Copyright Act of 1976; notice of copyright; restored copyright under GATT.

Copyright Act of 1976

This comprehensive federal statute governs copyright protection for original works of authorship created after January 1, 1978. Found in Title 17, United States Code, Section 100 and following, the 1976 Copyright Act (as amended from time to time), is the exclusive source of copyright law in the United States for works published after January 1, 1978. It preempts (replaces) all state laws that affect rights covered by this Act.

Related terms: audiovisual works; Copyright Act of 1909; copyright, explained; infringement action, explained; original work of authorship.

copyright and patent compared

As a general matter, the copyright and patent laws cover entirely different kinds of items. Copyright law protects all forms of expression fixed in a tangible medium, but not the underlying ideas. Patents protect ideas that take the form of useful, novel and nonobvious inventions—for instance, production methods, devices, substances and mechanical processes.

Copyright and patent do intersect, however, in two important areas:

- *product design.* Both copyright and patent may be used to protect a product's design as long as the design does not affect how the product functions. A design patent is more difficult to obtain than a copyright, but a patent offers a broader scope of protection because it embraces the idea of the design as well as its literal expression. A copyright, however, only extends to the literal design. On the other hand, copyright protection lasts for the life of the author, whereas design patent protection lasts for only 14 years from the date the patent issues. As mentioned, these two approaches to protecting original designs are not exclusive of each other. For instance, a truly innovative but functionless design for a computer might qualify for both copyright protection (as a pictorial, graphic or sculptural work) and for a design patent (as a purely ornamental design of an article of manufacture).

- *computer software.* Both copyright and patent may be used to protect computer software. A copyright may protect the program's literal expression and perhaps its structure, sequence and organization. A patent may issue on the program's innovative approach to solving a particular problem or producing a particular result in a computer or other type of machine, such as a robot or remote vehicle. As with designs, patent protection is broader than that afforded by copyright because the patent creates a monopoly over the ideas covered by the patent, whereas the copyright only protects the expression itself. In addition, a copyright owner can only stop someone who has *copied* the software. A patent owner can stop anyone who is making, selling or using the software, regardless of whether it has been copied or developed independently.

Related terms: computer software, copyright of; pictorial, graphic and sculptural works.
See also Part 3 (Patent Law): design patents; software patents.

copyright claimant

A copyright claimant is the party considered to be the basic owner of the copyright in a work being registered with the U.S. Copyright Office. The copyright claimant may be any of the following:

- the actual author of the work
- an employer (also considered the actual author) whose employee created the work in the scope of employment
- a party who commissioned a work made for hire, as defined in the Copyright Act of 1976 (also considered the actual author)

- a party to whom all rights in a work have been assigned, or
- a party who has come to own all of the exclusive rights that make up the copyright.

The name of the copyright claimant must be put in the copyright registration form filed with the U.S. Copyright Office as part of the registration process.

Related terms: registration of copyright, defined.

copyright infringement, defined

Any unauthorized use of a copyrighted work that violates the copyright owner's exclusive rights in the work constitutes an infringement. Common examples of infringement are:

- making unauthorized copies of an original work for commercial purposes
- using a composer's tune in a song with different words
- including in a computer program important software subroutines authored by someone else
- adapting another's work in one medium (such as a book or play) for use in another medium (such as a movie or CD-ROM), and
- outright plagiarism of somebody else's prior original copyrighted work.

Once a copyright owner suspects infringement, the owner may file a lawsuit against the infringer for damages in a federal court, provided that the copyright has been registered with the U.S. Copyright Office. An expedited registration process is available for those who have not previously registered and need to get into court right away. But the fact that the infringement began before the registration occurred will diminish the rights and remedies available in court unless the work was first published less than three months previously.

Whether or not a work will be found to have infringed an earlier copyrighted work largely depends on three factors:

- *Was the first work the subject of a proper copyright?* This factor is satisfied if the first work was independently created, has enough creativity and is fixed in a tangible medium.
- *Did the infringer copy the work?* In the absence of an admission that copying occurred, this factor depends on whether the author of the second work had access to the earlier work and whether there is a substantial similarity between the two works. The stronger the similarity, the greater the chance that a court will find that infringement occurred. Generally, a greater similarity is required for factual or nonfiction works to be considered infringing than is required for works of fiction.
- *Did the infringer improperly use the copied material?* The third factor addresses whether the infringer copied by paraphrasing or by repeating the expression verbatim, and how much was copied. Again, the key determination is how substantially similar are the two works. An infringement might be found based on several paraphrased passages of a few hundred words each, or just 20 words copied verbatim.

Some courts use a three-step approach to decide whether the substantial similarity element (in the second factor) has been shown. First, they identify the aspects of the two works that are subject to copyright protection. Then they make an objective comparison of these aspects to see how alike they are. If they are similar enough to warrant a suspicion of infringement, the courts then make a subjective determination as to whether the works are substantially similar enough to justify a finding of infringement.

Below are two examples showing the basic principles involved in copyright infringement.

EXAMPLE 1: *Infringement of the Right to Make Derivative Works.* Beverly uses the computer language BASIC and writes a copyrighted program that gives legal advice on divorce procedures in Michigan. Jeff, deciding that the program would sell equally well in Colorado, alters the program to apply Colorado law, and distributes it under his own name. Because in essence Jeff's program is a copy of Beverly's program, he has infringed on Beverly's exclusive right (as part of her copyright) to make copies of, and prepare derivative works from, the original work. However, if Jeff had only borrowed Beverly's idea and written his own program covering Colorado divorce law (or even Michigan divorce law), it would not be a copyright violation. In other words, if Jeff's program was not based on Beverly's (not simply translated or substantially programmed on the basis of the structure, sequence and organization of

Definitions

Beverly's program), but instead was an independent creation, Jeff will not have infringed Beverly's copyright.

EXAMPLE 2: *Infringement of the Right to Make Copies.* Joseph writes a book on media law which is used widely as a textbook. Peter, a media law teacher, wants to use the book as a textbook, but doesn't want his students to have to pay the $30 cover price. Accordingly, Peter makes 25 photocopies of the book and distributes them to his students for the cost of the copying. Peter has infringed Joseph's copyright. Although Peter did not make the copies for personal profit, Joseph has been deprived of income because of the unauthorized copying of his book. While the fair use provisions of the Copyright Act of 1976 allows some unauthorized copying for strictly educational purposes, copying a large portion of a textbook to avoid purchasing it probably exceeds what is allowed under the fair use doctrine.

Related terms: derivative work; fair use, defined; infringement action, explained; registration of copyright, defined.

copyright management information, defined

The Digital Millennium Copyright Act of 1998 prohibits the falsification of copyright management information and the distribution of such falsified information. The Act defines copyright management information as: "(1) The title and other information identifying the work, including the information set forth on a notice of copyright. (2) The name of, and other identifying information about, the author of a work. (3) The name of, and other identifying information about, the copyright owner of the work, including the information set forth in a notice of copyright. (4) With the exception of public performances of works by radio and television broadcast stations, the name of, and other identifying information about, a performer whose performance is fixed in a work other than an audiovisual work. (5) With the exception of public performances of works by radio and television broadcast stations, in the case of an audiovisual work, the name of, and other identifying information about, a writer, performer, or director who is credited in the audiovisual work."

Related terms: Digital Millennium Copyright Act of 1998.

copyright notice

See notice of copyright.

copyright office

See U.S. Copyright Office.

copyright owner, defined

Under the Copyright Act of 1976, the term "copyright owner" has two distinct meanings. First, it refers to the person or entity who is listed as the owner in the U.S. Copyright Office and on any notice attached to the copyrighted work. This is either the original author or developer, or a person or entity to whom all rights under the copyright have been transferred.

Second, "copyright owner" also refers to a person or entity who owns one or more of the five exclusive rights that make up the whole copyright, and who therefore has a right to sue infringers of that right. These constituent rights, which may be separately owned and assigned (sold), consist of the following:

- the right to reproduce (copy) the work
- the right to prepare derivative works
- the right to distribute copies of the work
- the right to perform the work, and
- the right to display the work.

EXAMPLE: June writes a novel and owns the copyright on the expression contained in it. June grants an exclusive worldwide license (permission) to Henry to publish and distribute her novel. She also gives Ernest the exclusive right to prepare a screenplay (a derivative work) based on the novel. Because these rights are exclusive, both Henry and Ernest are legally considered copyright owners.

In addition to separately licensing basic copyright rights, a copyright owner can separately license subparts of each right.

EXAMPLE: Vixen Publications purchases the entire copyright in Andrew Fox's book, *Teethmarks,* before it is written, in exchange for a royalties advance. Vixen is now the copyright owner, and has the right to transfer parts of its copyright ownership to others. Vixen licenses exclusive German language book rights to a German publisher, exclusive French language book rights to a French publisher and exclusive Russian language book rights to a Russian publisher. Vixen also licenses exclusive movie rights worldwide to a film producer and exclusive worldwide electronic publication rights to a CD-ROM developer. Each of the entities receiving exclusive rights under these licenses would also be considered a copyright owner.

Although different people or entities can own different rights based on a copyright and be considered copyright owners, there is only one actual "copyright."

Definitions

Unless the original developer (the author, employer, commissioner of a work made for hire or assignee of all rights) transfers *all* of the five exclusive rights set out above to one or more parties, that original developer is still considered by the U.S. Copyright Office to be *the* copyright owner.

Related terms: author as owner of copyright; copyright claimant; transfers of copyright ownership, generally.

copyright protection

See affirmative rights.

copyright registration

See registration of copyright, defined.

copyright registration forms

Forms published by the U.S. Copyright Office must be used to register copyrights with that agency. The most commonly used forms are Form TX for nondramatic literary works, including computer programs; Form PA for audiovisual works; Form VA for graphic art and sculptural works; Form SR for sound recordings; and Form SE for serials and periodicals. Samples are included in the Sample Forms section at the end of the copyright law part of the book. Copyright forms can be downloaded from the copyright office website (http://lcweb.loc.gov/copyright).

Related terms: registration of copyright, defined.

copyrighted work

A copyrighted work is any work that is entitled to copyright protection. For works publicly distributed after March 1, 1989, copyright protection is automatically available to any original work of expression that is fixed in a tangible medium. Putting a copyright notice on the work and registering it with the U.S. Copyright Office affords a copyright owner additional protection, but neither is required for basic copyright protection.

Related terms: Berne Convention; GATT (General Agreement on Tariffs and Trade); registration of copyright, defined.

creation of work, when protected by copyright

Under the Copyright Act of 1976, the following three rules determine when a work is first entitled to copyright protection—that is, when it is first "created":

Rule 1: Creation of a work occurs when it first becomes "fixed" in some form.

Rule 2: Drafts and other intermediate forms in the development of a work receive copyright protection just like the underlying work does.

Rule 3: Each new version of an original work is a separate creation.

EXAMPLE: Todd creates complex charts showing the relationships between scientific concepts in different fields. Todd often carries an idea for a particular chart around in his head for weeks before he jots it down in physical (tangible) form. Once his idea becomes fixed in a tangible form, whether on paper, programmed on a computer or constructed out of plastic or other materials, Todd has created a work of authorship. Todd typically changes and improves the physical representation of his original idea. Each new version of Todd's chart becomes an original work as of the moment it becomes fixed in a tangible form. As long as Todd is working on a given chart, he has created only one work despite a number of incremental changes. If, however, Todd produces his chart both in a print version and in a specially tailored computerized slide show, he would have two different versions of the same work and could obtain separate copyright protection for each. Separate copyrights may also be available for two different charts based on the same idea, regardless of the medium used.

Related terms: derivative work; fixed in a tangible medium of expression.

credit line

A written acknowledgment of authorship is referred to as a credit line. When authors give permission for somebody else to use a portion or an entire work, they commonly condition the permission on including a line crediting the original author in the new work.

criminal copyright infringement

Infringement of a copyright can be treated as a federal crime under the Copyright Act of 1976 (17 United States Code, Section 506) if it is done intentionally and with full knowledge that an infringement is occurring. As a practical matter, the U.S. Department of Justice only brings criminal charges against copyright infringers when a large amount of money is at stake, and the purpose of the infringement is commercial gain.

Most enforcement of the copyright laws is civil in nature, which involves detecting infringing activity and, if necessary, bringing copyright infringement lawsuits in federal court.

customs, preventing importing of infringing works

See importing of infringing works.

cyberspace, copyrights in

Cyberspace refers to the electronic world that has been created by linking millions of computers through the Internet and millions of business and home computer users to the Internet and such gigantic online services as America Online. Copyright law is supposed to work the same in this electronic world as it does in the more tangible worlds of print and the fine arts. However, once works are put into digital form and uploaded into cyberspace, keeping track of copyright ownership and enforcing copyright rights becomes difficult.

Works cast in digital form can more easily be copied and modified than when they exist on paper or canvas, and it can be difficult to know when the line between copyright violation and permissible copying of ideas has been crossed. Also, once a work is posted in cyberspace, it can simultaneously be copied by millions of users in many different countries, even if the copying is illegal. There is no practical way to reassert control over the work so that the copyright can be meaningfully enforced.

In an attempt to establish some regulation and predictability for copyrights on the Internet, Congress enacted the Digital Millenium Copyright Act of 1998 (DMCA). The DMCA prohibits circumvention of digital anti-piracy devices and the removal of secret codes known as digital watermarks from digital files. The DMCA also limits liability for companies that provide access to the Internet (Internet Service Providers—ISPs) in the event that an infringing copy is offered online. In addition, the DMCA establishes licensing standards by which companies can webcast music (broadcast over the Internet).

Despite passage of the DMCA, technology has continued to outpace copyright legislation and new unresolved issues have emerged in cyberspace such as linking, framing and file sharing. For example, website owners may be liable as copyright infringers for creating links to infringing materials. One company ran into problems when framing—placing the contents of one website within a frame of another website—because the process resulted in the creation of a derivative work. Downloading music, particularly through the use of an Internet technology known as MP3 has triggered litigation and debate as to what constitutes infringement and fair use. Napster and MP3.com, two websites that fostered distribution of unauthorized MP3 music files, were sued by the recording industry in 2000 and were forced to modify their methods of distributing MP3s. More issues will be resolved over time in the courts and, possibly, in Congress through further amendments to the Copyright Act.

Related terms: Digital Millenium Copyright Act of 1998; MP3; Linking; Framing.

damages for copyright infringement

Money damages in copyright infringement actions are commonly awarded under three legal theories:

- *Actual damages.* Also called compensatory damages, this consists of the dollar amount of any demonstrable loss the owner suffered as a result of the infringing activity.
- *Profits.* This consists of any money made by the infringer as a result of the infringement. These damages are only awarded if they exceed the amount of profits lost by the copyright owner as a result of the infringement.

   EXAMPLE: A book on self-defense, authored by Susan Lopez, contains a practical chapter on how to purchase and care for a handgun. Rachel Sanders also writes a book on self-defense and substantially borrows from Susan's chapter on handguns without first obtaining her permission. Rachel has infringed Susan's copyright. A court could award Susan actual damages if Susan proves that she lost sales of her book because people bought Rachel's book instead, at least in part because of the handgun chapter. In addition, the court could award Susan any profits that Rachel realized from the infringement to the extent such profits exceeded the amount of Susan's lost profits.

- *Statutory damages.* In many copyright cases, both actual damages and profits are difficult to prove. For that reason, the Copyright Act provides for statutory damages—that is, damages set by law. However, only a person who has registered a work with the U.S. Copyright Office before the infringement (or within three months of publication) may receive statutory damages. Such a plaintiff in an infringement action may opt for either actual damages (and the infringer's profits, if appropriate) or statutory damages, but not both.

   For infringements that can't clearly be proven as either innocent or willful, statutory damages may be from $750 to $30,000 per infringement depending on the circumstances. The amount will depend on the seriousness of the infringing act and the financial worth of the infringer. On the other hand, an innocent infringer may have to pay as little as $200, while an intentional infringer may have to pay as much as $150,000 for a single infringement of one work.

Related terms: criminal copyright infringement; infringement action, explained; injunctions, copyright infringement; innocent infringement of copyright; profits as damages.

databases, copyright of

See computer databases, copyright of.

Definitions

defective copyright notice

Until March 1, 1989, works published in the United States needed a copyright notice for the copyright to remain in force. A defective notice could and did permanently nullify copyright protection for many works. However, after the March 1, 1989, date, no notice is required, but only recommended (to give people notice that the work is protected by copyright).

A correct notice is either the little "©" or the words "Copyright" or "Copr." followed by the date and the author's name. In the case of a sound recording, the proper symbol is a "P" in a circle (℗).

A defective copyright notice might be one with an error in or omission of the author's name, the copyright symbol or the date (an error of more than one year).

Related terms: innocent infringement of copyright; international copyright protection; notice of copyright; omission of copyright notice.

defenses to copyright infringement

The main defenses to an allegation of copyright infringement are:

- The use was what the courts consider, and the Copyright Act defines as, a "fair use." In essence, the use was for a nonprofit or educational purpose, for a parody or in a critical commentary.
- The allegedly infringing work was independently created.
- The statute of limitations has run (the plaintiff waited too long to file suit— within three years of discovering the infringement).
- The work copied was in the public domain.
- The use was authorized.

Related terms: authorized use of copyrighted material; fair use, defined; independent creation, defense to infringement action; innocent infringement of copyright; public domain—copyright context; statute of limitations.

de minimis, defined

This term is used by the U.S. Copyright Office to characterize changes in an existing work that are too small to warrant a separate registration. U.S. Copyright Office regulations allow only one registration per version of a work. If an author makes several minor changes to a work and tries to register the new version, the U.S. Copyright Office will consider the changes "de minimis" and reject the attempted new registration.

The term is also used in copyright litigation. If a court determines that the infringement is insubstantial, the copying will be excused as *de minimis*. This is not a fair use defense; it is a defense based solely upon the inconsequential amount of infringing material. For example, several photographs appeared briefly in the film *Seven*. A court determined that a lay observer would have been unable to identify them. Therefore, the momentary use of the photos was so insubstantial that the copyright was not infringed. (*Sandoval v. New Line Cinema Corp.*, 47 147 F.3d 215 (2d Cir. 1998).)

Related terms: derivative work; single registration rule.

deposit with U.S. Copyright Office

Part of the copyright registration process requires the deposit of actual copies, photographs or other representations of an original work of authorship with the U.S. Copyright Office. For most categories of published works, it is necessary to deposit two copies of the work's best edition. For some types of works, however, including computer programs, motion pictures and most unpublished works, only one copy need be deposited. The form a deposit must take differs according to the media in question, but must generally be sufficient to identify the work being registered.

Related terms: identifying material, defined; Library of Congress, deposit requirement; registration of copyright, defined.

derivative work

A derivative work is one based upon preexisting material to which enough original creative work has been added so that the new work represents an original work of authorship. The term (as defined in 17 United States Code, Section 101) encompasses any form into which a work may be recast, transformed or adapted. Examples of derivative works are:

- an English translation of a book written in French
- a computer program rewritten in a different programming language
- a movie based on a play or book
- condensed or abridged versions of articles such as those found in *Reader's Digest*
- annotations to literary works (for example, *Cliff Notes*), and
- a jazz version of a popular tune.

Derivative works may also be fictionalizations, recordings or even editorial revisions. Compilations and collective works are not normally considered derivative works because they are collections of different underlying works, rather than a new work based upon an original work.

The exclusive right to make derivative works is an important part of the bundle of rights that make up every copyright. Absent an explicit transfer of this right by a written license, or by permission from the owner (voluntary or forced in the case of a compulsory license), no one else can exercise it except for their personal use. This rule applies not only in the U.S., but in Turkey, Germany, Japan and Australia, all countries that have signed GATT or the Berne or Universal Copyright Conventions.

EXAMPLE: Joe wants to adapt a popular novel into an interactive computer program. Because the program will be based on the novel, it will constitute a derivative work, and therefore cannot legally be marketed without permission from the novel's copyright owner.

There is often a large gray area where difficulty exists in telling whether or not subsequent works are derivative of earlier ones.

EXAMPLE: Jack writes a book in English about Ecoterrorists that is similar to one Luis has written in Spanish but is not, strictly speaking, a translation. Is this a derivative work? Yes, if the court finds that Jack's book was "based on" the Spanish one, and no, if the court finds that Jack's book was an "independent creation." Which of these results will occur depends on the degree of similarity between the works, whether Jack had access to Luis's work, the probability of Jack's independently creating a similar work, and so on.

Related terms: collective work; copyright, explained; copyright infringement, defined; independent creation, defense to infringement action.

Digital Millennium Copyright Act of 1998

This federal statute addresses a number of copyright issues created by the increasing use of the Internet for commerce in materials protected by copyright. Because the Digital Millenium Copyright Act (DMCA) is so new, it is sure to undergo much interpretation by the courts and by copyright experts in the coming years.

The DMCA outlaws attempts to get around devices used by software publishers to keep their programs from being copied, but makes a number of exceptions, including:

- works exempted by the Copyright Office, under rules to be issued in the future
- nonprofit libraries, archives and educational institutions who need to decide whether to add the protected work to their collections
- reverse engineering for the purpose of determining interoperability (the ability of computer programs to exchange information, and of such programs mutually to use the information which has been exchanged)
- legitimate encryption research
- legitimate security testing

- law enforcement and intelligence activities, and
- legitimate consumer privacy needs (the need to disable the protective device in order to prevent the unwanted acquisition of personal information or the tracking of activities on the Internet.

The DMCA also prohibits the production, marketing or sales of a product or service designed to circumvent these technological protections.

Effective April 28, 2000, the DMCA puts restrictions on the import, distribution and sales of analog video cassette recorders and camcorders that don't have a certain type of copy-proof technology.

The DMCA prohibits the falsification of copyright management information and the distribution of works that contain such falsified information.

The DMCA contains a number of provisions relating to transmission of copyrighted materials over Internet services providers (ISPs). The DMCA takes ISPs off the hook for infringement for transient transmissions automatically passing through their computers. The DMCA also allows ISPs to escape liability for infringement regarding more permanent materials if they promptly remove infringing materials upon request. The DMCA sets up a procedure in case the owner of the removed materials protests. In exchange for escaping liability for infringement, service providers must designate an agent to accept service of legal papers. The DMCA also relieves ISPs from liability for unknowingly linking to a site that does contain infringing material. Finally, the DMCA authorizes U.S. District Court clerks to issue subpoenas to service providers requiring them to identify an alleged online infringer.

The DMCA allows a copy of a computer program to be made for the purpose of repairing or maintaining a computer. In addition, the DMCA contains new laws regarding the licensing of motion pictures and phonorecordings and to the innovative designs of vessel hulls.

Violations of the DMCA can result in civil remedies consisting of injunctive relief, actual damages and statutory damages. Repeat violators may be tagged with treble damages. A willful violation of the DMCA for personal or financial gain can result in stiff criminal penalties (up to 10 years in prison).

Related terms: cyberspace, copyrights in; linking.

display a work, defined

The exclusive right to display an original work of authorship is one of the bundle of rights that together form the overall copyright. (17 United States Code, Section 101.) The Copyright Act of 1976 defines "display" as: "to show a copy of it, either directly or by means of a film, slide, television image, or any other device or process or, in the case of a motion picture or other audiovisual work, to show individual images nonsequentially" (as in movie previews).

EXAMPLE: Marylou photographs Juan's copyrighted print for the purpose of using it in her photography show. Because Juan has the exclusive right to display his work, Marylou must obtain Juan's permission before she displays the photo.

This particular copyright right is certain to become increasingly important as more creative works are put into digital form for display through the Internet, and through the large online services which charge users for the time they spend viewing displayed materials.

Related terms: copyright, explained.

dramatic works, copyrights

In the copyright sense, a dramatic work is one that carries a story line and is intended to be performed before an audience, either directly or through use of a tangible medium such as paper, film, videotape or videodisc. Dramatic works include movies, plays, satires, comedies and pantomimes. Like other original works of authorship, they are fully protectable by copyright.

Related terms: original work of authorship.

duration of copyrights

How long a copyright lasts in the U.S. depends on when the work covered by the copyright was first created or published:

- *Works created on or after January 1, 1978.* Under the Copyright Act of 1976, copyrights on works created on or after January 1, 1978, last for a defined period of time. If the "author" is an individual, and the work appears under that person's name, the copyright lasts for the life of the author plus 70 years. If the "author" is an employer or the commissioner of a work made for hire, or uses a pseudonym or remains anonymous, the copyright lasts for 95 years from the date of publication or 120 years from the date the work was first created, whichever comes first.
- *Works created or published before January 1, 1978.* If the work was published before 1978, the copyright lasts for 95 years from the date of publication, assuming the copyright was (or is) timely renewed (by filing a renewal application with the U.S. Copyright Office). The copyright in works created before 1978 lasts at least until December 31, 2002, regardless of when they were created and at least to 2047 if published before December 31, 2002.

Countries that are members of the Berne Convention and countries that have signed the GATT treaty (which requires its members to honor the Berne Convention's copyright protection standards) extend copyright protection for the life of the author plus a minimum of 50 years. The countries in the European Union also extend copyright protection for the life of the author plus 70 years.

The value of works such as books, films, art and songs (that is, their ability to generate copyright fees) may last well beyond the term of the copyright, in which case the author's inheritors are out of luck. On the other hand, computer-related works seem likely to be more short-lived so copyright protection will probably last for more than enough time to protect them for their entire commercial life expectancy.

Related terms: GATT (General Agreement on Tariffs and Trade); international copyright protection; work made for hire, defined; Sonny Bono Copyright Term Extension Act.

Below is a chart which shows the duration of copyrights for different publishing dates.

Copyright Duration Chart

Date and Nature of Work	Copyright Terms
Published before 1923	The work is in the public domain
Published 1923-1963 and never renewed	The work is in the public domain
Published 1923-1963 and timely renewed	95 years from the date of first publication
Published between 1964-1977	95 years from the date of publication (renewal term automatic)
Created 1978 or later (whether or not published)	Single term of life plus 70 years (but if work is made for hire or anonymous or pseudonymous, 95 years from the date of publication or 120 years from date of creation, whichever ends first)
Created, but not published or registered, before 1978	Single term of at least life plus 70 years, but cannot expire before December 31, 2002 (if work remains unpublished) or December 31, 2047 (if work is published before December 31, 2002)

Reprinted with permission from *The Copyright Handbook* by Stephen Fishman (Nolo).

Definitions

ephemeral recording

Under some circumstances, the Copyright Act permits making copies of works for purposes of later transmission. For example, a disc jockey is permitted to copy a song from compact disc to tape in order to prepare a radio broadcast. These ephemeral recordings are commonly used in radio, cable and Internet broadcasting.

exclusive copyright rights

The entire bundle of rights that a copyright owner is exclusively entitled to exercise under the copyright laws. These rights consists of:

- the right to reproduce (copy) the work
- the right to prepare derivative works
- the right to distribute copies of the work
- the right to perform the work, and
- the right to display the work.

Related terms: copyright, explained; exclusive license, defined; infringement action, explained.

exclusive license, defined

An exclusive license, which must be in writing, is a valid contract in which a copyright owner authorizes another person or entity (called the licensee) to exclusively exercise one or more of the rights (or portion of such rights) that belong to the copyright owner under the copyright. The licensee is said to "own" the rights granted in the license and is often referred to as a "copyright owner."

> **EXAMPLE:** Jeanette Pulaski, a U.S. author, publishes a successful cookbook specializing in East African recipes. Aaron Smith believes the book will sell well in other countries, and approaches Jeanette for permission to sell it on the international market. Jeanette may choose to grant Aaron an exclusive license to copy, distribute and translate (prepare derivative works from) the book for marketing in all countries outside of the U.S. She might, instead, license Aaron to market the book only in one or a few countries—for example, France, the Canadian province of Quebec and all Caribbean and African countries where French is a primary language. In addition to foreign rights, Jeanette is interested in finding someone to help her market the book to cooking stores within the U.S. To reach this market, she grants an exclusive license to a cookware wholesaler. Finally, she exclusively licenses a cookbook publisher to publish and distribute the book to the book trade (exclusive of cooking stores) in the U.S.

Under an exclusive license, the licensee as a "copyright owner" has the right to file an infringement action in court to stop all infringing activities, assuming that the copyright was properly registered and the license was recorded with the U.S. Copyright Office.

Related terms: copyright owner, defined; transfers of copyright ownership, generally.

expedited registration

The U.S. Copyright Office has a special procedure to quickly register a work if a copyright owner needs the registration to pursue a copyright infringement action in federal court (no action may be filed without first registering the copyright). Expedited registration—called "special handling" by the U.S. Copyright Office—costs an additional $500 (as of August 2000).

Related terms: copyright infringement, defined; infringement action, explained.

expression, protection of, under copyright law

See copyright, explained; original work of authorship.

factual works, defined

Factual works are those that legitimately may be classified as nonfiction. Histories, instruction manuals, trade catalogs, travel guides and biographies are all examples of factual works. Under copyright law, factual works receive less protection than works of fiction because the underlying facts are legally considered to be in the public domain. Therefore, factual works do not contain as much protectable material as fictional works.

> **EXAMPLE:** Tim writes a travel book on the Comoros Islands, a small island country off the east coast of Africa. In this book, he catalogs all the usual items, including lodging, tourist sites and food. A year later, Alice publishes a competing book that contains much of the same information plus some additional facts about the Comorean political system. Tim writes Alice, accusing her of copyright infringement. Alice responds that she used Tim's book to visit the Comoros and that since his facts were remarkably accurate, she had no choice but to include them in her book. Because facts such as those found in Alice's and Tim's books are in the public domain, Alice has not infringed Tim's copyright.

Related terms: *Feist Publications Inc. v. Rural Telephone Service Co.*; merger doctrine.

failure to deposit work

To properly register a copyright with the U.S. Copyright Office, the registrant must deposit one or more copies of the underlying work. Failure to deposit within three months after a demand for the deposit is made by the Registrar of Copyrights will require the owner to forfeit the copyright application fee and reapply. In that case, the owner will not be entitled to the original filing date.

Related terms: copyright infringement, defined; registration of copyright, defined.

fair use, defined

Certain uses of a work protected by copyright do not require permission of the copyright owner when done for essentially noncommercial reasons.

The Copyright Act of 1976, as amended in 1992, authorizes any person to make "fair use" of a published or unpublished copyrighted work—including the making of unauthorized copies—in these contexts:

- in connection with criticism of or comment on the work
- in the course of news reporting
- for teaching purposes, or
- as part of scholarship or research activity.

As a practical matter, fair use is primarily an affirmative defense to a claim of copyright infringement—that is, the defense is that even if infringement occurred there is no liability because the infringing activity was excusable as a fair use of the original work.

Whether or not a particular instance of copying without permission qualifies as a fair use is decided on a case-by-case basis and depends on four basic factors. These are:

- the purpose and character of the use, including whether such use is of a commercial nature or for nonprofit, educational purposes
- the nature of the copyrighted work
- the amount and substantiality of the portion used in relation to the copyrighted work as a whole, and
- the effect of the use upon the potential market for, or value of, the copyrighted work.

Below we examine each of these factors separately. Note, that when we use the term "defendant" we are referring to the person accused of infringement.

The first factor is considered the most important and requires an analysis as to whether the use is transformative. That is, did the defendant change the original by adding new expression or meaning? Did the defendant add value to the original by creating new information, new aesthetics, new insights and understandings? If the use was transformative, this weighs in favor of a fair use finding. In a parody, for example, the parodist transforms the original by holding it up to ridicule. The brief use of photographs in a film was considered to be transformative because the images were used in furtherance of the creation of a distinct aesthetic and overall mood. The defendant's work doesn't have to transform the original work's expression as long as the purpose is transformative, for example, scholarship, research, education or commentary.

When considering the second factor—nature of the copyrighted work—a court will generally consider whether the work being copied is informational or entertaining in nature. As the Supreme Court indicated, "copying a news broadcast may have a stronger claim to fair use than copying a motion picture." Why? Because copying from informational works such as scholarly, scientific or news journals encourages the free spread of ideas and encourages the creation of new scientific or educational works, all of which benefits the public. In addition, a defendant has a stronger case of fair use if material is copied from a published work rather than an unpublished work. The scope of fair use is narrower with respect to unpublished works because of the author's right to control the first public appearance of his expression.

As for the third factor—amount and substantiality of portion used—the more that is taken from a work, the more difficult it becomes to justify it as a fair use. For example, in one case the court found that copying more than half of an unpublished manuscript was not considered a fair use. When considering the amount and substantiality of the portion taken, the court considers not just the quantity of the material taken but the quality of the material taken. Determinations regarding "quality" or "substantiality" are subjective and may be difficult to reconcile. For example, the copying of 1 minute and 15 seconds of a 72-two minute Charlie Chaplin film, used in a news report about the comedian's death, was considered substantial and not a fair use. However, in another case, the court determined that copying 41 seconds from a boxing match film was not substantial and permitted it as a fair use in a movie biography of Muhammed Ali.

In certain rare cases, copying of a complete work may be considered a fair use. (*Universal City Studios v. Sony Corp.,* 464 U.S. 417 (1984).) For example, the Supreme Court in the *Sony* case permitted the off-the-air copying of complete television programs by consumers who owned video recorders (VCRs).

As for the fourth factor—effect of the use on the potential market—a judge must consider the effect on the actual and potential market for the copyrighted work. This consideration goes beyond the past intentions of the author or the means by which the author is currently exploiting the work. For example, in one case a photograph was adapted into a wood sculpture without the authorization of the photographer. The fact that the photographer never considered converting

Definitions

the photograph into a sculpture was irrelevant. What mattered was that the *potential* market existed as demonstrated by the fact that the defendant earned hundreds of thousands of dollars selling such sculptures.

Some uses are not considered to undermine the potential market. Copying a magazine cover for purposes of a comparative advertisement is a fair use because the comparative advertisement does not undermine the sales or need for the magazine. Similarly, a court found that the appearance of a poster in the background of a television series for less than 30 seconds did not harm the potential market for the poster.

In addition to these four fair use factors, a court may consider other factors, if relevant. The drafters of the Copyright Act of 1976 were careful to advise that the four fair use factors were intended only as a guideline and the courts are free to adapt the doctrine to particular situations on a case-by-case basis.

Related terms: copyright infringement, defined; infringement action, explained; published work, defined.

false representation in copyright registration application

A deliberate lie on a copyright registration form, such as a false statement that no preexisting works are included in the work being registered, may invalidate the legal effect and benefits of the registration. On the other hand, an innocent mistake should not invalidate the registration if the copyright owner makes timely moves to correct it.

Related terms: supplemental registration.

Feist Publications Inc. v. Rural Telephone Service Co.

In this court case, a publisher of a residential telephone directory sued a competitor who had copied the directory verbatim. The Supreme Court ruled that the original phone directory was not protected under copyright because:
- it consisted of facts in the public domain (the residence and phone number of each person listed in the directory), and
- the information was not arranged in a creative manner (the listings were in alphabetical order).

Although Feist argued that it wasn't fair to allow a competitor to capitalize on the labor and expense that had gone into the original directory, the Supreme Court ruled that copyright only protects original expression, not labor and expense. *(Feist Publications Inc. v. Rural Telephone Service Co.,* 111 S.Ct. 1282 (1991).)

Related terms: compilations of original or unoriginal material; computer databases, copyright of.

filtration test for determining substantial similarity

See Computer Associates Int'l v. Altai.

first sale doctrine

Under the Copyright Act of 1976, the purchaser of a legal copy of a copyrighted work is generally entitled to treat that copy in any way he or she desires, as long as the copyright owner's exclusive copyright rights are not infringed. This means the copy can be destroyed, sold, given away or rented. A common example is the rental of movie videos, where the store purchasing the videotapes is entitled to rent them out without paying any royalties to the owner of the copyright rights in the movie. If, however, the store made additional copies of the movie and also rented them out, the underlying copyright would be infringed. The term "first sale doctrine" comes from the fact that the copyright owner maintains control over a specific copy only until it is first sold.

There are exceptions to the first sale doctrine. As a result of lobbying by the computer and music industries, the rental of computer programs and sound recordings is prohibited. It is also not permissible under the first sale doctrine to destroy a fine art or photographic work that meets the requirements of the Visual Artists Rights Act (for example, signed and numbered photographs created in limited editions of 200 or fewer copies) (*see* work of visual art).

fixed in a tangible medium of expression

In the U.S., and most other countries, an original work of authorship first qualifies for copyright protection when it is reduced to some physical form or representation—that is, when it is fixed in a tangible medium of expression. Under the Copyright Act of 1976, a work is considered fixed in a tangible medium of expression when "its embodiment in a copy or phonorecord, by or under the authority of the author, is sufficiently permanent or stable to permit it to be perceived, reproduced or otherwise communicated for a period of more than transitory duration."

When a computer program is first reduced to paper or electronic patterns on a disk, it becomes fixed in a tangible medium of expression and is protected under the copyright laws. Similarly, when a song is recorded, a holograph photographed, a movie filmed, a video game recorded on tape or an ornamental design molded, each is fixed in a tangible medium of expression and protected by copyright.

A work consisting of sounds, images, or both, that is being transmitted live, is considered "fixed" if some record of the work is being made simultaneously with its transmission. A live transmission of a baseball game is therefore subject

Definitions

to copyright protection at the instant of transmission, because the images being broadcast are also captured on videotape or sound recording.

Although copyright protection arises the instant a work becomes fixed, many countries, including the U.S., allow the copyright owner to take additional steps to strengthen this protection, such as including a correct notice of copyright and registering the copyright with a government agency.

Related terms: copyright, explained; international copyright protection; registration of copyright, defined.

flow charts, registration of

Flow charts that constitute original works of authorship qualify for copyright protection, and may be registered with the U.S. Copyright Office. When registering flow charts, it is necessary to determine whether a Form TX or a Form VA is more appropriate. Form TX (for nondramatic literary works) is used for flow charts that communicate information primarily through text. Form VA (for visual arts works) is used for charts that communicate information primarily through a graphic arrangement of symbols and boxes.

Related terms: Form TX, described; Form VA, described; registration of copyright, defined.

Form CA, described

The U.S. Copyright Office requires Form CA for supplemental registrations, including the correction of errors.

Related terms: registration of copyright, defined; supplemental registration; U.S. Copyright Office.

Form PA, described

The U.S. Copyright Office requires Form PA to register all works involving the performing arts, including dramatic works, audiovisual works (such as movies, audio tapes and training films) and CD-ROM based multimedia products that feature a graphical user interface. Samples of this and other copyright registration forms are in the Sample Forms section at the end of this part of the book.

Related terms: musical works and copyright protection; registration of copyright, defined; U.S. Copyright Office.

Form RE, described

The U.S. Copyright Office requires Form RE to renew copyrights on works first published prior to January 1, 1978.

Related terms: duration of copyrights; registration of copyright, defined; U.S. Copyright Office.

Form SE (short, regular and group), described

The U.S. Copyright Office provides several versions of the SE form for the registration of works consisting of newspapers, serials or periodicals, such as magazines. Which form to use depends on a number of factors, including the number of items to be registered, the period of time for which the items are to be registered, and whether the constituent parts of the items are works made for hire.

Related terms: registration of copyright, defined; U.S. Copyright Office.

Form SR, described

The U.S. Copyright Office requires Form SR to register published and unpublished sound recordings.

Related terms: musical works and copyright protection; registration of copyright, defined; U.S. Copyright Office.

Form TX, described

The U.S. Copyright Office requires Form TX to register all works classified as literary and nondramatic. These include books, poems, computer programs and documentation, essays and articles. Samples of this and other copyright registration forms are in the Sample Forms section at the end of this part of the book.

Related terms: registration of copyright, defined; U.S. Copyright Office.

Form VA, described

The U.S. Copyright Office requires Form VA to register all sculptural or graphic works, such as paintings, photographs and designs. Samples of this and other copyright registration forms are in the Sample Forms section at the end of this part of the book.

Related terms: pictorial, graphic and sculptural works; registration of copyright, defined; U.S. Copyright Office.

Definitions

framing

Framing occurs when one website displays a Web page of another company within a bordered area on its own site (similar to the "picture-in-picture" feature offered on some televisions). For example, when a user enters a search engine request, the search engine might display the contents of an online store within the search engine's website, framed by the search engine's text and logos. When a website is framed within another website, its URL or domain name of the website within the frame is not displayed and users are not able to bookmark the site.

Framing may trigger a dispute under copyright and trademark law theories because a framed site arguably alters the appearance of the content and creates the impression that its owner endorses or voluntarily chooses to associate with the framer. In a 1997 lawsuit, Totalnews was sued by news providers for framing news content from media outlets such as CNN, USA Today and Time. For example, the content of a CNN Web page appeared within a frame packed with advertising and information about Totalnews. The lawsuit settled and TotalNews agreed to stop framing and to use text-only links.

A subsequent court fight involving two dental websites also failed to fully resolve the issue. Applied Anagramic, Inc., a dental services website, framed the content of a competing site. The frames included information about Applied Anagramic as well as its trademark and links to all of its Web pages. A federal district court ruled that a website containing a link that reproduced Web pages within a frame may constitute an infringing derivative work. The court reasoned that the addition of the frame modified the appearance of the linked site and such modifications could, without authorization, amount to infringement. (*Futuredontics Inc. v. Applied Anagramic Inc.*, 46 U.S.P.Q. 2d 2005 (C.D. Calif. 1997).)

Related terms: cyberspace, copyrights in; Digital Millenium Copyright Act of 1998; linking.

freedom of speech and copyright protection

The First Amendment to the U.S. Constitution prohibits the government from placing restrictions on a person's freedom of speech, except in certain situations. One exception is found in the copyright laws, which prohibit speech that would infringe on somebody's copyright. For example, a court can issue an injunction to prevent the publication of material that would damage a copyright owner by infringing on a copyright.

But this protection is not absolute. Educators, news reporters and scholars can invoke the statutory defense of fair use when they use small amounts of copyrighted material as part of teaching, criticizing or commenting on the copy-righted material.

Related terms: fair use, defined.

GATT (General Agreement on Tariffs and Trade)

Commonly known as GATT, the General Agreement on Tariffs and Trade is a comprehensive free-trade treaty signed by 117 nations, including almost every developed country. GATT created an international regulatory body known as the World Trade Organization (WTO) to enforce compliance with the agreement.

GATT becomes effective in different countries at different times, depending on when they enact it and the strength of their economies. For instance, GATT's effective date in the U.S. was January 1, 1996, whereas the former Soviet Union and Warsaw Pact members had to comply beginning in 2000 and the least developed countries will have until 2006.

The part of GATT that affects copyright law (and other forms of intellectual property) is contained in a special agreement known as Trade Related Aspects of Intellectual Property Rights (TRIPS for short). Probably the most important provision of the TRIPS agreement is that all members of GATT must now adhere to the Berne Convention (except for the Berne requirement that moral rights be respected), even if they haven't signed it. This means that 12 countries that were not members of the Berne Convention—including Haiti, Indonesia, Kuwait, Malaysia and some of the countries of the former Soviet Union—now agree to offer basic copyright protection under that treaty because of their GATT membership.

Other important GATT provisions applicable to all members include:

- Live musical performances must be protected from unauthorized distribution (bootlegging) through the means of fixing the performance in a tangible medium (tape, video, etc.) or communicating the performance to the public by wireless means.
- Computer programs are to be treated as literary works under the Berne Convention.
- Works by foreign authors that entered the public domain in the U.S. because of their failure to comply with U.S notice requirements in effect prior to March 1989 are to have restored copyright protection.
- Substantive penalties for copyright infringement are to be provided, including injunctive relief that prevents further infringement and adequate monetary damages for past infringement.

Definitions

- Members must implement procedures that stop infringing materials from crossing the borders of other member countries.
- Software copyright owners may prevent the commercial rental of their protected works.

Related terms: Berne Convention; international copyright protection; restored copyright under GATT; Universal Copyright Convention (U.C.C.).

grant of rights

When an author assigns all copyright rights to his or her publisher in advance of publication, in exchange for future royalties or other payment, the phrase commonly used is "grant of rights."

Related terms: assignment of copyright; transfers of copyright ownership, generally.

graphic and pictorial works

See pictorial, graphic and sculptural works.

HTML

HTML (Hypertext Markup Language) is a collection of computer symbols and codes that are used to create documents that can be displayed on the World Wide Web. HTML works in conjunction with a Web browser—a software program such as Netscape or Internet Explorer that allows users to surf the Internet.

ideas, not protected under copyright

Ideas as such are not protected through the copyright process. Only the actual expression of an idea is subject to copyright protection.

> **EXAMPLE:** Janice La Beaux authors a new computer program that permits a homemaker to keep a running inventory of household goods. If Kim Rivera likes the idea and independently writes a competing program, no copyright infringement has occurred because Kim copied Janice's idea, but not the expressive aspect of the program.

Other legal doctrines, such as patent law and trade secret law, are available to protect some ideas in certain contexts. For example, an idea that adds to a business's competitive position and is not generally known or used in the trade may be treated as a trade secret, and others may be prevented from disclosing or using it without permission. Similarly, an idea may qualify for protection as a utility patent if it is novel, nonobvious and useful, and has either been reduced to practice (that is, demonstrated to work) or has been adequately described in a

Definitions

patent application. An idea for a design may also qualify for a patent if it is for a nonfunctional ornamental design of a manufactured product.

Related terms: copyright and patent compared.
See also Part 1 (Trade Secret Law): ideas as trade secrets.

identifying material, defined

To register a copyright, it generally is necessary to deposit at least one, and often two, complete copies of the work with the U.S. Copyright Office. However, some kinds of works (for instance, holographs and virtual reality scenarios) are not easy to deposit. In other cases, the author may wish to maintain certain ideas as trade secrets and fears their disclosure if a true or complete copy of the work is to be deposited.

To accommodate the needs of registrants in these types of situations, the U.S. Copyright Office will accept a deposit of only a portion of the work or a representation of the entire work. The portion deposited is labeled as "identifying material" in order to satisfy the deposit requirement in the copyright law. Examples of identifying material include photographic prints, transparencies, photostats, drawings or similar two-dimensional reproductions visible without the aid of a machine.

To deposit computer software, the U.S. Copyright Office will accept the first and last 25 pages of a program as identifying material, if the program runs beyond 50 pages. For databases, identifying material consists of a portion of each file in the database.

In addition to these rules, the U.S. Copyright Office is willing to provide special relief for individual deposits on a case-by-case basis. For instance, if a software developer wants to deposit source code but doesn't want to disclose certain trade secrets, the U.S. Copyright Office will allow the developer to black out certain portions of the code so that it cannot easily be understood and copied by potential infringers. Deposits accomplished under the special relief doctrine are also considered to be "identifying material."

Related terms: deposit with U.S. Copyright Office; object code, copyrights; source code, copyrights; special relief, defined.

importing of infringing works

U.S. copyright and customs laws authorize the U.S. Customs Service to prevent material that infringes a U.S. copyright from entering the U.S. Under GATT, all member countries are supposed to enact a similar procedure.

In the U.S., the procedure is supposed to work like this. The copyright owner records his or her work with the U.S. Customs Service. Any imported copies that are the same or highly similar to the recorded works are temporarily seized. The copyright owner is informed of the seizure, and provided time in which to obtain a court order barring the materials from being imported to the U.S.

As a practical matter, this remedy is seldom used due to the inability of the Customs Service to check imports carefully against recorded copyrights. However, Customs will act if alerted by the copyright owner.

The U.S. customs law also authorizes copyright owners to file a complaint with the International Trade Commission to have infringing works excluded from the U.S., on the ground their importation would constitute an unfair method of competition.

Related terms: international copyright protection; international rules on copyright protection.

indecent or immoral works, not protected

Copyright protection is not available for works that a court or the U.S. Copyright Office deems to be indecent or immoral. Although in the past, the U.S. Copyright Office was commonly willing to reject registration of works on these grounds, the tendency now is to accept registration for even fairly explicit material, and to let the courts decide the issue if anyone objects.

independent creation, defense to infringement action

When an author independently creates a work, it is considered original, even though it may be highly similar to another work created by someone else. Accordingly, if a defendant in an infringement lawsuit can prove independent creation, the infringement action will fail, even if the plaintiffs have proved the necessary elements for infringement (substantial similarity and access).

Although some situations are relatively clear-cut, there is also a large gray area where it is difficult to tell whether subsequent works are independent creations or derivatives of earlier ones. In the latter case, permission to use the earlier work would be required.

EXAMPLE: Tim writes a book in English that is similar to one Antoine has written in French but it is not, strictly speaking, a translation. Is this an independent creation? No, if the court finds that Tim's book was based on the French one, and yes, if the court finds that Tim's book was created without relying on or borrowing from Antoine's book. Which of these results will occur depends on the degree of similarity between the works, whether Tim had access to Antoine's work and the probability of Tim's independently creating a similar work.

Determining whether a work is an independent creation or a derivative work is especially difficult in the cases of:

- *computer graphics.* Expression can easily be reduced to digital form, allowing incremental modifications (called "morphing" in the case of moving images) to easily be made, with the result that one expression can be transformed into another without a clear line of demarcation.
- *musical sampling.* Sounds can be digitally captured and then modified and mixed to a point that the result has very little resemblance to any of the original material.

Related terms: based on an earlier work; copyright, explained; copyright infringement, defined; derivative work (copyright).

information in public domain

See public domain—copyright context.

infringement action, explained

A lawsuit brought against someone who uses a copyrighted expression without permission is commonly known as an infringement action. Under the Copyright Act of 1976, a copyright owner is entitled to file an infringement action in federal court against a person who, without proper authorization of the owner:

- makes copies of a copyrighted work
- prepares derivative works from a copyrighted work
- distributes copies of a copyrighted work
- displays a work protected by copyright, or
- performs any original work of authorship protected by the copyright.

To prevail in an infringement action, a plaintiff (copyright owner) must establish that copying occurred. Because direct evidence of copying is almost never available, the plaintiff usually must establish that the infringing work is substantially similar to the infringed work and that the alleged infringer could have had access to the infringed work in order to copy it.

If these elements are proven, the defendant (who allegedly infringed the copyright) has several defenses, including claims that:

- the work was the product of an independent conception, and is therefore an original work of authorship
- the use falls under the "fair use" exception, or
- the defendant had permission to use the work.

Infringement actions offer the successful plaintiff the possibility of a wide variety of judicial relief, depending on the circumstances and whether the work is registered with the U.S. Copyright Office. Most important, the court is authorized to grant immediate but temporary relief in the form of a temporary restraining order, and, pending a full scale trial, more extended relief in the form of a preliminary injunction. Either or both of these devices can halt publication or distribution of the offending work.

The preliminary injunction can be vital to a copyright owner's interests, since a regular injunction (or permanent injunction) can only be obtained as a part of a final judgment, which can take years. A preliminary injunction is relatively easy to obtain, once substantial evidence has been presented to the court showing a probability that an infringement is occurring.

In addition to court orders prohibiting further infringing activity, plaintiffs may be awarded a money award known as damages. This can consist of actual losses suffered as a result of the infringement and the profits realized by the defendant because of the infringement. As an alternative to seeking damages and profits, copyright owners who have timely registered their copyright may pursue statutory damages, which can be awarded without any proof of harm or defendant's profits.

Copyright owners who timely register their copyright and/or record their ownership interest also qualify to have their attorney fees and court costs paid by an unsuccessful defendant. This alone can be a powerful incentive to register the copyright at the earliest possible time.

Related terms: copyright infringement, defined; damages for copyright infringement; defenses to copyright infringement; injunctions, copyright infringement; registration of copyright, defined.

infringement of copyright

See copyright infringement, defined.

injunctions, copyright infringement

Once copyright infringement is established, courts often are willing to issue an order (termed an injunction) to prevent the infringer from making or distributing further unauthorized copies of the original work of authorship. To the extent that the infringing work heavily relies on the infringed work, an injunction can have a severely adverse economic impact on the infringer.

EXAMPLE: When Apple Computer Inc. obtained an injunction preventing Franklin Computer from further copying the Apple Computer operating system, Franklin was effectively unable to market its computers because they would not work without using the infringing material. *(Apple Computer, Inc. v. Franklin Computer Corporation,* 714 F.2d 1240 (3rd Cir. 1983).)

Injunctions come in three forms:

- *temporary injunctions or temporary restraining orders (TROs).* These are technically restricted to a situation when the plaintiff is on the brink of suffering irreparable injury and needs to stop some immediate action pending further consideration of the case. TROs generally only last for a week or two until the court can consider whether to grant a preliminary injunction.
- *preliminary injunctions.* Courts will issue a preliminary injunction if the plaintiff makes a strong showing that: the plaintiff is likely to prevail at the trial of the case, and the plaintiff will suffer greater economic harm than the defendant if such interim relief is not granted. Preliminary injunctions can last as long as it takes to get to trial—sometimes years.
- *permanent injunctions.* These are, as billed, permanent prohibition against using or distributing the unauthorized work.

Because courts generally presume that copyright infringement will cause irreparable injury, they often issue TROs and preliminary injunctions if infringement appears likely. Nevertheless, the court will usually require the plaintiff to post a bond to compensate the defendant for any harm caused by the injunction if later on the defendant ends up winning the case. Whether or not preliminary relief is granted, the court will determine after a trial whether injunctive relief is appropriate on a more permanent basis.

As a practical matter, losing a preliminary injunction often spells defeat for the defendant, regardless of the legal strength of the case. This is because few defendants can afford to keep the allegedly infringing work off the market pending trial and also meet the costs of a full blown defense to the infringement charges. Because by definition a judge has already determined that infringement will mostly likely be found to exist when the case goes to trial, defendants normally find it economically prudent to settle early on the plaintiff's terms and get on with their business.

Related terms: *Apple Computer, Inc. v. Franklin*; damages for copyright infringement; infringement action, explained.

innocent infringement of copyright

Because the copyright laws afford protection to an original work of authorship as soon as it has become fixed in a tangible medium of expression, copyright infringement can easily be accidental. This is especially true if the copyright owner has failed to place a copyright notice on the work.

EXAMPLE: Lester collects many materials from diverse sources while writing a book about robot law. Among these is a July 6, 1995, article by Timothy Witherspoon, a well-known employee of the National Institutes of Science.

No copyright notice is attached, and Lester assumes that the article is in the public domain because of Witherspoon's federal employment (works published by the federal government are in the public domain). Accordingly, Lester quotes freely from the article in his book, giving Timothy a full credit line, but no royalties.

As it turns out, Timothy wrote the article on his own time and owns the copyright in the article. Because the article was published after March 1, 1989, the lack of a copyright notice does not affect the underlying copyright in a work. However, since Lester's infringement was inadvertent, Timothy will probably not be able to collect damages from him for the use of the article that occurred before Lester discovered that the article was protected by copyright. Further, Timothy may not even be able to prevent further publication and sales of the infringing work (the book on robot law). But Timothy is likely to get a court to require Lester, as a condition of permitting Lester to continue his infringement, to pay Timothy a reasonable license fee for what is called a "judicially imposed compulsory license."

Whether a particular infringement qualifies as innocent varies from case to case. For example, if Timothy's article had a proper copyright notice on it, or if the article had been registered with the U.S. Copyright Office, Lester could not have claimed innocence. It is always wise either to get an author's permission for a work prior to use, or, if it lacks a copyright notice, to check with the U.S. Copyright Office to see if a work is registered.

Innocent infringement should be distinguished from the fair use doctrine, where infringement is excused because of the nature of the material and the context in which it was used.

Related terms: fair use, defined; international rules on notice of copyright; omission of copyright notice.

instructional text

A literary, pictorial or graphic work that is prepared for use in day-to-day instructional activities is an instructional text. For example, a textbook would be an instructional text, but a novel used in a literature class would not be an instructional text. Instructional texts are one of the enumerated categories listed for determining whether a work can qualify as a commissioned work made for hire. This distinction is important because if a work was commissioned and it did not fall within one of the enumerated categories, it would not be a work made for hire even if there was a signed agreement stating that the work was made for hire. If a work qualifies as a work made for hire, the copyright is owned by the hiring party, not the author.

Related terms: work made for hire, defined.

international copyright protection

Over 120 nations have signed treaties in which they agree to extend reciprocal copyright protection to works authored by nationals of the other signing countries as well as works first published in one of the other signing countries. This reciprocal approach is commonly called "national treatment."

The two main copyright treaties are the Berne Convention and the Universal Copyright Convention (U.C.C.), both of which the U.S. has signed. To the extent the provisions of these two treaties overlap, the author is entitled to the most liberal protection available—usually found in the Berne Convention.

In 1994-1995, most countries of the world ratified GATT (General Agreement on Tariffs and Trade), which binds them to comply with the provisions of the Berne Convention (except for its moral rights provision) whether or not they are already members. The GATT treaty makes the Berne Convention by far the most important international treaty; the U.C.C. will play an increasingly minor role in international copyright protection.

Besides establishing reciprocal protection rights, the Berne Convention also establishes the minimum protections that must be afforded, and specifies that no formalities—such as copyright notice—are required for gaining such protection. The Berne Convention does not impose on any country a definition of what can and cannot be copyrighted, but virtually all of the signatory countries (and GATT members) will fully protect such traditional items as books, art works, movies and plays. In addition, GATT requires that all members treat computer programs as literary works under the Berne Convention.

Related terms: Berne Convention; GATT (General Agreement on Tariffs and Trade); international rules on notice of copyright; Universal Copyright Convention (U.C.C.).

international rules on notice of copyright

Authors seeking to invoke international protection under the Berne Convention (authors in the U.S. and in most large industrialized nations, including all nations that ratify the GATT treaty) need not apply any copyright notice to their works.

Authors seeking to invoke international copyright protection under the Universal Copyright Convention (the relatively few countries that have not signed the Berne Convention or the GATT treaty) must use the following notice: "© (year of publication) (author or other basic copyright owner)."

Definitions

For example, the correct U.C.C. notice for this book would be: "© 2000 Stephen Elias and Richard Stim." Or, if Nolo owned the copyright, the correct notice would be: "© 2000 Nolo."

Related terms: Berne Convention; international copyright protection.

Internet and copyright

See cyberspace and copyright, and Digital Millennium Copyright Act of 1998.

Internet service provider (ISP)

America Online, MSN and Mindspring are all ISPs—businesses that provide access to the Internet. ISPs may also offer services such as website hosting. ISPs can sometimes be held accountable for copyright violations for material posted by subscribers and users, but are usually protected by the provisions of the Digital Millennium Copyright Act.

Related terms: cyberspace, copyrights in; Digital Millenium Copyright Act.

joint copyright ownership

See joint work.

joint work

Under the Copyright Act of 1976, a joint work is defined as "a work prepared by two or more authors who intend to merge their contributions into inseparable or interdependent parts of the whole." (17 United States Code, Section 101.) The U.S. Copyright Office will accept for registration works that meet this statutory definition, and will treat the authors as having equal rights to register and enforce the copyright, regardless of what the joint authors arrange among themselves.

EXAMPLE: Tom Maris and Mary Tiger have a partnership agreement, under which Tom owns three-fourths of the copyright and Mary one-fourth. If the copyright is registered with the U.S. Copyright Office with Tom and Mary listed as coauthors, they will be simply listed as coauthors without reference to their independent, unequal ownership arrangement. However, the partnership agreement will govern issues that may arise between Tom and Mary, such as who gets what share of the any royalties earned on the work, who is entitled to license the work to others and who can sue to enforce the copyright.

Related terms: co-authors.

Library of Congress, deposit requirement

With few exceptions, under the Copyright Act of 1976, an author is required to deposit at least one copy of his or her published work with the Library of Congress. This requirement is automatically met if the work is registered with the U.S. Copyright Office, which requires a deposit of either one or two copies of the best edition of the work, depending on the type of work. However, even if an author decides not to register a work with the U.S. Copyright Office, the author generally has an obligation to make the Library of Congress deposit, except for computer programs and certain other types of works. Failure to make the deposit carries no penalty unless the Library of Congress makes a demand. In that case, failure to deposit within three months may result in a relatively nominal fine.

Related terms: best edition of a work; deposit with U.S. Copyright Office.

license fee, payable by innocent infringer

See innocent infringement of copyright.

license recordation

See recordation of copyright transfers.

licensing of copyrights

A copyright license is a method by which the owner of a copyright gives permission for another to use or copy an original work of authorship. Because the essence of a copyright is the exclusive right to make copies, in order to commercially exploit the product, a copyright owner often needs to pass this and associated rights to a publisher or distributor.

A license may be either exclusive or non-exclusive and can be restricted by territory, by time, by media, by purpose, or by virtually any other factor desired by the parties. Exclusive licenses must almost always be in writing to be valid. In all cases, licenses should be recorded with the U.S. Copyright Office.

Related terms: exclusive license, defined; transfers of copyright ownership, generally.

Definitions

linking

Any component of a Web page that connects to another Web page or another portion of the same Web page is a link. Clicking on underlined text or a graphic image activates most links. For example, if a user clicks on the words Financial Calculator or an image of a calculator, the user will be transported to a page that contains a calculator. Links are sometimes called "hyperlinks." Although it is not a copyright violation to create a link, it is a violation of the law to create a link that contributes to unauthorized copying of a copyrighted work if the linking party knew or had reason to know of the unauthorized copying and encouraged it.

> **EXAMPLE:** A website posted infringing copies of a church's copyrighted handbook at its site. The website was ordered to remove the handbook but subsequently provided links to other sites that contained infringing copies of the handbook. These links were different from traditional links because the website knew and encouraged the use of the links to obtain unauthorized copies. The linking activity constituted contributory copyright infringement. (*Intellectual Reserve, Inc. v. Utah Lighthouse Ministry, Inc.*, 75 F. Supp. 2d 1290 (D. Utah 1999).)

literary works, copyrights

"Literary works" is one of the broad categories of material protected under the copyright laws. The phrase has little legal significance, and is used primarily to classify materials that must be registered with the U.S. Copyright Office on a Form TX.

According to the U.S. Copyright Act of 1976, literary works are "works, other than audiovisual works, expressed in words, numbers, or other verbal or numerical symbols or indicia, regardless of the nature of the material objects, such as books, periodicals, manuscripts, phonorecords, film, tapes, disks or cards in which they are embodied." (17 United States Code, Section 101.)

Examples of literary works include computer programs, books, poems, plays, newspapers, magazines, software documentation, training films consisting primarily of dialogue and flowcharts consisting primarily of text.

Related terms: registration of copyright, defined.

manufacturing clause

The manufacturing clause is a now defunct U.S. statute that barred the importation of more than 2,000 copies of any nondramatic literary material written in English by an American author, unless it had been manufactured in the U.S. or Canada. The manufacturing clause has not been in effect since the 1980s.

mask work

See Semiconductor Chip Protection Act of 1984.

mechanical rights

The right to reproduce a song on vinyl recordings, cassette tape, compact disc or DVD (collectively known as phonorecords) is referred to as a mechanical right. In contrast, broadcasting a song over the radio, TV or Internet or incorporating a song in a movie, video or video game are not mechanical rights; they are performance rights.

Every time a song is "pressed" (or fixed) on a phonorecord, the songwriter is entitled to a payment for this mechanical right, known as a mechanical royalty. Mechanical royalty rates are set by law (known as the statutory rate) but artists and songwriters are free to negotiate a lower rate. The advantage of paying the statutory rate is that an artist does not have to seek permission to record the song provided that certain requirements are met (*see* compulsory license).

Why would a songwriter accept less than the statutory rate? Sometimes the songwriter has no choice because it is a condition of a recording agreement or because it is the only way to attract a specific artist to record the song.

Mechanical royalty rates are constantly changing. For example, it was common in the 1970s for a songwriter to receive $.02. For every song pressed on a recording. Below are the rates expected through the year 2006. The current mechanical rate can be determined by calling the Copyright Office Licensing Division (202-707-8150) or consulting the Code of Federal Regulations at 37 C.F.R. § 255. Two rates are provided: per song and per minute. The song owner is paid whichever rate is higher.

Table of Mechanical Royalty Rates

Years	Per Song	Per Minute
Jan. 1, 1998 - Jan. 1, 2000	7.1 cents	1.35 cents
Jan. 1, 2000 - Jan. 1, 2002	7.55 cents	1.45 cents
Jan. 1, 2002 - Jan. 1, 2004	8 cents	1.55 cents
Jan. 1, 2004 - Jan. 1, 2006	8.5 cents	1.65 cents
After Jan. 1, 2006	9.1 cents	1.75 cents

Related terms: compulsory license; music publisher.

Definitions

merger doctrine

This rule was developed in and followed by the courts. It severely limits copyright protection—or denies it altogether—to a work that involves very little creativity if its ways of expressing the ideas in the work are very limited. When it is very difficult to separate the expression in a work from the underlying ideas, the two are said to merge. Under the merger doctrine, a work will only be protected against verbatim copying, assuming there is any protectable expression at all in the work.

The merger doctrine has been the basis for a series of court decisions that deny protection to computer user interfaces, the best known of which is *Computer Associates Int'l v. Altai*, 982 F.2d 693 (2nd Cir. 1992). The merger doctrine also applies to factual works such as histories, biographies and scientific treatises.

Related terms: *Computer Associates Int'l v. Altai; Feist Publications Inc. v. Rural Telephone Service Co.*

microcode and copyright

Microcode is software embedded in a computer chip for the purpose of performing the computer's basic purpose—to process information. One court has ruled that microcode is subject to copyright protection. (*NEC Corp. v. Intel Corp.*, 10 U.S. P.Q. 2d 1177 (N.D. Cal. 1989).) However, this protection is likely to be limited to "virtually identical copying," as it was in the *Intel* case, since microcode is very much determined by external constraints such as heat and space, and the underlying unprotectable idea would therefore be merged with any protectable expression in the code.

Related terms: computer software, copyright of; merger doctrine.

mistakes in registration, correction of

See supplemental registration.

money damages in infringement action

See damages for copyright infringement.

moral rights

Every copyright owner who lives or publishes in a country that has signed the Berne Convention is supposed to have moral rights that are personal to the author and that cannot, therefore, be taken away or abridged. Sometimes referred to by the French term "droit moral," these rights include the author's right to:

- proclaim authorship of a work
- disclaim authorship of a work, and

- object to any distortion, mutilation or other modification of the work that would be injurious to the author's reputation as an author.

Even though the U.S. is a signatory nation to the Berne Convention, it doesn't specifically recognize moral rights, taking the position that a number of different U.S. statutes provide equivalent and adequate protection. For instance, Section 106 of the Copyright Act of 1976, as amended, provides that the artist of a work of visual art (as defined by the statute) can control whether his or her name is on the art and object if the integrity of the work is threatened. And under a federal statutory scheme that primarily governs trademarks (known as the Lanham Act), an author may sue anyone who misrepresents authorship.

Most art law experts believe this piecemeal approach to moral rights leaves the moral rights provision in the Berne Convention largely unimplemented in the U.S. Although the moral rights provision of the Berne Convention applies to all works of expression, it is seldom an issue in any area other than the visual arts.

Related terms: Berne Convention; international copyright protection; work of visual art. *See also* Part 3 (Trademark Law): Lanham Act.

motion pictures, copyrights

According Section 101 of the Copyright Act of 1976, as amended, "Motion pictures are audiovisual works consisting of a series of related images which, when shown in succession, impart an impression of motion, together with accompanying sounds, if any." Motion pictures are entitled to copyright protection under the audiovisual work category and may be registered with the U.S. Copyright Office by using Form PA and depositing the best edition of one complete copy.

Related terms: best edition of a work; registration of copyright, defined.

MP3

The most common system for music downloads from the Internet is known as MPEG 1 Layer 3 or "MP3" for short. MP3 technology compresses sound files so that approximately 60 minutes of music can be stored on 32 megabytes of computer memory. The distribution of MP3 files is an infringement unless authorized by the respective copyright owners. In 1998, the Rio appeared, the first handheld MP3 storage device. The music industry attempted to halt sales of the Rio, arguing that the Rio failed to meet standards established in the Audio Home Recording Act (AHRA). In 1998, a judge refused to issue an injunction halting the sale.

Internet sites that facilitate the copying, transfer or sale of unauthorized MP3s have been the subject of lawsuits from the recording Industry. In 2000, both MP3.com and Napster.com—a file sharing system—were the subjects of record company litigation. In both cases, judges rejected fair use arguments and found that the websites facilitated the distribution of unauthorized recordings. In other words, even though a company does not store or offer unauthorized recordings at its website, the company is still violating copyright law because if it has established a system that allows others to infringe copyrights.

Related terms: Audio Home Recording Act, cyberspace, copyrights in.

music publisher

Music publishers own song copyrights and collect revenue, handle business formalities, sue infringers and look for new ways to exploit songs. Music publishers acquire ownership of song copyrights when the songwriter transfers copyright ownership in exchange for payments or an ongoing royalty. Most music publishers offer an upfront sum or "advance" to the songwriter and share the revenue with the songwriter as the song earns money. That is, the songwriter continues to earn a percentage of the revenue through the life of the copyright. For example, even though Paul McCartney does not own the copyright in the Beatles songs, he still receives revenue from the music publisher that now owns the copyright.

musical works and sound recordings distinquished

There are two types of copyrights for music: musical works copyrights, which protect songs and compositions; and sound recording copyrights, which protect the manner in which music is arranged and recorded—that is, the sounds fixed on the recording. These forms of copyright protection create two overlapping sources of income. Songwriters earn income from the exploitation of songs. Recording artists and record companies earn money from the sale of recordings. The same person or business can own both types of copyrights, but the musical works copyright is usually owned by the songwriter or a music publisher, and the sound recording copyright is usually owned by a record company.

Form PA is used to register published or unpublished musical works. Form SR is used to register published or unpublished sound recordings such as a record, cassette recording or compact disc. In addition, Form SR would be used if the author also wishes to simultaneously register the sound recording and underlying musical work embodied on the sound recording.

national treatment

This approach to international copyright protection, taken by the Berne Convention and other major copyright treaties, requires a signatory country to extend to nationals of other signatory countries the same copyright protection as is extended to its own citizens.

Related terms: Berne Convention; international copyright protection.

new version

See derivative work; single registration rule.

news reporting, fair use

See fair use, defined.

non-exclusive license

A copyright owner grants a non-exclusive license when the owner (licensor) authorizes another person or institution (the licensee) to exercise one or more of the rights belonging to the owner under the copyright on a shared (non-exclusive) basis. Legally, no transfer of copyright ownership takes place under a non-exclusive license, since the licensee shares the right with the original owner and perhaps with additional non-exclusive licensees. Although a non-exclusive license need not be in writing to be valid, most are.

> **EXAMPLE:** Steve Rogers builds an electronic legal dictionary featuring intellectual property terminology for the purpose of selling it to law firms. Rather than sell the dictionary outright, Steve distributes it under non-exclusive licenses that permit licensee law firms to make copies for use in personal computers belonging to the law office staff (a site license). The non-exclusive license prohibits a licensee from transferring the dictionary to another firm, and requires payment of a set amount each year for renewal of the license. Under this arrangement, thousands of law firms might be non-exclusive licensees, but none of them would be considered as a copyright owner, since none has the exclusive right to use and therefore enforce the copyright.

Related terms: exclusive license, defined; licensing of copyrights.

notice of copyright

Often referred to as a "legend" or "bug," a notice of copyright is the little "©" plus the date of publication and author's name.

For works published in the U.S. after March 1, 1989, no such copyright notice is required for copyright protection within the U.S. Nor is a notice required in any of the other countries that have either signed the Berne Convention or GATT. However, the notice is still useful to:

- remind others that the work is protected by copyright
- preclude the use of the "innocent infringer" defense in a copyright infringement case, and
- point a would-be user of the work in the right direction if he or she wants permission to use it.

For works published in the U.S. prior to March 1, 1989, a copyright notice is required to preserve the copyright in the work.

To provide adequate notice where such notice is desired, the copyright notice must be placed where it will easily be seen by a person viewing the work—that is, it must provide "reasonable notice of the claim of copyright." Under guidelines published by the U.S. Copyright Office:

- For literary works, notice may appear either on the front or back of the title page.
- For computer software, notice may appear on the disk or cassette, in the program itself, or it may be placed to appear when the program appears on the computer screen.
- For audiovisual works, notice may appear on the screen with the credits.
- For phonorecords, audiotapes and CD-ROMs, notice may appear on the record cover or CD-ROM and tape enclosures.

There is no limit to the number of different places a copyright notice can appear.

Related terms: defective copyright notice; innocent infringement of copyright; international rules on notice of copyright; omission of copyright notice.

object code, copyrights

Most computers work through the use of compilers, which translate programs written in a programming language (called source code) into a language that the computer can recognize (called object code). The source code typically consists of words and a formal grammatical syntax. The object code consists of ones and zeros which, in all respects, are equivalent to the source code's meaning and syntax, but feed the program to the computer in a binary form (one=on and zero=off) which the computer can then process and act on. This is very much like translating a written message into short and long Morse Code signals for telegraphic transmission.

Although object code is unintelligible to most human readers, the courts have held that it qualifies for copyright protection as a form of expression, and as such can be registered with the U.S. Copyright Office. The reason to register object code rather than source code is that because source code can be readily understood by skilled readers, registering it may give away trade secrets that have been maintained in the software.

When someone registers object code rather than source code, the U.S. Copyright Office places the registration under what's termed "the rule of doubt." This means that because the U.S. Copyright Office can't read or understand what was deposited, it expresses no opinion on whether the object code qualifies for copyright protection. In short, the U.S. Copyright Office does not consider the object code deposit the best edition of the underlying work and expressly favors the source code as a computer program deposit instead.

The U.S. Copyright Office offers a number of alternatives to the deposit of pure object code, which are designed to preserve trade secrets in a program while providing the U.S. Copyright Office with something intelligible to its employees. For example, acceptable deposits include parts of the source code with strategic sections blacked out, or a mix of source code and object code.

Related terms: computer software, copyright of; deposit with U.S. Copyright Office; source code, copyrights.
See also Part 1 (Trade Secret Law): trade secret, defined.

omission of copyright notice

Although a copyright notice is no longer required in the U.S. as of March 1, 1989, for many years previous to that, omission of the notice voided copyright protections. A work of authorship published prior to January 1, 1978, without the proper notice of copyright qualified for no copyright protection. A work published between January 1, 1978, and March 1, 1989, without the proper notice of copyright lost its copyright protection unless the work was republished after March 1, 1989. But even then, the old copies remained unprotected unless the work was registered with the U.S. Copyright Office within five years of its original publication and an earnest attempt was made to have correct notices placed on all copies that were already distributed.

While works publicly distributed in the U.S. after March 1, 1989, do not need a notice to protect the copyright, it is still a good idea to include one. If a copyright infringement lawsuit becomes necessary and the work has the correct notice on it, the infringer will not be able to claim an innocent infringement—a legal status that makes it far harder for the copyright owner to recover damages.

Under GATT, works that entered into the public domain in the U.S. because they lacked a proper copyright notice may have their copyright restored if they were otherwise protected by the Berne Convention when created.

Related terms: defective copyright notice; innocent infringement of copyright; notice of copyright.

original work of authorship

Under the Copyright Act of 1976, an "original work of authorship" encompasses, with a few exceptions, any type of expression independently conceived of by its creator. Authorship embodies a certain minimum level of creativity and originality. But as long as a particular expression has been independently arrived at, it need not be original in the sense of "new." For example, if Thomas Dowel never heard of or read *One Flew Over the Cuckoo's Nest*, by Ken Kesey, but somehow managed to write a play very similar to it, Dowel's play would qualify as "original," and would thus be subject to copyright protection. Of course, when one work is very much like another, the odds favor the likelihood that copying occurred.

Among the many creations that qualify as works of authorship are sheet music, movies, records, tape recordings, video disk productions, laser disk games, cartoons, artistic designs, magazines and books. Computer software also counts as a work of authorship, in both source code and object code form.

A few categories of expression do not qualify as "original works of authorship" either because they are too short to deserve copyright protection or they involve little or no creativity or originality. Among these are titles of books, movies and songs; short phrases and slogans; printed forms; compilations of facts; and works consisting entirely of information that is public domain property—for instance, lists and tables taken from public documents or other common sources.

Related terms: compilations of original or unoriginal material; *Feist Publications Inc. v. Rural Telephone Service Co.*

output of computer, copyrightability of

Many computer programs produce original works of authorship on the screen that are individually protectable by copyright apart from the underlying program code. For example, the computer game "Doom" produces characters that may qualify for independent copyright protection. Other examples of protectable computer output are computer-generated slides, music produced by a computerized synthesizer and laser light shows.

Related terms: computer software, copyright of.

overlapping transfers of copyright

Overlapping transfers of copyright rights occur when a copyright owner:
- transfers all or part of the same exclusive right to two or more separate parties
- transfers an exclusive right when that right has already been the subject of a non-exclusive license, or
- grants a non-exclusive license involving a right that has already been transferred by an exclusive license.

The following rules determine ownership in these situations:
- In a case of conflicting exclusive rights, the first right granted is entitled to the protection if the right is recorded in the U.S. Copyright Office within one month of the underlying work's publication (within two months if the right was granted outside of the U.S.).
- If the exclusive right is not recorded on time, the first transfer recorded is entitled to protection (even if it was the second one granted), as long as the grantee received it in good faith (without knowledge of the earlier one).
- Whether recorded or not, a non-exclusive written license will coexist with a later transfer of an exclusive right.
- Whether recorded or not, a non-exclusive written license will coexist with an exclusive right that was transferred earlier if both the grant of the non-exclusive license occurred before the earlier transfer was recorded, and the recipient of the non-exclusive license did not know of the earlier exclusive-rights transfer.

A chart delineating overlapping transfers of copyright rights is set out below.

Related terms: exclusive license, defined; non-exclusive license; recordation of copyright transfers.

ownership of copyright

See copyright owner, defined.

pantomimes and choreographic works, copyrights

Pantomimes and choreographic productions are among the forms of expression that can qualify for copyright protection when fixed in a tangible medium of expression such as film, video, written score or recording. To register these types of works with the U.S. Copyright Office, the owner must use Form PA.

Related terms: Form PA, described; registration of copyright, defined.

Parody and fair use

Parody occurs when one work ridicules another well-known work by imitating it in a comedic way. Because parody is a type of critique—that is, it comments on the work being parodied— it constitutes speech protected under the First Amendment of the U.S. Constitution. However, to the extent that the parody copies material protected by copyright, its publication may also be considered a copyright infringement. How do the courts reconcile these two opposite interests? The courts first decide whether a particular work qualifies as parody. If so, the court then determines whether the work qualifies as a fair use. If it does, then there is no copyright infringement.

To determine whether a work is a parody, the courts decide whether the work actually comments on the original work or just invokes the original work as a means of calling attention to itself in the marketplace. For example, in one case involving a poem by a Dr. Juice called "The Cat NOT in the Hat," the court held that the poem was not a parody of the original Dr. Seuss work "The Cat in the Hat" because the purpose of the poem, which imitated the famous Dr. Seuss style without substantial alteration, was to comment on the O.J. trial rather than the original Dr. Seuss work. (*Dr. Seuss Enterprises v. Penguin Books USA Inc.,* 109 F.3d 1394 (9th Cir. 1997).) To quote from a leading U.S. Supreme Court case in this area (*Campbell v. Acuff-Rose,* 510 U.S. 569 (1994)), the key question to be addressed in deciding whether a work is a parody is whether the new work "adds something new, with a further purpose or different character altering the first with new expression, meaning, or message; it asks in other words whether and to what extent the new work is transformative."

A good example of what makes a work transformative can be seen in the case of *Leibovitz v. Paramount Pictures Corp.,* 137 F3d 109 (2nd Cir. 1998). In this case the Paramount motion picture company released an advertisement for the movie "Naked Gun 33 1/3" that showed Leslie Neilson's face superimposed on the famous nude photo of a pregnant Demi Moore (which originally appeared on the cover of *Vanity Fair* magazine). Annie Leibovitz, the photographer, sued Paramount for copyright infringement. In holding the work to be a parody, the

Court held that the "ad may reasonably be perceived as commenting on the seriousness and even pretentiousness of the original." The Court went on to note that the parody differed from the original "in a way that may, reasonably, be perceived as commenting, through ridicule, on what a viewer might reasonably think is the undue self-importance conveyed by the subject of the Leibovitz photograph."

Once a work is found to be a parody, the court then must go on to decide whether the other tests used to determine fair use apply to the case. Briefly these tests are:

- the purpose and character of the use, including whether such use is of a commercial nature or is for nonprofit educational purposes
- the nature of the copyrighted work
- the amount and substantiality of the portion used in relation to the copyrighted work as a whole, and
- the effect of the use upon the potential market for or value of the copyrighted work.

Related terms: copyright infringement, fair use.

patent and copyright

See copyright and patent, compared.

performing a work

The exclusive right to perform a work is one of the bundle of rights that make up a copyright. Performing a copyrighted work without obtaining permission from the copyright owner constitutes an infringement of copyright.

To perform a work publicly has a much broader meaning under copyright law than the common concept of a performance. The drafters of the Copyright Act of 1976 stated that "to perform a work means to recite, render, play, dance, or act it, either directly or by means of any device or process or, in the case of a motion picture or other audiovisual work, to show its images in any sequence or to make the sounds accompanying it audible." Section 101 of the Copyright Act states that to perform a work "publicly" means that there is performance of the work where the public is gathered *or* the work is transmitted or otherwise communicated to the public. (17 United States Code, Section 101.)

Examples of public performance include:

- A disc jockey plays a phonorecord in a nightclub.
- A novelist reads aloud from her work at a bookstore.
- A dancer presents a performance during halftime at a football game.

- A motion picture company authorizes a showing of its latest film.
- A songwriter performs an original composition at a nightclub.
- A radio station plays a record containing a copyrighted song.
- A television station broadcasts a television show.
- A cable TV company receives a television station broadcast and rebroadcasts it via cable transmission.

The performance right does not extend to pictorial, graphic or sculptural works because these works cannot be *performed*; they can only be *displayed* so these rights are covered by the display right. In 1994, the Copyright Act was amended to include digital performance rights for sound recordings and to prevent the bootlegging of live musical performances.

Related terms: copyright infringement, defined; exclusive copyright rights; public performance of a work.

performing music at a business

Performing rights societies collect fees from establishments where music is performed, such as clothing stores, bars or restaurants. The "performance" of a song has a broad meaning encompassing live concerts, playing of a recording at a business or club and transmission of a song via radio, television, cable or digital signals.

Some businesses are exempt from these pay-for-play rules. Businesses that play the radio or television do not have to pay performances fees if they meet the criteria below:

- the business is a restaurant or bar under 3,750 square feet;
- the business is a retail establishment under 2,000 square feet; or
- the business, regardless of size, has no more than six external speakers, but not more than four per room, or four televisions measuring 55 inches or less, but not more than one per room.

The exemptions above apply only to establishments that play radio and television. Establishments playing pre-recorded music, such as compact discs, must still pay performance fees. Permission is not required to play a song in a record store or if the song is played via licensed jukebox.

Related terms: performing a work; performing rights societies; mechanical rights; musical works and sound recordings distinguished.

performing rights societies

The owner of a song controls the right to publicly perform it (known as the "performance right"). The "performance" of a song has a broad meaning encompassing live concerts, playing of a recording at a business or club and transmission of a song via radio, television, cable or digital signals. Song owners earn money whenever their song is performed (known as "performance royalties").

It would be impractical if the proprietors of radio and TV stations or nightclubs had to contact each song owner for permission each time a song was publicly performed. Performing rights societies were established in order to negotiate and collect these fees. In the U.S. a song owner affiliates with one of three performing rights societies, ASCAP, BMI or SESAC. These societies act as agents for song owners, surveying radio stations on a regular basis and using the surveys as a basis for payments to songwriters. TV stations furnish logs of music played and agreements are also made with club owners where phonorecords are played, or with concert halls where live music is performed.

Related terms: performing a work; performing music at a business; mechanical rights; musical works and sound recordings distinguished.

permission, getting

Many kinds of media publications—small and large—use words, music and imagery that are protected by copyright laws. Is permission required for all uses of someone else's work? For example, is permission needed to reproduce a photo taken by a club member, a friend or a relative? The short answer is: "Yes." Copyright protection extends to any original work regardless of who created it and permission is required for reproduction, display or distribution of the work.

The reason for acquiring permission is to avoid a lawsuit. The copyright owner controls the use of the work and a person who uses it without permission could be sued for financial damages. If a friend or family member has consented to the use, the concern over a lawsuit diminishes, as does the need for a written permission agreement. An oral consent is valid, although an email or written consent is preferred as it is easier to prove in the event of a dispute. Sometimes the process of acquiring consent can be simplified by using the services of a copyright clearinghouse.

It is wise to operate under the assumption that all art, music and writings are protected by copyright law. A work is not in the public domain simply because it has been posted on the Internet (a popular fallacy) or because it lacks a copyright notice (another fallacy). As a general rule permission is needed to reproduce copyrighted materials including photos, writing, music and artwork.

Do not assume that clip art, shareware, freeware or materials labeled "royalty-free" or "copyright-free" can be distributed or copied without authorization. Read the terms and conditions in the "click to accept" agreement or "readme" files ordinarily accompanying such materials to be certain that an intended use is permitted. One company failed to honor the terms of a click-wrap agreement and was found liable for illegally distributing three volumes of software clip art. Also don't assume that because a site permits the download of a story that this story can be posted on another website. Each type of activity—emailing, copying, printing and posting—requires authorization.

Permission is sometimes needed to reproduce a trademark including any word, symbol or device that identifies and distinguishes a product or service. For example, the word "McDonald's," the distinctive yellow arches and the Ronald McDonald character are all trademarks of the McDonald's company. Permission would be needed to use these trademarks at a commercial website if consumers are likely to be confused by the use or if the commercial use damages the reputation of McDonald's.

Related terms: clearinghouse, copyright; shrink-wrap and click-wrap license.

phonorecords, defined

The U.S. Copyright Act of 1976 defines phonorecords not only as the traditional "record" but also as audio tape recordings, compact discs, laser discs and any future technology for reproducing sound. The statute covers "material objects in which sounds, other than those accompanying … [an] audiovisual work, are fixed by any method now known or later developed, and from which the sounds can be perceived, reproduced or otherwise communicated, either directly or with the aid of a machine or device. [It] … includes the material object in which the sounds are first fixed." (17 United States Code, Section 101.)

An original work of authorship contained on a phonorecord may be registered with the U.S. Copyright Office on Form SR.

Related terms: compulsory license; Form SR, described; registration of copyright, defined; musical works and sound recordings distinguished.

photocopies and copyright law

With some exceptions, making even one copy of an original work of authorship requires the copyright owner's permission; copying without permission constitutes infringement of the copyright and may entitle the copyright owner to seek damages in federal court. However, the photocopy machine is a very familiar part of life in America and copyrights are frequently and massively infringed by its use. Also, when the copying is very limited and not for the purpose of making money, the copying will usually be considered a fair use should an infringement lawsuit be brought.

Because much photocopying occurs in private and doesn't involve commercial distribution, this type of infringement is seldom discovered. Also, unless the copyright owner has been damaged in some manner or profits were gained from the infringement, an infringement lawsuit is usually out of the question.

EXAMPLE: Philbert writes an article and sends copies to several newspapers and periodicals requesting payment if the article is used. Upon receiving the article, a senior editor for one of the periodicals makes three photocopies and distributes them to the editorial staff for comment. Because Philbert's copyright gives him the exclusive right to make copies, the senior editor's act of making the three copies technically constitutes a copyright infringement. However, if Philbert tried to do anything about it, the periodical would be able to raise the fair use defense and escape any consequences.

Nevertheless, in situations where photocopying is discovered by a copyright owner and it appears that sales of the item being copied may be adversely affected, a copyright lawsuit may be the result. For instance, in the case of *Basic Books, Inc. v. Kinko's Graphics Corp.,* 758 F. Supp. 1522 (S.D. N.Y. 1991), a group of seven major publishers obtained a $510,000 judgment against a duplicating business for copying excerpts from books without permission, compiling them into "course packets," and selling them to college students.

Related terms: copies, meaning under copyright law; fair use, defined; infringement action, explained.

pictorial, graphic and sculptural works

Works of expression using graphic and physical representations of objects and ideas, rather than text, are entitled to copyright protection. The Copyright Act of

Definitions

1976 covers "two-dimensional and three-dimensional works of fine, graphic, and applied art, photographs, prints and art reproductions, maps, globes, charts, technical drawings, diagrams and models." (17 United States Code, Section 101.) To register pictorial, graphic or sculptural works with the U.S. Copyright Office, the owner should use Form VA.

The original design of a toy, package, implement or other product can qualify for copyright protection if it is created for expressive rather than functional purposes. For instance, a pitcher designed as a unicorn may be subject to copyright protection as long as the unicorn shape is not directly related to the pitcher's function—that is, the unicorn shape does not affect how the pitcher stores and pours liquids. Whether or not a design is functional or expressive can only be decided on a case-by-case basis.

Designs of an article of manufacture that are not functional may also qualify for patent protection under a design patent.

Related terms: copyright and patent, compared; Form VA, described; registration of copyright, defined.
See also Part 3 (Patent Law): design patents; Part 4 (Trademark Law); trade dress.

piracy, defined

A colloquial term without legal significance, piracy is used to describe the illegal activity of willful copyright infringers.

Related terms: copyright infringement, defined; criminal copyright infringement.

placement of copyright notice

See notice of copyright.

plagiarism, defined

Deliberately passing off somebody else's original expression or creative ideas as one's own is colloquially known as plagiarism. Plagiarism can be a violation of the federal Lanham Act (it's called "palming off" activity) if the plagiarism involves commercial gain. Plagiarism can be a copyright violation under the copyright laws if original expression is copied.

More often, however, plagiarism does not violate any law but marks the plagiarist as an unethical person in the political, academic or scientific community where the plagiarism occurs.

Plagiarism should not be confused with a copyright violation. The two concepts can occur simultaneously, but don't need to.

EXAMPLE 1: Harry receives John's unconditional permission to use an article that John authored. If Harry puts his own name on the article and distributes it in some form, he has plagiarized the article but not violated the copyright law because he had John's unrestricted permission. Conversely, if Harry attributes the article to John but doesn't get John's permission to use it, Harry has committed a copyright infringement but has not plagiarized.

EXAMPLE 2: Suppose John grants Harry permission to use the article on the condition that John be given credit as the author. If Harry later puts his own name on the article and distributes it, Harry would both be guilty of both plagiarism and of violating John's copyright. This is because the failure to credit John violates the non-exclusive license granted to Harry by John, which in turn constitutes a copyright infringement.

Related terms: copyright infringement, defined; original work of authorship.

preliminary injunctions

See injunctions, copyright infringement.

printed forms, not copyrightable

Printed forms do not usually qualify for copyright protection because they are designed for recording information and do not in themselves convey information.

Related terms: copyright, explained; original work of authorship.

profits as damages

Profits reaped by an infringer as a result of a copyright infringement (called defendant's profits) are one possible element of monetary damages a court may require the infringer to pay the copyright owner. Defendant's profits will only be awarded where these profits exceed the amount of profits lost by the copyright owner as a result of the infringement.

To establish the amount of an infringer's profits, the plaintiff copyright owner first must prove the defendant's gross profits from the sales of the infringing goods or services. The defendant then is entitled to deduct his or her demonstrable costs from the gross revenues from selling the infringing material. The resulting amount is then compared with the plaintiff's lost profits, if any. Damages that will be awarded will be the greater of defendant's profits attributable to the infringement or the plaintiff's lost profits.

EXAMPLE: Janet clearly infringed Jeffrey's copyright by stealing his dissertation and publishing it first. Jeffrey proves that he lost $20,000 in publishers' advances and royalties based on the reasonably anticipated sale of the dissertation as a scholarly book. Because Janet's publisher did a super job selling foreign rights, she ended up with $35,000. Janet would have to pay Jeffrey $35,000, because her profits were greater. However, if instead Janet's net profits were only $15,000, she would have to pay him $20,000 in his lost profits, because his lost profits were greater than her actual ones.

Related terms: damages for copyright infringement.

programs, computer, copyright of

See computer software, copyright of.

pseudonym, copyright under a

The copyright laws define a "pseudonymous work" as one on which the author is identified under a fictitious name. Copyright laws protect an author who publishes a work under a pseudonym almost as well as (and in some cases better than) they do an author who uses his or her real name. The main difference is that the copyright will last 75 years for a pseudonymous work, instead of the author's life plus 50 years for an author-identified work.

Related terms: anonymous, author as owner of copyright; duration of copyrights.

WHAT'S HE SO SMUG ABOUT?

I HEAR HE JUST ENTERED THE PUBLIC DOMAIN.

public domain—copyright context

Any work of authorship that is not protected under copyright law is said to fall within the public domain. This means that anyone can use the work without obtaining permission from the author or the author's heirs. There are several common reasons why works may be considered to be in the public domain:

- The work was published before 1923.
- The work consists solely of facts or ideas. (Facts and ideas are not protected by copyright, although the means used to express them may be protected to some extent.)
- The work was published before 1978 and lacked a proper copyright notice. (But the copyright in many of these works has been restored.)

- The work was published between 1978 and 1989, the notice on the work was defective and inadequate efforts were made to correct the defects. (Copyrights by non-U.S. authors covered by the Berne Convention that expired for this reason can be restored under GATT.)
- The copyright owner deliberately placed the work in the public domain by making a statement to that effect.
- The work was created by the federal government.

Related terms: factual works, defined; *Feist Publications Inc. v. Rural Telephone Service Co.*; original work of authorship; work of the U.S. Government, public domain; restored copyrights under GATT.

public performance of a work

Among the bundle of rights making up a copyright is the exclusive right to publicly perform or display an original work of authorship. The Copyright Act of 1976 considers in part the right to: "1) perform or display it at a place open to the public or at any place where a substantial number of persons outside of a normal circle of a family and its social acquaintances is gathered; or 2) transmit or otherwise communicate a performance or display of the work ... to the public, by means of any device or process...." (17 United States Code, Section 101.)

Related terms: copyright, explained; copyright infringement, defined; exclusive license, defined.

published work, defined

Published and unpublished works are both entitled to copyright protection, but some of the rules differ, such as:

- The fair use defense is harder to use when unpublished works are involved, because use of an unpublished work deprives its copyright owner of the right to determine its publication date.
- The duration of a copyright in an unpublished work that is a work made for hire or an anonymous or pseudonymous work can last up to 25 years longer than if the work were published.
- The publication date sets the time running for a timely registration of the copyright with the U.S. Copyright Office.
- A valid copyright notice on a published work can prevent the claim of innocent infringement from being raised in a copyright infringement lawsuit.

An original work of authorship is only considered published under the Copyright Act of 1976 when it is first made available to the public on an unrestricted basis. It is thus possible to display a work, or distribute it with restrictions on disclosure of its contents, without actually "publishing" it. However, if the work is displayed online, so that access by computer is widespread, the work would be considered published.

EXAMPLE: Andres Miczslova writes an essay called "Blood Bath" about the war in Bosnia, and distributes it to five human rights organizations under a non-exclusive license that places restrictions on their right to disclose the essay's contents. "Blood Bath" has not been "published" in the copyright sense. However, if Miczslova authorizes posting of the essay on the Internet, it would be considered published.

Related terms: fair use, defined; international copyright protection; notice of copyright; registration of copyright, defined.

recordation of copyright transfers

When one or more exclusive copyright rights is transferred, it is important for the recipient of the rights to record the transfer immediately with the U.S. Copyright Office. This is because the first to record has greater rights in the event of conflicting or overlapping transfers.

Recordation also provides all persons with "constructive notice" of the transfer of rights. This means that the law will presume infringers should have found out about it, even if they didn't actually know. Without recordation, although the owner of transferred rights can sue an infringer, it may be hard to prove that the infringement was not innocent.

To record a transfer, the new owner must file with the U.S. Copyright Office a written document describing the work involved and the transfer granted, and bearing the signature of the person granting the transfer.

Related terms: overlapping transfers of copyright; transfers of copyright ownership, generally.

recordings, copyright of

The U.S. Copyright Office calls all sound recordings "phonorecords," no matter what medium is actually used.

Related terms: phonorecords, defined.

Registrar of Copyrights

This is the official title of the person who heads the U.S. Copyright Office.

Related terms: registration of copyright, defined; U.S. Copyright Office.

registration of copyright, defined

Copyright protection automatically attaches to any work of authorship when it is fixed in a tangible medium of expression. In other words, registration is not required to obtain copyright. The author acquires copyright automatically once the work is fixed. Such protection can be strengthened if certain affirmative steps are taken, such as attaching a correct notice of copyright to the work and registering the work with the U.S. Copyright Office. In fact, when one speaks of copyrighting a work, this often means registering it.

Registration provides several distinct advantages in case of infringement:

- Registration is required before the copyright owner may file an infringement action in court. If the copyright is not already registered, and litigation becomes necessary, there will be a delay while the registration application process goes forward (although expedited registration is possible for $500). Registration is not required to file an infringement lawsuit for non-U.S. works that meet the definition of Berne Convention works (that is, when the author is a national of a Berne Convention country and the work was first published in a Berne Convention country). (*See* 17 United States Code, Section 101.) Registration is also not required to file an infringement lawsuit for works of visual art (fine art limited editions of 200 or fewer copies as defined in 17 United States Code, Sections 101 and 106A).).
- If a copyright is registered either before an infringing activity has begun, or within three months of first publication of the work, the copyright owner may collect statutory damages for the infringement, plus attorney's fees, if the issue ends up in court. These benefits often make the difference between an owner being able to afford litigation and having to forego copyright rights.
- In an infringement action, the registered copyright owner is presumed to be the actual owner, and the statements in the registration application are presumed to be true. Such presumptions make it easier to present a viable court case, because they put the burden on the other side to disprove the plaintiff's right to relief.

The registration process is relatively simple. The U.S. Copyright Office provides a number of preprinted forms, with instructions, for different types of works:

- Form TX is used for all nondramatic literary works, including software code
- Form PA is used for published and unpublished works of the performing arts such as musical and dramatic works, pantomimes, motion pictures and graphically based multimedia works on CD-ROM
- Form VA is used for the visual arts
- Form SR is used for sound recordings, and
- Form SE (there are several variations) is used for serials, like newspapers, periodicals and journals.

Several sample registration forms are contained in the Sample Forms section at the end of this part of the book. You can download these forms from the U.S. Copyright Office's website at http://www.loc.gov/copyright/forms.

Once the form is filled out, it must be sent to the U.S. Copyright Office with a proper deposit of the work itself, or with material that satisfactorily identifies the work (called identifying material), and a relatively small filing fee ($30 as of September 2000). The U.S. Copyright Office has specific regulations governing what form the deposit must take for different types of works and, in the case of items such as computer software, phonorecordings and mask works, what kind of identifying material will be accepted.

In individual cases, upon application for a good reason, the U.S. Copyright Office grants "special relief" by waiving formal deposit or other registration requirements. This means, for example, that the U.S. Copyright Office will accept deposits in a different medium or form than is normally required. There are no specific rules for when specific relief will and will not be granted.

Assuming that the registration materials are properly completed, the U.S. Copyright Office will normally register the work and send a certificate of registration. On the other hand, if information is either left out of the form or is clearly erroneous on its face (for instance, the date of publication is 100 years off), the U.S. Copyright Office will send the form back and indicate how to correct it.

If, after registration, information provided in the initial registration is incorrect or needs to be updated, it is usually possible to correct it by filing a supplemental registration form (Form CA).

Related terms: copyright infringement, defined; copyright owner, defined; deposit with U.S. Copyright Office; identifying material, defined; infringement action, explained; special relief, defined; timely registration, defined.

registration of copyright license

See recordation of copyright transfers.

registration of copyrights in unpublished works

See unpublished work, copyrightability of.

reliance party, when copyright restored

See restored copyright under GATT.

renewal of copyright

See duration of copyrights.

restored copyright under GATT

Until the U.S. became a member of the Berne Convention in March 1989, works originating in Berne Convention countries often lost their copyright in the U.S. because they failed to observe certain formalities required by the U.S. copyright laws, such as copyright notices. Under the General Agreement on Tariffs and Trade (GATT), copyright protection has been restored in all such works. However, parties who used these restored works without permission in reliance on the fact that they weren't protected by copyright (called reliance parties) cannot be sued for copyright infringement, and may continue using the works under certain circumstances if they pay a reasonable license fee to the restored copyright owner under a type of compulsory license.

Related terms: GATT (General Agreement on Tariffs and Trade).

revocation of license

Most copyright licenses contain conditions under which the license must be exercised. If these conditions are broken, the copyright owner generally has a right to revoke the license. The license revocation should always be done in writing. Any exercise of the licensed right after revocation will constitute an infringement of the copyright.

Revocation of a license should not be confused with the right to terminate transfers under the Copyright Act of 1976. In that situation (and in addition to any provisions in the license itself), the original copyright owner (or his or her heirs) has a legal right to terminate any transfer after 35 to 40 years have passed.

Related terms: licensing of copyrights; termination of transfers.

rule of doubt

The U.S. Copyright Office allows object code to be deposited in connection with a computer program registration. There is, however, an express understanding that doubt exists as to whether the code qualifies for copyright protection should litigation later ensue. In essence, the U.S. Copyright Office is saying, "We will let you deposit object code, but since we can't read or understand it, we won't commit ourselves as to its copyrightability."

If the registration is accomplished under the rule of doubt, the copyright owner may be unable to claim the presumption of ownership—an important benefit of registration—should the issue end up in court because of an alleged copyright infringement.

Related terms: computer software, copyright of; special relief, defined.

sampling

The digital recording process has made it possible to "sample" a portion of a sound recording. These digital samples can be manipulated to replay once or twice or repeat as a "loop" throughout a new recording. The use of a musical sample may infringe both the musical works and sound recording copyright held on the sampled music. Whether the use qualifies as an infringement depends upon the portion sampled and its qualitative or quantitative importance to the copyrighted work. Initially, the courts took a rigid approach prohibiting any use of digital samples. However, in a 1997 case, a court determined that the rap group Run DMC's use of a drum sample from a 1973 recording was not infringing. (*Ruff 'N' Rumble Mgmt. v. Profile Records, Inc.*, 42 U.S.P.Q.2d 1398 (S.D. NY 1997).)

Sound recordings were not protected by copyright law until 1972. The use of a musical sample from a work created prior to 1972 would not be an infringement of a sound recording copyright, although it may be a violation of applicable state laws. In order to avoid claims of infringement, popular artists seek sample clearance from copyright owners.

Semiconductor Chip Protection Act of 1984

This statute protects semiconductor chip manufacturers against the unauthorized copying or use of semiconductor chips and the templates that are used to manufacture them.

Semiconductor chips are a complex combination of tiny circuits that are designed to manipulate electronic data. They are mass-produced from multi-layered three-dimensional templates that are called "chip masks" in the trade, and "mask works" under the Semiconductor Chip Protection Act.

Mask works (and the resulting semiconductor chips) are very difficult and expensive to design, but very easy to copy. Accordingly, semiconductor chip manufacturers have long sought protection of these devices as a form of intellectual property. Because technological advances in these chips have been incremental in nature, most improvements have been considered obvious and, therefore, not patentable. Before 1984, the chips did not qualify for copyright protection, due to the fact that their design was considered functional rather than expressive. To plug this gap, Congress passed the Semiconductor Chip Protection Act.

Under this statute, the owner of the exclusive rights in the mask work (generally the manufacturer) is given an exclusive ten-year right to:

- reproduce the mask work
- import or distribute a semiconductor chip product in which the mask work is embodied, and
- license others to exercise these rights.

These rights are forfeited, however, if the owner fails to register the mask work with the U.S. Copyright Office within two years of its commercial exploitation anywhere in the world.

A party who innocently purchases a semiconductor chip product that has been manufactured in violation of these exclusive rights is not liable for copyright infringement, but must pay a reasonable royalty for each unit the innocent party imports or distributes after notice of the infringement.

Related terms: computer software, copyright of; innocent infringement of copyright.

shrink-wrap and click-wrap license

Software publishers often wish to limit how purchasers use the software. For example, they may want the software used only for personal rather than commercial purposes. To impose this and other restrictions, most publishers employ a type of contract legally known as a non-exclusive license and popularly known as a "shrink-wrap license" (because you can't read it until you break the box's shrink wrapping). When the software is sold online, the license is referred to as a "click-wrap agreement" since the buyer must click to accept. The license may also appear on the screen when the program first boots up. Under the terms of the typical license the user is deemed to accept the terms of the license if she proceeds to use the program. If she doesn't agree, she may return the program for a refund.

From the beginning there was doubt as to whether this type of license could be enforced in court, especially if the provisions were inconsistent with the Copyright Act. The reason for this doubt is that the license isn't really a result of a negotiation between seller and purchaser at the time of sale, and so the purchaser shouldn't be held to its terms, especially if it means that he or she is waiving rights under the Copyright Act as a result. For example, many licenses prohibit the user from modifying the software, even though the Copyright Act permits the purchaser to modify one copy for his or her own use.

Many of these doubts have now been laid to rest in a federal Court of Appeal Case (7th Cir.) decided in June 1996. That court ruled that shrink-wrap licenses are perfectly valid contracts as long as the user has the option of returning the product for a refund if he or she doesn't agree to the terms of the license. Further, the court ruled that there was no legal problem with the license restricting rights that a purchaser would have otherwise had under the Copyright Act if not for the license. (*ProCD v. Zeidenberg*, 86 F.3d 1447 (7th Cir. 1996).) Effective October 1, 2000, click-wrap agreements are expected to become as enforceable as traditional paper contracts. Federal legislation—the Electronic Signatures in Global and International Commerce Act—removes the uncertainty that previously plagued e-contracts and prevents a contract from being challenged simply because it was created electronically.

Related terms: computer software, copyright of; licensing of copyrights.

simultaneous publication

Previous to March 1, 1989, the U.S. belonged to the Universal Copyright Convention (U.C.C.) but not to the Berne Convention. If an author wished to obtain protection under both the Berne Convention and the U.C.C., it could do so by causing the initial publication of the work to simultaneously occur in the U.S. and a Berne Convention country, such as Canada. In March 1989, however, the U.S. joined the Berne Convention, so U.S. authors have no further reason for simultaneous publication.

Related terms: Berne Convention; international copyright protection; Universal Copyright Convention (U.C.C.).

single registration rule

The U.S. Copyright Office generally allows only one registration for each original work of authorship. There are exceptions, however. A new registration is permitted when an unpublished work is later published. A new registration is also allowed to substitute an author's name.

Changes, updates or translations of a given work will merit a second registration only if they are substantial enough in quantity or quality to qualify the work as a new version. Practically, unless the modified work is significantly changed or contains a great deal of new material, the original registration should provide adequate protection. However, certain minor or technical changes in an existing registration sometimes warrant filing a supplemental registration.

If a new version is registered, that registration only applies to the new material contained in the work. The material taken from the original work is still covered under the original registration.

Related terms: best edition of a work; supplemental registration.

site license

Some software publishers grant a single license to a company, which allows a set number of copies of the software to be installed on individual computers. For instance, if a company with 100 employees wants its employees to use a particular graphics program, it can either buy 100 copies of the program, or try to get a site license that would permit use of 100 copies of the software at a reduced rate per copy.

Related terms: computer software, copyright of; licensing of copyrights.

software and copyrights

See computer software, copyright of.

Sonny Bono Copyright Term Extension Act

This Act, signed by the President on October 26, 1998, extends the copyright term in the United States by 20 years of all works published after January 1, 1998. The act also extended the duration of the copyright term on works created or published prior to 1978.

Related terms: Duration of Copyright.

sound recordings, copyrights

See phonorecords, defined.

source code, copyrights

The computer program written by a programmer is usually called source code. Source code is commonly written in a programming language (for instance, COBOL, C++, Visual Basic) and contains not only the commands for the computer, but also the programmer's comments regarding the purpose and meaning of the different lines of code. It is relatively easy for a skilled computer programmer to examine the source code for a particular program and figure out how to produce the same result with a technically different program. Thus, access to source code will reveal a program's trade secrets and allow a competitor to use its ideas in a competing program.

For this reason, programmers like to keep their source code as confidential as possible. Accordingly, when registering a program with the U.S. Copyright Office, many software authors prefer to deposit only object code, which is extremely difficult to decipher because it appears in the form of ones and zeros, hexadecimal or some other inscrutable form.

Nevertheless, the U.S. Copyright Office considers a program's source code to be the best edition of the work, and accordingly prefers it as a deposit. In fact, the U.S. Copyright Office will accept a deposit of portions of the source code with critical parts blacked out, or a mixture of source code and object code. But the U.S. Copyright Office will also accept a deposit of the object code under what is called the rule of doubt—that is, it has no opinion as to whether the registered code qualifies for copyright protection, since it can't read it.

Related terms: computer software, copyright of; object code, copyrights; registration of copyright, defined; rule of doubt.

special relief, defined

The U.S. Copyright Office sometimes gives a special variance to depart from its usual requirements for copyright registration or deposit. This variance is known as "special relief." Applicants for copyright registration may have one or many reasons to seek exemptions from the formal requirements for registration and deposits—for example, an unusual shape, size or composition of the work to be deposited or the need to maintain a trade secret expressed by the work. Often the U.S. Copyright Office will grant such special relief to applicants who request it and explain in a cover letter to their registration application why they need it.

Related terms: best edition of a work; deposit with U.S. Copyright Office; registration of copyright, defined.

statute of limitations

A person accused of infringing another's copyright, patent or trademark may argue in defense that the plaintiff waited too long to file suit—that is, they violated the statute of limitations. In civil copyright cases, this limit provides that you can't file suit more than three years after the discovery of the infringement, or after it reasonably should have been discovered. (In criminal copyright cases, the government must bring an action within 5 years after the infringement occurred.) The theory behind the statute of limitations defense is that plaintiffs can't be allowed to "sit on their rights" and accumulate damages, but must act reasonably promptly to prevent further damage once it is discovered.

Because it is not always easy to discover the existence of a copyright infringement, it's fairly common to file a lawsuit after the three-year deadline, claiming recent discovery. Unfortunately, the courts do not agree on what types of acts start the calendar running for purposes of the three-year statute of limitations period.

statutory damages under copyright act

See damages for copyright infringement.

substantial similarity, infringement

See copyright infringement, defined.

supplemental registration

Certain errors in a copyright registration may be corrected, changed or amplified by filing a supplemental registration. Form CA is available from the U.S. Copyright Office for this purpose.

Supplemental registration is appropriate for both trivial mistakes and more serious errors, such as where:

- the author's name was misspelled
- the author's birth date was incorrect
- the title of the work has changed since the original registration
- the owner's address has changed
- an unpublished work was registered as published
- the author or copyright claimant was misidentified, omitted or has a changed name (not because of a transfer), or
- some aspect of the application information needs clarification.

The first three of these situations are trivial and need not be changed for the copyright to remain valid. An address change need not be noted for legal purposes, but an accurate address will obviously enable potential licensees and transferees to locate the copyright owner. The other errors, and the need to correct them, are more important because they affect both the validity of the copyright and the owner's ability to vindicate his or her rights in court.

Related terms: single registration rule.

temporary restraining order (TRO)

See infringement action, explained; injunctions, copyright infringement.

termination of transfers

For works published after January 1, 1978, any exclusive copyright right that has been transferred by the author eventually may be terminated by the author, the author's surviving spouse or the author's children or grandchildren. The termination must occur after 35 years from publication of the work, or 40 years after the transfer is made, whichever comes first. However, such termination must occur within five years of the date the author or heirs become eligible to do so, or the right to terminate is lost forever. This termination right does not apply to works made for hire.

EXAMPLE: Bill Haywoode composes a song about robots who take over factory jobs. Bill grants the rights to record and market the song to Ecotopia Enterprises. The transfer takes effect January 1, 1995. When first published in

January 1996, the song becomes a classic, continuously recorded by a succession of artists. In 2031, Bill will have the right to terminate the "grant of rights" and recapture full ownership of the copyright. However, if Bill fails to exercise this option to terminate by 2036, he will lose it.

Although all copyright transfers may be terminated through this process, any derivative works that have been legally prepared in the meantime will continue to belong to their authors, rather than reverting to the original copyright owner. For instance, if under a broad grant of rights from Bill (which included the right to use the song for all legal purposes) Ecotopia had prepared and marketed a television series based on the song, all rights to the television series will remain with Ecotopia or anyone to whom it transferred the series.

Related terms: exclusive license, defined; licensing of copyrights.

timely registration, defined

To obtain all the benefits of registration, a work must be registered with the U.S. Copyright Office within certain time limits. Timely registration entitles a copyright owner to statutory damages and attorney fees in an infringement suit, which may make affordable a suit that is otherwise prohibitively expensive and risky.

For a published work, timely registration must occur within three months of first publication or before the infringement begins. For unpublished works, registration is timely as long as it occurs before the infringement begins.

Related terms: copyright, explained; registration of copyright, defined.

Trade Related Aspects of Intellectual Property Rights (TRIPS)

See GATT (General Agreement on Tariffs and Trade).

transfers of copyright ownership, generally

According to the Copyright Act of 1976, a transfer of copyright ownership is any grant of an exclusive right, or an assignment, mortgage, exclusive license or any other conveyance of a copyright or of any of the exclusive rights constituting a copyright. A transfer includes almost any assignment of rights except a non-exclusive license.

A transfer can involve the entire copyright or only a portion of it, since a copyright consists of a bundle of rights that can be divided. For example, a grant of rights may be limited by time, geography or media. The right to make copies of an original work, the right to sell the work, the right to display the work, and the right to make derivative works of the work are also separate transferable rights.

EXAMPLE: Ruth Gottfried writes a book called *Nurse Ruth*. She registers the copyright with the U.S. Copyright Office and lists herself as the owner. Although Ruth could publish and market the book herself, more likely she will let others do the job for her. For example, she might execute a written license giving Able Publishers the exclusive right to sell, display and make copies of the book. She may also transfer some or all of the remaining rights (for instance, film, radio and TV, magazine, CD-ROM, Polish-speaking countries) to Able, or she can choose to transfer some of them to others, retaining for herself only a few or perhaps only the exclusive right to make derivative works.

In fact, an almost infinite number of transfers can occur for a copyrighted work. The only prerequisites for a transfer of ownership are that:
- the transfer must be in writing
- the transfer must be signed by the owner, and
- the right transferred must be an exclusive one.

EXAMPLE 1: Ruth retains at least one of the exclusive copyright rights in the book *Nurse Ruth*, so she remains the owner of the "copyright" as far as the U.S. Copyright Office is concerned, and continues to have her name on the notice of copyright. Although Able Publishers may own a number (but not all) of the rights and is considered a legal copyright owner, it owns only the exclusive rights transferred in the license, and is not named as owner in the U.S. Copyright Office or on the notice of copyright.

EXAMPLE 2: Ruth decides to transfer all of her copyright rights in *Nurse Ruth* to Able Publishers (including the right to make derivative works). Able is the new "owner" in the U.S. Copyright Office and on the copyright notice. On the

Definitions

other hand, if Ruth transfers all rights to Able except the derivative works, which she transfers to someone else (her sister Edna, perhaps), Ruth will still be the "owner," even though she has transferred all her rights to other people. This is because the U.S. Copyright Office considers the original owner to remain the owner unless all of the copyright rights are transferred together to a single person or entity.

Although transfers can be valid without being recorded with the U.S. Copyright Office, it is better practice to record them. This record will serve as evidence in case of an argument about the scope of the rights granted. Also, the date of recordation helps determine which transfer prevails in case of overlapping transfers.

Related terms: overlapping transfers of copyright; recordation of copyright transfers.

translation rights

See compulsory license; derivative work.

Universal Copyright Convention (U.C.C.)

This is an international copyright treaty that offers national treatment to any work first published in a U.C.C. member country or by a national of any U.C.C. country. In addition, it limits the formalities that a U.C.C. country may require to confer copyright protection. A member country may require only that the work carry this notice of copyright: "© (year of first publication) (name of the author)."

The U.C.C. also requires that each member country offer a minimum copyright duration of at least the life of the author plus 25 years. With one exception, each author is also given the exclusive right to translate his or her own work. If, however, the work is imported to another U.C.C. treaty country and not translated within seven years of the work's original publication, the government of that country may authorize a translation into that country's language under a compulsory licensing system (along with payment of a fair fee).

Although the U.C.C. continues to have some importance in areas not covered by the Berne Convention, the Berne Convention is normally the governing international treaty, especially since the GATT treaty provides that all of its signatories agree to be bound by the Berne Convention.

Related terms: Berne Convention; GATT (General Agreement on Tariffs and Trade); international copyright protection.

unpublished work, copyrightability of

An original work of authorship that is fixed in a tangible medium of expression but has not yet been published (made available to the general public without restriction) automatically qualifies for copyright protection. Unpublished works may be registered with the U.S. Copyright Office, but the more common practice is to wait until a work is published before registering. If the registration occurs before an infringement of the unpublished works begins, the copyright owner may recover statutory damages and possibly attorney's fees.

Related terms: fair use, defined; published work, defined; registration of copyright, defined.

U.S. Copyright Office

Established by Congress, the U.S. Copyright Office—a branch of the Library of Congress—oversees the implementation of the federal copyright laws. It issues regulations, processes applications for registration of copyrights, accepts and (for some types of works) stores deposits made in connection with registration. The U.S. Copyright Office also issues opinions on whether certain types of items are subject to copyright protection.

The U.S. Copyright Office may be reached at:

Registrar of Copyrights
U.S. Copyright Office
Library of Congress
Washington, D.C. 20559
Information Line: 202-707-3000
Forms Hotline: 202-707-9100

The U.S. Copyright Office also has a website (http://www.loc.gov/copyright) where you can download forms and find a great deal of information.

version

See derivative work; single registration rule.

visual artists' rights

See work of visual art.

website

A website is a collection of pages or documents located on the World Wide Web. The website is usually written in a computer language known as HTML and is accessed by typing in a domain name such as http://www.nolo.com. Although the website is written in computer code, it incorporates, displays and performs many media, including text, photography, music, animation, sound, artwork and movies. All of these media may contain copyrightable expressions. To that extent, the website's creator must obtain permission to use these media. The unauthorized use of these materials is an infringement unless permitted as a fair use.

Definitions

In turn, a website or Web page is protected under copyright law and may be registered with the Copyright Office. The procedure for registration is established in Copyright Circular 66, which is available at the Copyright Office website (http://www.loc.gov/copyright). Copyright protection for a website does not extend to the layout or "look and feel" or design of the site. In other words, the website's style cannot be protected under copyright law. But it is possible that the style or style features may be protected as trade dress under trademark laws.

work made for hire, defined

For purposes of the Copyright Act of 1976, a work made for hire is:

- a work created by an employee within the scope of employment, or
- certain works specified in the Copyright Act (see below) created by an independent author under a written contract specifying that the project is a work made for hire.

The importance of the work-made-for-hire concept is that copyright of a work made for hire belongs either to the party who commissioned it or the employer (depending on the situation), not the party who created it.

Works made for hire most typically result when an employee authors an article, computer program or another original work of authorship within the scope of employment. This generally means that it is the kind of work the employee is paid to perform, it is prepared substantially within work hours at the workplace and it is prepared, at least in part, to serve the employer.

Unless an employer and employee agree otherwise, anything an employee creates outside the scope of employment is not a work made for hire. This is so even if the work arises out of the employee's activities on the employer's behalf.

EXAMPLE: Ned Sugimoto uses company time to write a training manual for his employer. The employer owns the copyright in the manual as a work made for hire. By contrast, if Ned used his own time to write the manual, Ned would own the copyright, even though the manual's main purpose was to help Ned's employer.

Who is an employee for purposes of the work made for hire rule? If a court determines that an employment relationship exists, even if the author is not technically employed, the work made for hire rule treats the author as an employee for the purpose of determining copyright ownership. The courts examine 11 factors to decide whether an employment relationship exists. All of the factors address who has the right to control the manner and means by which the work is created:

1. the skill required to do the work
2. the source of tools and materials used to create the work
3. the duration of the relationship
4. whether the commissioning person has the right to assign additional projects to the creative party
5. who determines when and how long the creative party works
6. the method of payment
7. who decides which assistants will be hired and who pays them
8. whether the work is in the ordinary line of business of the person who commissions it
9. whether the creative party has his/her own business
10. whether the creative party receives employee benefits from the commissioning person, and
11. the tax treatment of the creative party.

If there is no employment relationship, a work will still be considered a "work made for hire" if both parties sign a written work for hire agreement and the work fits within one of the following nine categories of works (17 United States Code, Section 101):

1. a work specially ordered or commissioned for use as a contribution to a collective work
2. a part of a motion picture or other audiovisual work, such as a screenplay
3. a translation
4. a supplementary work
5. a compilation
6. an instructional text
7. a test or answer material for a test
8. an atlas, or
9. a sound recording.

EXAMPLE: The law firm of Elias & Stim plan to publish a series of educational texts on copyright, trademark and patent law. They hire Charles Contractor, an author who is not employed by the law firm, to write the books. For the law firm to own copyright as work made for hire, Charles Contractor will have to sign a work-made-for-hire agreement and the resulting texts must fall within one of the enumerated work made for hire categories. It's possible that the texts may qualify as "instructional texts," but only if they are intended to be used in day-to-day teaching activities. If the texts do not fall within one of the enumerated categories, the works will not be works made for hire even though a work-made-for-hire agreement has been signed. In that event, the only other method by which the law firm could acquire copyright ownership is if Charles granted an assignment.

The duration of copyrights on works for hire is different than on copyrights for author-owners. A copyright on a work made for hire lasts for the shorter of 75 years from the date of publication or 100 years from the date of creation.

Related terms: copyright, explained; duration of copyrights.

work of the U.S. government, public domain

All works prepared by an officer or employee of the U.S. government as part of that person's official duties are considered part of the public domain, and are not entitled to copyright protection. This rule does not apply to state or local governmental employees.

Related terms: public domain—copyright context.

work of visual art

All art works (photos, paintings, etc.) are protected under copyright. But visual art that is produced in a single copy or limited edition of 200 copies or fewer signed and numbered copies receives special protection under an amendment to the Copyright Act known as the Visual Artists Rights Act (VARA) (17 United States Code, Section 106A).

VARA amends the Copyright Act by defining a "work of visual art" is (1) a painting, drawing, print, or sculpture, existing in a single copy, in a limited edition of 200 copies or fewer that are signed and consecutively numbered by the author, or, in the case of a sculpture, in multiple cast, carved, or fabricated sculptures of 200 or fewer that are consecutively numbered by the author and bear the signature or other identifying mark of the author; or (2) a still photographic image produced for exhibition purposes only, existing in a single copy that is signed by the author, or in a limited edition of 200 copies or fewer that are signed and consecutively numbered by the author.

VARA incorporates certain rules developed in Europe to protect the moral rights of artists. European law grants certain rights to artists based upon moral principles. For example, the creator of a work of fine art (or the artist's heirs) can share in subsequent sales of the work and can prevent the destruction or mutilation of a work. Under these principles, known as *droit de moral*, the artist's rights continue after the sale of the art. An unknown artist who sold a work inexpensively could share in revenues if the work later appreciated in value.

The U.S. refused to recognize moral rights for most of the twentieth century. However, in order to join in an international treaty known as the Berne Convention, Congress amended the Copyright Act in 1990 to include VARA. VARA incorporates two of the features of European *droit de moral*—attribution and integrity. Attribution is the right to claim or disclaim authorship of a work. That is, the artist has a right to demand that credit be given or that credit be removed from an artwork. The right of integrity is the right to prevent distortion, mutilation or other modification of the work. These rights are independent of the other rights granted under copyright law.

What's Protected & What's Not Protected by VARA

Protected by VARA	Not Protected by VARA
A limited edition of 20 copies of a silkscreen, numbered and signed by the artist.	A silkscreen image reprinted on 1,000 posters.
A sculpture of Noah's ark.	Miniature replicas of Noah's ark sold by a mail-order company.

What happens if an oil painting is reproduced in a museum booklet or in a magazine review? Does that mass production remove the work from VARA status? No, the artist could still exert VARA rights over the oil painting. However, the artist could not prevent destruction or mutilation of the reprints in the booklet because these would not be covered by VARA, although they would still be covered under normal copyright principles.

Definitions

Under Section 106A, the creator of a work of visual arts can prevent the "intentional distortion, mutilation, or other modification of that work which would be prejudicial to his or her honor or reputation." This is the most powerful right granted under the VARA provisions. For example, if a collector buys a limited edition photograph (that is, less than 200 prints were made), the collector cannot destroy it without permission from the artist. If the work is destroyed, the artist can sue under VARA and recover damages.

The rule regarding destruction does not apply if: (1) the work was created prior to enactment of the VARA provisions on December 1, 1990; (2) the artist specifically waives the rights in a written statement signed by the artist and owner of the artwork; or (3) the destruction or modification results from the passage of time or because of the materials used to construct the work. For example, certain works such as ice sculptures and sand sculptures self-destruct and the owner would have no obligation to affirmatively prevent such destruction.

Under certain circumstances, the person who employs an artist or commissions artwork acquires copyright ownership. This principle is known as work made for hire. If artwork is created as work made for hire, there are no VARA rights. That is, although normal copyright law applies to the work, neither the artist nor the person commissioning the work can claim rights of integrity or attribution under VARA.

The rights granted under VARA—attribution and integrity—are not transferable. Only the artist can exert these rights. Although copyright protection normally lasts for the life of the author plus 70 years, the rights granted under VARA only last for the life of the artist. That is, once the artist has died, the work can be destroyed under VARA without the destroyer seeking consent from the artist's estate.

Some states such as California have passed more comprehensive statutes regarding art preservation and resale. Under the California statute (California Civil Code Sections 986-989), for example, an artist is entitled to five percent of the resale of a work of fine art. These rights survive for 20 years after the death of the artist. New York and eight other states also have laws that grant certain rights to artists.

Related terms: Copyright Act of 1976, work made for hire.

World Trade Organization (WTO)

See GATT (General Agreement on Tariffs and Trade).

World Wide Web and copyright

See cyberspace and copyright.

Copyright Law

Sample Form PA (front)

FEE CHANGES
Fees are effective through June 30, 2002. After that date, check the Copyright Office Website at www.loc.gov/copyright or call (202) 707-3000 for current fee information.

FORM PA
For a Work of the Performing Arts
UNITED STATES COPYRIGHT OFFICE

REGISTRATION NUMBER

PA   PAU

EFFECTIVE DATE OF REGISTRATION

Month   Day   Year

DO NOT WRITE ABOVE THIS LINE. IF YOU NEED MORE SPACE, USE A SEPARATE CONTINUATION SHEET.

1

TITLE OF THIS WORK ▼

And Then You Die

PREVIOUS OR ALTERNATIVE TITLES ▼

NATURE OF THIS WORK ▼ See instructions

Screenplay

2

a NAME OF AUTHOR ▼

David Griffith

DATES OF BIRTH AND DEATH
Year Born ▼   Year Died ▼
1935

Was this contribution to the work a "work made for hire"?
☐ Yes
☒ No

AUTHOR'S NATIONALITY OR DOMICILE
Name of Country
OR { Citizen of ▶ U.S.A.
Domiciled in ▶

WAS THIS AUTHOR'S CONTRIBUTION TO THE WORK
Anonymous?   ☐ Yes ☒ No
Pseudonymous? ☐ Yes ☒ No
If the answer to either of these questions is "Yes," see detailed instructions.

NATURE OF AUTHORSHIP Briefly describe nature of material created by this author in which copyright is claimed. ▼
Entire text

NOTE

Under the law, the "author" of a "work made for hire" is generally the employer, not the employee (see instructions). For any part of this work that was "made for hire" check "Yes" in the space provided, give the employer (or other person for whom the work was prepared) as "Author" of that part, and leave the space for dates of birth and death blank.

b NAME OF AUTHOR ▼

DATES OF BIRTH AND DEATH
Year Born ▼   Year Died ▼

Was this contribution to the work a "work made for hire"?
☐ Yes
☐ No

AUTHOR'S NATIONALITY OR DOMICILE
Name of Country
OR { Citizen of ▶
Domiciled in ▶

WAS THIS AUTHOR'S CONTRIBUTION TO THE WORK
Anonymous?   ☐ Yes ☐ No
Pseudonymous? ☐ Yes ☐ No
If the answer to either of these questions is "Yes," see detailed instructions.

NATURE OF AUTHORSHIP Briefly describe nature of material created by this author in which copyright is claimed. ▼

c NAME OF AUTHOR ▼

DATES OF BIRTH AND DEATH
Year Born ▼   Year Died ▼

Was this contribution to the work a "work made for hire"?
☐ Yes
☐ No

AUTHOR'S NATIONALITY OR DOMICILE
Name of Country
OR { Citizen of ▶
Domiciled in ▶

WAS THIS AUTHOR'S CONTRIBUTION TO THE WORK
Anonymous?   ☐ Yes ☐ No
Pseudonymous? ☐ Yes ☐ No
If the answer to either of these questions is "Yes," see detailed instructions.

NATURE OF AUTHORSHIP Briefly describe nature of material created by this author in which copyright is claimed. ▼

3

a YEAR IN WHICH CREATION OF THIS WORK WAS COMPLETED
2001
◀ Year
This information must be given in all cases.

b DATE AND NATION OF FIRST PUBLICATION OF THIS PARTICULAR WORK
Complete this information ONLY if this work has been published.
Month ▶ _____ Day ▶ _____ Year ▶ _____
◀ Nation

4

See instructions before completing this space.

COPYRIGHT CLAIMANT(S) Name and address must be given even if the claimant is the same as the author given in space 2. ▼
David Griffith
666 Hollywood Blvd.
Hollywood, CA 90000

TRANSFER If the claimant(s) named here in space 4 is (are) different from the author(s) named in space 2, give a brief statement of how the claimant(s) obtained ownership of the copyright. ▼

DO NOT WRITE HERE
OFFICE USE ONLY

APPLICATION RECEIVED

ONE DEPOSIT RECEIVED

TWO DEPOSITS RECEIVED

FUNDS RECEIVED

MORE ON BACK ▶
• Complete all applicable spaces (numbers 5-9) on the reverse side of this page.
• See detailed instructions.
• Sign the form at line 8.

DO NOT WRITE HERE
Page 1 of _____ pages

Sample Form PA (back)

EXAMINED BY

FORM PA

CHECKED BY

CORRESPONDENCE
Yes

FOR
COPYRIGHT
OFFICE
USE
ONLY

DO NOT WRITE ABOVE THIS LINE. IF YOU NEED MORE SPACE, USE A SEPARATE CONTINUATION SHEET.

PREVIOUS REGISTRATION Has registration for this work, or for an earlier version of this work, already been made in the Copyright Office?

☐ Yes ☒ No If your answer is "Yes," why is another registration being sought? (Check appropriate box.) ▼ If your answer is "no," go to space 7.

a. ☐ This is the first published edition of a work previously registered in unpublished form.

b. ☐ This is the first application submitted by this author as copyright claimant.

c. ☐ This is a changed version of the work, as shown by space 6 on this application.

If your answer is "Yes," give: **Previous Registration Number** ▼ **Year of Registration** ▼

5

DERIVATIVE WORK OR COMPILATION Complete both space 6a and 6b for a derivative work; complete only 6b for a compilation.
Preexisting Material Identify any preexisting work or works that this work is based on or incorporates. ▼

Material Added to This Work Give a brief, general statement of the material that has been added to this work and in which copyright is claimed. ▼

6 a b

See instructions before completing this space.

DEPOSIT ACCOUNT If the registration fee is to be charged to a Deposit Account established in the Copyright Office, give name and number of Account.
Name ▼ Account Number ▼

7 a

CORRESPONDENCE Give name and address to which correspondence about this application should be sent. Name/Address/Apt/City/State/ZIP ▼

David Griffith
666 Hollywood Blvd.
Hollywood, CA 90000

Area code and daytime telephone number ▶ (213) 666-6666 Fax number ▶ ( )
Email ▶

b

CERTIFICATION* I, the undersigned, hereby certify that I am the

Check only one ▶

☒ author
☐ other copyright claimant
☐ owner of exclusive right(s)
☐ authorized agent of _____

Name of author or other copyright claimant, or owner of exclusive right(s) ▲
of the work identified in this application and that the statements made by me in this application are correct to the best of my knowledge.

8

Typed or printed name and date ▼ If this application gives a date of publication in space 3, do not sign and submit it before that date.

David Griffith Date ▶ May 1, 2000

Handwritten signature (X) ▼

x _____

Certificate will be mailed in window envelope to this address:

Name ▼
David Griffith
Number/Street/Apt ▼
666 Hollywood Blvd.
City/State/ZIP ▼
Hollywood, CA 90000

YOU MUST:
• Complete all necessary spaces
• Sign your application in space 8
SEND ALL 3 ELEMENTS IN THE SAME PACKAGE:
1. Application form
2. Nonrefundable filing fee in check or money order payable to *Register of Copyrights*
3. Deposit material
MAIL TO:
Library of Congress
Copyright Office
101 Independence Avenue, S.E.
Washington, D.C. 20559-6000

As of July 1, 1999, the filing fee for Form PA is $30.

9

*17 U.S.C. § 506(e): Any person who knowingly makes a false representation of a material fact in the application for copyright registration provided for by section 409, or in any written statement filed in connection with the application, shall be fined not more than $2,500.
June 1999—200,000
WEB REV: June 1999

☆U.S. GOVERNMENT PRINTING OFFICE: 1999-454-879/68

Sample Forms

Sample Form TX (front)

FEE CHANGES
Fees are effective through June 30, 2002. After that date, check the Copyright Office Website at www.loc.gov/copyright or call (202) 707-3000 for current fee information.

FORM TX
For a Nondramatic Literary Work
UNITED STATES COPYRIGHT OFFICE

REGISTRATION NUMBER

_____

TX   TXU
EFFECTIVE DATE OF REGISTRATION

Month   Day   Year

DO NOT WRITE ABOVE THIS LINE. IF YOU NEED MORE SPACE, USE A SEPARATE CONTINUATION SHEET.

1

TITLE OF THIS WORK ▼

A Fish Story

PREVIOUS OR ALTERNATIVE TITLES ▼

PUBLICATION AS A CONTRIBUTION If this work was published as a contribution to a periodical, serial, or collection, give information about the collective work in which the contribution appeared.   **Title of Collective Work ▼**

If published in a periodical or serial give: **Volume ▼**   **Number ▼**   **Issue Date ▼**   **On Pages ▼**

2

a

NAME OF AUTHOR ▼

Felix Founder

DATES OF BIRTH AND DEATH
Year Born ▼   Year Died ▼
1955

Was this contribution to the work a "work made for hire"?
☐ Yes
☒ No

AUTHOR'S NATIONALITY OR DOMICILE
Name of Country
OR { Citizen of ▶ U.S.A.
Domiciled in ▶

WAS THIS AUTHOR'S CONTRIBUTION TO THE WORK
Anonymous?   ☐ Yes ☒ No
Pseudonymous?   ☐ Yes ☒ No
If the answer to either of these questions is "Yes," see detailed instructions.

NATURE OF AUTHORSHIP Briefly describe nature of material created by this author in which copyright is claimed. ▼
Entire text of unpublished novel

NOTE

Under the law, the "author" of a "work made for hire" is generally the employer, not the employee (see instructions). For any part of this work that was "made for hire" check "Yes" in the space provided, give the employer (or other person for whom the work was prepared) as "Author" of that part, and leave the space for dates of birth and death blank.

b

NAME OF AUTHOR ▼

DATES OF BIRTH AND DEATH
Year Born ▼   Year Died ▼

Was this contribution to the work a "work made for hire"?
☐ Yes
☐ No

AUTHOR'S NATIONALITY OR DOMICILE
Name of Country
OR { Citizen of ▶
Domiciled in ▶

WAS THIS AUTHOR'S CONTRIBUTION TO THE WORK
Anonymous?   ☐ Yes ☐ No
Pseudonymous?   ☐ Yes ☐ No
If the answer to either of these questions is "Yes," see detailed instructions.

NATURE OF AUTHORSHIP Briefly describe nature of material created by this author in which copyright is claimed. ▼

c

NAME OF AUTHOR ▼

DATES OF BIRTH AND DEATH
Year Born ▼   Year Died ▼

Was this contribution to the work a "work made for hire"?
☐ Yes
☐ No

AUTHOR'S NATIONALITY OR DOMICILE
Name of Country
OR { Citizen of ▶
Domiciled in ▶

WAS THIS AUTHOR'S CONTRIBUTION TO THE WORK
Anonymous?   ☐ Yes ☐ No
Pseudonymous?   ☐ Yes ☐ No
If the answer to either of these questions is "Yes," see detailed instructions.

NATURE OF AUTHORSHIP Briefly describe nature of material created by this author in which copyright is claimed. ▼

3

a YEAR IN WHICH CREATION OF THIS WORK WAS COMPLETED   This information must be given in all cases.
2001   ◀ Year

b DATE AND NATION OF FIRST PUBLICATION OF THIS PARTICULAR WORK
Complete this information ONLY if this work has been published.   Month ▶ _____ Day ▶ _____ Year ▶ _____   ◀ Nation

4

See instructions before completing this space.

COPYRIGHT CLAIMANT(S) Name and address must be given even if the claimant is the same as the author given in space 2. ▼
Felix Founder
1000 Bonito Way
Tampa, FL 10000

APPLICATION RECEIVED

ONE DEPOSIT RECEIVED

TWO DEPOSITS RECEIVED

FUNDS RECEIVED

DO NOT WRITE HERE OFFICE USE ONLY

TRANSFER If the claimant(s) named here in space 4 is (are) different from the author(s) named in space 2, give a brief statement of how the claimant(s) obtained ownership of the copyright. ▼

MORE ON BACK ▶   • Complete all applicable spaces (numbers 5-9) on the reverse side of this page.
• See detailed instructions.   • Sign the form at line 8.

DO NOT WRITE HERE
Page 1 of _____ pages

Sample Form TX (back)

EXAMINED BY	FORM TX
CHECKED BY	
☐ CORRESPONDENCE Yes	FOR COPYRIGHT OFFICE USE ONLY

DO NOT WRITE ABOVE THIS LINE. IF YOU NEED MORE SPACE, USE A SEPARATE CONTINUATION SHEET.

PREVIOUS REGISTRATION Has registration for this work, or for an earlier version of this work, already been made in the Copyright Office?

☐ Yes ☒ No If your answer is "Yes," why is another registration being sought? (Check appropriate box.) ▼

a. ☐ This is the first published edition of a work previously registered in unpublished form.

b. ☐ This is the first application submitted by this author as copyright claimant.

c. ☐ This is a changed version of the work, as shown by space 6 on this application.

If your answer is "Yes," give: **Previous Registration Number** ▶   **Year of Registration** ▶

5

DERIVATIVE WORK OR COMPILATION

Preexisting Material Identify any preexisting work or works that this work is based on or incorporates. ▼

a

6

See instructions before completing this space.

Material Added to This Work Give a brief, general statement of the material that has been added to this work and in which copyright is claimed. ▼

b

DEPOSIT ACCOUNT If the registration fee is to be charged to a Deposit Account established in the Copyright Office, give name and number of Account.

Name ▼   **Account Number** ▼

a

7

CORRESPONDENCE Give name and address to which correspondence about this application should be sent.   Name/Address/Apt/City/State/ZIP ▼

b

Felix Founder
1000 Bonito Way
Tampa, FL 10000

Area code and daytime telephone number ▶ **(813) 123-4567**   Fax number ▶

Email ▶

CERTIFICATION* I, the undersigned, hereby certify that I am the

Check only one ▶

☒ author
☐ other copyright claimant
☐ owner of exclusive right(s)
☐ authorized agent of _____

of the work identified in this application and that the statements made by me in this application are correct to the best of my knowledge.

Name of author or other copyright claimant, or owner of exclusive right(s) ▲

8

Typed or printed name and date ▼ If this application gives a date of publication in space 3, do not sign and submit it before that date.

Felix Founder   Date ▶ May 1, 2001

☞ Handwritten signature (X) ▼

X _____

Certificate will be mailed in window envelope to this address:	Name ▼ Felix Founder
	Number/Street/Apt ▼ 1000 Bonito Way
	City/State/ZIP ▼ Tampa, FL 10000

YOU MUST:
• Complete all necessary spaces
• Sign your application in space 8

SEND ALL 3 ELEMENTS IN THE SAME PACKAGE:
1. Application form
2. Nonrefundable filing fee in check or money order payable to *Register of Copyrights*
3. Deposit material

MAIL TO:
Library of Congress
Copyright Office
101 Independence Avenue, S.E.
Washington, D.C. 20559-6000

As of July 1, 1999, the filing fee for Form TX is $30.

9

*17 U.S.C. § 506(e): Any person who knowingly makes a false representation of a material fact in the application for copyright registration provided for by section 409, or in any written statement filed in connection with the application, shall be fined not more than $2,500.

June 1999—200,000
WEB REV: June 1999

☆U.S. GOVERNMENT PRINTING OFFICE: 1999-454-879/49

Sample Form VA (front)

FEE CHANGES
Fees are effective through June 30, 2002. After that date, check the Copyright Office Website at www.loc.gov/copyright or call (202) 707-3000 for current fee information.

FORM VA
For a Work of the Visual Arts
UNITED STATES COPYRIGHT OFFICE

REGISTRATION NUMBER

VA   VAU

EFFECTIVE DATE OF REGISTRATION

Month   Day   Year

DO NOT WRITE ABOVE THIS LINE. IF YOU NEED MORE SPACE, USE A SEPARATE CONTINUATION SHEET.

1

TITLE OF THIS WORK ▼

All About Everything

NATURE OF THIS WORK ▼ See instructions

Photographs

PREVIOUS OR ALTERNATIVE TITLES ▼

Publication as a Contribution If this work was published as a contribution to a periodical, serial, or collection, give information about the collective work in which the contribution appeared.   **Title of Collective Work ▼**

If published in a periodical or serial give: Volume ▼   Number ▼   Issue Date ▼   On Pages ▼

2

NOTE
Under the law, the "author" of a "work made for hire" is generally the employer, not the employee (see instructions). For any part of this work that was "made for hire" check "Yes" in the space provided, give the employer (or other person for whom the work was prepared) as "Author" of that part, and leave the space for dates of birth and death blank.

a NAME OF AUTHOR ▼
Mike Minolta

DATES OF BIRTH AND DEATH
Year Born ▼   Year Died ▼
1940

Was this contribution to the work a "work made for hire"?
☐ Yes
☒ No

Author's Nationality or Domicile
Name of Country
OR { Citizen of ▶ U.S.A.
Domiciled in ▶

Was This Author's Contribution to the Work
Anonymous?   ☐ Yes ☒ No
Pseudonymous? ☐ Yes ☒ No
If the answer to either of these questions is "Yes," see detailed instructions.

NATURE OF AUTHORSHIP Check appropriate box(es). **See instructions**
☐ 3-Dimensional sculpture   ☐ Map   ☐ Technical drawing
☐ 2-Dimensional artwork   ☒ Photograph   ☐ Text
☐ Reproduction of work of art ☐ Jewelry design   ☐ Architectural work

b NAME OF AUTHOR ▼

DATES OF BIRTH AND DEATH
Year Born ▼   Year Died ▼

Was this contribution to the work a "work made for hire"?
☐ Yes
☐ No

Author's Nationality or Domicile
Name of Country
OR { Citizen of ▶
Domiciled in ▶

Was This Author's Contribution to the Work
Anonymous?   ☐ Yes ☐ No
Pseudonymous? ☐ Yes ☐ No
If the answer to either of these questions is "Yes," see detailed instructions.

NATURE OF AUTHORSHIP Check appropriate box(es). **See instructions**
☐ 3-Dimensional sculpture   ☐ Map   ☐ Technical drawing
☐ 2-Dimensional artwork   ☐ Photograph   ☐ Text
☐ Reproduction of work of art ☐ Jewelry design   ☐ Architectural work

3

a Year in Which Creation of This Work Was Completed
2000
◀ Year This information must be given in all cases.

b Date and Nation of First Publication of This Particular Work
Complete this information ONLY if this work has been published.
Month ▶ May   Day ▶ 11   Year ▶ 2000
U.S.A.   ◀ Nation

4

See instructions before completing this space.

COPYRIGHT CLAIMANT(S) Name and address must be given even if the claimant is the same as the author given in space 2. ▼

Mike Minolta
100 Grant St.
Chicago, IL 50000

Transfer If the claimant(s) named here in space 4 is (are) different from the author(s) named in space 2, give a brief statement of how the claimant(s) obtained ownership of the copyright. ▼

APPLICATION RECEIVED

ONE DEPOSIT RECEIVED

TWO DEPOSITS RECEIVED

FUNDS RECEIVED

DO NOT WRITE HERE
OFFICE USE ONLY

MORE ON BACK ▶   • Complete all applicable spaces (numbers 5-9) on the reverse side of this page.
• See detailed instructions.   • Sign the form at line 8.

DO NOT WRITE HERE

Page 1 of _____ pages

Sample Form VA (back)

EXAMINED BY	FORM VA
CHECKED BY	
☐ CORRESPONDENCE Yes	FOR COPYRIGHT OFFICE USE ONLY

DO NOT WRITE ABOVE THIS LINE. IF YOU NEED MORE SPACE, USE A SEPARATE CONTINUATION SHEET.

PREVIOUS REGISTRATION Has registration for this work, or for an earlier version of this work, already been made in the Copyright Office?

☐ Yes ☒ No If your answer is "Yes," why is another registration being sought? (Check appropriate box.) ▼

a. ☐ This is the first published edition of a work previously registered in unpublished form.

b. ☐ This is the first application submitted by this author as copyright claimant.

c. ☐ This is a changed version of the work, as shown by space 6 on this application.

If your answer is "Yes," give: **Previous Registration Number** ▼   **Year of Registration** ▼

5

DERIVATIVE WORK OR COMPILATION Complete both space 6a and 6b for a derivative work; complete only 6b for a compilation.
a. Preexisting Material Identify any preexisting work or works that this work is based on or incorporates. ▼

b. Material Added to This Work Give a brief, general statement of the material that has been added to this work and in which copyright is claimed. ▼

6

a

b

See instructions before completing this space.

DEPOSIT ACCOUNT If the registration fee is to be charged to a Deposit Account established in the Copyright Office, give name and number of Account.
Name ▼   **Account Number** ▼

CORRESPONDENCE Give name and address to which correspondence about this application should be sent.   Name/Address/Apt/City/State/ZIP ▼

Mike Minolta
100 Grant St.
Chicago, IL 50000

Area code and daytime telephone number ▶ (312) 555-5555   Fax number ▶ (   )

Email ▶

7

a

b

CERTIFICATION* I, the undersigned, hereby certify that I am the

check only one ▶
☒ author
☐ other copyright claimant
☐ owner of exclusive right(s)
☐ authorized agent of _____
Name of author or other copyright claimant, or owner of exclusive right(s) ▲

of the work identified in this application and that the statements made by me in this application are correct to the best of my knowledge.

8

Typed or printed name and date ▼ If this application gives a date of publication in space 3, do not sign and submit it before that date.

Mike Minolta   Date ▶ July 1, 2000

Handwritten signature (X) ▼

☞ X _____

Certificate will be mailed in window envelope to this address:	Name ▼ Mike Minolta	YOU MUST: • Complete all necessary spaces • Sign your application in space 8
	Number/Street/Apt ▼ 100 Grant St.	SEND ALL 3 ELEMENTS IN THE SAME PACKAGE: 1. Application form 2. Nonrefundable filing fee in check or money order payable to *Register of Copyrights* 3. Deposit material
	City/State/ZIP ▼ Chicago, IL 50000	MAIL TO: Library of Congress Copyright Office 101 Independence Avenue, S.E. Washington, D.C. 20559-6000

As of July 1, 1999, the filing fee for Form VA is $30.

9

June 1999—100,000
WEB REV: June 1999

☆U.S. GOVERNMENT PRINTING OFFICE: 1999-454-879/71

Sample Forms

Copyright Law

COPYRIGHT ACT OF 1976. The following selected federal statutes are part of the Copyright Act of 1976, as amended, set out in Title 17 United States Code, Sections 101-810; 1001-1010.

§ 101. Definitions

This statute defines commonly used terms in the Copyright Act of 1976, as amended.

Except as otherwise provided in this title, as used in this title, the following terms and their variant forms mean the following:

An "anonymous work" is a work on the copies or phonorecords of which no natural person is identified as author.

An "architectural work" is the design of a building as embodied in any tangible medium of expression, including a building, architectural plans, or drawings. The work includes the overall form as well as the arrangement and composition of spaces and elements in the design, but does not include individual standard features.

"Audiovisual works" are works that consist of a series of related images which are intrinsically intended to be shown by the use of machines or devices such as projectors, viewers, or electronic equipment, together with accompanying sounds, if any, regardless of the nature of the material objects, such as films or tapes, in which the works are embodied.

The "Berne Convention" is the Convention for the Protection of Literary and Artistic Works, signed at Berne, Switzerland, on September 9, 1886, and all acts, protocols, and revisions thereto.

The "best edition" of a work is the edition, published in the United States at any time before the date of deposit, that the Library of Congress determines to be most suitable for its purposes.

A person's "children" are that person's immediate offspring, whether legitimate or not, and any children legally adopted by that person.

A "collective work" is a work, such as a periodical issue, anthology, or encyclopedia, in which a number of contributions, constituting separate and independent works in themselves, are assembled into a collective whole.

A "compilation" is a work formed by the collection and assembling of preexisting materials or of data that are selected, coordinated, or arranged in such a way that the resulting work as a whole constitutes an original work of authorship. The term "compilation" includes collective works.

"Copies" are material objects, other than phonorecords, in which a work is fixed by any method now known or later developed, and from which the work can be perceived, reproduced, or otherwise communicated, either directly or with the aid of a machine or device. The term "copies" includes the material object, other than a phonorecord, in which the work is first fixed.

"Copyright owner," with respect to any one of the exclusive rights comprised in a copyright, refers to the owner of that particular right.

The "country of origin" of a Berne Convention work, for purposes of section 411, is the United States if—

> (1) in the case of a published work, the work is first published—
>> (A) in the United States;
>> (B) simultaneously in the United States and another nation or nations adhering to the Berne Convention, whose law grants a term of copyright protection that is the same as or longer than the term provided in the United States;
>> (C) simultaneously in the United States and a foreign nation that does not adhere to the Berne Convention; or
>> (D) in a foreign nation that does not adhere to the Berne Convention, and all of the authors of the work are nationals, domiciliaries, or habitual residents of, or in the case of an audiovisual work legal entities with headquarters in, the United States;
> (2) in the case of an unpublished work, all the authors of the work are nationals, domiciliaries, or habitual residents of the United States, or, in the case of an unpublished audiovisual work, all the authors are legal entities with headquarters in the United States; or
> (3) in the case of a pictorial, graphic, or sculptural work incorporated in a building or structure, the building or structure is located in the United States.

For the purposes of section 411, the "country of origin" of any other Berne Convention work is not the United States.

A work is "created" when it is fixed in a copy or phonorecord for the first time; where a work is prepared over a period of time, the portion of it that has been fixed at any particular time constitutes the work as of that time, and where the work has been prepared in different versions, each version constitutes a separate work.

A "derivative work" is a work based upon one or more preexisting works, such as a translation, musical arrangement, dramatization, fictionalization, motion picture version, sound recording, art reproduction, abridgment, condensation, or any other form in which a work may be recast, transformed, or adapted. A work consisting of editorial revisions, annotations, elaborations, or other modifications which, as a whole, represent an original work of authorship, is a "derivative work."

A "device," "machine," or "process" is one now known or later developed.

A "digital transmission" is a transmission in whole or in part in a digital or other non-analog format.

To "display" a work means to show a copy of it, either directly or by means of a film, slide, television image, or any other device or process or, in the case of a motion picture or other audiovisual work, to show individual images nonsequentially.

An "establishment" is a store, shop, or any similar place of business open to the general public for the primary purpose of selling goods or services in which the majority of the gross square feet of space that is nonresidential is used for that purpose, and in which nondramatic musical works are performed publicly.

The term "financial gain" includes receipt, or expectation of receipt, of anything of value, including the receipt of other copyrighted works.

A work is "fixed" in a tangible medium of expression when its embodiment in a copy or phonorecord, by or under the authority of the author, is sufficiently permanent or stable to permit it to be perceived, reproduced, or otherwise communicated for a period of more than transitory duration. A work consisting of sounds, images, or both, that are being transmitted, is "fixed" for purposes of this title if a fixation of the work is being made simultaneously with its transmission.

A "food service or drinking establishment" is a restaurant, inn, bar, tavern, or any other similar place of business in which the public or patrons assemble for the primary purpose of being served food or drink, in which the majority of the gross square feet of space that is non-residential is used for that purpose, and in which nondramatic musical works are performed publicly.

The "Geneva Phonograms Convention" is the Convention for the Protection of Producers of Phonograms Against Unauthorized Duplication of Their Phonograms, concluded at Geneva, Switzerland, on October 29, 1971.

The "gross square feet of space" of an establishment means the entire interior space of that establishment, and any adjoining outdoor space used to serve patrons, whether on a seasonal basis or otherwise.

The terms "including" and "such as" are illustrative and not limitative.

An "international agreement" is—

(1) the Universal Copyright Convention;

(2) the Geneva Phonograms Convention;

(3) the Berne Convention;

(4) the WTO Agreement;

(5) the WIPO Copyright Treaty;

(6) the WIPO Performances and Phonograms Treaty; and

(7) any other copyright treaty to which the United States is a party.

A "joint work" is a work prepared by two or more authors with the intention that their contributions be merged into inseparable or interdependent parts of a unitary whole.

"Literary works" are works, other than audiovisual works, expressed in words, numbers, or other verbal or numerical symbols or indicia, regardless of the nature of the material objects, such as books, periodicals, manuscripts, phonorecords, film, tapes, disks, or cards, in which they are embodied.

"Motion pictures" are audiovisual works consisting of a series of related images which, when shown in succession, impart an impression of motion, together with accompanying sounds, if any.

To "perform" a work means to recite, render, play, dance, or act it, either directly or by means of any device or process or, in the case of a motion picture or other audiovisual work, to show its images in any sequence or to make the sounds accompanying it audible.

A "performing rights society" is an association, corporation, or other entity that licenses the public performance of nondramatic musical works on behalf of copyright owners of such works, such as the American Society of Composers, Authors and Publishers (ASCAP), Broadcast Music, Inc. (BMI), and SESAC, Inc.

"Phonorecords" are material objects in which sounds, other than those accompanying a motion picture or other audiovisual work, are fixed by any method now known or later developed, and from which the sounds can be perceived, reproduced, or otherwise communicated, either directly or with the aid of a machine or device. The term "phonorecords" includes the material object in which the sounds are first fixed.

"Pictorial, graphic, and sculptural works" include two-dimensional and three-dimensional works of fine, graphic, and applied art, photographs, prints and art reproductions, maps, globes, charts, diagrams, models, and technical drawings, including architectural plans. Such works shall include works of artistic craftsmanship insofar as their form but not their mechanical or utilitarian aspects are concerned; the design of a useful article, as defined in this section, shall be considered a pictorial, graphic, or sculptural work only if, and only to the extent that, such design incorporates pictorial, graphic, or sculptural features that can be identified separately from, and are capable of existing independently of, the utilitarian aspects of the article.

For purposes of Section 513, a "proprietor" is an individual, corporation, partnership, or other entity, as the case may be, that owns an establishment or a food service or drinking establishment, except that no owner or operator of a radio or television station licensed by the Federal Communications Commission, cable system or satellite carrier, cable or satellite carrier service or programmer, provider of online services or network access or the operator of facilities therefor, telecommunications company, or any other such audio or audiovisual service or programmer now known or as may be developed in the future, commercial subscription music service, or owner or operator of any other transmission service, shall under any circumstances be deemed to be a proprietor.

A "pseudonymous work" is a work on the copies or phonorecords of which the author is identified under a fictitious name.

"Publication" is the distribution of copies or phonorecords of a work to the public by sale or other transfer of ownership, or by rental, lease, or lending. The offering to distribute copies or phonorecords to a group of persons for purposes of further distribution, public performance, or public display, constitutes publication. A public performance or display of a work does not of itself constitute publication.

To perform or display a work "publicly" means—

(1) to perform or display it at a place open to the public or at any place where a substantial number of persons outside of a normal circle of a family and its social acquaintances is gathered; or

(2) to transmit or otherwise communicate a performance or display of the work to a place specified by clause (1) or to the public, by means of any device or process, whether the members of the public capable of receiving the performance or display receive it in the same place or in separate places and at the same time or at different times.

"Registration," for purposes of sections 205(c)(2), 405, 406, 410(d), 411, 412, and 506(e), means a registration of a claim in the original or the renewed and extended term of copyright.

"Sound recordings" are works that result from the fixation of a series of musical, spoken, or other sounds, but not including the sounds accompanying a motion picture or other audiovisual work, regardless of the nature of the material objects, such as disks, tapes, or other phonorecords, in which they are embodied.

"State" includes the District of Columbia and the Commonwealth of Puerto Rico, and any territories to which this title is made applicable by an Act of Congress.

A "transfer of copyright ownership" is an assignment, mortgage, exclusive license, or any other conveyance, alienation, or hypothecation of a copyright or of any of the exclusive rights comprised in a copyright, whether or not it is limited in time or place of effect, but not including a non-exclusive license.

A "transmission program" is a body of material that, as an aggregate, has been produced for the sole purpose of transmission to the public in sequence and as a unit.

To "transmit" a performance or display is to communicate it by any device or process whereby images or sounds are received beyond the place from which they are sent.

A "treaty party" is a country or intergovernmental organization other than the United States that is a party to an international agreement.

The "United States," when used in a geographical sense, comprises the several States, the District of Columbia and the Commonwealth of Puerto Rico, and the organized territories under the jurisdiction of the United States Government.

A "useful article" is an article having an intrinsic utilitarian function that is not merely to portray the appearance of the article or to convey information. An article that is normally a part of a useful article is considered a "useful article."

The author's "widow" or "widower" is the author's surviving spouse under the law of the author's domicile at the time of his or her death, whether or not the spouse has later remarried.

A "work of visual art" is—

    (1) a painting, drawing, print, or sculpture, existing in a single copy, in a limited edition of 200 copies or fewer that are signed and consecutively numbered by the author, or, in the case of a sculpture, in multiple cast, carved, or fabricated sculptures of 200 or fewer that are consecutively numbered by the author and bear the signature or other identifying mark of the author; or

    (2) a still photographic image produced for exhibition purposes only, existing in a single copy that is signed by the author, or in a limited edition of 200 copies or fewer that are signed and consecutively numbered by the author.

A work of visual art does not include—

    (A)   (i) any poster, map, globe, chart, technical drawing, diagram, model, applied art, motion picture or other audio-visual work, book, magazine, newspaper, periodical, data base, electronic information service, electronic publication, or similar publication;

         (ii) any merchandising item or advertising, promotional, descriptive, covering, or packaging material or container;

         (iii) any portion or part of any item described in clause (i) or (ii);

    (B) any work made for hire; or

    (C) any work not subject to copyright protection under this title.

A "work of the United States Government" is a work prepared by an officer or employee of the United States Government as part of that person's official duties.

A "work made for hire" is—

    (1) a work prepared by an employee within the scope of his or her employment; or

    (2) a work specially ordered or commissioned for use as a contribution to a collective work, as a part of a motion picture or other audiovisual work, as a translation, as a supplementary work, as a compilation, as an instructional text, as a test, as answer material for a test, or as an atlas, if the parties expressly agree in a written instrument signed by them that the work shall be considered a work made for hire. For the purpose of the foregoing sentence, a "supplementary work" is a work prepared for publication as a secondary adjunct to a work by another author for the purpose of introducing, concluding, illustrating, explaining, revising, commenting upon, or

assisting in the use of the other work, such as forewords, afterwords, pictorial illustrations, maps, charts, tables, editorial notes, musical arrangements, answer material for tests, bibliographies, appendixes, and indexes, and an "instructional text" is a literary, pictorial, or graphic work prepared for publication and with the purpose of use in systematic instructional activities.

The terms "WTO Agreement" and "WTO member country" have the meanings given those terms in paragraphs (9) and (10), respectively, of section 2 of the Uruguay Round Agreements Act. A "computer program" is a set of statements or instructions to be used directly or indirectly in a computer in order to bring about a certain result.

§ 102. Subject matter of copyright: In general

This statute sets out the types of creative works that are and are not protected by copyright.

(a) Copyright protection subsists, in accordance with this title, in original works of authorship fixed in any tangible medium of expression, now known or later developed, from which they can be perceived, reproduced, or otherwise communicated, either directly or with the aid of a machine or device. Works of authorship include the following categories:

(1) literary works;

(2) musical works, including any accompanying words;

(3) dramatic works, including any accompanying music;

(4) pantomimes and choreographic works;

(5) pictorial, graphic, and sculptural works;

(6) motion pictures and other audiovisual works;

(7) sound recordings; and

(8) architectural works.

(b) In no case does copyright protection for an original work of authorship extend to any idea, procedure, process, system, method of operation, concept, principle, or discovery, regardless of the form in which it is described, explained, illustrated, or embodied in such work.

§ 103. Subject matter of copyright: Compilations and derivative works

This statute describes when and how copyright protection applies to works consisting in whole or in part of preexisting materials.

(a) The subject matter of copyright as specified by section 102 includes compilations and derivative works, but protection for a work employing preexisting material in which copyright subsists does not extend to any part of the work in which such material has been used unlawfully.

(b) The copyright in a compilation or derivative work extends only to the material contributed by the author of such work, as distinguished from the preexisting material employed in the work, and does not imply any exclusive right in the preexisting material. The copyright in such work is independent of, and does not affect or enlarge the scope, duration, ownership, or subsistence of, any copyright protection in the preexisting material.

§ 104. Subject matter of copyright: National origin

This statute addresses when works created by citizens or nationals of other countries, or works first published in other countries, are entitled to protection under the U.S. copyright laws.

(a) **Unpublished Works.**—The works specified by sections 102 and 103, while unpublished, are subject to protection under this title without regard to the nationality or domicile of the author.

Statutes

(b) **Published Works.**—The works specified by section 102 and 103, when published, are subject to protection under this title if—

    (1) on the date of first publication, one or more of the authors is a national or domiciliary of the United States, or is a national, domiciliary, or sovereign authority of a foreign nation that is a party to a copyright treaty to which the United States is also a party, or is a stateless person, wherever that person may be domiciled; or

    (2) the work is first published in the United States or in a foreign nation that, on the date of first publication, is a treaty party; or

    (3) the work is a sound recording that was first fixed in a treaty party; or

    (4) the work is a pictorial, graphic, or sculptural work that is incorporated in a building or other structure, or an architectural work that is embodied in a building and the building or structure is located in the United States or a treaty party; or

    (5) the work is first published by the United Nations or any of its specialized agencies, or by the Organization of American States; or

    (6) the work comes within the scope of a Presidential proclamation. Whenever the President finds that a particular foreign nation extends, to works by authors who are nationals or domiciliaries of the United States or to works that are first published in the United States, copyright protection on substantially the same basis as that on which the foreign nation extends protection to works of its own nationals and domiciliaries and works first published in that nation, the President may by proclamation extend protection under this title to works of which one or more of the authors is, on the date of first publication, a national, domiciliary, or sovereign authority of that nation, or which was first published in that nation. The President may revise, suspend, or revoke any such proclamation or impose any conditions or limitations on protection under a proclamation.

For purposes of paragraph (2), a work that is published in the United States or a treaty party within 30 days after publication in a foreign nation that is not a treaty party shall be considered to be first published in the United States or such treaty party, as the case may be.

(c) **Effect of Berne Convention.**—No right or interest in a work eligible for protection under this title may be claimed by virtue of, or in reliance upon, the provisions of the Berne Convention, or the adherence of the United States thereto. Any rights in a work eligible for protection under this title that shall not be expanded or reduced by virtue of, or in reliance upon, the provisions of the Berne Convention, or the adherence of the United States thereto.

(d) **Effect of phonograms treaties.**—Notwithstanding the provisions of subsection (b), no works other than sound recordings shall be eligible for protection under this title solely by virtue of the adherence of the United States to the Geneva Phonograms Convention or the WIPO Performances and Phonograms Treaty. [Note: This subsection takes effect upon the entry into force of the WIPO Performances and Phonograms Treaty with respect to the United States.]

§ 106. Exclusive rights in copyrighted works

This statute specifies the separate rights that make up the bundle of rights protected by copyright.

Subject to sections 107 through 120, the owner of copyright under this title has the exclusive rights to do and to authorize any of the following:

    (1) to reproduce the copyrighted work in copies or phonorecords;

    (2) to prepare derivative works based upon the copyrighted work;

(3) to distribute copies or phonorecords of the copyrighted work to the public by sale or other transfer of ownership, or by rental, lease, or lending;

(4) in the case of literary, musical, dramatic, and choreographic works, pantomimes, and motion pictures and other audiovisual works, to perform the copyrighted work publicly; and

(5) in the case of literary, musical, dramatic, and choreographic works, pantomimes, and pictorial, graphic, or sculptural works, including the individual images of a motion picture or other audiovisual work, to display the copyrighted work publicly.

(6) in the case of sound recordings, to perform the copyrighted work publicly by means of a digital audio transmission.

§ 106A. Rights of certain authors to attribution and integrity

This statute provides authors of works of visual art with certain rights commonly known as moral rights—such as the right to claim or disclaim authorship and the right to prevent mutilation or distortion of a work. It addresses such issues as the duration of these rights and the circumstances under which they may be waived.

(a) **Rights of Attribution and Integrity.**—Subject to section 107 and independent of the exclusive rights provided in section 106, the author of a work of visual art—

    (1) shall have the right—

        (A) to claim authorship of that work, and

        (B) to prevent the use of his or her name as the author of any work of visual art which he or she did not create;

    (2) shall have the right to prevent the use of his or her name as the author of the work of visual art in the event of a distortion, mutilation, or other modification of the work which would be prejudicial to his or her honor or reputation; and

    (3) subject to the limitations set forth in section 113(d)[not provided in this desk reference], shall have the right—

        (A) to prevent any intentional distortion, mutilation, or other modification of that work which would be prejudicial to his or her honor or reputation, and any intentional distortion, mutilation, or modification of that work is a violation of that right, and

        (B) to prevent any destruction of a work of recognized stature, and any intentional or grossly negligent destruction of that work is a violation of that right.

(b) **Scope and Exercise of Rights.**—Only the author of a work of visual art has the rights conferred by subsection (a) in that work, whether or not the author is the copyright owner. The authors of a joint work of visual art are co-owners of the rights conferred by subsection (a) in that work.

(c) **Exceptions.**—(1) The modification of a work of visual art which is a result of the passage of time or the inherent nature of the materials is not a distortion, mutilation, or other modification described in subsection (a)(3)(A).

    (2) The modification of a work of visual art which is the result of conservation, or of the public presentation, including lighting and placement, of the work is not a destruction, distortion, mutilation, or other modification described in subsection (a)(3) unless the modification is caused by gross negligence.

    (3) The rights described in paragraphs (1) and (2) of subsection (a) shall not apply to any reproduction, depiction, portrayal, or other use of a work in, upon, or in any connection with any item described in subparagraph (A) or (B) of the definition of

"work of visual art" in section 101, and any such reproduction, depiction, portrayal, or other use of a work is not a destruction, distortion, mutilation, or other modification described in paragraph (3) of subsection (a).

(d) **Duration of Rights.**—(1) With respect to works of visual art created on or after the effective date set forth in section 610(a) of the Visual Artists Rights Act of 1990, the rights conferred by subsection (a) shall endure for a term consisting of the life of the author.

   (2) With respect to works of visual art created before the effective date set forth in section 610(a) of the Visual Artists Rights Act of 1990, but title to which has not, as of such effective date, been transferred from the author, the rights conferred by subsection (a) shall be coextensive with, and shall expire at the same time as, the rights conferred by section 106.

   (3) In the case of a joint work prepared by two or more authors, the rights conferred by subsection (a) shall endure for a term consisting of the life of the last surviving author.

   (4) All terms of the rights conferred by subsection (a) run to the end of the calendar year in which they would otherwise expire.

(e) **Transfer and Waiver.**—(1) The rights conferred by subsection (a) may not be transferred, but those rights may be waived if the author expressly agrees to such waiver in a written instrument signed by the author. Such instrument shall specifically identify the work, and uses of that work, to which the waiver applies, and the waiver shall apply only to the work and uses so identified. In the case of a joint work prepared by two or more authors, a waiver of rights under this paragraph made by one such author waives such rights for all such authors.

   (2) Ownership of the rights conferred by subsection (a) with respect to a work of visual art is distinct from ownership of any copy of that work, or of a copyright or any exclusive right under a copyright in that title work. Transfer of ownership of any copy of a work of visual art, or of a copyright or any exclusive right under a copyright, shall not constitute a waiver of the rights conferred by subsection (a). Except as may otherwise be agreed by the author in a written instrument signed by the author, a waiver of the rights conferred by subsection (a) with respect to a work of visual art shall not constitute a transfer of ownership of any copy of that work, or of ownership of a copyright or of any exclusive right under a copyright in that work.

§ 107. Limitations on exclusive rights: Fair use

This statute describes the circumstances under which a work protected by copyright may be used without the copyright owner's permission—commonly known as the fair use doctrine.

Notwithstanding the provisions of sections 106 and 106A, the fair use of a copyrighted work, including such use by reproduction in copies or phonorecords or by any other means specified by that section, for purposes such as criticism, comment, news reporting, teaching (including multiple copies for classroom use), scholarship, or research, is not an infringement of copyright. In determining whether the use made of a work in any particular case is a fair use the factors to be considered shall include—

   (1) the purpose and character of the use, including whether such use is of a commercial nature or is for nonprofit educational purposes;

   (2) the nature of the copyrighted work;

   (3) the amount and substantiality of the portion used in relation to the copyrighted work as a whole; and

(4) the effect of the use upon the potential market for or value of the copyrighted work.

The fact that a work is unpublished shall not itself bar a finding of fair use if such finding is made upon consideration of all the above factors.

§ 108. Limitations on exclusive rights: Reproduction by libraries and archives

This statute sets out the conditions under which libraries may legally copy materials protected by copyright without permission from the copyright owner.

    (a) Except as otherwise provided in this title and notwithstanding the provisions of section 106, it is not an infringement of copyright for a library or archives, or any of its employees acting within the scope of their employment, to reproduce no more than one copy or phonorecord of a work, except as provided in subsections (b) and (c), or to distribute such copy or phonorecord, under the conditions specified by this section, if—

        (1) the reproduction or distribution is made without any purpose of direct or indirect commercial advantage;

        (2) the collections of the library or archives are (i) open to the public, or (ii) available not only to researchers affiliated with the library or archives or with the institution of which it is a part, but also to other persons doing research in a specialized field; and

        (3) the reproduction or distribution of the work includes a notice of copyright that appears on the copy or phonorecord that is reproduced under the provisions of this section, or includes a legend stating that the work may be protected by copyright if no such notice can be found on the copy or phonorecord that is reproduced under the provisions of this section.

    (b) The rights of reproduction and distribution under this section apply to three copies or phonorecords of an unpublished work duplicated solely for purposes of preservation and security or for deposit for research use in another library or archives of the type described by clause (2) of subsection (a), if—

        (1) the copy or phonorecord reproduced is currently in the collections of the library or archives; and

        (2) any such copy or phonorecord that is reproduced in digital format is not otherwise distributed in that format and is not made available to the public in that format outside the premises of the library or archives.

    (c) The right of reproduction under this section applies to three copies or phonorecords of a published work duplicated solely for the purpose of replacement of a copy or phonorecord that is damaged, deteriorating, lost, or stolen, or if the existing format in which the work is stored has become obsolete, if—

        (1) the library or archives has, after a reasonable effort, determined that an unused replacement cannot be obtained at a fair price; and

        (2) any such copy or phonorecord that is reproduced in digital format is not made available to the public in that format outside the premises of the library or archives in lawful possession of such copy.

For purposes of this subsection, a format shall be considered obsolete if the machine or device necessary to render perceptible a work stored in that format is no longer manufactured or is no longer reasonably available in the commercial marketplace.

    (d) The rights of reproduction and distribution under this section apply to a copy, made from the collection of a library or archives where the user makes his or her request or from that of another library or archives, of no more than one article or other contribution to a copyrighted collection or periodical issue, or to a copy or phonorecord of a small part of any other copyrighted work, if—

    (1) the copy or phonorecord becomes the property of the user, and the library or archives has had no notice that the copy or phonorecord would be used for any purpose other than private study, scholarship, or research; and

    (2) the library or archives displays prominently, at the place where orders are accepted, and includes on its order form, a warning of copyright in accordance with requirements that the Register of Copyrights shall prescribe by regulation.

(e) The rights of reproduction and distribution under this section apply to the entire work, or to a substantial part of it, made from the collection of a library or archives where the user makes his or her request or from that of another library or archives, if the library or archives has first determined, on the basis of a reasonable investigation, that a copy or phonorecord of the copyrighted work cannot be obtained at a fair price, if—

    (1) the copy or phonorecord becomes the property of the user, and the library or archives has had no notice that the copy or phonorecord would be used for any purpose other than private study, scholarship, or research; and

    (2) the library or archives displays prominently, at the place where orders are accepted, and includes on its order form, a warning of copyright in accordance with requirements that the Register of Copyrights shall prescribe by regulation.

(f) Nothing in this section—

    (1) shall be construed to impose liability for copyright infringement upon a library or archives or its employees for the unsupervised use of reproducing equipment located on its premises: *Provided,* That such equipment displays a notice that the making of a copy may be subject to the copyright law;

    (2) excuses a person who uses such reproducing equipment or who requests a copy or phonorecord under subsection (d) from liability for copyright infringement for any such act, or for any later use of such copy or phonorecord, if it exceeds fair use as provided by section 107;

    (3) shall be construed to limit the reproduction and distribution by lending of a limited number of copies and excerpts by a library or archives of an audiovisual news program, subject to clauses (1), (2), and (3) of subsection (a); or

    (4) in any way affects the right of fair use as provided by section 107, or any contractual obligations assumed at any time by the library or archives when it obtained a copy or phonorecord of a work in its collections.

(g) The rights of reproduction and distribution under this section extend to the isolated and unrelated reproduction or distribution of a single copy or phonorecord of the same material on separate occasions, but do not extend to cases where the library or archives, or its employee—

    (1) is aware or has substantial reason to believe that it is engaging in the related or concerted reproduction or distribution of multiple copies or phonorecords of the same material, whether made on one occasion or over a period of time, and whether intended for aggregate use by one or more individuals or for separate use by the individual members of a group; or

    (2) engages in the systematic reproduction or distribution of single or multiple copies or phonorecords of material described in subsection (d): *Provided,* That nothing in this clause prevents a library or archives from participating in interlibrary arrangements that do not have as their purpose or effect, that the library or archives receiving such copies or phonorecords for distribution does so in such aggregate quantities as to substitute for a subscription to or purchase of such work.

(h) (1) For purposes of this section, during the last 20 years of any term of copyright of a published work, a library or archives, including a nonprofit educational institution that functions as such, may reproduce, distribute, display, or perform in facsimile or digital form a copy or phonorecord of such work, or portions thereof, for purposes of preservation, scholarship, or research, if such library or archives has first determined, on the basis of a reasonable investigation, that none of the conditions set forth in subparagraphs (A), (B), and (C) of paragraph (2) apply.

(2) No reproduction, distribution, display, or performance is authorized under this subsection if—

(A) the work is subject to normal commercial exploitation;

(B) a copy or phonorecord of the work can be obtained at a reasonable price; or

(C) the copyright owner or its agent provides notice pursuant to regulations promulgated by the Register of Copyrights that either of the conditions set forth in subparagraphs (A) and (B) applies.

(3) The exemption provided in this subsection does not apply to any subsequent uses by users other than such library or archives.

(i) The rights of reproduction and distribution under this section do not apply to a musical work, a pictorial, graphic or sculptural work, or a motion picture or other audiovisual work other than an audiovisual work dealing with news, except that no such limitation shall apply with respect to rights granted by subsections (b) and (c), or with respect to pictorial or graphic works published as illustrations, diagrams, or similar adjuncts to works of which copies are reproduced or distributed in accordance with subsections (d) and (e).

§ 109. Limitations on exclusive rights: Effect of transfer of particular copy or phonorecord

This statute:

- *sets out what is known as the first sale doctrine—which permits the rightful owner of a copy of a copyrighted work to sell the copy to another party, and*

- *describes the circumstances under which a copy of a protected work may be rented, leased or displayed to others without the copyright owner's permission.*

(a) Notwithstanding the provisions of section 106(3), the owner of a particular copy or phonorecord lawfully made under this title, or any person authorized by such owner, is entitled, without the authority of the copyright owner, to sell or otherwise dispose of the possession of that copy or phonorecord. Notwithstanding the preceding sentence, copies or phonorecords of works subject to restored copyright under section 104A that are manufactured before the date of restoration of copyright or, with respect to reliance parties, before publication or service of notice under section 104A(e), may be sold or otherwise disposed of without the authorization of the owner of the restored copyright for purposes of direct or indirect commercial advantage only during the 12-month period beginning on—

(1) the date of the publication in the Federal Register of the notice of intent filed with the Copyright Office under section 104A(d)(2)(A), or

(2) the date of the receipt of actual notice served under section 104A(d)(2)(B), whichever occurs first.

(b)(1)(A) Notwithstanding the provisions of subsection (a), unless authorized by the owners of copyright in the sound recording or the owner of copyright in a computer program (including any tape, disk, or other medium embodying such program), and in the case of a sound recording in the musical works embodied therein, neither the owner of a particular phonorecord nor any person in possession of a particular copy of a computer program (including any tape, disk, or other medium embodying such program), may, for the purposes of direct or indirect commercial advantage, dispose of, or authorize the disposal of, the possession of that phonorecord or computer program (including any tape, disk, or other medium embodying such program) by rental, lease, or lending, or by any other act or practice in the nature of rental, lease, or lending. Nothing in the preceding sentence shall apply to the rental, lease, or lending of a phonorecord for nonprofit purposes by a nonprofit library or nonprofit educational institution. The transfer of possession of a lawfully made copy of a computer program by a nonprofit educational institution to another nonprofit educational institution or to faculty, staff, and students does not constitute rental, lease, or lending for direct or indirect commercial purposes under this subsection.

    (B) This subsection does not apply to—

        (i) a computer program which is embodied in a machine or product and which cannot be copied during the ordinary operation or use of the machine or product; or

        (ii) a computer program embodied in or used in conjunction with a limited purpose computer that is designed for playing video games and may be designed for other purposes.

    (C) Nothing in this subsection affects any provision of chapter 9 of this title.

  (2)(A) Nothing in this subsection shall apply to the lending of a computer program for non-profit purposes by a nonprofit library, if each copy of a computer program which is lent by such library has affixed to the packaging containing the program a warning of copyright in accordance with requirements that the Register of Copyrights shall prescribe by regulation.

    (B) Not later than three years after the date of the enactment of the Computer Software Rental Amendments Act of 1990, and at such times thereafter as the Register of Copyright considers appropriate, the Register of Copyrights, after consultation with representatives of copyright owners and librarians, shall submit to the Congress a report stating whether this paragraph has achieved its intended purpose of maintaining the integrity of the copyright system while providing nonprofit libraries the capability to fulfill their function. Such report shall advise the Congress as to any information or recommendations that the Register of Copyrights considers necessary to carry out the purposes of this subsection.

  (3) Nothing in this subsection shall affect any provision of the antitrust laws. For purposes of the preceding sentence, 'antitrust laws' has the meaning given that term in the first section of the Clayton Act and includes section 5 of the Federal Trade Commission Act to the extent that section relates to unfair methods of competition.

  (4) Any person who distributes a phonorecord or a copy of a computer program (including any tape, disk, or other medium embodying such program) in violation of paragraph (1) is an infringer of copyright under section 501 of this title and is subject to the remedies set forth in sections 502, 503, 504, 505, and 509. Such violation shall not be a criminal offense under section 506 or cause such person to be subject to the criminal penalties set forth in section 2319 of title 18.

    (c) Notwithstanding the provisions of section 106(5), the owner of a particular copy lawfully made under this title, or any person authorized by such owner, is entitled, without the authority of the copyright owner, to display that copy publicly, either directly or by the projection of no more than one image at a time, to viewers present at the place where the copy is located.

(d) The privileges prescribed by subsections (a) and (c) do not, unless authorized by the copyright owner, extend to any person who has acquired possession of the copy or phonorecord from the copyright owner, by rental, lease, loan, or otherwise, without acquiring ownership of it.

(e) Notwithstanding the provisions of sections 106(4) and 106(5), in the case of an electronic audiovisual game intended for use in coin-operated equipment, the owner of a particular copy of such a game lawfully made under this title, is entitled, without the authority of the copyright owner of the game, to publicly perform or display that game in coin-operated equipment, except that this subsection shall not apply to any work of authorship embodied in the audiovisual game if the copyright owner of the electronic audiovisual game is not also the copyright owner of the work of authorship.

§ 117. Limitations on exclusive rights: Computer programs

This statute governs when copies of computer programs may be made without permission from the copyright owner.

(a) **Making of additional copy or adaptation by owner of copy.**—Notwithstanding the provisions of section 106, it is not an infringement for the owner of a copy of a computer program to make or authorize the making of another copy or adaptation of that computer program provided:

(1) that such a new copy or adaptation is created as an essential step in the utilization of the computer program in conjunction with a machine and that it is used in no other manner, or

(2) that such new copy or adaptation is for archival purposes only and that all archival copies are destroyed in the event that continued possession of the computer program should cease to be rightful.

(b) **Lease, sale, or other transfer of additional copy or adaptation.**—Any exact copies prepared in accordance with the provisions of this section may be leased, sold, or otherwise transferred, along with the copy from which such copies were prepared, only as part of the lease, sale, or other transfer of all rights in the program. Adaptations so prepared may be transferred only with the authorization of the copyright owner.

(c) **Machine maintenance or repair.**—Notwithstanding the provisions of section 106, it is not an infringement for the owner or lessee of a machine to make or authorize the making of a copy of a computer program if such copy is made solely by virtue of the activation of a machine that lawfully contains an authorized copy of the computer program, for purposes only of maintenance or repair of that machine, if—

(1) such new copy is used in no other manner and is destroyed immediately after the maintenance or repair is completed; and

(2) with respect to any computer program or part thereof that is not necessary for that machine to be activated, such program or part thereof is not accessed or used other than to make such new copy by virtue of the activation of the machine.

(d) **Definitions.**—For purposes of this section—

(1) the "maintenance" of a machine is the servicing of the machine in order to make it work in accordance with its original specifications and any changes to those specifications authorized for that machine; and

(2) the "repair" of a machine is the restoring of the machine to the state of working in accordance with its original specifications and any changes to those specifications authorized for that machine.

§ 120. Scope of exclusive rights in architectural works

This statute governs when architectural works may be reproduced, altered or destroyed.

(a) **Pictorial representations permitted.**—The copyright in an architectural work that has been constructed does not include the right to prevent the making, distributing, or public display of pictures, paintings, photographs, or other pictorial representations of the work, if the building in which the work is embodied is located in or ordinarily visible from a public place.

(b) **Alterations to and destruction of buildings.**—Notwithstanding the provisions of section 106(2), the owners of a building embodying an architectural work may, without the consent of the author or copyright owner of the architectural work, make or authorize the making of alterations to such building, and destroy or authorize the destruction of such building.

§ 201. Ownership of copyright

This statute explains who initially owns the copyright in a work.

(a) **Initial Ownership.**—Copyright in a work protected under this title vests initially in the author or authors of the work. The authors of a joint work are co-owners of copyright in the work.

(b) **Works Made for Hire.**—In the case of a work made for hire, the employer or other person for whom the work was prepared is considered the author for purposes of this title, and, unless the parties have expressly agreed otherwise in a written instrument signed by them, owns all of the rights comprised in the copyright.

§ 204. Execution of transfers of copyright ownership

This statute sets out the requirements for transfers of copyright ownership (assignments).

(a) A transfer of copyright ownership, other than by operation of law, is not valid unless an instrument of conveyance, or a note or memorandum of the transfer, is in writing and signed by the owner of the rights conveyed or such owner's duly authorized agent.

(b) A certificate of acknowledgement is not required for the validity of a transfer, but is prima facie evidence of the execution of the transfer if—

(1) in the case of a transfer executed in the United States, the certificate is issued by a person authorized to administer oaths within the United States; or

(2) in the case of a transfer executed in a foreign country, the certificate is issued by a diplomatic or consular officer of the United States, or by a person authorized to administer oaths whose authority is proved by a certificate of such an officer.

§ 205. Recordation of transfers and other documents

This statute sets out the procedures for recording a copyright transfer and establishes a set of priorities in case of conflicting transfers.

(a) **Conditions for Recordation.**—Any transfer of copyright ownership or other document pertaining to a copyright may be recorded in the Copyright Office if the document filed for recordation bears the actual signature of the person who executed it, or if it is accompanied by a sworn or official certification that it is a true copy of the original, signed document.

(b) **Certificate of Recordation.**—The Register of Copyrights shall, upon receipt of a document as provided by subsection (a) and of the fee provided by section 708, record the document and return it with a certificate of recordation.

(c) **Recordation as Constructive Notice.**—Recordation of a document in the Copyright Office gives all persons constructive notice of the facts stated in the recorded document, but only if—

(1) the document, or material attached to it, specifically identifies the work to which it pertains so that, after the document is indexed by the Register of Copyrights, it would be revealed by a reasonable search under the title or registration number of the work; and

(2) registration has been made for the work.

(d) **Priority Between Conflicting Transfers.**—As between two conflicting transfers, the one executed first prevails if it is recorded, in the manner required to give constructive notice under subsection (c), within one month after its execution in the United States or within two months after its execution outside the United States, or at any time before recordation in such manner of the later transfer. Otherwise the later transfer prevails if recorded first in such manner, and if taken in good faith, for valuable consideration or on the basis of a binding promise to pay royalties, and without notice of the earlier transfer.

(e) **Priority Between Conflicting Transfer of Ownership and Non-exclusive License.**—A non-exclusive license, whether recorded or not, prevails over a conflicting transfer of copyright ownership if the license is evidenced by a written instrument signed by the owner of the rights licensed or such owner's duly authorized agent, and if—

(1) the license was taken before execution of the transfer; or

(2) the license was taken in good faith before recordation of the transfer and without notice of it.

§ 302. Duration of copyright: Works created on or after January 1, 1978

This statute sets out the duration of copyright protection for works created in or after 1978. The duration depends on the date of creation or the date of publication, and on the nature of the authorship. The statute governing the duration of works created before 1978 is not included in this desk reference.

(a) **In General.**—Copyright in a work created on or after January 1, 1978, subsists from its creation and, except as provided by the following subsections, endures for a term consisting of the life of the author and 70 years after the author's death.

(b) **Joint Works.**—In the case of a joint work prepared by two or more authors who did not work for hire, the copyright endures for a term consisting of the life of the last surviving author and 70 years after such last surviving author's death.

(c) **Anonymous Works, Pseudonymous Works, and Works Made for Hire.**—In the case of an anonymous work, a pseudonymous work, or a work made for hire, the copyright endures for a term of 95 years from the year of its first publication, or a term of 120 years from the year of its creation, whichever expires first. If, before the end of such term, the identity of one or more of the authors of an anonymous or pseudonymous work is revealed in the records of a registration made for that work under subsections (a) or (d) of section 408, or in the records provided by this subsection, the copyright in the work endures for the term specified by subsection (a) or (b), based on the life of the author or authors whose identity has been revealed. Any person having an interest in the copyright in an anonymous or pseudonymous work may at any time record, in records to be maintained by the Copyright Office for that purpose, a statement identifying one or more authors of the work; the statement shall also identify the person filing it, the nature of that person's interest, the source of the information recorded, and the particular work affected, and shall comply in form and content with requirements that the Register of Copyrights shall prescribe by regulation.

(d) Records Relating to Death of Authors.—Any person having an interest in a copyright may at any time record in the Copyright Office a statement of the date of death of the author of the copyrighted work, or a statement that the author is still living on a particular date. The statement shall identify the person filing it, the nature of that person's interest, and the source of the information recorded, and shall comply in form and content with requirements that the Register of Copyrights shall prescribe by regulation. The Register shall maintain current records of information relating to the death of authors of copyrighted works, based on such recorded statements and, to the extent the Register considers practicable, on data contained in any of the records of the Copyright Office or in other reference sources.

(e) Presumption as to Author's Death.—After a period of 95 years from the year of first publication of a work, or a period of 120 years from the year of its creation, whichever expires first, any person who obtains from the Copyright Office a certified report that the records provided by subsection (d) disclose nothing to indicate that the author of the work is living, or died less than 70 years before, is entitled to the benefit of a presumption that the author has been dead for at least 70 years. Reliance in good faith upon this presumption shall be a complete defense to any action for infringement under this title.

§ 401. Notice of copyright: Visually perceptible copies

This statute explains the proper form for a copyright notice, as well as when, where and why a copyright notice should be placed on a work of expression.

(a) General Provisions.—Whenever a work protected under this title is published in the United States or elsewhere by authority of the copyright owner, a notice of copyright as provided by this section may be placed on publicly distributed copies from which the work can be visually perceived, either directly or with the aid of a machine or device.

(b) Form of Notice.—If a notice appears on the copies, it shall consist of the following three elements:

(1) the symbol © (the letter C in a circle), or the word "Copyright," or the abbreviation "Copr."; and

(2) the year of first publication of the work; in the case of compilations or derivative works incorporating previously published material, the year date of first publication of the compilation or derivative work is sufficient. The year date may be omitted where a pictorial, graphic, or sculptural work, with accompanying text matter, if any, is reproduced in or on greeting cards, postcards, stationery, jewelry, dolls, toys, or any useful articles; and

(3) the name of the owner of copyright in the work, or an abbreviation by which the name can be recognized, or a generally known alternative designation of the owner.

(c) Position of Notice.—The notice shall be affixed to the copies in such manner and location as to give reasonable notice of the claim of copyright. The Register of Copyrights shall prescribe by regulation, as examples, specific methods of affixation and positions of the notice on various types of works that will satisfy this requirement, but these specifications shall not be considered exhaustive.

(d) Evidentiary Weight of Notice.—If a notice of copyright in the form and position specified by this section appears on the published copy or copies to which a defendant in a copyright infringement suit had access, then no weight shall be given to such a defendant's interposition of a defense based on innocent infringement in mitigation of actual or statutory damages, except as provided in the last sentence of section 504(c)(2).

§ 402. Notice of copyright: Phonorecords of sound recordings

This statute governs how, when, where and why to place a copyright notice on a phonorecord (the media on which sounds are fixed for the purpose of distribution essentially, and reproduction).

(a) **General Provisions.**—Whenever a sound recording protected under this title is published in the United States or elsewhere by authority of the copyright owner, a notice of copyright as provided by this section may be placed on publicly distributed phonorecords of the sound recording.

(b) **Form of Notice.**—If a notice appears on the phonorecords, it shall consist of the following three elements:

(1) the symbol ℗ (the letter P in a circle); and

(2) the year of first publication of the sound recording; and

(3) the name of the owner of copyright in the sound recording, or an abbreviation by which the name can be recognized, or a generally known alternative designation of the owner; if the producer of the sound recording is named on the phonorecord labels or containers, and if no other name appears in conjunction with the notice, the producer's name shall be considered a part of the notice.

(c) **Position of Notice.**—The notice shall be placed on the surface of the phonorecord, or on the phonorecord label or container, in such manner and location as to give reasonable notice of the claim of copyright.

(d) **Evidentiary Weight of Notice.**—If a notice of copyright in the form and position specified by this section appears on the published phonorecord or phonorecords to which a defendant in a copyright infringement suit had access, then no weight shall be given to such a defendant's interposition of a defense based on innocent infringement in mitigation of actual or statutory damages, except as provided in the last sentence of section 504(c)(2).

§ 405. Notice of copyright: Omission of notice on certain copies and phonorecords

This statute describes the legal consequences of failing to put a valid copyright notice on a published work. The consequences are different for works published before and after March 1, 1989.

(a) **Effect of Omission on Copyright.**—With respect to copies and phonorecords publicly distributed by authority of the copyright owner before the effective date of the Berne Convention Implementation Act of 1988, the omission of the copyright notice described in sections 401 through 403 from copies or phonorecords publicly distributed by authority of the copyright owner does not invalidate the copyright in a work if—

(1) the notice has been omitted from no more than a relatively small number of copies or phonorecords distributed to the public; or

(2) registration for the work has been made before or is made within five years after the publication without notice, and a reasonable effort is made to add notice to all copies or phonorecords that are distributed to the public in the United States after the omission has been discovered; or

(3) the notice has been omitted in violation of an express requirement in writing that, as a condition of the copyright owner's authorization of the public distribution of copies or phonorecords, they bear the prescribed notice.

(b) **Effect of Omission on Innocent Infringers.**—Any person who innocently infringes a copyright, in reliance upon an authorized copy or phonorecord from which the copyright notice has been omitted and which was publicly distributed by authority of the copyright owner before the effective date of the Berne Convention Implementation Act of 1988, incurs no liability for actual or statutory damages under section 504 for any infringing acts committed before receiving actual notice that registration for the work has been made under section 408, if such person proves that he or she was misled by the omission of notice. In a suit for infringement in such a case the court may allow or disallow recovery of any of the infringer's profits attributable to the infringement, and may enjoin the continuation of the infringing undertaking or may require, as a condition of permitting the continuation of the infringing undertaking, that the infringer pay the copyright owner a reasonable license fee in an amount and on terms fixed by the court.

(c) **Removal of Notice.**—Protection under this title is not affected by the removal, destruction, or obliteration of the notice, without the authorization of the copyright owner, from any publicly distributed copies or phonorecords.

§ 407. Deposit of copies or phonorecords for Library of Congress

This statute covers requirements for depositing a published work with the Library of Congress, which is done through the U.S. Copyright Office.

(a) Except as provided by subsection (c), and subject to the provisions of subsection (e), the owner of copyright or of the exclusive right of publication in a work published in the United States shall deposit, within three months after the date of such publication—

   (1) two complete copies of the best edition; or

   (2) if the work is a sound recording, two complete phonorecords of the best edition, together with any printed or other visually perceptible material published with such phonorecords.

Neither the deposit requirements of this subsection nor the acquisition provisions of subsection (e) are conditions of copyright protection.

(b) The required copies or phonorecords shall be deposited in the Copyright Office for the use or disposition of the Library of Congress. The Register of Copyrights shall, when requested by the depositor and upon payment of the fee prescribed by section 708, issue a receipt for the deposit.

(c) The Register of Copyrights may by regulation exempt any categories of material from the deposit requirements of this section, or require deposit of only one copy or phonorecord with respect to any categories. Such regulations shall provide either for complete exemption from the deposit requirements of this section, or for alternative forms of deposit aimed at providing a satisfactory archival record of a work without imposing practical or financial hardships on the depositor, where the individual author is the owner of copyright in a pictorial, graphic, or sculptural work and (i) less than five copies of the work have been published, or (ii) the work has been published in a limited edition consisting of numbered copies the monetary value of which would make the mandatory deposit of two copies of the best edition of the work burdensome, unfair, or unreasonable.

(d) At any time after publication of a work as provided by subsection (a), the Register of Copyrights may make written demand for the required deposit on any of the persons obligated to make the deposit under subsection (a). Unless deposit is made within three months after the demand is received, the person or persons on whom the demand was made are liable—

(1) to a fine of not more than $250 for each work; and

(2) to pay into a specially designated fund in the Library of Congress the total retail price of the copies or phonorecords demanded, or, if no retail price has been fixed, the reasonable cost of the Library of Congress of acquiring them; and

(3) to pay a fine of $2,500, in addition to any fine or liability imposed under clauses (1) and (2), if such person willfully or repeatedly fails or refuses to comply with such a demand.

(e) With respect to transmission programs that have been fixed and transmitted to the public in the United States but have not been published, the Register of Copyrights shall, after consulting with the Librarian of Congress and other interested organizations and officials, establish regulations governing the acquisition, through deposit or otherwise, of copies or phonorecords of such programs for the collections of the Library of Congress.

(1) The Librarian of Congress shall be permitted, under the standards and conditions set forth in such regulations, to make a fixation of a transmission program directly from a transmission to the public, and to reproduce one copy or phonorecord from such fixation for archival purposes.

(2) Such regulations shall also provide standards and procedures by which the Register of Copyrights may make written demand, upon the owner of the right of transmission in the United States, for the deposit of a copy or phonorecord of a specific transmission program. Such deposit may, at the option of the owner of the right of transmission in the United States, be accomplished by gift, by loan for purposes of reproduction, or by sale at a price not to exceed the cost of reproducing and supplying the copy or phonorecord. The regulations established under this clause shall provide reasonable periods of not less than three months for compliance with a demand, and shall allow for extensions of such periods and adjustments in the scope of the demand or the methods for fulfilling it, as reasonably warranted by the circumstances. Willful failure or refusal to comply with the conditions prescribed by such regulations shall subject the owner of the right of transmission in the United States to liability for an amount, not to exceed the cost of reproducing and supplying the copy or phonorecord in question, to be paid into a specially designated fund in the Library of Congress.

(3) Nothing in this subsection shall be construed to require the making or retention, for purposes of deposit, of any copy or phonorecord of an unpublished transmission program, the transmission of which occurs before the receipt of a specific written demand as provided by clause (2).

(4) No activity undertaken in compliance with regulations prescribed under clauses (1) or (2) of this subsection shall result in liability if intended solely to assist in the acquisition of copies or phonorecords under this subsection.

§ 411. Registration and infringement actions

This statute requires, with some exceptions, that a copyright be registered with the U.S. Copyright Office before a lawsuit for copyright infringement may be filed.

(a) Except for an action brought for a violation of the rights of the author under section 106A(a), and subject to the provisions of subsection (b), no action for infringement of the copyright in any work shall be instituted until registration of the copyright claim has been made in accordance with this title. In any case, however, where the deposit, application, and fee required for registration have been delivered to the Copyright Office in proper form and registration has been refused, the applicant is entitled to institute an action for infringement if notice thereof, with a copy of the complaint, is served on the Register of

Copyrights. The Register may, at his or her option, become a party to the action with respect to the issue of registrability of the copyright claim by entering an appearance within sixty days after such service, but the Register's failure to become a party shall not deprive the court of jurisdiction to determine that issue.

(b) In the case of a work consisting of sounds, images, or both, the first fixation of which is made simultaneously with its transmission, the copyright owner may, either before or after such fixation takes place, institute an action for infringement under section 501, fully subject to the remedies provided by sections 502 through 506 and sections 509 and 510, if, in accordance with requirements that the Register of Copyrights shall prescribe by regulation, the copyright owner—

   (1) serves notice upon the infringer, not less than ten or more than thirty days before such fixation, identifying the work and the specific time and source of its first transmission, and declaring an intention to secure copyright in the work; and

   (2) makes registration for the work, if required by subsection (a), within three months after its first transmission.

§ 412. Registration as prerequisite to certain remedies for infringement

This statute establishes the penalty for failure to timely register a copyright with the U.S. Copyright Office and states when a registration will be considered timely.

In any action under this title, other than an action brought for a violation of the rights of the author under section 106A(a) or an action instituted under section 411(b), no award of statutory damages or of attorney's fees, as provided by sections 504 and 505, shall be made for—

   (1) any infringement of copyright in an unpublished work commenced before the effective date of its registration; or

   (2) any infringement of copyright commenced after first publication of the work and before the effective date of its registration, unless such registration is made within three months after the first publication of the work.

§ 502. Remedies for infringement: Injunctions

This statute authorizes the federal court to order the cessation of any activities that constitute copyright infringement.

(a) Any court having jurisdiction of a civil action arising under this title may, subject to the provisions of section 1498 of title 28, grant temporary and final injunctions on such terms as it may deem reasonable to prevent or restrain infringement of a copyright.

(b) Any such injunction may be served anywhere in the United States on the person enjoined; it shall be operative throughout the United States and shall be enforceable, by proceedings in contempt or otherwise, by any United States court having jurisdiction of that person. The clerk of the court granting the injunction shall, when requested by any other court in which enforcement of the injunction is sought, transmit promptly to the other court a certified copy of all the papers in the case on file in such clerk's office.

§ 503. Remedies for infringement: Impounding and disposition of infringing articles

This statute allows the court to order the seizure of any articles that are alleged to infringe a copyright (in a lawsuit). If the court finds in a final judgment that infringement occurred, it may order that the articles be destroyed.

(a) At any time while an action under this title is pending, the court may order the impounding, on such terms as it may deem reasonable, of all copies or phonorecords claimed to have been made, or used in violation of the copyright's owner's exclusive rights, and of all plates, molds, matrices, masters, tapes, film negatives, or other articles by means of which such copies or phonorecords may be reproduced.

(b) As part of a final judgment or decree, the court may order the destruction or other reasonable disposition of all copies or phonorecords found to have been made or used in violation of the copyright owner's exclusive rights, and of all plates, molds, matrices, masters, tapes, film negatives, or other articles by means of which such copies or phonorecords may be reproduced.

§ 504. Remedies for infringement: Damages and profits

This statute describes the types of money damages that a court may award a copyright owner in a copyright infringement lawsuit: normally either actual damages and profits or statutory damages. It also addresses damages awarded against innocent infringers.

(a) **In General.**—Except as otherwise provided by this title, an infringer of copyright is liable for either—

    (1) the copyright owner's actual damages and any additional profits of the infringer, as provided by subsection (b); or

    (2) statutory damages, as provided by subsection (c).

(b) **Actual Damages and Profits.**—The copyright owner is entitled to recover the actual damages suffered by him or her as a result of the infringement, and any profits of the infringer that are attributable to the infringement and are not taken into account in computing the actual damages. In establishing the infringer's profits, the copyright owner is required to present proof only of the infringer's gross revenue, and the infringer is required to prove his or her deductible expenses and the elements of profit attributable to factors other than the copyrighted work.

(c) **Statutory Damages.**—

    (1) Except as provided by clause (2) of this subsection, the copyright owner may elect, at any time before final judgment is rendered, to recover, instead of actual damages and profits, an award of statutory damages for all infringements involved in the action, with respect to any one work, for which any one infringer is liable individually, or for which any two or more infringers are liable jointly and severally, in a sum of not less than $750 or more than $30,000 as the court considers just. For the purposes of this subsection, all the parts of a compilation or derivative work constitute one work.

    (2) In a case where the copyright owner sustains the burden of proving, and the court finds, that infringement was committed willfully, the court in its discretion may increase the award of statutory damages to a sum of not more than $150,000. In a case where the infringer sustains the burden of proving, and the court finds, that such infringer was not aware and had no reason to believe that his or her acts constituted an infringement of copyright, the court in its discretion may reduce the award of statutory damages to a sum of not less than $200. The court shall remit statutory damages in any case where an infringer believed and had reasonable grounds for believing that his or her use of the copyrighted work was a fair use under section 107, if the infringer was: (i) an employee or agent of a nonprofit educational institution, library, or archives acting within the scope of his or her employment who, or such institution, library, or archives itself, which infringed by reproducing the work in copies or phonorecords; or (ii) a public broadcasting entity which or a person who, as a regular part of the nonprofit activities of a public broadcasting entity (as defined in subsection (g) of section 118) infringed by

performing a published nondramatic literary work or by reproducing a transmission program embodying a performance of such a work.

(d) **Additional damages in certain cases.**—In any case in which the court finds that a defendant proprietor of an establishment who claims as a defense that its activities were exempt under section 110(5) did not have reasonable grounds to believe that its use of a copyrighted work was exempt under such section, the plaintiff shall be entitled to, in addition to any award of damages under this section, an additional award of two times the amount of the license fee that the proprietor of the establishment concerned should have paid the plaintiff for such use during the preceding period of up to 3 years.

§ 505. Remedies for infringement: Costs and attorney's fees

This statute authorizes a court to:

- *award full costs to a party in an infringement lawsuit, and*
- *award attorney's fees to the prevailing party as part of the costs.*

In any civil action under this title, the court in its discretion may allow the recovery of full costs by or against any party other than the United States or an officer thereof. Except as otherwise provided by this title, the court may also award a reasonable attorney's fee to the prevailing party as part of the costs.

§ 506. Criminal offenses

This statute authorizes criminal penalties for certain types of copyright infringement and establishes fines for certain dishonest copyright-related activities.

(a) **Criminal Infringement.**—Any person who infringes a copyright willfully either—
　(1) for purposes of commercial advantage or private financial gain, or
　(2) by the reproduction or distribution, including by electronic means, during any 180-day period, of 1 or more copies or phonorecords of 1 or more copyrighted works, which have a total retail value of more than $1,000,
　　shall be punished as provided under section 2319 of title 18, United States Code. For purposes of this subsection, evidence of reproduction or distribution of a copyrighted work, by itself, shall not be sufficient to establish willful infringement.

(b) **Forfeiture and Destruction.**—When any person is convicted of any violation of subsection (a), the court in its judgment of conviction shall, in addition to the penalty therein prescribed, order the forfeiture and destruction or other disposition of all infringing copies or phonorecords and all implements, devices, or equipment used in the manufacture of such infringing copies or phonorecords.

(c) **Fraudulent Copyright Notice.**—Any person who, with fraudulent intent, places on any article a notice of copyright or words of the same purport that such person knows to be false, or who, with fraudulent intent, publicly distributes or imports for public distribution any article bearing such notice or words that such person knows to be false, shall be fined not more than $2,500.

(d) **Fraudulent Removal of Copyright Notice.**—Any person who, with fraudulent intent, removes or alters any notice of copyright appearing on a copy of a copyrighted work shall be fined not more than $2,500.

(e) **False Representation.**—Any person who knowingly makes a false representation of a material fact in the application for copyright registration provided for by section 409, or in any written statement filed in connection with the application, shall be fined not more than $2,500.

(f) **Rights of Attribution and Integrity.**—Nothing in this section applies to infringement of the rights conferred by section 106A(a).

§ 507. Limitations on actions

This statute governs the time limit within which criminal and civil copyright lawsuit can be filed.

(a) **Criminal proceedings.**—Except as expressly provided otherwise in this title, no criminal proceeding shall be maintained under the provisions of this title unless it is commenced within 5 years after the cause of action arose.

(b) **Civil actions.**—No civil action shall be maintained under the provisions of this title unless it is commenced within three years after the claim accrued.

Part 3

Patent Law

The basic concept underlying patents is very simple. Patents allow the creator of certain kinds of inventions that contain new ideas to keep others from making commercial use of those ideas without the creator's permission. This right of control over the idea lasts between 14 and 20 years, depending on the type of invention.

1. What is a patent?

A patent is a document issued by the U.S. Patent and Trademark Office (PTO) that grants a monopoly for a limited period of time on the use and development of an invention which the PTO finds to qualify for patent protection.

Related terms: co-inventors; in-force patent; invention, defined; inventor, defined; patent, defined; patent attorneys; patent deed; patent owner; senior party in interference proceedings; shop rights.

2. How do inventors benefit by holding a patent?

Most inventors do not themselves develop the invention covered by a patent. Rather, they make arrangements with an existing company to do this for them. Typically, the arrangement takes the form of a license (contract) under which the developer is authorized to commercially exploit the invention in exchange for paying the patent owner royalties for each invention sold.

A license may be exclusive (only one manufacturer is licensed to develop the invention) or non-exclusive (a number of manufacturers are licensed to develop it). The license may be for the duration of the patent or for a shorter period of time. Sometimes the patent is sold outright to the developer for a lump sum up front.

The developer itself may license other companies to market or distribute the invention. The extent to which the inventor will benefit from these sublicenses depends on the terms of the agreement between the inventor and the developer. Especially when inventions result from work done in the course of employment, the employer-business usually ends up owning the patent rights, and receives all or most of the royalties based on subsequent licensing activity.

These distribution licenses are often limited by geography (for instance, different licenses for different countries or for different parts of one country) and by use. In many cases, the developer will trade licenses with other companies—called cross-licensing—so that companies involved in the trade will benefit from each other's technology.

Related terms: anti-shelving clause; anti-trust law (federal) and patents; assignment of a patent; compulsory licensing of a patent; concerted refusal to deal; cross-licensing; defensive disclosure; exclusive patent license; geographic patent license; licensing of an invention; march-in rights;

marking of an invention; misuse of patent; non-exclusive patent license; not invented here (NIH) syndrome; patent number; patent pools; price fixing; working a patent.

3. What kinds of patents may be issued?

The U.S. Patent and Trademark Office (PTO) issues three different kinds of patents:

- utility patents. Useful inventions may qualify for a utility patent if they fit into at least one of these five categories: a process, a machine, a manufacture, a composition of matter or an improvement of an existing idea that falls into one of these categories. Often, an invention that qualifies for a patent because of its usefulness will fall into more than one of the categories. For instance, computer software can usually be described both as a process (the steps that it takes to make the computer do something) and as a machine (a device that takes information from an input device and moves it to an output device). Regardless of the number of categories an invention falls under, only one utility patent may be issued on it.
- design patents. To qualify for a patent under the design test, a design must be innovative, nonfunctional and part of a functional manufactured article. For example, a new shape for a car fender, bottle or flashlight that doesn't improve its functionality would qualify.
- plant patents. Patents may be issued for any asexually or sexually reproducible plants (such as flowers) that are both novel and nonobvious. Plant patents are the least frequently issued type of patent.

Related terms: combination patent; composition of matter; design patents; improvement inventions; machines as patentable subject matter; manufactures as patentable subject matter; new-use invention; non-statutory subject matter; operability; patentability; plant patents; processes (or methods) as patentable subject matter; public domain; public use; software patents; statutory bar; statutory subject matter; utility patents, defined.

4. What types of inventions qualify for a patent?

Most types of inventions (the term we'll use for innovative ideas) qualify for a patent if they offer something new (are novel) and are particularly clever (that is, nonobvious). However, some types of inventions do not qualify for a patent, no matter how nonobvious they are. For instance, mathematical formulas, newly discovered laws of nature and newly discovered substances that occur naturally in the world traditionally have been considered to be unpatentable.

When deciding whether an invention qualifies for a patent, the U.S. Patent and Trademark Office (PTO) first must determine whether the invention was novel in some way—that is, a new development in at least one or more of its constituent

Overview

elements—as of the date the inventor conceived it or when the patent application was filed.

If the PTO determines that the invention was novel, it then must make another more difficult decision: was the invention nonobvious? To make this determination, the PTO asks this question: Would someone who was skilled in the particular field as of the invention date consider the invention to be an unexpected or surprising development?

If the invention is found to be both novel and nonobvious, and it fits within one or more of the five statutory categories discussed earlier (question 3, above), it may qualify to receive a patent.

Among the many types of creative works that might qualify for a patent are: biological inventions; carpet designs; new chemical formulas, processes or procedures; clothing accessories and designs; computer hardware and peripherals; computer software; containers; cosmetics; decorative hardware; electrical inventions; electronic circuits; fabrics; fabric designs; food inventions; furniture design; games (board, box and instructions); housewares; jewelry; laser light shows; machines; magic tricks or techniques; mechanical inventions; medical accessories and devices; medicines; musical instruments; odors; plants; recreational gear; sporting goods (designs and equipment).

Related terms: algorithms; anticipation; building and testing an invention; classification of patents; design around; exhibiting an unpatented invention; experimental use of an unpatented invention; field of invention; fully met by a prior art reference; genetic engineering and patents; *Graham v. John Deere* case; Internet, U.S. Patent and Trademark Office site; laws of nature exception to patents; naturally occurring substances as nonpatentable; nonobviousness, defined; novelty, defined; obviousness, defined; on sale statutory bar; one-year rule; Patent and Trademark Depository Library; patent search; patent search, computerized; patent searcher; patentability search; patents as prior art; person with ordinary skill in the art; preliminary look at prior art; printed publication as statutory bar; prior art, defined; prior art reference; Software Patent Institute; Statutory Invention Registration (SIR); submarine patent; teach; thesis as prior art.

5. What is the procedure for applying for a patent?

There is no such thing as an automatic patent through creation or usage of an invention; the inventor must file an application (and pay a filing fee) and be issued a patent. To apply for a U.S. patent, the inventor files an application with a branch of the U.S. Department of Commerce, known as the U.S. Patent and Trademark Office (PTO).

For the purpose of obtaining an early filing date, the inventor may file what is known as a Preliminary Patent Application (PPA). The only requirement for a PPA is that it must adequately describe the invention. However, to obtain a patent, the

inventor must file a formal patent application (within one year of the PPA date if one is filed) that follows technical conventions and contains words and drawings to clearly:

- teach how to make and use the basic invention
- explain why the invention is different from all previous and similar developments (known as the prior art), and
- precisely describe what aspects of the invention deserve the patent (the patent claims).

This patent application will be the subject of much push and pull between the applicant and the patent examiner employed by the PTO to screen it.

Related terms: abandonment of patent; abstract; application filing fees; certificate of correction; claims, defined; confidentiality of patent application; dependent claim; disclosure requirement for patents; drawings, patent application; duty of candor and good faith; enabling disclosure; fraud on the U.S. Patent and Trademark Office; group art unit; independent claim; Information Disclosure Statement; large entity; limiting reference; means plus function clause; multiple claims; new matter; patent agents; patent applicant; patent application; Patent Application Declaration (PAD); Provisional Patent Application (PPA); read on; recite; small entity; specification, defined.

6. What happens if there are multiple applications for the same invention?

If the patent examiner discovers that another pending application involves the same invention, and that both inventions appear to qualify for a patent, the patent examiner will declare that a conflict (called an interference) exists between the two applications. In that event, a hearing is held to determine who is entitled to the patent. Affidavits or declarations are submitted and often live testimony is taken.

Who may be awarded the patent depends on such variables as who first conceived of the invention and worked on it diligently, who first actually built and tested the invention and who filed the first provisional or regular patent application.

Related terms: constructive reduction to practice; diligence in reducing to practice; Disclosure Document Program (DDP); filing date; infringement search; interference, defined; interference proceeding; junior party in interference proceedings; patent notebook; reduction to practice; reexamination of patent; swearing behind a prior art reference.

7. Under what circumstances is a patent application approved?

Once a patent application is received by the U.S. Patent and Trademark Office (PTO), a patent examiner is assigned to the application. He or she is responsible for deciding whether the application meets all technical requirements, whether the invention qualifies for a patent and, assuming it does, what the scope of the patent should be.

Usually, back and forth communications occur between the applicant and the examiner regarding these issues. Typically this takes between one and three years and involves significant amendments by the applicant. The most serious and difficult issue to fix is whether the invention qualifies for a patent in light of previous developments—that is, whether the invention is novel and nonobvious in light of the prior art.

Eventually, if the examiner's objections are overcome by the applicant, the invention is approved for a patent. Then, the applicant pays a patent issue fee ($355 for independent inventors, nonprofit corporations and for-profit corporations with fewer than 500 employees or $710 for for-profit companies with 500 or more employees; current as of October 1, 2000), and receives an official (ribboned) copy of the patent.

To keep a patent in effect, three additional fees must be paid over the life of the patent. The total patent fee for a small inventor, from application to issue to expiration, is approximately $3,000 (current as of October 1, 2000). For large corporations, it is twice this amount.

Overview

Related terms: allowance; amendment of patent application; Board of Appeals; Board of Patent Appeals and Interferences; Board of Patent Interferences; CCPA (Court of Customs and Patent Appeals); Director of the U.S. Patent and Trademark Office; continuation application; continuation-in-part application (CIP); divisional application; double patenting; file wrapper; final office action; first office action; grant of patent; issue fee; Manual of Patent Examining Procedure (MPEP); narrowing a claim; nonelected claims; notice of allowance; notice of references cited; office action; Official Gazette (OG); parent application; patent examiners; patent pending; prosecution of a patent application; reconsideration request; reissue patent; shotgun rejection of claims; substitute patent application; supplemental declaration.

8. How are patent rights enforced?

Once a patent is granted, the owner may enforce it by bringing a patent infringement action (lawsuit) against anyone who uses the invention without the patent owner's permission. Normally, when a patent infringement action is filed, the alleged infringer counters by attacking the validity of the patent. Patents may be held invalid on a number of grounds, such as fraud on the U.S. Patent and Trademark Office during the application period; a violation of the anti-trust laws that curb restraints of trade and monopolistic practices; or—as is most common—if an alleged infringer can show that the invention really wasn't novel or nonobvious, that the patent examiner simply made a mistake in issuing the patent.

Assuming, however, that the patent is upheld, the court will take one of two approaches. It may issue a court order (injunction) preventing the infringer from any further use or sale of the infringing device and award damages to the patent owner. The court may instead work with the parties to hammer out an agreement under which the infringing party will pay the patent owner royalties in exchange for permission to use the infringing device.

Related terms: admissions by inventor; breaking a patent; contributory infringement of patent; Court of Appeals for the Federal Circuit (CAFC); declaratory judgment of non-infringement, invalidity and unenforceability of patent; defenses to a patent infringement claim; doctrine of equivalents; file wrapper estoppel; infringement action; infringement of patent; intervening right; lay judge; negative doctrine of equivalents; presumption of validity; smart money; statute of limitations, infringement action; validity search.

9. When does a patent expire or otherwise come to an end?

The most common reason for a patent to come to an end is that the statutory period during which it is in force expires. For utility and plant patents, the statutory period is 20 years after the application date (21 years after the Provisional Patent Application date if one is filed). For design patents, the statutory period is 14 years from date of issuance.

Another common reason why patents expire is that the patent owner fails to pay required maintenance fees. Usually this occurs because attempts to commercially exploit the underlying invention have failed and the patent owner chooses not to throw good money after bad.

A patent may also be declared invalid (and no longer in force) if it is later shown that the patent application was insufficient, that the applicant committed fraud on the U.S. Patent and Trademark Office (usually by lying about or failing to disclose the applicant's knowledge about prior art that would legally preclude issuance of the patent), or that the inventor engaged in illegal conduct when using the patent—such as conspiring with a patent licensee to exclude other companies from competing with them.

Once a patent has expired for any reason, the invention described by the patent falls into the public domain: it can be used by anyone without permission and the patent owner has no more rights to the invention than any member of the public. The basic technologies underlying television and personal computers are good examples of valuable inventions that are no longer covered by in-force patents.

The fact that an invention is in the public domain does not mean that subsequent developments based on the original invention are also in the public domain. Rather, new inventions that improve public domain technology are constantly being conceived and patented. For instance, televisions and personal computers that roll off today's assembly lines employ many recent inventions that are covered by in-force patents.

Related terms: duration of patents; maintenance fees; patent term extension.

10. What about international protection for U.S. patents?

The right to control, or monopolize, an invention that a patent owner enjoys in the U.S. originates in the U.S. Constitution and is implemented exclusively by federal laws passed by Congress. These laws define the kinds of inventions that are patentable and the procedures that must be utilized to apply for, receive and maintain the patent in full force for its entire period.

All other industrialized countries also offer inventors protection in the form of a patent. While the standards of what is patentable and the period that patents last differ from country to country, several international treaties (including the Patent Cooperation Treaty and the Paris Convention) allow U.S. inventors to obtain patent protection in these other countries if they take certain required steps, such as filing a patent application in the countries on a timely basis and paying required patent fees.

Related terms: Convention application; European Patent Convention; Federal Trade Commission proceeding; first to file countries; first to invent countries; GATT (General Agreement on Tariffs and Trade); International Bureau of the World Intellectual Property Organization; international patent protection for U.S. inventions ; opposing a patent (international rules); Patent Cooperation Treaty (PCT); Plant Variety Protection Act; Title 35 of the United States Code; U.S. Patent and Trademark Office (PTO); utility model; World Trade Organization (WTO).

11. Patent resources

If you're interested in hands-on, step-by-step instructions on applying for a patent, you may want to consult one of these Nolo resources:

- *Patent It Yourself*, by David Pressman
- *The Patent Drawing Book*, by Jack Lo and David Pressman
- *The Inventor's Notebook*, by Fred Grissom and David Pressman
- *License Your Invention*, by Richard Stim
- *Patent Searching Made Easy*, by David Hitchcock, and
- *Nolo's Patents for Beginners*, by David Pressman and Richard Stim.

A detailed description of these resources is provided in the Introduction, Section C. (Order information is at the back of this book.)

If you have access to the World Wide Web, you may find valuable information related to patents in the following sites:

1) **Nolo at http://www.nolo.com.** Nolo offers self-help information about a wide variety of legal topics, including patent law. (See the intellectual property topic in the Legal Encyclopedia, which incidentally includes selected entries from this part of the book.)

2) **The U.S. Patent and Trademark Office at http://www.uspto.gov.** This is the place to go for recent policy and statutory changes and transcripts of hearings on various patent law issues. You may also use this site to conduct a search of of patents issued since 1971.

3) **IBM's Intellectual Property Network at http://www.patents.ibm.com.** This site offers free patent searching for patents issued since 1971.

4) **Software Patent Institute at http://www.spi.org.** This site lets you search for previous software developments that may affect whether a particular software item qualifies for a patent.

Overview

Patent Law

B elow are definitions of the words and phrases commonly used in patent-related activities.

abandonment of patent

The U.S. Patent and Trademark Office (PTO) considers a patent application abandoned if the applicant fails to respond in a timely manner to actions or requests initiated by the PTO.

The PTO's response to most patent applications is to send the applicant a notice (called an office action), rejecting one or more aspects of the application. The applicant must then amend the application—usually the claims, which are precise descriptions of the invention—or provide some other suitable response within three months to keep the application alive.

In the event an application is treated by the PTO as abandoned, the applicant may:

- petition the director of the PTO to set aside the abandonment decision
- file a substitute application—which means paying additional fees and being given a later filing date (harmful if another applicant files an application for a similar invention between the first and second filing dates), or
- forget about the patent and utilize another available method of protection such as trade secrecy or trademark (that is, you can use a clever name for the invention to capture market share, such as "pet rock").

Related terms: claims, defined; prosecution of a patent application; substitute patent application.

abstract

This paragraph in the patent application concisely summarizes the general nature, structure and purpose of the invention. When a patent is issued, the abstract appears on the front page of the patent.

Related terms: Official Gazette (OG); patent application.

actual reduction to practice

See reduction to practice.

admissions by inventor

Statements by an inventor about his or her invention may be used by the U.S. Patent and Trademark Office (PTO) to reject a patent application or cause a court to rule against the invention's validity. An inventor should never write anything in a patent application or in correspondence with the PTO that derogates the invention, since the statement will constitute an admission that can later be introduced by the PTO or by a competitor to fight the patent.

Related terms: certificate of correction; duty of candor and good faith; file wrapper estoppel.

algorithms

An algorithm is a mathematical procedure that can be used to solve a problem or class of problems. Common examples of algorithms are mathematical formulas, geometry axioms and algebraic equations. Algorithms as such are not patentable because the patent would create a huge and fundamental monopoly over laws of nature.

EXAMPLE: The Heisenberg uncertainty principle, a well-known law of nature, states that you cannot design an apparatus to simultaneously determine the location and momentum of a subatomic particle. This principle is relevant to many scientific and electrical engineering applications, thus a patent on it would give exclusive control of the development of these applications to the owner of the patent. Effectively, a patent on the Heisenberg uncertainty principle would either halt progress in any field where the principle applies, or force all would-be developers to pay license fees to the patent holder.

Until recently, the rule against patenting algorithms was applied to computer software, because software largely consists of procedural instructions in mathematical form that make a computer accomplish a certain and definite result. Now, however, the U.S. Patent and Trademark Office will allow patents on that aspect of software that accomplishes a useful, concrete and tangible result.

Related terms: laws of nature exception to patents; software patents.
See also Part 2 (Copyright Law: computer software, copyright of).

allowance

The decision by the U.S. Patent and Trademark Office (PTO) to award a patent
to an applicant is referred to as an allowance (the application is "allowed"). The
applicant is sent a notice of allowance by the PTO; this usually occurs after the
initial claims were amended at least once during the prosecution of the patent
application.

Related terms: certificate of correction; prosecution of a patent application.

amendment of patent application

A patent application may be amended (changed) in response to an initial rejection
by the U.S. Patent and Trademark Office. Patent examiners often reject the initial
application as filed, most commonly because the scope of the patent being
applied for is too broad in light of previous developments in that field (the prior
art). Other common reasons for rejection are noncompliance with certain rules
governing how the invention must be described in words or portrayed in drawings.

This initial rejection includes an explanation and copies of any patents that
seem very similar (called prior art references) and have contributed to the
rejection. Upon receiving a rejection, an applicant usually files an amendment, in
one part changing the application in accordance with the examiner's requirements
and in the other part contesting such requirements. Alternatiavely, an applicant
may contest the examiner's decisions completely or file an amendment that
completely conforms the application to the examiner's requirements.

Related terms: office action; prosecution of a patent application.

anticipation

An invention is said to be anticipated when it is too similar to an earlier invention
to be considered novel. Because novelty is a requirement for patentability,
anticipated inventions are not patentable.

An invention may be anticipated in any of the following ways:

- *prior publication in such writings as a news article, trade journal article,
  academic thesis or prior patent.* For example, Fred Jones invents a low-cost
  kit that permits a car's driver to monitor ten different engine functions
  while driving. If all of the primary characteristics (elements) of this kit had
  been described by someone else in a publication or patent before Fred
  invented his kit, the invention would be considered anticipated by the
  published reference, and would be barred from receiving a patent.

Definitions

- *by existence of a prior invention, if all significant elements of the later invention are found in an earlier one prior to the date of invention or the application's filing date.* Suppose Sammy "invents" an electric generator that is driven by the kinetic energy of a car's moving wheels. If all basic elements used by Sammy in his "invention" can be found in a prior invention (whether patented or not) by Jake, who used his invention openly—without suppressing or concealing it—Sammy's generator has been anticipated.
- *by placing the invention on sale more than one year prior to an application's being filed.* "On sale" means not only an actual sale, but any offer of sale. For example, if Sammy offers to sell his invention to a major car manufacturer more than one year previous to his filing a patent application on it, the offer will anticipate the invention even if the sale never takes place.
- *by public use or display of the invention more than a year prior to filing the patent application.* For example, if Fred publicly demonstrated his kit a year or more prior to filing for a patent, the invention would be considered "anticipated" because the earlier public display would render the invention no longer "novel" at the time of filing the application. However, if the public demonstrations were predominately for experimental purposes, the one-year period might not apply. In fact, anticipation through public use or display rarely occurs.

Anticipation by a prior invention or printed publication—that is, a prior art reference—can only occur if all of the later invention's basic elements are contained in a single invention or a single publication. For example, if a news article describes some elements of an invention, and a prior invention shows the rest, no anticipation has occurred, because no single reference contained all the elements.

Related terms: novelty, defined; printed publication as statutory bar; prior art reference; public use.

anti-shelving clause

This provision in a licensing agreement makes permission to use a patented invention contingent on the willingness of the party receiving the license to use the patent commercially within a designated period of time (rather than "putting it on the shelf"). For obvious reasons, this type of provision is especially important when a license is granted in exchange for the payment of royalties based on the number of products sold.

antitrust law (federal) and patents

Federal antitrust laws generally prohibit businesses from engaging in monopolistic activities—that is, to engage in practices purposely designed to give the business dominant control over a particular market segment. However, by definition, a patent is a legal monopoly over the production, use and distribution of an invention. In an attempt to reconcile these conflicting legal goals, the U.S. (and most countries) restricts the ways companies holding patents may use them in the marketplace.

In addition to preventing monopolistic activities, antitrust laws prohibit business practices that restrain the free flow of commerce (called restraint of trade). Among the more common types of patent-related activity that may potentially cause antitrust violations are:

- price fixing—for example, a patent owner requiring licensees of a patent to charge certain prices for goods manufactured under the patent
- exclusive dealing agreements—for example, a patent owner encouraging patent licensees not to deal with certain customers
- "tying agreements"—that is, requiring a customer who wishes to purchase the patented invention to also purchase other goods or services as a condition of the purchase. For instance, putting a provision in a license agreement that requires the licensee of a mainframe computer to use the licensor to service the computer would tie the purchase of the computer to the purchase of the service
- requirements contracts, whether mandatory or encouraged by price reductions—for example, prohibiting a purchaser of goods covered by a patent from purchasing comparable items from another source
- territorial restrictions—for example, restricting licensees to certain geographical areas in their marketing of goods covered by the patent, and
- concerted refusal to deal—for example, excluding some potential customers from use of the device or process covered by the patent while including others.

Practically speaking, antitrust laws should not be a concern for most patent owners, as few patents have a large enough impact on the related market or industry to raise the antitrust warning flag. If, however, a patent is so broad in its coverage that the actual ebb and flow of commerce might be affected by it, there is no substitute for good knowledge of antitrust law. This is especially true when important inventions are involved in patent infringement lawsuits, because

Definitions

defendants often charge that the plaintiff committed an antitrust violation and therefore cannot enforce the patent.

Related terms: defenses to a patent infringement claim; misuse of patent; price fixing.

appeals

See Board of Patent Appeals and Interferences.

application filing fees

Fees must be paid to file a patent application with the U.S. Patent and Trademark Office. The fees are twice as much for large entities as for small entities. Generally, independent inventors, nonprofit corporations and businesses with fewer than 500 employees qualify for small entity status. However, if an assignment has or will be made by a small entity to a large entity, large entity fees must be paid.

Patent application fees are currently (as of October 1, 2000):

- for utility patents, $710 for large entities and $355 for small entities
- for design patents, $320 for large entities and $160 for small entities, and
- for plant patents, $490 for large entities and $245 for small entities.

Related terms: issue fee.

application issue fees

See issue fee.

assignment of a patent

Because a patent is a type of property, it can be sold (assigned) to others. An assignment is a document that transfers a patent owner's rights in exchange for money payable in a lump sum or royalties on future sales of the invention.

Many inventors assign their invention, either to the company they work for under an employment agreement or, in the case of independent inventors, to outside development or manufacturing companies. These assignments typically transfer ownership of any patent that issues on the invention and may provide for compensation for the inventor, although employed inventors often receive little or no additional compensation because they are getting paid to invent.

Related terms: licensing of an invention; patent owner.

attorney fees, infringement action

See infringement action.

Attorneys and Agents Registered to Practice Before the U.S. Patent and Trademark Office

See patent attorneys.

best mode disclosure requirement

See disclosure requirement for patents.

biotechnology and patents

See genetic engineering and patents.

Board of Appeals

Formerly, this administrative body within the U.S. Patent and Trademark Office handled appeals from decisions by patent examiners to disallow one or more claims in patent applications. Appeals are now handled by the Board of Patent Appeals and Interferences.

Related terms: Board of Patent Appeals and Interferences.

Board of Patent Appeals and Interferences

A tribunal of administrative judges of the U.S. Patent and Trademark Office handles appeals of rejected applications and decides who is entitled to a patent when an interference occurs (when two or more inventors lay claim to the same invention). This administrative body combines the former functions of the Board of Appeals and the Board of Patent Interferences.

Related terms: Court of Appeals for the Federal Circuit (CAFC); final office action; interference, defined; interference proceeding; prosecution of a patent application.

Board of Patent Interferences

Formerly, this administrative body within the U.S. Patent and Trademark Office decided who was entitled to a patent when an interference occurred (when two or more inventors laid claim to the same invention in pending patent applications).

Interference decisions are now handled by the Board of Patent Appeals and Interferences.

Related terms: Board of Patent Appeals and Interferences.

breaking a patent

To break a patent means to establish that an existing patent is invalid or unenforceable because:

- it was improperly issued by the U.S. Patent and Trademark Office in the first place, or
- it was legally misused by the patent owner.

Patents are normally broken in the course of defending against a patent infringement charge brought by the patent owner.

Related terms: antitrust law (federal) and patents; defenses to a patent infringement claim; infringement action; misuse of patent.

building and testing an invention

After conceiving of an invention, an inventor's next step is usually to build and test a working model (called "actually reducing an invention to practice"). Although not necessary to get a patent, building and testing an invention before applying for a patent on it is strongly advised, because a working model will:

- more definitively establish the exact nature of the invention
- make it much easier to describe the invention in the patent application
- help to sell the invention to a company, and
- prove a crucial date in case of an interference or a prior use reference having a date up to one year before the applicant's filing date.

Related terms: experimental use of an unpatented invention; interference, defined; reduction to practice.

business methods as statutory subject matter

For many years it has been assumed that methods of doing business are not patentable subject matter. This assumption has been strained in recent years by the PTO's practice of allowing patents for computer programs that carried out complex business functions. Finally, in the case of *State Street Bank and Trust v. Signature* (CAFC 7/23/98), the Court of Appeals for the Federal Circuit ruled that there is no logical basis for the business methods exception, and that a business method constitutes statutory subject matter if it produces a useful, concrete and tangible result. The business method approved of in the *State Street* case was part of a computer program that facilitates mutual fund investing.

The term "business method patent" has also been used to describe a group of utility patents whose inventions combine software programs and methods of doing business, most of which relate to Internet uses. These are also sometimes referred to as "Internet Patents" and the most well known example is Amazon.com's "One-Click" system, a method that allows a repeat customer to bypass address and credit card data entry forms when placing an online order. (U.S. Pat. No. 5,960,411).

Although the terms "business method patent" and "Internet patent" have been used interchangeably in the media, these patents may deal with mutually exclusive concepts. For example, a patented method of doing business does not have to pertain to an online application. Likewise, a patent for a process used on the Internet may be more accurately described as a software patent than a business method.

Regardless of their categorization, all of these patents seem to have one thing in common: They expand ways of doing business in new technologies. In the six months following the *State Street* ruling, patent filings for software and Internet business methods increased by 40%. In response to the development of these new methods, the PTO created a new classification for such applications: "Data processing: financial, business practice, management or cost/price determination."

Following the *State Street* case, patents have been issued for business methods such as:

- an online shopping rewards program, referred to as the "ClickReward" (U.S. Pat. No. 5,774,870)
- a system that provides financial incentives for citizens to view political messages on the Internet (U.S. Pat. No. 5,855,008)
- an online auction system by which consumers name the price they are willing to pay and the first willing seller gets the sale (also known as "name your price" or as a "reverse auction," U.S. Pat. No. 5,794,207) and
- a process that supposedly blocks the auction practices described in the previous patent (U.S. Pat. No. 5,845,265)

Sometimes a business may have been using a particular business method prior to another company acquiring a patent on that method. For example, if Business A files for a business method patent, but Business B can show that it implemented and commercially used the method publicly more than a year prior to the filing. Business B has a good defense against the patent. This defense was created under a 1999 amendment to the patent law. (35 United States Code, Section 273(b).)

Many critics contend that patent examiners simply do not have the tools and resources to competently investigate whether an Internet business method is novel or nonobvious. One reason that the PTO is ill-equipped is that when determining novelty, patent examiners have traditionally reviewed past patents and other information in the PTO library. Because the Internet revolution is new, this almost guarantees that the PTO will not detect similar Web-based methods and software processes developed recently.

In response to this criticism, the PTO announced in March 2000 that it is adding an additional "layer of review" to business method patent applications and is hiring technology specialists to aid examiners in the areas of finance, e-commerce, insurance and Internet infrastructure.

Related terms: software patents; statutory subject matter.

CCPA (Court of Customs and Patent Appeals)

Formerly, this court handled appeals from determinations by the U.S. Patent and Trademark Office. Appeals are now heard by the Court of Appeals for the Federal Circuit (CAFC).

Related terms: Court of Appeals for the Federal Circuit (CAFC).

certificate of correction

The U.S. Patent and Trademark Office (PTO) issues a certificate of correction form when an inventor wishes to make minor technical or clerical corrections in an application after the PTO has decided to issue the patent. These corrections may not, however, consist of new matter that changes the invention covered by the patent.

Related terms: new matter; prosecution of a patent application.

chemicals as patentable subject matter

See composition of matter.

CIP

See continuation-in-part application (CIP).

claims, defined

Claims are statements included in a patent application that describe (or "recite") the structure of an invention in precise and exact terms, using a long established formal style and precise terminology. Claims serve as a way:

- for the U.S. Patent and Trademark Office (PTO) to determine whether an invention is patentable, and

- for a court to determine whether a patent has been infringed (someone has made, used or sold a patented device without the patent owner's permission).

Most patent applications contain more than one claim, each of which describes the invention from a slightly different viewpoint. Claims may be "independent" (standing on their own) or "dependent" (referring to other claims on which they depend for some or all of their elements). Examples of independent and dependent claims are below.

Each claim must "particularly point out and distinctly claim" the invention for which the patent is being sought. To this end, the PTO requires that each claim be:

- stated in one unit (a sentence fragment which can and almost always does have numerous clauses and subclauses)
- very specific
- clear
- distinct from other claims, and
- consistent with the narrative description of the patent contained in the patent application.

Claims may be broad or narrow in terms of the scope of the invention they address. The greater the scope of the invention defined in the claims (that is, the broader the claims), the wider the reach of the patent. Similarly, the narrower the scope of a patent claim, the more restricted is the reach of the patent—and the easier it is for another inventor to come up with a somewhat similar invention that does not infringe the claim.

EXAMPLE 1: A claim to a new type of writing implement states that the invention is "a hand-held device containing means by which marks may be made on a surface." Because the language of this claim literally reaches every writing implement that ever has been or ever could be manufactured, it would be considered extremely broad. If a patent were issued (extremely unlikely, as discussed below), any subsequent invention that was held by hand and made marks on a surface would infringe the claim and therefore the patent.

EXAMPLE 2: Suppose the inventor of a type of writing implement claims the invention as follows: "A 3-inch by 1/2-inch plastic tube containing liquid and for making an indelible 1/32-inch line on a flat paper surface." If another company makes a 4-inch by 1/4-inch metal tube containing a charcoal substance capable of making variable width lines on any flat surface, the claim is not infringed because it recited very specific elements that are different than the elements of the later invention.

Although broad claims promise to give the inventor more protection, there is a rub: they may preclude the issuance of a patent. To qualify for a patent, an invention must be both novel (different in some way from previous inventions) and nonobvious (produce an unexpected or surprising result). The broader the claims, the more likely that they overlap with previous developments and the greater risk that the invention described in the claims won't be considered novel and nonobvious. (The writing implement discussed above is a good example.) Conversely, narrower claims for an invention provide a greater chance that the invention will be considered novel and nonobvious, because the claims are less likely to overlap with previous developments.

EXAMPLE: The first writing implement claim described earlier was so broad that it clearly read on (described) prior inventions (such as pencil, chalk, pen, quill, crayon). This fact should preclude the issuance of a patent and would make invalid any patent that did issue on the invention described in that claim. The narrower version of the writing implement claim, however, tended to exclude many prior inventions. For instance, by limiting the claim to a liquid means, the claim excluded pencils and chalk. The narrower claim would therefore have a better chance of being considered novel and nonobvious.

Because claims must be narrow enough to distinguish the invention from previous developments, but broad enough to provide meaningful protection, the primary goal of all patent claim drafters is to draft claims as broadly as possible, given the constraints of the state of prior knowledge or art (inventions and developments).

Related terms: dependent claim; independent claim; infringement of patent; limiting reference; means plus function clause; multiple claims; patent application; prior art, defined; specification, defined.

Class Definitions manual

See classification of patents.

classification of patents

The U.S. Patent and Trademark Office (PTO) assigns numbered classes and subclasses to inventions for the purpose of classifying patents issued on them and facilitating retrieval of these patents in the course of a patent search. To conduct a search for prior patents relevant to an invention, one must first determine its proper classification.

Example of Independent and Dependent Claims

Independent Claim	I claim:
	1. A target comprising substrate means and target pattern means formed on one side of said substrate means in a layer substantially covering said one side of said substrate means, said substrate means and said target pattern means being mutually contrasting visually, said substrate means and said target pattern means being arranged such that when struck by a high speed projectile, a substantially larger-than-projectile-size portion of said target pattern means at the projectile's point of impact will be physically separated and remove from the rest of said target pattern means, and a hole, of a size smaller than said removed portion of said target pattern means, will be made in said substrate means, whereby a portion of said substrate means around said hole will be exposed by the impact of said projectile.
Dependent Claims	**2.** The target of claim **1** wherein said substrate means is contrastingly colored to said target pattern means by means of a fluorescent dye.
	3. The target of claim **1** wherein said substrate means comprises a transparent film backed by a layer of material having a contrasting color to said target pattern means.
	4. The target of claim **1** wherein said substrate means comprises an ionomer resin and said target pattern means comprises an ink layer.
	5. The target of claim **4** wherein said ionomer resin is transparent and is backed by layer of material having a contrasting color to said target pattern means.
	6. The target of claim **4** wherein said ionomer resin has a contrasting color to said target pattern means.
	7. The target of claim **1** wherein said substrate means has a target pattern congruent with the target pattern on said target pattern means.
	8. The target of claim **7** wherein said substrate means comprises a transparent film backed by a layer of material having contrasting color to said target pattern means, said congruent target pattern being formed on said layer of material.
	9. The target of claim **8** wherein said layer of material is paper which is dyed with a brightly-colored fluorescent ink.
	10. The target of claim **1** wherein said target pattern means comprises at least one substantially larger-than-bullet-size flat member adhesively secured to said substrate means.
	11. The target of claim **1** wherein said target pattern means comprises a mosaic of substantially larger-than-bullet-size flat members adhesively secured to and covering said substrate means and carries a target pattern thereon.

There are roughly 300 main classes, and an average of more than 200 sub-classes under each main class. An invention will fall within at least one of the 66,000 separate classifications, and sometimes several.

Fortunately, the PTO publishes resources, available at the PTO website (www.upto.gov) and in all patent and trademark depository libraries, to help a patent searcher find the correct classification(s):

- *Index of U.S. Patent Classification.* All 66,000 categories (classes and sub-classes) used to classify patented U.S. inventions are listed alphabetically. To conduct a patent search for prior patents relevant to an invention, it is useful to first determine the class and subclass within which the invention falls.
- *Manual of Classification.* This loose-leaf manual lists by number the 66,000 classes and subclasses used by the PTO to categorize inventions.
- *Class Definitions.* This loose-leaf manual contains brief definitions of each classification and subclassification used to categorize patents. The manual helps a patent searcher determine the appropriate categories to search in.

Related terms: patent search.

co-inventors

In situations where an invention is attributable to the creative effort of more than one person, everyone who makes a creative contribution to the invention (as described in at least one claim in the patent application) is considered a co-inventor.

> **EXAMPLE:** Tom Haberfeld and Bonnie Rand jointly conceive of and design a miniature EEG machine (a machine that measures brain waves), which allows its wearer to monitor his or her own brain waves via a wrist watch-like device. To make sure the concept is viable, Tom and Bonnie get their engineer friend, Clark Bromsky, to build a test model according to their specifications. Bonnie and Tom would be listed as "co-inventors" of the invention because they were the sole creative contributors to the invention's structure. Clark would not be considered a co-inventor, assuming his model was made according to set specifications and did not encompass creative additions to the invention. If, on the other hand, Clark had significantly altered the invention's basic specifications and design while building the test model, he also might qualify as a co-inventor.

When filing a patent application, it is extremely important to accurately identify the inventor or co-inventors. Leaving an inventor out or listing someone who doesn't qualify may later cause an issued patent to be declared invalid and unenforceable (if an action is brought in court to enforce the patent) because an accurate description of the true inventors in the patent application is one of the basic requirements for a valid patent.

Related terms: inventor, defined; patent application.

combination patent

This is a colloquial phrase for patents on inventions that are combinations of prior existing inventions or technology. Suppose an inventor combines a public domain bicycle frame with a public domain movable tread design previously utilized on a snowmobile, and creates a new type of device that travels efficiently on sand. Because the invention combines two public domain inventions, a patent issued on it will commonly be referred to as a "combination patent."

Earlier court decisions in patent cases suggested that a combination invention must demonstrate a new or surprising result, called "synergism," before it could qualify for a patent. However, the Court of Appeals for the Federal Circuit has ruled that the phrase "combination patent" has no operational meaning under the patent laws, and that virtually all inventions can be said to be combinations of prior existing technology. In short, under the reasoning of this decision, an invention need only meet the basic requirements for a patent (statutory subject matter, novelty, nonobviousness and utility). The fact that it is a combination of prior developments has no legal effect, and no showing of synergism is required.

Commissioner for Patents

The Commissioner for Patents is the title of the person who manages the patent division of the U.S. Patent and Trademark Office. The previous title for this position was "The Assistant Commissioner for Patents."

Related terms: Director of the U.S. Patent and Trademark Office; U.S. Patent and Trademark Office.

community patent

See European Patent Convention.

composition of matter

A composition of matter is one of the five categories of things (collectively, statutory subject matter) that qualify for a patent. Generally, compositions of matter consist of chemical compositions, conglomerates, aggregates or other chemically significant substances that are usually supplied in bulk, in liquid, gas or solid form. They include most new chemicals, new forms of life created by gene splicing techniques (the genetic mixing constitutes the composition), drugs, road-building compositions, gasoline, fuels, glues and paper.

Related terms: non-statutory subject matter; statutory subject matter.

compulsory licensing of a patent

In some countries, a patent owner is legally required to allow others to utilize his or her invention in exchange for reasonable compensation. Compulsory licensing of a patent doesn't happen in the U.S., because a U.S. patent owner has the right to not produce, manufacture, create or implement his or her invention. This, of course, means that the public may never benefit from the invention—at least until the patent has expired.

Under the General Agreement on Tariffs and Trade (GATT), compulsory patent licenses are disfavored and will probably disappear from the countries that used to provide for them.

Related terms: GATT (General Agreement on Tariffs and Trade); licensing of an invention; working a patent.

computer programs and patents

See software patents.

computerized patent search

See patent search, computerized.

conception

There are two foundations of patent rights: conception and reduction to practice. Conception is the mental part of inventing, including how an invention is formulated or how a problem is solved. Reduction to practice means that the inventor can demonstrate that the invention works for its intended purpose. These two events and the dates upon which they occur can affect determinations of prior art and the date of invention.

Inventors can document conception by maintaining a notebook or by filing a document disclosure under the PTO's Disclosure Document Program. It is a common myth that an inventor can document conception by mailing a description of the invention to him or herself by certified or registered mail and keeping the sealed envelope. The PTO has ruled that such "Post Office Patents" have little legal value.

Related terms: reduction to practice; Disclosure Document Program, date of invention.

concerted refusal to deal

If two or more businesses jointly boycott (discriminate against, refuse to buy from or refuse to sell to) one or more other businesses, such activity can be an antitrust violation if commerce has been significantly affected. If a concerted refusal to deal stems from the selective use of one or more patents, these patents may be declared invalid if the antitrust laws have been violated.

> **EXAMPLE:** The three largest genetic engineering laboratories agree to share their patents through a patent pool arrangement. Competitors are not allowed to use the patents. This exclusion of competitors may constitute a concerted refusal to deal, resulting in the patents being unenforceable.

Related terms: antitrust law (federal) and patents; breaking a patent.

confidentiality of patent application

The U.S. Patent and Trademark Office (PTO) treats all patent applications as confidential at least for the first 18 months of the patent application process. Effective December 2000, the PTO will publish a patent application 18 months after its filing date if the applicant intends to seek patent rights outside the U.S. (The 18-month publication statute was enacted in order to make U.S. patent laws more like those of foreign countries.) Publication terminates trade secret rights in the material claimed in the application.

If an applicant states, at the time of filing, that the application will not be filed abroad, the information in the patent application is kept confidential and is only published if the patent is approved by the PTO. At that point, the applicant gives up trade secret rights in order to obtain patent rights. If the applicant is not filing abroad and the patent application is rejected, the PTO will not publish the application. In that case, the trade secret will remain intact and the competition will not know about the invention.

If an applicant states that the application will not be filed abroad and then later files abroad, the applicant must notify the PTO within 45 days of the foreign filing. The PTO will then publish the application 18 months after the U.S. filing date (or as soon as possible after the 18-month period) and the applicant must pay a publication fee. If the PTO is not notified within 45 days, the application will be abandoned unless the applicant can demonstrate that the delay was unintentional and a stiff fee is paid.

Related terms: patent search; submarine patent.
See also Part 1 (Trade Secret Law): patent application, effect on trade secrets.

constructive reduction to practice

An invention may legally be considered to have been reduced to practice even though no actual building and testing has occurred.

An invention is considered reduced to practice when any one of the following three events occurs:

- the inventor actually builds and tests the invention (actual reduction to practice)
- the inventor files a patent application on the invention (constructive reduction to practice), or
- the inventor files a Provisional Patent Application (PPA) on the invention (also a constructive reduction to practice).

The timing of when an invention was reduced to practice is important because in the event of a conflict between inventions, it is necessary to identify the first inventor, who is entitled to the patent. This determination depends on a number of important factors, including:

- who first conceived the invention
- after conception, who was most diligent in developing the invention, and
- who first reduced the invention to practice.

Related terms: building and testing an invention; diligence in reducing to practice; interference proceeding; reduction to practice.

continuation application

This type of patent application may keep an original patent application alive after the patent examiner has issued a final office action rejecting one or more of the claims. A "continuation application" must be filed within three months after a patent application is rejected, unless an extension is obtained by filing an extension application and paying the appropriate fee.

A continuation application requires a new fee and new claims and will receive a new serial number and filing date. However, in the event an interference occurs (a conflict between two pending applications), and for purposes of determining the existence of prior art, the inventor will be entitled to the benefit of the original filing date. In other words, if someone else comes up with the same invention between an applicant's original filing date and the continuation application filing date, the original filing date will control and the corresponding invention will be given priority.

The term "continuation application" is often used interchangeably with a "file wrapper continuing application (FWC)."

Related terms: continuation-in-part application (CIP); prosecution of a patent application; Request for Coninued Examination.

continuation-in-part application (CIP)

A continuation-in-part application (CIP) is an application filed subsequent to an original application which includes new material not covered in the original application. A CIP provides a way for an inventor to supplement an earlier patent application with new matter to cover improvements made since the first application was filed. The CIP receives the same filing date for matter that it and the original (or parent) application have in common. However, any claim in the CIP that covers the new subject matter is treated as being filed as of the date of the CIP.

Note that a continuation-in-part application should be distinguished from a continuation application, where the applicant reformulates his or her claims after a rejection by the PTO.

Related terms: continuation application; final office action; prosecution of a patent application; Request for Coninued Examination.

contributory infringement of patent

The sale of an item that has been especially designed to work as a material part of a patented invention may be considered an infringement of the patent, called a contributory infringement, if the item itself lacks independent non-infringing use. Contributory infringement can occur even when the item being sold is itself not patentable. In essence, the contributory infringement doctrine recognizes that items especially modified for a patented invention will not generally be sold unless they are being used for an infringing purpose.

> **EXAMPLE:** Bionics, Inc., a manufacturer of artificial human organs, patents and manufactures an artificial kidney containing several unique (but non-patentable) valves. If Empire Hospital Equipment Ltd. starts selling the modified valve separately, they may be held to be a contributory infringer of the kidney patent, unless they can show that the valves have an independent use that does not infringe the kidney invention.

Related terms: infringement action; infringement of patent.

Convention application

A patent application may be filed in accordance with the Convention for the Protection of Industrial Property, sometimes known as the Paris Convention. Under this treaty, a patent application must be filed in every country where patent protection is desired, within one year of the date that an application is first filed in any other member country. So, if a U.S. patent application has a filing date of February 5, 1997, all additional Convention filings in other countries or

Definitions

jurisdictions, including the Patent Cooperation Treaty and the European Patent Office, must be made by February 5, 1998.

Each Convention filing must be made in the language of the country where it takes place, and separate filing and search fees must be paid. Generally speaking, Convention applications in individual countries utilize a different and more costly procedure than do Convention applications under the Patent Cooperation Treaty.

Related terms: international patent protection for U.S. inventions; Patent Cooperation Treaty (PCT).

Convention for the Protection of Industrial Property

See Convention application.

Court of Appeals for the Federal Circuit (CAFC)

Often referred to as "Kafka," this special federal court of appeals is responsible for hearing and deciding all appeals from patent infringement actions decided in the U.S. District Courts, as well as all appeals from decisions by the Board of Patent Appeals and Interferences (a branch of the PTO). The CAFC convenes in Washington, D.C., and also hears cases in other parts of the U.S.

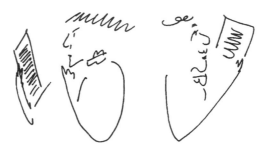

cross-licensing

In a cross-licensing arrangement, two or more owners of separate patents cooperate so that each may use the other's inventions. Because technologies such as automobile manufacturing, genetic engineering and semiconductor chip fabrication depend heavily on many inventions owned by a number of different companies, these companies commonly share their patents through cross-licensing agreements. By doing this, they can benefit from the state-of-the-art improvements in the particular field without having to pay royalties to all the relevant patent owners.

Related terms: improvement inventions; patent pools.

damages for patent infringement

See infringement action.

date of invention

In order to decide what prior art is with respect to any given invention, it's first necessary to determine the date of invention. Most inventors think it's the date on which one files a patent application. However, the date of invention is the earliest of the following dates:

- the date an inventor filed the patent application (provisional or regular)
- the date an inventor can prove that the invention was built and tested (known as "reduction to practice") in the U.S. or a country that is a member of North American Free Trade Association (NAFTA) or the World Trade Organization (WTO) (35 United States Code, Section 104) or
- the date an inventor can prove that the invention was conceived in a NAFTA or WTO country, provided the inventor can also prove diligence in building and testing it or filing a patent application on it. Most industrial countries are members of the WTO and a listing of WTO signatories is provided at the PTO website (http://www.uspto.gov).

An inventor who maintains proper records and is diligent afterwards in the invention process will be able to use the date of conception, which is usually several months before the filing date. Once the date of invention is determined, the relevant prior art comprises everything available before that date or anything available about the invention more than one year prior to filing the application.

Related terms: reduction to practice.

declaratory judgment of non-infringement, invalidity and unenforceability of patent

This is a court ruling that allows a business to proceed making or using a device without fear that it might later be held to infringe a particular patent. This type of ruling is commonly sought when a business desires to commercially utilize a device or process arguably described in a patent owned by someone else, but is unable to reach a satisfactory licensing agreement with that party. The business files an action in court, requesting a judge to declare (issue a declaratory judgment) that the patent is either invalid or unenforceable, or that it doesn't apply to the device or process in question. If the business wins, it can go ahead to develop the invention unless the patent owner appeals the case. If the business loses, it can appeal, but most likely will end up having to license the invention from the patent owner.

Related terms: infringement of patent; licensing of an invention.

Definitions

defenses to a patent infringement claim

When a patent owner takes legal action to enforce a patent by alleging that it has been infringed (that is, the invention described in the patent has been made, used or sold without the patent owner's permission), there are a number of possible defenses.

Depending on the facts in dispute, some defenses attempt to render the patent unenforceable; others challenge its basic validity. The primary difference between an unenforceable patent and an invalid one is that an unenforceable patent's owner can usually take steps to make it enforceable, whereas an invalid patent cannot be made valid. In either event, if a party accused of infringement can establish that at that time the patent is either invalid or unenforceable, the alleged infringer will win the lawsuit and may continue to use the invention without paying the patent owner.

Because of the variety of potential defenses to an infringement action, many observers feel that a patent is not worth a great deal if there's significant economic motivation to infringe it. According to this view, the more valuable a patent, the more likely it is that large economic interests will mount a fierce and expensive court challenge to the patent's validity. And the more difficult it is to enforce a patent, the less it is worth to its rightful owner. (Sound like a paradox? Welcome to patent law.)

On the other hand, billions of dollars are awarded to patent owners every year as a result of successful infringement actions, and numerous inventors (both small and institutional) make good money from licensing others to use the inventions covered by their patents.

Related terms: infringement action; infringement of patent; intervening right; statute of limitations, infringement action; unenforceable patent.

defensive disclosure

Publishing the details of an invention legally transforms the invention into prior art, which in turn precludes others from obtaining a patent on it. A defensive disclosure consists of publishing a description of an invention in the Official Gazette or another publication that is likely to be noticed by the U.S. Patent and Trademark Office (PTO), prior to a patent being issued.

A defensive disclosure is often used after an inventor files a patent application and decides not to pursue it further, but also doesn't want a subsequent filer of an application on the same or similar invention to have monopoly rights. Defensive disclosures are also used by companies that don't think a particular area of technology (such as software) should be subject to the patent laws, and therefore disclose their technology to prevent others from patenting it and extracting royalties.

There are two basic approaches to making a defensive disclosure: a Statutory Invention Registration procedure offered by the PTO and a preemptive private publication. The PTO procedure is much more expensive than the private approach.

To publish defensively under the Statutory Invention Registration program, an inventor can file a document with the PTO that:

- requests the PTO to publish the patent application's abstract in the Official Gazette
- formally abandons the patent application, and
- authorizes the PTO to open the patent application to public inspection.

EXAMPLE: Lou Swift invents a new form of portable energy source that allows most residential users of electricity to disconnect from the common electrical grid. After Lou applies for a patent, she comes to believe that the cause of peace and freedom would best be served by the invention being placed in the public domain, therefore becoming unpatentable. She utilizes the procedures described above to turn her application into a prior art reference that precludes anybody else from obtaining a patent on her invention. (This example is based on a theme developed in *Ecotopia Emerging*, by Ernest Callenbach.)

The private and less expensive approach to making a defensive disclosure is to publish the invention in journals published just for this purpose, such as *International Technical Disclosure* and *Research Disclosure*. Also, the Software Patent Institute provides a defensive disclosure program for software-based inventions.

Related terms: confidentiality of patent applications; Official Gazette (OG); prior art reference; Software Patent Institute; Statutory Invention Registration (SIR).

dependent claim

The scope of a patent is determined by the way the underlying invention is described in the patent claims (precise single sentence statements that articulate the exact nature of the invention). There are two basic types of patent claims: independent and dependent. Independent claims are statements that stand by themselves. Dependent claims are statements that rely on another claim for part of their description. In other words, each dependent claim must be read (interpreted) by incorporating the wording of each claim to which it refers, which may be an independent claim or another dependent claim.

The typical patent application contains several independent claims, each of which are referred to by several additional dependent claims. (Samples of dependent and independent claims are provided in "claims, defined.")

Related terms: claims, defined; independent claim.

design around

To design or build a device or process that is similar to but doesn't infringe on an invention protected by a patent is referred to as "designing around" the patent. The scope of protection acquired under a patent is determined by the wording of the patent's claims. Thus, any device, process, or substance containing the same elements described in a patent's claims can be said to infringe the patent. Conversely, a device or process that contains fewer or different elements does not infringe the patent (technically, the patent's claims do not "read on," or literally describe, the infringing device). Therefore, by studying the claims associated with a specific patent, it is often possible to build or design a device or process very similar to that described in the patent without legally infringing the patent's claims.

> **EXAMPLE:** Fred Akama invents and patents a small radiator-type device that uses hot water to dry and warm towels. One of the claims for his invention describes it as consisting of plastic. Bonanza Bathroom Products (BBP) creates a similar device, but uses a metal alloy that doubles the ability of the device to retain heat. BBP probably has not infringed Fred's patent, because it designed around the invention by using a different element that produces a different result.

To try to prevent such "designing around" activity, Fred's patent claim should have been broader to start with. Instead of limiting his invention to plastic, Fred's claim might have described "an inflexible means through which hot water can be channeled at normal domestic water pressures, the heat retained over a period of time, and towels folded over for the purpose of drying."

There is one important legal restriction on the ability to design around a patent claim. A court can decide that the differences in the basic elements of the two inventions—in the previous example, the type of substance used and the extra heat retention—are immaterial (unimportant) to the overall invention. In that event, infringement will have occurred under the doctrine of equivalents, which allows infringement to be found when two inventions work in the same way to produce substantially the same result.

Related terms: claims, defined; doctrine of equivalents.

design patents

A design patent may be issued on an inventive design that is novel, nonobvious and purely ornamental or aesthetic in nature (rather than useful or functional, which are requirements for a utility patent).

> **EXAMPLE:** A personal computer designed to resemble a classical robot might qualify for a design patent as long as the robot characteristics were purely ornamental. But if the robot characteristics were functional in some way—for instance, they provided the computer with mobility—a design patent on these characteristics would be precluded.

Often, two patents will be submitted for the same device: a utility patent covering the device's functional characteristics, and a design patent protecting the device's ornamental characteristics. In our robot-computer example, it might be possible to obtain both types of patents if they cover different aspects of the device.

Although design patents are relatively easy to obtain, the fact that the design by definition lacks utility normally makes it easy to create another design that will also be novel and interesting without violating the design patent.

Related terms: design around.

diligence in reducing to practice

An inventor's diligence in reducing an invention to practice consists of steady progress toward the goal of either:

- *actual reduction to practice*—building and testing a working model of the invention, or
- *constructive reduction to practice*—filing a provisional or regular patent application on it.

If two inventors come up with the same invention about the same time, the first inventor who can also show diligence in reducing the invention to practice, usually through documentation of building and testing activity or activity related to the preparation of a patent application, is most likely to get the patent.

> **EXAMPLE 1:** In March 2000, Joe Vermont conceives of an invention that produces heat from a car heater the instant the car is started. Joe steadily applies himself during the next six months to building a working model of the insta-heater, and in October 2000 applies for a patent on it. Sal Fortuna independently conceives of the same invention in June 2000, but rather than building and testing a working model, Sal files a patent application on the

invention in July 2000. Under these facts, Joe should get the patent because he was first to conceive of the invention and was diligent in reducing the invention to practice, even though his patent application was later than Sal's. Although Sal was also diligent in reducing the invention to practice (called constructive reduction to practice in this case) by filing the patent application a month after he conceived of the invention, he wasn't the first to invent, so he would lose out to Joe.

EXAMPLE 2: Using the same insta-heater invention, assume now that Joe didn't get around to building and testing his working model until September 2000. He then filed a patent application in December 2000. Under these facts, the patent would probably go to Sal, because Joe was not diligent in reducing the invention to practice, while Sal was.

Related terms: constructive reduction to practice; interference proceeding; reduction to practice.

direct infringement of patent

See infringement of patent.

Director of the U.S. Patent and Trademark Office

This is the title of the person who runs the U.S. Patent and Trademark Office, a branch of the U.S. Department of Commerce. The full title is actually: Under-secretary of Commerce for Intellectual Property and Director of the U.S. Patent and Trademark Office." Prior to 2000 the title for this position was the Commissioner of Patents and Trademarks.

Related terms: Commissioner for Patents; U.S. Patent and Trademark Office.

Disclosure Document Program (DDP)

This U.S. Patent and Trademark Office (PTO) program allows inventors, for a nominal fee, to file a signed document, called a disclosure, that preliminarily describes their invention. Later, when the inventor applies for a patent on the invention, the disclosure can be used to prove the date of conception of the invention, should this become necessary because of an interference with another patent application.

There are other ways to document inventive efforts, such as keeping a notebook or producing disclosures that are signed and witnessed. Some experts prefer these other methods and think the Document Disclosure Program should not be used unless an inventor has no witnesses.

The DDP should not be confused with a Provisional Patent Application (PPA), which may be filed with the PTO on an invention for a $75 fee ($150 for large entities). A PPA is the legal equivalent of constructive reduction to practice as long as it meets the standards for disclosure required in the specification portion of a regular patent application.

Related terms: disclosure requirement for patents; interference, defined; interference proceeding; notebook; Provisional Patent Application (PPA).

disclosure requirement for patents

A patent application must disclose enough about the invention to enable a person with ordinary skill in the art (technology used in the invention) to build or develop it. The reason for the disclosure requirement is simple. A disclosure that is detailed enough to enable the invention to be built enhances the public's knowledge of the technology and ideas involved in the invention. In exchange for this public benefit, an inventor earns the right to a statutory monopoly over the right to make, use and sell the invention.

If the information necessary to build the invention is not sufficiently disclosed in the application, a patent that is issued on the invention may be declared invalid and the patent therefore not enforceable. As a practical matter, the fact that the U.S. Patent and Trademark Office approved the application in the first place is generally relied on by courts to reject this particular defense.

Related terms: patent application.

divisional application

If a patent examiner rejects a patent application because it claims two or more inventions (a patenting no-no), the common inventor response is to restrict the application to one invention of the inventor's choosing. But if the inventor doesn't wish to abandon the other "nonelected" invention, he or she can file a separate divisional application to cover it. The divisional application will be entitled to the filing date of the original application (which is referred to as the parent application, once a divisional application is filed).

What happens if the patent examiner was wrong, and a court later finds that there was, in fact, only one invention, even though the U.S. Patent and Trademark Office (PTO) issued two (or more) patents on it? Although this violates another patenting rule (the statutory rule against double patenting), both patents will be upheld because the restriction of the original patent application was imposed by the PTO.

Related terms: abandonment of patent; double patenting; nonelected claims; prosecution of a patent application.

Definitions

doctrine of equivalents

A secondary method for deciding whether a patent is being infringed, the doctrine of equivalents considers whether a later device or process does the same work in substantially the same way, to accomplish the same result as a patented invention. If it does, then patent infringement will be found to exist.

The primary method used by the courts to assess possible patent infringement is to compare the literal language of each element of the patent's claims with each element of the device or process claimed to be infringing. (In patent jargon, do the patent claims "read on" the infringing device or process?) However, even if a patent's claims don't literally "read on" an allegedly infringing device or process, infringement may be found under the doctrine of equivalents so long as the element of the device is the "equivalent" of the claimed element. A device element is equivalent if it performs the same function in the same way to achieve the same result as the claim element, or the role of the device element is substantially the same as that of the claim element.

The doctrine of equivalents is intended to prevent designing around a patent on hyper-technical grounds. Unfortunately, there is no logical dividing line between 1) non-infringement based on legitimate designing around an invention, and 2) infringement based on the doctrine of equivalents. It is up to the courts to decide, on a case-by-case basis, if inventions are substantially equivalent.

Related terms: design around; infringement of patent; negative doctrine of equivalents.

double patenting

If two patents are obtained on (or claim) a single invention, it's referred to as double patenting. Double patenting is not allowed under the patent laws and both patents can later be invalidated. However, if double patenting results from a divisional application required by the U.S. Patent and Trademark Office (PTO) because of the PTO's misperception that two inventions were being described in the original patent application, under a special statute (35 United States Code, Section 121) this rule does not apply and the patents will be considered valid.

Related terms: divisional application.

drawings, patent application

Visual representations of an invention must be included in the patent application. These drawings should show all the features recited (described) in the claims.

If an invention is a thing (including machines or articles of manufacture), the drawings must show features of the invention that are different from those known in the prior art. A drawing for a process should consist of a flowchart showing its sequence of steps.

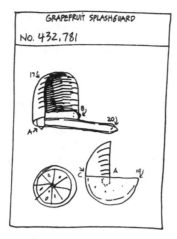

Drawings are generally not required for inventions consisting of compositions of matter unless:

- the inventions consist of structures that can be shown in a cross-sectional representation, or
- a flowchart showing the process of manufacture is relevant.

Related terms: disclosure requirements for patents; patent application.

duration of patents

Utility patents—the most common kind—expire 20 years after the filing date of the regular formal patent application. This means that the period of time the patent is actually in force will depend on how long it takes the patent to be examined. For instance, if the regular patent application is filed on December 1, 1997, and the patent issues on December 1, 1999, the patent will be in force for 18 years.

Effective June 2000, every patent is guaranteed an in-force period of at least 17 years. The patent term will be extended for as long as necessary to compensate for any of the following:

- any delay caused by the PTO failing to examine a new application within 14 months from filing
- any delay caused by the PTO failing to take any one of the following actions within four months:
  - reply to an amendment or to an appeal brief
  - issue an allowance or office action after a decision on appeal, or
  - issue a patent after the issue fee is paid and any required drawings are filed

- any delay caused by the PTO failing to issue a patent within three years from filing, unless the delay was due to the applicant filing a continuation application or buying a delay to reply to an Office Action, or
- any delay due to secrecy orders, appeals, or interferences.

Because the law creating the 20-year patent term became effective June 8, 1995, patents issued prior to that date—or which were pending on that date—will expire 20 years from their filing date or 17 years from their issue date, whichever period is longer. (35 USC §154(c)(1).)

Design patents last for 14 years from the date the patent issues, and plant and utility patents last for 20 years from the date of filing.

Related terms: filing date; in-force patent; patent term extension.

duty of candor and good faith

This duty is owed to the U.S. Patent and Trademark Office (PTO) by every patent applicant in connection with the information and disclosures contained in the patent application. Under rules issued by the PTO, the applicant must disclose:

- all known instances of anticipation (events or references that might cause the PTO to determine that the invention isn't novel)
- pertinent prior art that might bear on the question of nonobviousness
- the preferred embodiment (best mode) of the invention, and
- any other information known to the applicant that bears on the patentability of the invention and the proper scope of the patent claims.

Failure to comply fully with the duty of candor and good faith can result in rejection of the patent application by the PTO, or a later finding in an infringement action that the applicant committed fraud on the PTO (if the noncompliance was willful or negligent). In the latter case, the patent may be declared invalid even if the undisclosed information would not have invalidated the patent as such.

EXAMPLE: In 2000, Patricia invented a device and a process that allowed wind velocities to be differentially measured according to very small portions of space. The results of the measurements could then be fed into a computer, and the best placement for windmills could be determined. Patricia made the invention for her own home in the country and decided not to patent it, due to the plentiful supply of centralized electrical energy at that time. Patricia let some of her neighbors use the invention on an as-needed basis, which may have constituted prior public use of the invention, which in turn could be considered prior art.

Three years later, oil prices soar and Patricia applies for and receives a patent. In her patent application, she neglects to mention the use of the device by her neighbors, a fact she should have disclosed under the applicant's duty to disclose known relevant prior art. In 2005, a leading power company begins to market Patricia's device across the country without a license from Patricia. If Patricia sues the company for infringement or her patent, she may find that her patent cannot be enforced. Why? Because she failed to disclose relevant prior art to the PTO, even though the information in question, if disclosed at the time, might not have barred issuance of the patent. If this information comes out at trial, the judge may find that she violated her duty of candor and good faith.

Related terms: anticipation; defenses to a patent infringement claim; disclosure requirement for patents; fraud on the Patent and Trademark Office.

elements of invention

See claims, defined.

enabling disclosure

The description of an invention included ("disclosed") in a patent application must be in sufficient detail as to "enable" a person with ordinary skill in the art to build or develop it ("work it") without having to apply any inventiveness of his or her own.

Related terms: disclosure requirement for patents.

equivalents, doctrine of

See doctrine of equivalents.

European Patent Convention

This treaty covers patent law relationships, primarily among the members of the European Community (the Common Market), plus a few other countries.

Under the European Patent Convention (EPC), an inventor need make only one filing and undergo one examination procedure to obtain patent protection in all member countries. Filings and examinations are conducted by the European Patent Office in Munich, Germany, and The Hague, Netherlands. A patent issued under the EPC, called a community patent, lasts for 20 years from the date of application, but must be registered in each country.

Related terms: Convention application; Patent Cooperation Treaty (PCT).

European Patent Office

See European Patent Convention.

examiners, patent

See patent examiners.

exclusive patent license

A binding agreement in which a patent owner (the licensor) grants another party (the licensee) the sole (exclusive) right to make, use and/or sell an invention covered by the patent is known as an exclusive patent license.

Sometimes the grant of rights is for all purposes, but often it is limited to a specific context. For example, sales may be restricted to the U.S., to a particular period of time, or for a particular purpose. However, the particular right is granted exclusively to the person or business receiving it. For example, a patent owner could grant one company the exclusive right to make and sell the invention in the United States and another company the exclusive right to make and sell it in the European Community.

Related terms: geographic patent license; non-exclusive patent license.

exhibiting an unpatented invention

Using or exhibiting an unpatented invention in public in an unrestricted (nonconfidential) context prior to filing a provisional or regular patent application can constitute a public use, which would qualify as prior art and later bar a patent from being issued under the anticipation doctrine.

Related terms: anticipation; experimental use of an unpatented invention; public use.

experimental use of an unpatented invention

An unpatented invention may be used or exhibited in public for experimental purposes—that is, to test or improve the invention. Experimental use is not considered a public use or a disclosure, and therefore won't bar a patent under the anticipation rule.

Many inventions need to be tested in public one or more times before the inventor is ready to file a patent application. However, if the public use is not truly experimental in nature, such use may bar a patent unless an application for the patent is filed within one year of the use.

Related terms: anticipation; exhibiting an unpatented invention; public use.

expiration of patent

See duration of patents.

false marking of invention

See marking of an invention.

Federal Circuit Court of Appeals

See Court of Appeals for the Federal Circuit (CAFC).

Federal Trade Commission proceeding

Under this administrative process, a patent owner can get an order barring devices that infringe the patent from being imported into the U.S.

Related terms: international patent protection for U.S. inventions.

field of invention

The "field" of an invention is colloquial for the classification or subclassification into which an invention falls. For instance, an invention involving gene splicing might be said to be in the "genetic engineering field," while an invention involving computers would fall within the "electronics field."

These terms have no legal significance. The similar phrase "field of search" is related to how patents are categorized for search purposes.

Related terms: classification of patents; patent search.

file wrapper

The file the U.S. Patent and Trademark Office (PTO) maintains for each patent application is known as a file wrapper. This file contains the application itself, as well as copies and notes of all correspondence between the PTO and the applicant regarding amendment and issuance of the patent. For example, if a letter is sent to the PTO regarding a pending patent application, it will be added to the applicant's file wrapper.

Related terms: continuation application; file wrapper estoppel; patent application.

file wrapper continuing application (FWC)

See continuation application.

file wrapper estoppel

This is a rule of court under which patent applicants are bound by the statements they make in their patent application and subsequent correspondence and documents filed with the U.S. Patent and Trademark Office (PTO) in the course of prosecuting the application. The term "file wrapper" is jargon for the file the PTO maintains on an invention and the term "estoppel" is a legal principle that holds people to their words even if they later want to weasel out of them.

The file wrapper estoppel rule becomes pertinent if the patent owner should ever seek enforcement of his or her patent in court. In that event, the inventor would be prevented from describing the scope of the invention differently from

Definitions

how it was described in earlier documents in the PTO patent file (again, colloquially referred to as the "file wrapper"). In short, an inventor is stuck with what's already been told to the PTO—and cannot later try to broaden a patent's coverage that has been surrendered by original claim language, or in an amendment or a written argument during the earlier prosecution stage.

Because of the file wrapper estoppel rule, it is good practice to follow these two rules:

- Do not say anything negative about an invention in a patent application (your words may come back to haunt you).
- Draft patent claims as broadly as possible in light of the pertinent prior art.

EXAMPLE: Otto Makespence invents a medical tool that uses a fiber optic strand, laser light, specially cloned antibodies and certain chemicals to detect the presence of various substances in human tissue. In his patent application, Otto drafts his claims very broadly, without a limiting reference to his use of fiber optics. After the PTO rejects the initial claims, Otto amends his application so that the claims now specify fiber optics as the method of transmitting the laser light. In his cover letter transmitting the amendment to the PTO, Otto admits that his original claim was wildly overbroad and thanks the examiner for helping him pare his claim down to the appropriate scope. The patent is then granted. Ten years later, Lewis Opalenik, a famous heart surgeon, makes and uses a similar diagnostic tool, using a magnetic rather than fiber optic means for transmitting the laser light waves. If Otto brings an infringement action against Lewis, alleging that his patent is sufficiently broad in scope to preclude Lewis's device, the court will hold Otto to his admission about the overly broad scope of his original claim, as found in the file wrapper, which clearly limits his patent to a fiber optic means.

Related terms: claims, defined; prosecution of a patent application.

filing date

Assigned to every application by the U.S. Patent and Trademark Office (PTO), the filing date is indicated on a "filing receipt" that the PTO sends to the applicant. The date is usually one to four days after the patent application was mailed, or the date it's mailed if sent by U.S. Postal Service Express Mail.

The filing date is crucial for a number of reasons, including the following:

- The filing date starts the period within which a patent application must be filed in other countries to receive patent protection. If a Convention application in Germany, for instance, is not filed within one year after the U.S.

filing date, German patent protection will be precluded. If, however, the applicant files under the Patent Cooperation Treaty within one year of the U.S. filing date, the applicant is allowed a longer time period to file in Germany.

- The filing date closes the one-year period during which an inventor can publicly use, work, describe, or place the invention on sale in the U.S. without the anticipation rule being applied to bar a patent on it.

- The filing date shuts the door on all subsequent developments by other inventors from being considered as prior art. That is, any developments that occur after the filing date will not be considered as prior art that would preclude a patent (which must be novel or nonobvious).

- The filing date is when the law considers an invention to be first reduced to practice (called constructive reduction to practice), absent evidence that it was actually reduced to practice at an earlier time by building and testing it. In the event of an interference (pending applications by different inventors covering the same invention), the inventor who filed first will receive the patent unless another inventor can show that he or she conceived of the invention first and then diligently set about to reduce it to practice or actually reduced it practice first by building and testing it.

A Provisional Patent Application (PPA) may be filed up to one year prior to filing a regular patent application. The PPA filing date will count as a constructive reduction to practice, and serve as the date for deciding whether the invention has been anticipated by prior art. However, the regular patent application filing date—not the PPA filing date—will count as the beginning of the patent term, which expires 20 years from date of "filing," and will also begin the year period in which a patent application must be filed in many foreign jurisdictions—if patent protection is sought in them.

To take advantage of the earlier filing date, the regular patent application must specifically claim that date, and the PPA must meet the rigorous standard for disclosure of the invention required of regular patent applications.

Related terms: anticipation; interference, defined; international patent protection for U.S. inventions; prosecution of a patent application; Provisional Patent Application (PPA).

filing fees

See application filing fees; issue fee.

final office action

The patent examiner's decision as to whether or not to issue a patent is known as a final office action. Despite the name, final office actions are not necessarily "final." A patent examiner can be petitioned to reconsider the application. And, even if the examiner refuses to budge, the applicant can:

- file a continuation application
- agree to amend the application to exclude a claim altogether (if the argument is about a particular claim), or
- appeal the decision to the Board of Patent Appeals and Interferences.

Normally, the final office action occurs after the patent applicant has been afforded at least one opportunity to amend the application (in response to a first office action which raised problems with the application). Most commonly, the applicant will be expected to revise one or more of the claims in the amendment, thereby avoiding an overlap with prior art that otherwise would preclude a patent from issuing. Also, technical mistakes in how the application describes the invention, how the claims are constructed and how the drawings depict the invention are typical subjects of an amendment.

Related terms: Board of Patent Appeals and Interferences; continuation application; prosecution of a patent application.

first office action

This term refers to the patent examiner's first response to a patent application. Often, the first office action involves the rejection of all or most of the claims in an application (in the trade, humorously termed a "shotgun rejection") on the ground that one or more prior art references render the invention obvious. The applicant can file a response within three months (extendable for up to six months) that either amends the claims or satisfactorily explains to the patent examiner why the prior art references found troublesome by the examiner are not pertinent.

Related terms: prosecution of a patent application; swearing behind a prior art reference.

first to file countries

Under the first to file system, an inventor who is the first to file an application for a patent on an invention is given absolute priority over other inventors. All countries except the U.S. use the first to file system.

The laws providing for this absolute priority are sometimes termed "race statutes," because they award a patent to the inventor who wins the race to the patent office. Because the first to file is the one who gets the patent, interference hearings (to determine priority of inventorship) do not exist in first to file countries, as they do in the U.S.

Related terms: first to invent countries; international patent protection for U.S. inventions.

first to invent countries

The U.S. awards a patent to the first party to actually come up with an invention (first to invent), as opposed to the first party to file a patent application (first to file). All other countries use the first to file system.

Related terms: first to file countries; international patent protection for U.S. inventions.

fraud on the U.S. Patent and Trademark Office

Any behavior by an applicant for a patent that attempts to mislead the U.S. Patent and Trademark Office (PTO) in regard to whether the invention deserves a patent is known as fraud. The most common type of fraud is failure to inform the PTO about one or more relevant prior art references known to the applicant. This issue is usually raised by an alleged infringer as a defense to court litigation seeking enforcement of a patent. Once found to exist by a court, fraud on the PTO usually results in the patent being judged unenforceable or invalid.

Related terms: defenses to a patent infringement claim; duty of candor and good faith; infringement action; unenforceable patent.

fully met by a prior art reference

When any single previous development or publication (prior art reference) contains all of the specific elements and limitations set out in a patent claim, the claim is said to be fully met by the prior art. If a claim is fully met, the invention is considered anticipated and is therefore not entitled to a patent.

> **EXAMPLE:** Unaware of prior developments, Gary invents a mechanical match. When he tries to patent it, however, the U.S. Patent and Trademark Office points out a patent that shows (teaches) all of the elements in the claim describing Gary's device. Because Gary's claims are fully met, his device has been "anticipated" and is not entitled to a patent.

Related terms: claims, defined; novelty, defined; prior art reference.

GATT (General Agreement on Tariffs and Trade)

The General Agreement on Tariffs and Trade (GATT) is among the most important international trade treaties in our history. And it will have a large effect on U.S. patent law.

Under GATT, for patents filed after June 7, 1995, the U.S. patent monopoly ends 20 years from the application's filing date, regardless of when the patent issues. However, effective June 2000, every patent is guaranteed an in-force period of at least 17 years. Previously, the patent monopoly lasted for 17 years from the date of issue, regardless of when the application was filed. (Patent

Definitions

applications that were pending—and patents which were in force—as of June 8, 1995, expire 20 years from filing or 17 years from issue, whichever period is longer.)

Another GATT-related change involves the Provisional Patent Application or PPA. Filing a PPA will legally "reduce an invention to practice," provided that the inventor files an actual patent application a year after filing the PPA. The reduction to practice date is crucial if an inventor is faced with a competing patent application or a prior art reference with a close date. Formerly, an invention could be reduced to practice only by building and testing it or by filing a regular patent application.

Another GATT-related change involves foreign inventors. Under current U.S. law, an inventor may establish a date of invention earlier than the filing date of the inventor's patent application in order to:

- obtain the patent in the face of a competing application ("win an interference"), or
- show that the invention predates a particular prior art reference ("swear behind cited prior art").

    But to do this, the inventor must show conception of the invention and either:

- actual reduction to practice (building and testing), or
- diligent efforts to reduce the invention to practice or file a patent application.

Before GATT, inventors could rely on activities only in the U.S., Mexico or Canada. For applications filed on or after Jan. 1, 1996, inventors will also be able to rely on activities in any GATT country.

The final GATT-related change enhances protection against patent infringement. Prior to GATT, a patent only gave its owner the right to exclude others from making, using or selling the patented invention. GATT expanded this right to include the situation when anyone else offers for sale or imports a patented invention, or, in the case of a process patent, to imports of products made abroad by the patented process.

genetic engineering and patents

Ordinarily, patents will not be issued on "inventions" consisting of items or substances that are found to exist in a natural state. The reason for this is obvious. Something occurring in nature without human intervention cannot have been the product of inventive activity.

There are several categories of patentable inventions that do, however, involve "natural" materials. One category is novel and nonobvious plants created through asexual breeding. Plant patents for new plants involving human inventiveness (breeding skill) are specifically authorized by statute (the patent laws and the Plant Variety Protection Act) in the U.S.

Genetic engineering is another field where "natural" materials (that is, bacteria, DNA, RNA) have been manipulated by humans through gene splicing and cloning techniques (such as Polymerase Chain Reaction or PCR) to produce new organic materials and life forms. These new substances and forms, and the processes used to create them, are also considered to be patentable under authority of the U.S. Supreme Court's decision in the case of *Diamond v. Chakrabarty,* 447 U.S. 303 (1980), as long as they meet the basic patent requirements of novelty, nonobviousness and utility.

Because Congress wants basic research in biotechnology to develop as quickly as possible, federal law permits a company to utilize biotechnical inventions patented by another company if the purpose of the use is strictly for research. This is an exception to the general rule that a patent prohibits the manufacture or use of an invention covered by an in-force patent. If, however, the company doing the research desires to commercially exploit the substance or process being utilized, it must obtain permission from the patent owner (usually accomplished by paying a license fee).

Related terms: laws of nature exception to patents; non-statutory subject matter.

geographic patent license

This type of exclusive license grants its holder (the licensee) the right to make, use or sell a patented invention within a specified geographic region only. For example, one license might allow its holder to exploit the invention commercially in the U.S., while another license might provide similar rights to another company, to be exercised solely in the European Community countries.

Related terms: exclusive patent license.

Graham v. John Deere case

This 1966 Supreme Court case created the guidelines for determining when an invention is nonobvious—a statutory requirement for an invention to be patentable. (The text of this case can be located in 383 U.S. 1.)

According to the *Deere* case, the following steps help to determine if an invention is nonobvious:

- Determine the scope and content of the prior art.
- Determine the novelty of the invention.
- Determine the skill level of artisans in the pertinent technology (art).

Definitions

- Against this background, determine the obviousness or nonobviousness of the inventive subject matter.
- Consider relevant secondary factors, such as the commercial success experienced with the invention, whether there was a long-felt but unsolved need for the invention and whether others tried but failed to produce the invention.

In practice, these guidelines boil down to whether, taking all relevant factors into account, a person reasonably skilled in the art involved in the invention would find the invention to be a surprising or unexpected development at the time it was made.

Related terms: nonobviousness, defined; obviousness, defined.

grant of patent

A patent is granted when the U.S. Patent and Trademark Office issues a patent on an invention.

group art unit

The group art unit is an internal division of the U.S. Patent and Trademark Office to which a filed patent application is assigned for examination.

Related terms: prosecution of a patent application; U.S. Patent and Trademark Office (PTO).

improvement inventions

Technically, almost all inventions are "improvement inventions"—that is, inventions that improve upon other prior inventions.

Patent protection for small improvements on existing inventions in well-developed fields (many technological developments) are relatively easy to obtain. Conversely, in relatively new fields such as genetic engineering, small improvements may be considered too trivial or obvious to be granted a patent. This is true primarily because new fields of invention are much more supportive of new developments than are established fields, where the areas of potential improvement in existing techniques are more obvious.

A patent on an improvement invention only covers the improvement itself, and is thus subject to the rights of any holders of in-force patents on the other technology involved. This means that to commercially exploit the improvement invention, its owner must license the right to use the underlying invention. Often this is accomplished by cross-licensing (you can use mine if I can use yours) the two patents. Cross-licensing is extremely common throughout the industrial world.

EXAMPLE: A computer manufacturer makes an unexpected and novel improvement on an existing patented data bus (a device included in most microcomputers to move data from one part of the computer to another in an orderly way). The value of this improvement patent will depend heavily upon the degree to which appropriate arrangements can be made with the owner of the patent on the original data bus. This may not be difficult, because the original patent owner will likely want the right to commercially exploit the improvement patent. If so, the parties can enter into a cross-license agreement permitting them to use each other's inventions for agreed upon compensation. If there are two in-force patents covering the original data bus, the improvement patent owner would have to come to terms with both patent owners to exploit the invention.

Related terms: cross-licensing; patent pools.

independent claim

An independent claim by itself describes an aspect of the invention without reference to any other claim. By contrast, a dependent claim refers to another independent or dependent claim. (Samples of dependent and independent claims are provided in "claims, defined.")

Related terms: claims, defined; dependent claim.

Index of U.S. Patent Classification

See classification of patents.

in-force patent

A patent is said to be in-force (in effect) if all of the following are true:
- the patent's statutory term has not yet has expired
- appropriate maintenance fees have been paid when due, and
- the patent has not been ruled invalid by the U.S. Patent and Trademark Office or a court.

Even when a patent is no longer in-force, it still is considered prior art when determining if a later invention qualifies for a patent.

Related terms: patent term extension; reexamination of patent.

Information Disclosure Statement

A statement must be filed with a regular patent application (or within the following three months) that describes all relevant prior art references known to the applicant, and also provides actual copies of such references when they have

Definitions

appeared in print. Known as an Information Disclosure Statement, an IDS or PTO Form 1449, this statement provides the U.S. Patent and Trademark Office (PTO) with a head start in determining whether the invention deserves a patent. An IDS need not be filed with a Provisional Patent Application.

An applicant's knowing failure to disclose any known and relevant prior art reference is considered fraud on the PTO. If a patent was granted in this circumstance, it may be held unenforceable in court, although the deliberately omitted prior art reference might not have resulted in any claim being disallowed.

When examining a patent application, the PTO conducts its own patent search in addition to what it learns from an applicant's IDS, and often picks up omitted prior art references. These references may then be used to reject the application on novelty or nonobviousness grounds, but the PTO seldom presumes that the omission was intentional. If, however, the PTO fails to find the omitted prior art reference and proceeds in its ignorance to issue a patent, the reference will usually only be brought to light if an infringement lawsuit is filed. This is because the infringer, as part of its defense, can be counted on to do an exhaustive prior art search (called a validity search) to prove that the patent was improvidently issued and therefore invalid. If the prior art reference is found in the course of this search, the infringer can then be expected to argue that the omission was deliberate. If the court agrees, it will invalidate the patent because of fraud on the PTO, without regard to how the reference affects the invention's novelty and nonobviousness.

Related terms: defenses to a patent infringement claim; patent search; Provisional Patent Application (PPA); validity search.

infringement action

An infringement action is a lawsuit alleging that one or more parties (defendants) have, without permission, made, used or sold an invention protected under a patent owned by the party bringing the lawsuit (plaintiff). Patent infringement actions must be filed in the U.S. District Court within a maximum of six years after the date the infringement occurred—or sooner, if a delay in filing would obviously cause undue hardship to the defendant.

Although it is possible to have a jury trial in a patent infringement case, the judge alone is responsible for interpreting the patent claims. (*Markman v. Westview Instruments, Inc.*, 517 US 370 (1996).) The judge or jury then examines the plaintiff's patent and compares the elements recited in its claims with those of the accused infringer's device or process. On this basis, the judge or jury decides whether the plaintiff's claims, as interpreted by the judge, cover the defendant's device or process—that is, fully describe the elements contained in the device or process. If the plaintiff's claims cover (read on) the device or process, infringement is found. If the claims do not cover the defendant's device or process, then no infringement has occurred.

Even if the claims don't literally read on the infringing device, the judge or jury could find infringement by applying the doctrine of equivalents: the two devices are sufficiently equivalent in what they do and how they do it to warrant a finding of infringement. Also possible, but extremely rare, is the converse: finding no infringement because the two devices are sufficiently dissimilar in what they accomplish or how they work, even though the claims are the same (in patent speak, the negative doctrine of equivalents).

If infringement is found to exist, the judge may:

- issue an injunction (court order) preventing further infringement
- award the patent owner damages for loss of income or for profits resulting from the infringement from the time the invention was properly marked (when the word "patent" and the patent number were affixed to the invention) or from when the infringer was first put on actual notice of the infringement, whichever occurred first, and
- in the event the infringement was willful or flagrant (it continued without a reasonable defense after notification by the patent owner or infringement occurred through a direct copying without any ground to believe the plaintiff's patent was invalid), the court may award the plaintiff three times the actual damages established in court and reasonable attorney fees.

Patent infringement lawsuits are risky for the patent owner, because the defendant will almost always attack the underlying validity of the patent on such grounds as:

- the invention was obvious or lacked novelty when the patent issued by introducing relevant prior art references not picked up by the PTO in the course of examining the patent application
- the patent application failed to fully disclose the best mode of the invention, as is required by the patent laws, or
- the patent applicant failed to disclose relevant prior art known to the applicant (fraud on the PTO).

Until the late 1980s, courts ruled against the validity of the patent in over half of all patent infringement cases. Lately, however, under leadership of the U.S. Court of Appeals for the Federal Circuit, the courts are upholding significantly more patents than they strike down.

Related terms: breaking a patent; contributory infringement of patent; defenses to a patent infringement claim; infringement of patent.

infringement of patent

Infringement occurs when someone makes, uses or sells an item covered by the claims of an in-force patent without the patent owner's permission. If a court finds that infringement occurred, every patent infringer can be ordered by a court to stop all infringing activity. Any of the infringers who profited from the infringement may also be found liable for money damages. Only an infringer who had reason to know that a patent was being infringed can be held liable for treble damages as a willful infringer.

> **EXAMPLE:** Owens Organic Products invents and patents a simple computerized sprinkler system that turns on and off according to the moisture level of the soil. Although Phil Prendergast has been independently working on the same invention, he failed to beat Owens to the Patent and Trademark Office and is unable to prove that he was the first to invent. However, figuring that Owens will probably never find out, Phil licenses Garden Development Corp. to construct and market his invention in exchange for royalties. Garden Development manufactures and distributes the system on a wholesale basis to a chain of retail garden-supply stores, which then sell the sprinklers to consumers, who use them in their gardens. Phil, Garden Development, the retail stores and the consumers are all guilty of patent infringement—even though none except Phil knew about Owens's patent. Phil, Garden Development and the retail stores may be ordered to stop infringing and to pay money damages. However, only Phil would be liable for treble damages, unless Garden Development and the retail stores knew, or should have known, that their activity infringed Owens's patent.

Related terms: contributory infringement of patent; infringement action.

infringement search

Colloquial for a type of patent search, an infringement search is conducted for the purpose of discovering whether an invention infringes any in-force patent. This type of search is typically conducted by an invention developer as a preliminary step to deciding whether to develop a particular invention. It is much narrower in scope than a patentability search, which is concerned with all prior art—including expired patents and relevant unpatented technology. It also differs from a validity search, which typically is conducted by a defendant in a patent infringement lawsuit for the purpose of discovering information that would invalidate the patent.

Related terms: patent search.

injunctions and injunctive relief

See infringement action.

interference, defined

An "interference" is patent jargon for an administrative proceeding scheduled by the U.S. Patent and Trademark Office to determine who gets the patent in situations where two pending applications (or a pending application and a patent issued within one year of the pending application's filing date) both claim the same invention.

Related terms: Board of Patent Appeals and Interferences; interference proceeding.

interference proceeding

An administrative hearing is conducted by the Board of Patent Appeals and Interferences to determine the priority of inventionship when the same invention is claimed in two or more pending patent applications, or in a pending patent application and a patent issued within a year of the application's filing date.

The Board of Patent Appeals and Interferences determines the priority of inventorship according to the following analytical steps.

Step 1: The Board decides which inventor was the first to reduce the invention to practice. This will be the first inventor to either:

- constructively reduce the invention to practice by filing a provisional or regular patent application (the senior party), or
- actually reduce the invention to practice by building and testing a working model of the invention.

Step 2: Based on evidence introduced in the interference proceeding, the Board decides whether the inventor who was second to reduce to practice can prove both that: 1) he or she was first to conceive of the invention, and 2) he or she was also diligently attempting to reduce the invention to practice at the time the other inventor conceived the invention.

The inventor who can prove both prior conception and diligence in reduction to practice will be awarded the patent; otherwise, the inventor who was first to reduce the invention to practice (either actually or constructively) gets the patent.

The reasoning behind these priorities is relatively simple. The patent laws attempt to balance three goals:

- get the inventor to file as quickly as possible so the invention can become known to the public
- get the inventor to come up with the best possible version of the invention, and
- reward the inventor who is first to conceive of the invention.

By initially presuming that the first inventor to reduce the invention to practice should get the patent, the patent laws serve the first two goals. But all three goals can be served by giving the patent to the first to conceive the invention if that inventor also worked diligently to reduce the invention to practice.

Because an inventor may later be called on to prove when an invention was first conceived, and what steps were taken to reduce it to practice, most inventors maintain detailed records of their inventive activities in notebooks or in disclosure documents that are signed and witnessed.

EXAMPLE: Bellingham Medical Supplies and Boca Raton Pharmaceuticals both have pending applications for a patent on a painkilling device designed to allow patients to self-medicate small doses of certain opiates without running the risk of an overdose or addictive reaction. An interference is declared and a hearing scheduled. At the hearing, the research scientists at Bellingham Medical produce their notebooks showing that they were the first to conceive of the invention. Boca Raton, on the other hand, establishes that it filed its patent application first, and was thus the first to constructively reduce the invention to practice.

If Bellingham can establish that it was the first to actually reduce the invention to practice by building a working model before Boca Raton filed its application, or that it was diligently working to reduce the invention to practice at the time Boca Raton first conceived of the invention, Bellingham will be awarded the patent. If neither of these showings is made, however, Boca Raton will be awarded the patent (even though it was the second to conceive the invention), because it was the first to reduce the invention to practice by filing the patent application, and Bellingham failed to show the necessary diligence towards reduction to practice after its initial conception of the invention.

Related terms: Disclosure Document Program (DDP); filing date; interference, defined; notebook; Provisional Patent Application (PPA); reduction to practice.

How the PTO Decides a Patent Interference Proceeding

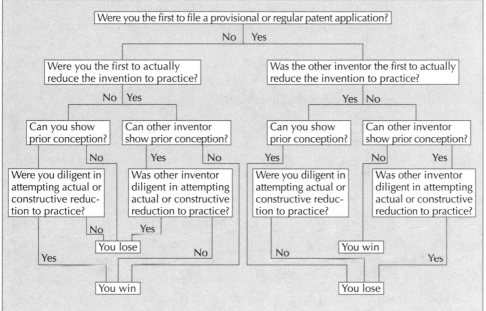

International Bureau of the World Intellectual Property Organization

This administrative arm of the World Intellectual Property Organization (WIPO) in Geneva, Switzerland, is designated by the Patent Cooperation Treaty of 1970 as the clearinghouse for international patent applications.

Related terms: Patent Cooperation Treaty (PCT).
See also Part 1 (Trade Secret Law): World Intellectual Property Organization (WIPO).

international patent protection for U.S. inventions

U.S. inventors can gain patent protection in countries outside the U.S. in two ways:

- by filing separately in each country where protection is desired under certain rules established by the Paris Convention, or
- by filing an "international application" with the International Bureau of the World Intellectual Property Organization, an office established under the Patent Cooperation Treaty (PCT). This single filing establishes a filing date

good in all member countries, although the patent owner must file separate "national" applications in each member country where the owner wants coverage. The European Patent Office is considered a single entity for the purpose of the PCT.

Although other treaties exist between the U.S. and certain countries pertaining to reciprocal patent protection, the two mentioned above provide the primary international protection for U.S. inventors.

Related terms: Convention application; European Patent Convention; Federal Trade Commission proceeding; Patent Cooperation Treaty (PCT).

Internet, patent searching

See patent search, computerized.

Internet patent

The term "Internet patent" has been used to describe a group of utility patents issued for software programs and for methods of doing business, most of which relate to Internet uses. The most well-known example of an Internet patent is Amazon.com's "One-Click" system, a method that allows a repeat customer to bypass address and credit card data entry forms when placing an online order. (U.S. Pat. No. 5,960,411).

What *is* different about Internet patents is the subject matter—a method of doing business. For most of the 20th century, the courts and the PTO believed that business methods could not be patented. But in 1998 a federal court ruled that patent laws were intended to protect any method, whether or not it required the aid of a computer, so long as it produced a "useful, concrete and tangible result." (*State Street Bank & Trust Co. v. Signature Financial Group, Inc.*, 149 F.3d 1368 (Fed. Cir. 1998).) Thus, with one stroke, the court legitimized both software patents and methods of doing business, opening the way for these so-called Internet patents. Regardless of their categorization, business method, software or Internet patents have one thing in common: they expand ways of doing business in new technologies.

Related terms: business methods as statutory subject matter; software patents.

intervening right

When an in-force patent is reissued on the basis of broadened claims, there exists the possibility that someone relying on the wording of the claims in the original patent developed or used a device that would not have infringed the original patent, but that does infringe the reissue patent. When this occurs, the infringing business is said to have "intervening" rights, which preclude an infringement suit under the new broadened claims. However, these intervening rights are considered personal to the business in question and cannot be transferred to another business or owner.

Related terms: defenses to a patent infringement claim; reissue patent.

invalid patent

See defenses to a patent infringement claim; unenforceable patent.

invention, defined

As defined by patent attorney David Pressman in his book, *Patent It Yourself* (Nolo), an invention is any thing, process or idea that:

- is not generally and currently known
- without too much skill or ingenuity can exist or be reduced to tangible form or used in a tangible thing
- has some value or use to society, and
- was thought up or discovered by someone.

In addition to this description, an invention is said to happen when the thing, process or idea being invented is first conceived of, if efforts are then continually made to build a working model of the invention or file a patent application on it—that is, reduce it to practice.

Related terms: inventor, defined; patent, defined.

inventor, defined

An inventor is a person who contributes significant creative input into an invention. An application for a patent on an invention must be made in the name of the inventor (or names of all inventors if more than one), even if a commercial or nonprofit organization actually owns the invention. Failing to accurately name the true inventor or inventors in a patent application can result in an issued patent later being declared invalid.

Related terms: co-inventors; patent applicant; patent owner; prosecution of a patent application; shop rights.

issue fee

In addition to the fees required for filing a patent application, additional fees also must be paid for the patent to issue after allowance by the U.S. Patent and Trademark Office. The fees are twice as much for large entities as for small entities. Generally, independent inventors, nonprofit corporations and businesses with fewer than 500 employees qualify for small entity status. However, if an assignment has or will be made by a small entity to a large entity, large entity fees must be paid.

Definitions

Currently (October 2000), fees for a patent to issue are:
- for utility patents, $710 for large entities and $355 for small entities
- for design patents, $320 for large entities and $160 for small entities, and
- for plant patents, $490 for large entities and $245 for small entities.

Related terms: application filing fees; prosecution of a patent application.

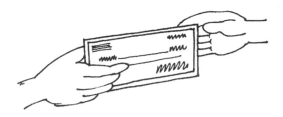

joint inventors

See co-inventors.

junior party in interference proceedings

When an interference is scheduled by the U.S. Patent and Trademark Office, the inventor who was last to file a patent application is known as the junior party.

Related terms: interference proceeding; senior party in interference proceedings.

jury, role of in patent infringment cases

See infringement action.

laboratory notebook

See notebook.

large entity

A for-profit company that has over 500 employees is considered a large entity by the U.S. Patent and Trademark Office (PTO). When a large entity owns the patent rights to an invention, or is entitled to have ownership of these rights transferred to it, the fees payable to the PTO for various aspects of the patent application and prosecution process are double those for small entities.

Related terms: issue fee; maintenance fees; small entity.

laws of nature exception to patents

This rule states that general scientific and mathematical principles are not patentable, even if they meet the other required statutory requirements for patentability (such as utility, novelty and nonobviousness). Laws of nature are considered to be part of the public domain rather than products of human inventiveness.

Related terms: algorithms; genetic engineering and patents; naturally occurring substances as nonpatentable; non-statutory subject matter; statutory subject matter.

lay judge

This term is used by patent law practitioners to refer to any judge sitting in a patent case who is not a patent attorney or especially experienced in patent law.

lay patent searchers

See patent searcher.

letters patent

See patent deed.

licensing of an invention

The process by which an owner gives permission to another party to make, use or sell his or her patented invention is most often given in the form of a written document called a license. A license of patent rights can either be an exclusive license (only the licensee is entitled to exercise the rights set out in the license) or a non-exclusive license (the licensee may exercise the rights set out in the license but cannot prevent others from exercising the same right under a different license).

Related terms: assignment of a patent; exclusive patent license; non-exclusive patent license.

limiting reference

A limiting reference consists of any element in a patent claim that operates to both define the invention and, by defining it, limit its scope.

Related terms: claims, defined.

machines as patentable subject matter

Generally any devices with moving parts, machines are one of the five categories of inventions (called statutory subject matter) that can be patented. Electronic circuits are also considered machines, even though their parts, strictly speaking, don't move.

Related terms: statutory subject matter.

maintenance fees

Fees must be paid to the U.S. Patent and Trademark Office (or the patent office of another country where a patent has been obtained) to keep an issued patent in effect. Currently (October 2000), the maintenance fees for U.S. utility patents (there are no maintenance fees for design or plant patents) are as follows:

Definitions

- to keep a patent in-force for the fourth through eighth year, $850 for large entities and $420 for small entities
- to keep a patent in-force for the ninth through the twelfth year, $1,950 for large entities and $975 for small entities
- to keep a patent in-force for the rest of the patent term (20 years from the filing date), $2,990 for large entities and $1,495 for small entities.

Effective with applications filed after June 7, 1995, the patent term changes from 17 years from the date of issue to 20 years from the date of filing. This means that the final maintenance fee may extend beyond the seventeenth year until the patent term actually expires. As of August 2000, the PTO will accept credit card payments online for maintenance fees at its website (http://www.uspto.gov).

A number of other industrialized countries require inventors to pay even larger maintenance fees, reaching into the thousands of dollars per renewal period, in order to maintain the validity of their patent.

Related terms: large entity; small entity.

Manual of Classification

See classification of patents.

Manual of Patent Examining Procedure (MPEP)

The MPEP is a large, loose-leaf manual of internal procedures followed by U.S. Patent and Trademark Office (PTO) examiners in processing patent applications. Many large libraries carry this volume (often termed "The Examiner's Bible"), which will answer most questions that arise in the course of applying for a patent. Also, the MPEP may be obtained from the PTO, for a fee, in both hard copy form and on CD-ROM.

Related terms: classification of patents; patent application.

manufactures as patentable subject matter

Relatively simple objects that don't have working or moving parts, "manufactures" are one of the five categories of inventions (statutory subject matter) that can be patented. Sometimes called "articles of manufacture," there can be some overlap between the "machine" and "manufacture" categories—especially in the case of inventions involving electronic circuits, which lack moving parts but which are frequently classified as machines because of how they operate.

Examples of more typical manufactures include: erasers, desks, houses, wire, tires, books, cloth, chairs, containers and transistors.

Related terms: statutory subject matter.

Definitions

march-in rights

The U.S government retains the right to use an invention that has been developed as a result of a government contract if the actual inventor fails to develop and exploit the invention sufficiently.

Related terms: patent owner; shop rights.

marking of an invention

Affixing the marks "Patent Pending" or "Pat. Pend." to an invention after a patent application or provisional patent application has been filed, or affixing the patent number after a patent has issued, is known as marking the invention.

The marks "Patent Pending" or "Pat. Pend." have no immediate legal significance, but do place potential infringers on notice that, should a patent ultimately issue, they will not be allowed to make, use or sell the invention without the patent owner's permission. During the patent pending period, an inventor cannot stop an infringer or collect damages. However, under the new 18-month publication statute (see confidentiality of patent applications), an inventor whose application is published prior to issuance may obtain royalties from an infringer from the date the application is published. There are two requirements: (1) the application later issues as a patent; and (2) the infringer had actual notice of the published application. (35 United States Code, Sections 122, 154.) An infringer will have actual notice of a publication if he or she sees the published application. This can be accomplished by sending a copy to the infringer by registered mail. Otherwise, the inventor has no rights whatsoever against infringers during the pendency period—only the hope of a future monopoly, which doesn't commence until a patent issues.

Marking an invention with a patent number (for example, "patent #4,040,387" or "pat. #4,040,387") after a patent is issued puts infringers on notice that any use of the invention may result in an injunction and damages. If an infringement action is later filed, the patent owner will be able to collect damages from the date he or she began properly marking the invention. By contrast, if the invention is not marked, damages may be collected only from the time the infringer received actual notice (usually a demand letter from the patent owner) or the date the patent infringement suit was first filed, whichever occurred earlier.

Many inventors prefer not to place the patent number on their invention. Why? Because marking the invention makes it easier for a competitor to obtain a copy of the patent and design around it. A competitor may have a much more difficult time locating the patent on an unmarked invention. In an attempt to avoid this problem, some patent holders just use the mark "patent," without an accompanying number. This doesn't have any legal clout, however, since this type of notice is not legally sufficient to start the period running for which damages may be recovered. As with an unmarked invention, damages on an inadequately marked invention are recoverable only for the period after the infringer received actual notice, or after the suit was filed.

Related terms: confidentiality of patent applications; infringement action; patent pending.

Markman v. Westview Instruments

This U.S. Supreme Court case (517 U.S. 370 (1976)) ruled that the judge rather than the jury is responsible for interpreting patent claims in a patent infringement case. Since the scope of the claims can often determine the outcome of an infringement case, the power of the jury in such cases has been sharply diminished.

mathematical formulas

See algorithms.

means plus function clause

This jargon refers to a way of defining an invention in a patent claim that describes an element of the invention in terms of its function (as the means by which a specific function is performed), rather than in terms of its specific structure.

The use of a means plus function clause broadens the claim, and makes the claim harder to design around (and therefore easier to infringe), since a patent on the "means" will then support all possible structures that can perform the specified function. A means plus function clause must include the term "means" followed by the specific function of the element.

> EXAMPLE: One of the claims in a patent application filed on fundamental multimedia search technology begins by stating: "A computer search system for retrieving information, comprising:... means for storing interrelated textual information and graphical information."

In this claim element, the words "means for storing... information" theoretically are broad enough to include CD-ROM, a computer hard disk or any other information storage method that exists now or may exist in the future. However, the scope of this or any other claim using a means plus clause is not as unlimited as the words may suggest. When determining the scope of a claim containing a means plus function clause, the U.S. Patent and Trademark Office (PTO) and courts look to other references to the invention contained in the patent or patent application and limit the reach of the claim to those references. Also, because historically there has been some dispute as to how broadly means plus function claims can read (that is, how many devices/processes they can cover), it is often wise to draft one set of claims using means plus function clauses and a duplicate set of claims citing specific devices and processes so that the patent will be both as broad and specific as the PTO will allow.

Related terms: claims, defined; prosecution of a patent application.

methods as patentable subject matter

See processes (or methods) as patentable subject matter.

misuse of patent

Use of a patent in a manner that violates federal patent or antitrust laws may result in the patent being declared invalid or unenforceable by a court. Most often, the issue of patent misuse is raised as a defense to a patent infringement action. If the court in such an action finds that the patent was misused, it will not enforce the patent unless the owner can show that the misuse was voluntarily and completely cured ("purged"). If the misuse was an antitrust violation, however, no such cure is possible and the patent will simply be declared invalid.

Related terms: antitrust law (federal) and patents; breaking a patent; defenses to a patent infringement claim; infringement of patent.

multiple claims

A single patent application may contain two or more claims describing a single invention. A patent application typically contains more than one claim, because there is often more than one way a single invention can be novel and/or useful.

> **EXAMPLE:** A robotics invention that keeps a running account of a kitchen's ingredients can be viewed as a device for maintaining general inventory, a specific process of managing a kitchen's stock of food and a new physical manifestation of certain robotics principles. At least three different independent claims might be used to describe the invention in these different ways.

Related terms: claims, defined; dependent claim; independent claim.

narrowing a claim

A claim in a patent application that was initially rejected by a patent examiner as being too broad (over the prior art) may be redrafted (narrowed) so that the claim no longer overlaps with the prior art, and therefore describes a novel and nonobvious invention. Narrowing can be done by adding more elements to the claim or by reciting the existing elements more specifically.

Related terms: claims, defined; first office action.

naturally occurring substances as nonpatentable

Items or substances that are found to exist in a natural state are not eligible for patent protection (they are non-statutory subject matter). In other words, the discovery of natural substances and processes does not by itself qualify as an invention. However, if natural substances are manipulated and repackaged to meet specific human needs—as is true with many drugs—they may qualify as patentable inventions.

The rule prohibiting the patenting of naturally occurring substances previously was used to bar patents on most living matter. However, the late twentieth century has seen the development of technologies that allow the genetic alteration of living plants and animals into something different from a "naturally occurring substance." Accordingly, patents have issued on such items as genetically manipulated DNA molecules, enzymes, proteins, bacteria, viruses, plants and even a mouse, as well as on the processes of manipulation themselves.

Related terms: genetic engineering and patents; non-statutory matter; plant patents.

negative doctrine of equivalents

Under this doctrine, a later device or process may be held to not infringe the patent on an earlier invention, even though the patent's claims fully cover (read on) the later device or process, if the structure, function or result of the two inventions are substantially different.

This is the rarely used converse of the doctrine of equivalents, which requires a finding of infringement when an invention and a later item are basically the same, even though the patent's claims do not, strictly speaking, cover the later item.

Related terms: doctrine of equivalents; infringement action.

new combinations of old inventions

See combination patent.

new matter

Technical information about an invention that was not included in the original patent application is referred to as new matter. Once an application has been filed, the U.S. Patent and Trademark Office (PTO) does not allow an applicant to add new matter that would change the scope and nature of the invention. This is because the filing date often determines the date of the invention, and if new matter could continually be added to an application, the filing date would no longer serve this purpose.

However, an applicant for a patent who wants to bring new matter before the PTO may do so by filing a special supplementary application, called a continuation-in-part application.

Related terms: continuation-in-part application (CIP); filing date; patent application.

new-use invention

A new-use invention consists of a new way to use an old device or process, such that the new use is nonobvious—generally remote or surprising to one skilled in the art.

> **EXAMPLE:** Utilizing a known physical property of color dyes that causes them to expand at a different rate when applied to cloth, Tony invents a new process for transferring color patterns into textiles. Assuming that the process is considered nonobvious, it will be entitled to a patent as a "new use" of an old principle.

Related terms: nonobviousness, defined; statutory subject matter.

nondisclosure of patent applications by U.S. Patent and Trademark Office

See confidentiality of patent application.

nonelected claims

A patent may only claim one invention. An applicant may voluntarily choose (elect) not to prosecute a claim or claims in a pending patent application in response to a patent examiner's decision that the application impermissibly claims two inventions. However, an applicant can file a "divisional application" on the nonelected claims, so that they are not abandoned.

Related terms: abandonment of patent; divisional application; double patenting.

non-exclusive patent license

A non-exclusive patent license is an agreement by which a patent owner (the "licensor") authorizes (licenses) another (the "licensee") to make, use and/or sell the patented invention, but retains the right to license it to others as well. For example, the inventor of a new, more efficient fuel injection system would most likely grant non-exclusive licenses to all the major car companies able to utilize the system, rather than just license it to one company on an exclusive basis.

Related terms: anti-shelving clause; exclusive patent license; infringement action.

Definitions

Definitions

nonobviousness, defined

The quality of nonobviousness refers to the ability of the invention to produce unexpected or surprising new results—results that were not anticipated by the prior art. (The statute that sets forth the nonobviousness requirements is found in 35 United States Code, Section 103.)

To be patentable, an invention must be nonobvious to a person with ordinary skill in the art. Thus, an invention involving video technology would need to be considered nonobvious to a video engineer thoroughly familiar with prior art in the video field.

Analyzing an invention for nonobviousness is difficult primarily because it is a subjective exercise. In addition, whether or not an invention is nonobvious is supposed to be determined as of the date of invention—which in most cases is considered to be the date a provisional or regular patent application is filed. This means that the U.S. Patent and Trademark Office (PTO) usually must decide whether an invention is nonobvious well after the date of the invention, because of delays inherent in the patent prosecution process. If the issue of nonobviousness is raised as a defense in a patent infringement lawsuit, the court must look back over an even longer period of time to decide whether the invention was nonobvious as of the date of invention.

The initial determination of whether an invention is (was) nonobvious is made by the patent examiner in the course of deciding whether a patent should issue. The patent examiner generally approaches this task by examining all pertinent prior art references that existed as of the date of invention. Because the patent examiner is usually knowledgeable in the area of the patent being examined, his or her expertise may also be brought to bear as a person with ordinary skill in the art.

However, once a patent issues, the patent may be attacked (usually in court) on the ground that the patent examiner made a mistake on the question of nonobviousness. In this situation, both sides will typically produce experts who provide opposing opinions ("Yes, it was nonobvious"; "No, it absolutely wasn't"). The inventor will also attempt to establish that the invention enjoyed commercial success or solved an unperceived need and should therefore be considered to be nonobvious on the basis of actual developments in the marketplace, regardless of what the experts say. In addition to this evidence, the court will evaluate from scratch the prior art existing at the time of the invention.

EXAMPLE: In August 1998, Future Enterprises invented a machine that could analyze chromosomes for multiple types of genetic damage and abnormalities.

A patent application was filed in October 1998. In April 2000, the PTO examined the prior art existing as of October 1998. That prior art indicated ("taught" in patent jargon) that gene identification procedures at that time only allowed one identification at a time, so the PTO determined that the invention was nonobvious in October 1998 and issued a patent on the invention in August 2000, without concern for intervening developments.

In October 2000, by which time multiple analysis procedures were in common use, Future Enterprises sued NewGene Inc., a molecular biology laboratory, for patent infringement, claiming that NewGene was using the multiple analysis procedure without Future's permission. NewGene defended the suit by alleging that multiple analysis procedures were obvious at the time of the invention, and that the PTO's decision to issue the patent should be overturned and the patent invalidated on obviousness grounds.

When the suit goes to trial in August 2002, Future and NewGene both introduce testimony by molecular biologists regarding the state of knowledge in October 1998, the date the of the challenged invention. One set of biologists testifies that the multiple analysis procedures described in the invention were the obvious next step and that their development was not a new and surprising result. Another group of biologists testifies that in October 1998, the molecular biology field was stuck in its single analysis mode and that the invention was a significant breakthrough that allowed molecular biologists to identify faulty genes at a much faster pace. In addition to presenting expert testimony, both sides also introduce reams of documents that try to prove their competing contentions. The court then considers all this evidence over four years after the date of the original invention and decides whether the invention was nonobvious.

One danger of relying on this type of retrospective analysis is that the experts and judge will be unconsciously affected by the intervening technical improvements, and the invention might later be considered obvious even though it wasn't at the time of invention.

Related terms: *Graham v. John Deere* case; obviousness, defined; person with ordinary skill in the art; statutory subject matter.

non-statutory subject matter

To qualify for a patent, an invention must fit into one or more categories established by the federal patent laws (statutes). The categories are compositions of matter, processes, machines, manufactures and new uses of inventions falling within any of the first four categories. Inventions that don't fall within any of these classes are said to be "non-statutory subject matter," and are not patentable. Examples of non-statutory subject matter are:

- processes done entirely by human motor coordination, such as choreographed dance routines
- printed matter that has no unique physical shape or structure associated with it
- naturally occurring matter, even though its external characteristics may be modified, and
- abstract scientific principles, mathematical formulas and natural laws (algorithms) or ideas that don't produce a useful, concrete or tangible result.

The term "non-statutory subject matter" has a second, less obvious meaning: any invention that doesn't qualify for a patent for any reason is also termed non-statutory subject matter. So even if an invention fits within one of the five statutory categories above, it would still be considered non-statutory subject matter if it failed to meet the additional basic patent qualifications of novelty, non-obviousness and utility.

Related terms: algorithms; genetic engineering and patents; laws of nature exception to patents; naturally occurring substances as nonpatentable; statutory subject matter.

not invented here (NIH) syndrome

A handicap to inventors trying to market their inventions is the refusal by many companies to buy, develop or distribute inventions owned by outside inventors—inventions that are "not invented here."

This all too common policy is often attributable to corporate ego: if it wasn't invented here, it can't be any good. But in addition, it can be the understandable result of the sincere desire to avoid potential and expensive disputes over who owns the patents held or applied for by the company. By never looking at out-siders' inventions, a business can at least partially protect itself from such claims.

Related terms: infringement action; patent owner.

notebook, inventor's

Many inventors maintain a journal in which they record when and how they conceived of an invention and specify all procedures, dates, actions, failures, successes, contacts and other events that occur in the course of building and testing the invention.

This information may be very important if there is a conflict between patent applications pending in the PTO. Every inventor is therefore well advised to

maintain such a journal, diary or notebook, and to have the notebook entries signed, dated and witnessed as they are made.

Two statutory alternatives to the patent notebook method of documenting an invention are:

- the Disclosure Document Program, a procedure in which an inventor can disclose the conception of his or her invention to the PTO for a nominal fee, and
- the Provisional Patent Application (PPA), a program effective June 8, 1995, under which an inventor may submit a full disclosure of his or her invention to the PTO up to a year prior to filing the actual patent application. A properly filed PPA operates as a (constructive) reduction to practice in case of an interference or conflicting prior art.

Related terms: Disclosure Document Program (DDP); interference proceeding; Provisional Patent Application (PPA).

notice of allowance

A notice of allowance is sent to an applicant when a patent examiner decides that a patent should issue on an invention (technically, the claims are allowed).

Related terms: office action; prosecution of a patent application.

notice of references cited

This form is sent by the U.S. Patent and Trademark Office (PTO) to a patent applicant citing the various prior art references used by the PTO as a basis for rejecting the application's claims. Copies of the references are also enclosed, so the applicant can respond to the rejection by either explaining why they don't apply or by amending the rejected claims.

Related terms: office action; prior art reference; prosecution of a patent application.

Definitions

novelty, defined

An invention must have novelty to qualify for a patent. In this context, "novelty" means that the invention is different from the prior art (that is, all previous products, devices, methods and documents describing these things). An invention is considered different from the prior art—and therefore novel—when no single prior art item describes all of the invention's elements. The statute setting out the novelty requirement is 35 United States Code, Section 102.

Even if an invention is novel in that it is different from the prior art, it can still flunk the novelty test if it has been described in a published document or put to public use more than one year prior to a patent application being filed on it (known as the one-year rule).

Although an invention may meet the novelty test, it still may be denied a patent if the patent examiner finds that the invention is obvious—that is, it isn't innovative enough to deserve a patent.

Related terms: anticipation; nonobviousness, defined; one-year rule.

obviousness, defined

The quality of an obvious invention is such that a person with ordinary skill in the art could reasonably believe that, at the time of its conception, the invention was to be expected. An obvious invention (that is, one that lacks the quality of nonobviousness) doesn't qualify for a patent.

> EXAMPLE: A new metal that is significantly lighter and stronger than current alloys hits the market. It is "obvious" that someone will build a bicycle containing the material, since lightness is a desirable aspect of high-quality bicycles. Thus, while the inventor of the metal may be entitled to a patent, the developer of the new bicycle made from that metal will not.

Related terms: nonobviousness, defined; person with ordinary skill in the art.

office action

A letter sent by a patent examiner to an applicant regarding the pending application is called an office action. Generally, one or two office actions are sent per patent application. The first office action typically describes what's wrong with the application and why it can't be allowed. Most often, the first office action rejects the application because of:

- lack of novelty (35 United States Code, Section 102)
- obviousness (35 United States Code, Section 103), or
- claim indefiniteness (35 United States Code, Section 112).

The applicant is permitted to amend the application to overcome the rejection as long as no new subject matter is added. If the application is acceptable as amended, a notice of allowance will be sent (that is, a patent is granted). If the application is still not acceptable, the patent examiner will send a final office action that partially or completely rejects the application.

Related terms: final office action; first office action; prosecution of a patent application.

Official Gazette (OG)

The Official Gazette consists of two weekly publications put out by the U.S. Patent and Trademark Office (PTO). There is one for trademarks and another for patents. Each is colloquially known as the OG.

The patent edition contains official announcements concerning PTO policy and patent rules, and information on patents issued that week. For each patent, the Official Gazette contains:

- its patent number
- all inventors' names and addresses
- the assignee (usually a company to which the inventor has transferred ownership of the patent), if any
- the filing date
- the application's serial number
- the international classification number
- the U.S. classification number
- the main figure or drawing
- the number of claims, and
- a sample claim or abstract.

The Official Gazette contains the essence of the invention, not the entire patent. The full text of the patent contains far more technical information.

Anyone wishing to keep up with the patents being issued in his or her field should regularly read the Official Gazette. Many major libraries subscribe to this publication and file back issues. It is now also possible to track issued patents by subscribing to an online new-patent service available through the Internet (located on the PTO's Internet site at http://www.uspto.gov).

Related terms: abstract; Internet, U.S. Patent and Trademark Office site; Patent and Trademark Depository Library; patent search.

on sale statutory bar

Part of the one-year rule, the on sale statutory bar holds that any invention that is placed on sale more than one year before a patent application is filed on it is not eligible for a patent. In this case, the patent is barred by statute from issuing. (35 United States Code, Section 102.)

"On sale" means not only the actual selling, but also any sales effort or solicitation. Such actions are considered public use in violation of the novelty requirement.

Related terms: anticipation; novelty, defined; one-year rule; statutory bar.

one-year rule

The one-year rule (35 United States Code, Section 102) requires a patent application on an invention to be filed within one year of:

- any public use of the invention by the inventor
- an actual sale of the invention
- an offer to sell the invention, or
- any description of the invention by the inventor in a published document.

Failure to file a patent application within this one-year period results in the invention passing into the public domain. An invention in the public domain is not considered novel, and is therefore not eligible for a patent.

The filing of a Provisional Patent Application (PPA) does not trigger the one-year rule for purposes of determining the invention's novelty in the U.S., but does trigger the one-year period for filing patent applications in other countries. Also, if a regular patent application is not filed within one year of the PPA's filing date, the PPA's date cannot be claimed as the filing date for purposes of deciding whether the invention has been anticipated by prior art or reduced to practice (in case of an interference).

Related terms: anticipation; filing date; novelty, defined; on sale statutory bar; patent application; Provisional Patent Application (PPA).

online patent searching

See patent search, computerized.

operability

An invention must (theoretically at least) work in order to qualify for a utility patent. Although this does not mean the device must actually be built and working, it does mean that the patent application must disclose sufficient information to demonstrate the theoretical operability of the invention.

A patent examiner who believes an invention will not work (is non-operable) can require proof of its operability (such as a demonstration) before the patent application will be allowed. However, the fact that a patent has been issued on an invention is not a guarantee that the invention will work—only that it appears to work on paper.

Related terms: disclosure requirement for patents; utility patents, defined.

opposing a patent (international rules)

In most countries, a party may register its opposition to a pending patent application after it has been officially published. If the opposing party can establish that relevant prior art exists, an opposition proceeding is held to determine whether a patent should be issued. This process opens up the initial patent determination to all interested parties.

Related terms: defenses to a patent infringement claim; infringement action; reexamination of patent.

ordinary skill in the art

See person with ordinary skill in the art.

ownership of patent

See patent owner.

PAD

See Patent Application Declaration (PAD).

PCT

See Patent Cooperation Treaty (PCT).

PTDL

See Patent and Trademark Depository Libraries.

PTO

See U.S. Patent and Trademark Office (PTO).

parent application

During the prosecution of a patent, an applicant may need to file additional applications, such as a divisional application, a substitute application, a continuation application, a continuation-in-part application or an application for a reissue patent. If one of these subsequent applications is filed, the original application will be referred to as the parent application.

> **EXAMPLE:** Rory applies for a patent for a tennis racket with an electronic device embedded in the handle that keeps track of the score. The patent examiner rejects the application because it claims two inventions—the racket/device combination and the device by itself. Rory then restricts his application by withdrawing or canceling the claims to the device itself, and files a divisional

application on it. In this scenario, the application that now only claims the combination will be considered the parent application.

Related terms: continuation application; divisional application; double patenting; prosecution of a patent application; reissue patent; substitute patent application.

Paris Convention

See Convention application; European Patent Convention.

patent, defined

Legally, a patent is a right provided by a government that allows an inventor to prevent others from manufacturing, selling or using the patent owner's invention. This right covers the invention as specifically described in the patent application's claims allowed by the U.S. Patent and Trademark Office (PTO) or other patent examining agencies in other countries.

Physically, a U.S. patent consists of the following:

- a cover sheet bearing the patent number; the name of the invention as provided by the inventor; the name of all inventors; the name of the assignee (the person or company to whom the patent has been assigned), if any; the application filing date; a list of the prior art references found by the patent examiner to be pertinent to the invention; and the patent abstract (a concise summary of the invention)
- one or more pages containing drawings of the invention submitted by the patent applicant
- the patent specification as submitted in the patent application (a detailed narrative description of the invention's structure and function), and
- the patent claims as finally approved by the patent examiner.

The original physical patent issued by the PTO is termed a "patent deed" or "letters patent" and has a blue ribbon and gold seal for adornment. The physical patent retained by the PTO and others interested in the patent is often termed a "patent copy" or a "soft copy" and lacks the adornment found on the patent deed. As with a college diploma or deed, the patent in any of its forms has no intrinsic value. The patent derives its value from the offensive rights it provides in the event of an infringement.

Related terms: claims, defined; infringement action; prosecution of a patent application.

patent agents

Patent agents are non-attorneys with technical training who are legally permitted—under a license issued by the PTO—to draft, file and prosecute patent applications on behalf of inventors. If necessary, a patent agent also can represent applicants before the Board of Patent Appeals and Interferences. However, if a patent becomes the subject of litigation in court, only a patent attorney may appear on behalf of the inventor.

Related terms: patent attorneys; patent searcher.

patent applicant

The inventor or organization who files the patent application (and often, who will own the patent if the application is granted) is termed the patent applicant. Patent applicants typically are independent inventors who choose to build and distribute their own inventions, companies to which independent inventors have sold (assigned) their invention, or large R&D companies that employ the actual inventor. Even if an entity other than the inventor will own the patent, the application must be filed in the name of the inventor.

Related terms: co-inventors; inventor, defined; patent application; patent owner.

patent application

A voluminous packet of papers must be mailed to the U.S. Patent and Trademark Office (PTO) to obtain a patent. Usually included in a patent application (now referred to as a regular or formal patent application to distinguish it from a Provisional Patent Application) are:

- a self-addressed receipt postcard
- a transmittal letter
- a check for the filing fee
- a fee transmittal form
- drawings
- a specification (a sample is provided in the Forms & Resources section at the end of this part of the book.)
- one or more patent claims
- an abstract
- a Patent Application Declaration (PAD)
- a Small Entity Declaration (SED), for independent inventors and small companies to obtain the lower application fee, and
- an Information Disclosure Statement (IDS).

A regular patent application can also include a Petition to Make Special (to speed the processing), an assignment and assignment cover sheet (if the invention was sold by its owner), a Disclosure Document Reference Letter (if a disclosure document was previously filed with the PTO) and a transmittal letter claiming the Provisional Patent Application filing date, if a PPA was filed.

Definitions

One to two weeks after the application is mailed, the applicant will receive the receipt postcard back from the PTO with the filing date and number stamped on it. The filing date applies to this application and will provide the starting date for determining the patent term (20 years from date of filing). However, if a Provisional Patent Application was filed, its filing date will provide the basis for determining the invention's novelty and deciding any interference that is declared by the PTO.

The receipt of the postcard means that the PTO has established a separate file (called a file wrapper) in which the application and all future correspondence between the applicant and the PTO is kept.

Once a regular patent application is on file, the applicant is said to be in the patent prosecution stage, which averages 18 months but which can take much longer in specific cases.

Related terms: prosecution of a patent application; Provisional Patent Application (PPA).

Patent Application Declaration (PAD)

A Patent Application Declaration (PAD) is a written statement, made under penalty of perjury, that must accompany a patent application. In the statement, the patent applicant states (avers) that:

- the applicant is the first and true inventor
- the applicant has reviewed and understands the specification and claims, and
- the applicant has disclosed all information material to the examination of the application.

Related terms: duty of candor and good faith; fraud on the U.S. Patent and Trademark Office; patent application; prosecution of a patent application.

patent attorneys

Patent attorneys must be licensed to practice law and also be licensed by the U.S. Patent and Trademark Office (PTO) to practice before it. Patent attorneys prepare and prosecute patent applications, represent clients in interference proceedings and bring and defend patent-related lawsuits in federal court.

Patent attorneys are required to have a technical higher education degree as well as a legal background, and must pass a PTO examination in order to obtain their license. A complete listing of all licensed patent attorneys can be obtained in the PTO publication, *Attorneys and Agents Registered to Practice Before the U.S. Patent and Trademark Office.*

Related terms: infringement action; interference, defined; patent agents.

patent claim

See claims, defined.

Patent Cooperation Treaty (PCT)

This international agreement establishes streamlined procedures for obtaining uniform patent protection in its member countries. The PCT is administered by the World Intellectual Property Organization (WIPO) in Geneva, Switzerland. U.S. inventors applying for PCT patent protection can file with the U.S. Patent and Trademark Office, which has been designated a receiving office of the International Bureau.

In addition to filing the one PCT application, an inventor must still file a national patent application in every country in which patent protection is desired. However, the primary advantages of using PCT's procedures are:

- By filing one PCT application, the applicant obtains a filing date that is good in every member country in which he or she ultimately seeks patent protection.

- An initial international patent search is conducted on the PCT application and the member countries will rely heavily on this search. Thus, the applicant is saved the great expense and delay that can result from having to conduct separate searches in each country and convince each country's patent examining agency that an invention is novel and nonobvious over the prior art.

- The PCT applicant need not decide whether to prosecute the international application in the individual countries until 18 months after the initial patent application filing date in his or her original country.

Currently (November 2000), PCT member countries or jurisdictions are: ARIPO (African Regional Industrial Property Organization, which includes Kenya, Malawi and Sudan), Armenia, Australia, Austria, Barbados, Belarus, Belgium, Brazil, Bulgaria, Canada, China (People's Republic), Czech Republic, Denmark, Estonia, European Patent Office, Finland, France, Georgia, Germany, Greece, Hungary, Ireland, Italy, Japan, Kazakhstan, Kenya, Korea (North), Korea (South), Kyrgyzstan, Latvia, Liberia, Lichtenstein, Lithuania, Luxembourg, Madagascar, Malawi, Moldovia (Republic of), Monaco, Mongolia, Netherlands, New Zealand, Niger, Norway, OAPI (Organization Africane Propriete Intellectual, which includes Benin, Burkina Faso, Cameroon, Central African Republic, Chad, Congo, Cote d'Ivoire, Gabon, Guinea, Mali, Senegal and Togo), Poland, Portugal, Romania, Russian Federation, Slovak Republic, Sri Lanka, Sudan,

Sweden, Switzerland, Tajikistan, Trinidad, Tobago, Ukraine, United Kingdom, United States, Uzbekistan and Vietnam.

For more specific information on filing under the Patent Cooperation Treaty, a booklet called the *PCT Applicant's Guide* can be obtained from the World Intellectual Property Organization.

Related terms: International Bureau of the World Intellectual Property Organization; international patent protection for U.S. inventions.
See also Part 1 (Trade Secret Law): World Intellectual Property Organization (WIPO).

patent deed

This official document, sometimes termed "letters patent," is sent to applicants by the U.S. Patent and Trademark Office, when their patent issues.

Related terms: final office action; notice of allowance; patent, defined.

patent examination process

See prosecution of a patent application.

patent examiners

U.S. Patent and Trademark Office examiners are employees who examine patent and trademark applications. On the patent side, the examiners correspond with applicants and decide whether inventions deserve patents. All patent examiners must have a technical degree in some field, such as electrical engineering, chemistry or physics. Many are also attorneys.

Related terms: U.S. Patent and Trademark Office (PTO).

patent infringement action

See infringement action.

patent issue fees

See issue fee.

patent license agreements

See exclusive patent license; non-exclusive patent license.

patent number

The number assigned to each patent by the U.S. Patent and Trademark Office is known as the patent number.

Related terms: marking of an invention.

patent number marking

See marking of an invention.

patent owner

The inventor is usually the patent owner unless the invention and patent rights were assigned (ownership rights were transferred to another person or entity—for instance, because the invention arose in the course of an employment relationship).

Many inventors assign ownership of their invention to development or manufacturing companies in exchange for compensation in the form of a lump sum or royalties on sales realized from the invention. These assignments typically also include ownership of the patent, whether already issued or to be issued in the future.

Large companies, and often universities and laboratories, usually require employees to assign their future inventions to the institution as a condition of employment. Under these assignments, the institution will be considered the patent owner. In some states, such requirements are prohibited for inventions that:

- were made on the employee's own time
- did not involve the use of the employer's equipment, supplies, facilities or trade secret information, and
- do not relate to the business of the employer and do not result from any work prepared by the employee for the employer or relate to the employer's actual or demonstrably anticipated research or development.

Even if an inventor retains the right to the invention and is therefore considered the patent owner, employers retain the right (called "shop rights") to make and use an invention created in the course of the employment relationship and with the employer's tools and facilities.

Related terms: assignment of patent; co-inventors; shop rights.

patent pending

Once a patent application (regular or provisional) has been filed in the U.S. Patent and Trademark Office, the invention has patent pending status. The inventor can then mark the device "patent pending" to deter potential competitors from copying it by informing them that it may soon receive a patent. However, unless and until a patent is actually issued, an inventor has no right to prevent others from making, using and selling the invention. In other words, simply applying for a patent does not earn the applicant the right to behave like a patent owner.

However, under the new 18-month publication statute (see confidentiality of patent applications), an inventor whose application is published prior to issuance may obtain royalties from an infringer from the date the application is published. There are two requirements: (1) the application later issues as a patent; and (2) the infringer had actual notice of the published application. (35 United States Code, Sections 122, 154.) An infringer will have actual notice of a publication if he or she sees the published application. This can be accomplished by sending a copy to the infringer by registered mail. Otherwise, the inventor has no rights whatsoever against infringers during the pendency period.

The patent pending label can also provide a way for an inventor to show the invention to a potential developer without fear that the developer will rip it off and later claim to be the true inventor. This is especially useful when a developer refuses to sign a nondisclosure agreement for fear of a later lawsuit by the inventor.

Before June 8, 1995, obtaining patent pending status involved the considerable expense of preparing and filing a full patent application. Under the Provisional Patent Application program, however, patent pending status costs considerably less ($75 for small entities, current as of September 2000).

Related terms: marking of an invention; not invented here (NIH) syndrome; office action; opposing a patent (international rules); Provisional Patent Application (PPA).

patent pools

Under a patent pool arrangement between two or more companies, the companies assign (sell) their patents to a third party which, in turn, licenses any or all of the patents back to participating companies. This allows the participating companies to share their patents by providing them with access to each other's patents on a reciprocal basis.

Patent pools run a substantial risk of violating the antitrust laws in the event they are not open to all competitors in a particular industry.

Related terms: antitrust law (federal) and patents; concerted refusal to deal; cross-licensing.

patent prosecution

See prosecution of patent application.

patent search

The term "patent search" generally means a search for documents that will help one decide whether a particular invention was novel and nonobvious when it was invented. While a patent search usually starts with the patent database (all previously issued patents), it also covers other types of documents that may describe the invention being searched, such as journal articles and scientific papers.

There are normally three discrete types of patent searches:

- *patentability searches.* This kind of search is normally conducted by, or on behalf of, an inventor to familiarize the inventor with previous developments in the field of invention and to help the inventor determine whether it is worthwhile to develop the invention and/or apply for a patent in the first place. Also, once a patent application is filed, the U.S. Patent and Trademark Office will conduct its own patentability search in the course of examining the application.
- *infringement searches.* An infringement search is usually much narrower in scope than a patentability search and is conducted for the purpose of deciding whether a particular invention will infringe an in-force patent.
- *validity searches.* This search is usually conducted by the defendant in a patent infringement case for the purpose of discovering documents that will adversely bear on the validity of the patent as issued.

Related terms: infringement search; nonobviousness, defined; novelty, defined; patent search, computerized; patent searcher; Patent and Trademark Depository Library (PTDL); patentability search; prior art, defined; validity search.

patent search, computerized

All patents issued by the U.S. Patent and Trademark Office (PTO) since 1972 now are available online through a number of different public and private services.

Here are several organizations that offer computer searching of patent records along with a description of their services. Several of the "for fee" databases also provide foreign patent information.

- The U.S. Patent & Trademark Office (http://www.uspto.gov/patft/index.html) is a free online full-text searchable database of patents and drawings that cover the period from January 1976 to the most recent weekly issue date (usually each Tuesday). In order to view the drawings, the user's computer must be able to view TIFF files. The PTO's site is linked to a source that provides a free downloadable TIFF reader program. For faster searching there is also a Bibliographic Database that contains only the text of each patent without drawings.
- IBM Intellectual Property Network (http://www.patents.ibm.com) is a free online searchable database with abstract, title, and claims searching capability for patents issued from 1974 to the present.
- Corporate Intelligence Corp (http://www.1790.com) is a commercial fee-based database of U.S. patents searchable from 1945 to the present. Users must first set up an account. CIC offers delivery of patent copies dating back to 1790 by U.S. mail, fax, or email.

Definitions

- Micropatent (http://www.micropatent.com) is a commercial fee-based database of U.S. and Japanese patents searchable from 1976 to the present, International PCT patents from 1983, European patents from 1988 and the Official Gazette (Patents).
- Patent Miner (http://www.patentminer.com) is a commercial fee-based database of U.S. patents searchable from 1970 to the present. Copies of any patent dating from 1790 (the year when U.S. patents were first issued) can be ordered.
- LexPat (http://www.lexis-nexis.com) is a commercial fee-based database of U.S. patents searchable from 1971 to the present. In addition, the LEXPAT library offers extensive prior-art searching capability of technical journals and magazines.
- QPAT (http://www.qpat.com) and Questel/Orbit (http://www.questel.orbit. com) are both commercial fee-based services which access the QPAT database that includes U.S. patents searchable from 1974 to the present and full-text European A (1987-present) and B (1991-present) patents.

The services described above are all accessible from a personal computer connected to the Internet. PTO computer databases can also be accessed through the terminals at the PTO and through the APS Search terminals at 12 of the Patent Trademark Deposit Libraries (PTDLs) listed in the Forms Appendix. The PTDLs at the Sunnyvale, California; Houston, Texas; and Detroit, Michigan public libraries can display the full text and drawings of all U.S. patents back to 1790.

All prior art is relevant to a patent application, even patents that were issued decades ago and which have long since expired. For this reason, it may be necessary to search for pre-1972 patents well as the patents in the computer database—all of which were issued after that date. This would especially be true for gadget-type inventions that might resemble something invented hundreds of years ago. For instance, the finger grooves in certain types of old swords were considered relevant prior art for the finger indentations found in many modern automobile steering wheels.

Pre-1972 patents are not normally relevant to patent searches involving inventions based on modern technologies such as computers and software, integrated circuits, superconductivity, nanotechnology, artificial intelligence, robotics and bio-engineering. For these types of inventions, an online computer search should do the entire job.

An excellent prior art software database can be searched at the Software Patent Institute (http://www.spi.org), 9225 Indian Creek Parkway, Suite 1100, Overland Park, KS 66210-2009 (913-451-3355; FAX: 913-451-3361). The SPI maintains, catalogs, and has the best software prior art database in the world. The SPI also likes to receive prior art on software inventions, such as old instruction books and manuals. Another software patent resource is the Source Translation and Optimization Patent Website (http://www.bustpatents.com). The STO is directed by Gregory Aharonian, one of the PTO's most vocal critics. The site provides critiques, legal reviews, file wrappers and information about infringement lawsuits relating to software patents. The STO also offers a free email newsletter.

Computerized patent searches are usually carried out by typing certain key words at a computer terminal, and instructing the computer to produce a list of all patents that contain those words in the order that you specify. For example, if your search involves a bicycle chain, you might ask for a listing of all patents that contain the words "bicycle" and "chain," where "bicycle" comes before "chain." When the list appears on your terminal, you can then view the full text of any entry on the list or any selected portion (such as the abstract of patent, drawing, claims or specification).

If you find that no patent contains the words "bicycle" and "chain" in that order, then you will need to reformulate your request (try "bipedal vehicle" and "wheel pulling device"). Often it takes a number of attempts to cover all possible words used in all relevant patents. Unless you come up with all the correct words, you may miss patents, and thus perform an incomplete search.

A copy of a patent can be acquired by:

- contacting the PTO (703-305-8716; FAX: 703-305-8759), ordering from the PTO website (http://www.uspto.gov/web/uspto/patsales/patsales.htm) or writing a letter listing the number of the patent to Commissioner for Patents, Washington, DC 20231, with a payment for the price per patent (see the Fee Schedule at the PTO website) times the total number of patents being ordered. The PTO can furnish copies by mail, fax, or FedEx. A copy of a patent can also be obtained from the PTO by clicking on "Order Copy" at the "Manual Search" page at the PTO website (http://www.uspto.gov)

- downloading a text copy or image copy of the patent, if available, from either the IBM or PTO search sites, or

- ordering a copy from a private supply company such as Faxpat (http://www.faxpat.com), Optipat (http://www.optipat.com), Reedfax (http://www.reedfax.com) or Corporate Intelligence Corp. (http://www.1790.com).

Definitions

Related terms: classification of patents; Internet, U.S. Patent and Trademark Office site; patent search; Patent and Trademark Depository Libraries.

patent searcher

A number of individuals and firms specialize in conducting patent searches. In the U.S., patent searchers tend to be concentrated in Arlington, Virginia, because the Patent and Trademark Office (PTO) library is located there and it therefore is the best place to conduct a patent search.

There are three options for getting a patent search done by someone else:

- patent attorneys
- patent agents, and
- lay searchers.

Patent attorneys usually have their favorite searchers and can help you assess the results of the search. However, this is the most expensive option.

The next most expensive option is a patent agent. Patent agents are licensed by the PTO and have demonstrated their competence by passing a PTO-administered test.

The least expensive option is a lay searcher. However, lay searchers are not licensed and you should be careful when selecting one to do your search.

The Yellow Pages are a good place to locate a patent searcher. Look under "patent searcher" for lay searchers and under "attorney," "legal" or "lawyer" for patent attorneys and patent agents.

Related terms: patent agents; patent attorneys; patent search.

patent term extension

Under 35 United States Code, Sections 155 and 156, the statutory period during which a patent is in-force can be extended if the inventor's ability to realize gain from the invention will be adversely affected by a regulatory process. For instance, a new drug or food may be withheld from the market for a number of years because of a requirement that the Food and Drug Administration must approve such items as safe and effective.

Related terms: duration of patents; in-force patent.

Patent and Trademark Depository Libraries

Over 80 libraries around the U.S. have been designated as Patent and Trademark Depository Libraries (PTDLs). These public or special libraries contain copies of patents and the reference tools necessary to carry out a reasonably informative U.S. patentability search.

Although PTDLs contain enough pertinent materials to enable an inventor or other patent searcher to get a reasonably complete picture of the relevant prior art, not all PTDLs have all patents issued from the earliest days of the country. And more seriously, no PTDL has patents physically separated by classification, as does the U.S. Patent and Trademark Office (PTO) library in Arlington, Virginia. Accordingly, most professional patentability searches are conducted by patent searchers situated in the general area of the PTO.

What PTDLs do provide is access to two CD-ROM databases known as CASSIS/CLASS and CASSIS/BIB. CASSIS/CLASS allows the searcher find the classification of any patent and the list of patents in any class. CASSIS/BIB allows the searcher to find bibliographic information about patents issued during the past 20 years as well as the field of search (class and subclass) for any type of invention. Together, these databases can be very helpful to the PTDL patent searcher.

In addition, 32 PTDLs are now providing online access to the PTO patent database, for patents issued after 1971, through a service known as APS (automated patent system), and three PTDLs—Sunnyvale, California; Rice University (Texas) and Detroit—offer access to the same database used by patent examiners.

A list of PTDLs is in the Forms section at the end of this part of the book.

Related terms: patent search; patent search, computerized.

Patent and Trademark Office

See U.S. Patent and Trademark Office (PTO).

patentability

Not all inventions qualify for a patent. To qualify for a utility patent, an invention must:

- fit within one of the five statutory subject matter classes
- have novelty
- be nonobvious, and
- have some usefulness.

To qualify for a plant patent, the plant must meet the first three of these tests. To qualify for a design patent, the novel features of a design must meet the first three qualifications and must be purely ornamental (have no practical function other than ornamental).

Related terms: non-statutory subject matter; statutory subject matter.

patentability search

Once an invention is conceived, the inventor will normally conduct (or have conducted) a search of previous and existing patents and other documents that

Definitions

might describe the invention, to discover whether the invention is novel and nonobvious enough over the prior art to qualify for a patent. A search conducted for this purpose is commonly termed a patentability search. The primary reason for a patentability search is to avoid wasting time and money developing an invention that is not patentable.

Related terms: classification of patents; novelty, defined; patent search; patent search, computerized; patent searcher, prior art reference.

patentable subject matter

See statutory subject matter.

patents as prior art

All patents, whether expired or in-force, and whether issued in the U.S. or in other countries, are considered prior art when determining whether an invention qualifies for a patent.

Related terms: anticipation; prior art, defined; prior art reference.

person with ordinary skill in the art

This is a hypothetical person whose educational or occupational credentials would make him or her competent in the field of the invention. For example, an electrical engineer would be a person with ordinary skill with respect to integrated circuits, whereas a prosthetics engineer would be a person with ordinary skill in the art of designing knee braces.

How this hypothetical person would view a particular invention is used as a standard to make some important determinations. Among the questions that must be answered in deciding whether a patent should issue, or whether an in-force patent is valid, are:

- whether a person with ordinary skill in the art would find the invention an obvious development in light of the relevant prior art (the technology and knowledge existing at the time the invention was first conceived), and
- whether the patent application sufficiently discloses the nature of the invention to permit a person with ordinary skill in the art to build it in a routine manner.

Related terms: disclosure requirement for patents; *Graham v. John Deere* case; nonobviousness, defined.

Petition to Make Special

An applicant can, under certain circumstances, have an application examined sooner than the normal course of PTO examination (one to three years). This is accomplished by filing a "Petition to Make Special" (PTMS), together with a Supporting Declaration.

Related terms: patent applicant; patent application.

plant patents

Since 1930, the U.S. has been granting plant patents under the Plant Patent Act to any person who first appreciates the distinctive qualities of a plant and reproduces it asexually. Asexual reproduction means reproducing the plant by a means other than seeds, usually by grafting or cloning the plant tissue. If a plant cannot be duplicated by asexual reproduction, it cannot be the subject of a plant patent. In addition, the patented plant must also be novel and distinctive. Generally, this means that the plant must have at least one significant distinguishing characteristic to establish it as a distinct variety. For example, a rose may be novel and distinctive if it is nearly thornless and has a unique two-tone color scheme. Tuber-propagated plants (such as potatoes) and plants found in an uncultivated state cannot receive a plant patent. (35 United States Code, Sections 161-164.)

There is a limit on the extent of plant patent rights. Generally, a plant patent can only be infringed when a plant has been asexually reproduced from the actual plant protected by the plant patent. In other words, the infringing plant must have more than similar characteristics—it must have the same genetics as the patented plant.

A man-made plant can also be the subject of a utility patent. These plants can be reproduced either sexually (by seeds) or asexually. For example, utility patents have been issued for elements of plants such as proteins, genes, DNA, buds, pollen, fruit, plant-based chemicals, and the processes used in the manufacture of these plant products. To obtain a utility patent, the plant must be made by humans and must fit within the statutory requirements (utility, novelty and nonobviousness). The patent must describe and claim the specific characteristics of the plant for which protection is sought. Sometimes the best way to meet this requirement is to deposit seeds or plant tissue at a specified public depository. For example, many countries have International Depositories for such purposes.

Although a utility patent is harder and more time-consuming to acquire than a plant patent, a utility patent is considered to be a stronger form of protection. For example, a plant protected by a utility patent can be infringed if it is reproduced either sexually or asexually. Since the utility patent owner can prevent others from making and using the invention, does this mean the purchaser of a patented

Definitions

seed cannot sell the resulting plants to the public? No, under patent laws, the purchaser can sell the plants but cannot manufacture the seed line.

Related terms: genetic engineering and patents; non-statutory subject matter.

Plant Variety Protection Act

This statute authorizes the U.S. Department of Agriculture to grant patent protection for certain types of plants.

Related terms: plant patents.

practicing an invention

See reduction to practice; working a patent.

preliminary look at prior art

This preliminary investigation by inventors consists of checking stores, catalogs, reference books, product directories and similar sources to discover whether a proposed invention already exists. Such preliminary looks should be done before investing time and money developing an invention.

If a preliminary look finds no relevant previous development, then work on the invention may be initiated, with a more serious patentability search to follow before significant resources are expended.

Related terms: patent search; patentability search.

presumption of validity

In an infringement suit brought by a patent owner against an alleged infringer, it is legally presumed that the patent owner's patent is valid. Practically, this means the legal responsibility (burden) is on the alleged infringer to prove that the patent is invalid, if he or she wants to raise this defense.

Related terms: defenses to a patent infringement claim; infringement action.

price fixing

If two or more separate businesses enter into an agreement (formal or informal) to maintain their prices at a certain level, it is known as price fixing. Price fixing is considered a restraint of trade, which is a violation of the antitrust laws. A patent owner who uses the patent monopoly for the purpose of fixing prices may also be deemed guilty of misusing the patent and accordingly lose the patent rights.

Related terms: antitrust law (federal) and patents; concerted refusal to deal; misuse of patent.

printed publication as statutory bar

Under patent law, published writings are considered prior art references, so a previous publication that discusses or describes the essential ideas, functional means or structures that underlie an invention can render that invention ineligible for a patent (the patent is barred by statute from issuing). This will happen if the article describing the invention was published:

- by someone other than the inventor anytime before the date of the invention, or
- by the inventor (or someone else) more than one year before the patent application for the patent was filed.

Related terms: anticipation; one-year rule; statutory bar; thesis as prior art.

prior art, defined

"Prior art" refers to all previous developments that are used by the U.S. Patent and Trademark Office and the courts (in the event of an infringement action) to decide whether a particular invention is sufficiently novel and nonobvious to qualify for a U.S. patent.

Prior art relevant to a particular invention generally includes:

- any description or discussion of the invention's essential characteristics in any printed publication anywhere in the world, in any language, that was made available to the public before the invention was conceived of
- any description or discussion of the invention in a printed publication, public use or sale of the invention occurring more than one year prior to the filing date of the patent application
- any public knowledge of the invention in the U.S. that can be shown to have existed at the time the invention was first conceived of
- any relevant expired or current foreign or U.S. patent issued at any time before the inventor conceived of the invention for which a patent is being sought, or
- any relevant U.S. patent application made prior to conception.

Any specific instance of prior art is generally referred to as a prior art reference.

Related terms: anticipation; nonobviousness, defined; novelty, defined; patentability; prior art reference.

prior art reference

Any printed publication, prior patent or other document that contains a discussion or description relevant to an invention for which a patent is currently being sought or enforced is a prior art reference.

When applying for a patent, an applicant who knows of any prior art references is required to submit an Information Disclosure Statement (IDS) in which all such references must be listed, and to which copies of these references must be appended.

In the event a patent examiner rejects one or more claims on the ground they are anticipated by (or are obvious over) the prior art, the U.S. Patent and Trademark Office sends out a Notice of Prior Art References, with copies of the actual references attached, which identifies the prior art references upon which the rejection is based.

Related terms: anticipation; Information Disclosure Statement; prior art, defined.

processes (or methods) as patentable subject matter

Ways of doing or making things (termed processes or methods) are one of the five categories of statutory subject matter—that is, types of inventions that can be patented. Processes always have at least two steps, each of which expresses some activity or occurrence. Examples of processes include heat-treatment processes, chemical reactions, surgical techniques, gene-splicing procedures, applied robotics and computer software.

To be patentable, a process must produce a useful, concrete and tangible result.

Related terms: non-statutory subject matter; software patents; statutory subject matter.

prosecution of a patent application

Once a regular patent application has been filed, the full gamut of procedures that must be followed to actually obtain the patent is referred to as the prosecution of a patent application. The patent prosecution process does not apply to Provisional Patent Applications (PPAs), which are only examined if the applicant wishes to claim the PPA filing date.

The first step in the patent prosecution process is when a PTO patent examiner who has been assigned to the application sends the applicant a written form (called the first office action), which sometimes takes place up to a year after the application is received. This form will typically deny all or most of the application's claims on a variety of grounds.

If the rejection was due to lack of novelty (35 United States Code, Section 102), the office action will identify the reasons. If the rejection was due to obviousness over the relevant prior art (35 United States Code, Section 103), the office action will list the prior art references in a Notice of Prior Art References. In both Sections 102 and 103 rejections, the PTO will attach copies of the relevant prior art references and designate the claims to which the references pertain.

If a valid PPA was previously filed on the invention, and the PPA filing date is claimed in the regular patent application, the examiner will use that earlier date

Prosecuting of a Patent Application

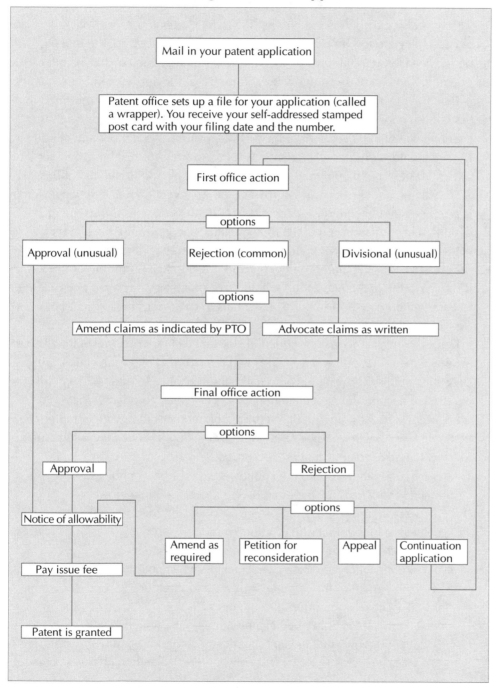

to assess the prior art and only base a rejection on prior art references that came before it.

Claims also may be rejected under 35 United States Code, Section 112, because they are too broad or are formulated incorrectly. If so, the inventor will be provided the opportunity to make amendments suggested by the examiner. On occasion, the patent examiner will determine that the application impermissibly claims two or more inventions. In this case, the applicant will be informed in the first office action that he or she must "elect" (choose to include) the claims covering one of the inventions in the original (parent) application, and optionally file one or more divisional applications for the nonelected claims (the ones that weren't kept in the parent application) that recite the additional inventions.

Sometimes, an inventor will improve his or her invention while the application is pending or will want to broaden or better define the claims. If so, he or she can file a continuation-in-part (CIP) application incorporating the changes.

Whatever the recommendations made by the patent examiner, and the reasons given for the claims being rejected, the applicant must either file a response to the first office action within three months or pay a fee and obtain up to a three-month extension. If he or she fails to do either, the application will be deemed abandoned.

Once the applicant has responded, the patent examiner will respond again, usually with a final office action. This will either reject all of the claims with suggested modifications that would make them allowable or reject some of the claims and accept others. If amended claims are rejected on anticipation or obviousness grounds, any pertinent prior art references that were not cited the first time around will be listed (and copies sent). Suggestions may also be made for how to narrow claims that are too broad.

After the final office action, the applicant has four basic choices:

- amend the claims as suggested by the patent examiner
- request that the patent examiner reconsider one or more of the decisions contained in the final office action
- appeal to the Board of Patent Appeals and Interferences, or
- file a continuation application (essentially a new application with new claims, with the benefit of the original filing date for the purpose of determining the effect of relevant prior art references).
- file a Request for Continued Examination (RCE), which effectively removes the final action so that the applicant can submit further amendments, for example, new claims, new arguments, a new declaration or new references.

Whatever the choice, it must be done within three months of the final office action, or up to a three-month extension must be obtained. Otherwise, the application will be deemed legally abandoned. If the application has not been published by the PTO, it won't serve as a prior art reference after being abandoned —unless a defensive publication is made by the applicant.

Assuming that the final action results in an allowance of one or more claims, either as drafted or as amended in response to the final office action, the applicant will receive a Notice of Allowability. This will be followed or accompanied by a formal Notice of Allowance and a form specifying the issue fee that is due. At this time it is still possible to file minor amendments. Also, if any amendments to claims that have occurred in the course of prosecution are not covered by the formal Patent Application Declaration signed by the applicant, a Supplemental Declaration should also be filed.

If the issue fee is sent to the PTO within three months of the formal Notice of Allowance, the applicant will receive a patent deed (a decorative document describing the patent with a PTO seal on the front) and a regular photocopy of the patent. Although the formal patent prosecution process is now over, the inventor may later wish to amend his or her in-force patent in some material way, perhaps because a new ramification is spotted or the inventor now sees that one or more of the claims could have been made broader. If the amendment broadens one or more claims, and the application is filed within two years of the patent issue date, a reissue patent may be obtained. This will carry the same issue date as the original patent, but will incorporate the claims as amended.

Related terms: claims, defined; continuation application; continuation-in-part application (CIP); filing date; issue fee; office action; patent application; Provisional Patent Application (PPA); reconsideration request; reissue patent; Request for Continued Examination; supplemental declaration; swearing behind a prior art reference.

Provisional Patent Application (PPA)

An inventor may file an interim patent application (called a provisional patent application or PPA) to constructively reduce his or her invention to practice. If the PPA sufficiently discloses the invention, and a regular patent application is filed within one year of the PPA's filing date, the inventor gets the benefit of the PPA filing date for the purpose of deciding whether prior art is relevant and, in the event an interference exists, who is entitled to the patent. In addition, the inventor gets the full 20-year term from the date the regular application is filed.

The PPA only need contain a portion of the information presently required in a patent application specification—a complete description of the invention (structure and operation) and any drawings that are necessary to understand the description. The PPA need not include claims, formal drawings, a Patent Application Declaration or an Information Disclosure Statement. In order to claim the benefit of the PPA's filing date, the applicant must file an amendment in the regular patent application referring to the earlier filed PPA.

The PPA currently (October 2000) costs $75 to file ($150 for large entities), which means an inventor can now afford to get an invention registered with the PTO and have a year to show the invention to potential developers before filing a regular patent application. An inventor who files a PPA may claim patent pending status.

Related terms: filing date; patent application; patent pending; prosecution of a patent application.

public domain

When an idea, design or expression does not belong to anyone under the patent (or copyright) laws, it is said exist in the public domain and may be used by anyone for any purpose without permission from its originator or author.

Any invention that is published, put in public use, sold or placed on sale more than one year prior to the filing of a patent application is considered to be in the public domain. Also in the public domain are inventions whose patents are no longer in force (that is, the patent period has expired).

Related terms: anticipation; defensive disclosure; on sale statutory bar; printed publication as statutory bar; prior art, defined; Statutory Invention Registration (SIR).

public use

When an invention is worked (used by the inventor in the presence of one or more members of the public in a non-confidential context), it is considered to have been publicly used. Public use of an invention constitutes a statutory bar to a patent under the anticipation doctrine, unless the patent application is filed within a one-year period after the public use.

There are exceptions to the public use rule for:

- experimental tests (to develop and improve an invention), and
- uses that are not, in fact, public (for instance, when witnesses to the use sign nondisclosure agreements or are otherwise required to maintain secrecy).

Whether any particular use of an invention is a public use must be determined on a case-by-case basis.

EXAMPLE: Julian David, a motel keeper, invents a counterweighting device that allows a king-size bed to be easily moved on very thick carpets. Julian actually constructs a bed that uses the device and uses it in his motel for a little over a year. If Julian then attempts to obtain a patent, the PTO will probably deny it. Why? The use of the bed in the motel probably would be considered a public use, and therefore a statutory bar to the patent, because the patent application was not filed within one year of the "use." Julian is required to disclose this use of the invention in his patent application.

What about the exception for experimental uses? If Julian can show that he was engaged in both monitoring the experiences of cleaning personnel with the bed, and actively modifying the bed's basic design according to what he learned, he might escape the statutory one-year bar. What if Julian only allowed one customer to use the bed, and only for two nights, but he still failed to file the patent application within one year? He will be barred from the patent unless he can establish that the two nights' use was really for experimental purposes or he had the user sign a nondisclosure agreement.

Related terms: anticipation; exhibiting an unpatented invention; experimental use of an unpatented invention; statutory bar.

race statutes

See first to file countries.

read on

In the patent context, "read on" means to literally describe. A patent is infringed if the patent's claims read on (literally describe) all elements of the infringing device.

Related terms: anticipation; claims, defined; infringement of patent.

recite

When the claims of a prior patent literally describe or "read on" the elements of a later invention, the claims are said to "recite" such elements.

Related terms: read on.

reconsideration request

A patent applicant may request that the patent examiner reconsider an application whose claims were rejected in the final office action. If this reconsideration request is rejected, the applicant may:

- amend the claims in the manner suggested by the patent examiner, if this option was presented to the applicant in the office action
- appeal to the Board of Patent Appeals and Interferences, or
- file a continuation application.

Related terms: continuation application; final office action; prosecution of a patent application.

Definitions

reduction to practice

After conceiving an invention, the inventor's next step is to reduce the invention to practice. This can be done in several ways:

- build and test the invention (called actual reduction to practice)
- file a Provisional Patent Application (PPA) on the invention (called constructive reduction to practice), or
- file a regular patent application (also a constructive reduction to practice).

While it's not legally required to get a patent, many inventors find that building and testing a working model of an invention is necessary to convince others to finance the invention's development. Also, if the invention consists of something generally thought highly improbable, such as a perpetual motion machine (a machine that will perpetually produce more energy than it uses), the U.S. Patent and Trademark Office (PTO) may ask that its operability be demonstrated.

The issue of when an invention was first reduced to practice can be extremely important if an interference occurs—that is, two or more pending applications claim the same underlying invention. In this situation, the inventor who was first to reduce the invention to practice, whether by building and testing it or by filing a provisional or regular patent application, will normally be entitled to the patent.

> **EXAMPLE:** Babette and Alain, working independently in different states, both invent a new type of ski binding that releases when sensors on the skier's leg muscles indicate potential for severe muscular or skeletal strain. Babette files a regular patent application one day earlier than Alain. Because there are now two pending regular patent applications covering the same underlying invention, the PTO declares an interference. Babette's filing date is one day earlier than Alain's, so she should be awarded priority (and the patent) unless Alain can establish that he successfully built and tested his invention before Babette filed her application. (If Alain is able to show that this occurred, the PTO will examine several additional factors when deciding who should get the patent.)

However, if the other inventor can prove that he or she was first to conceive the invention and thereafter was diligent in attempting to either build and test the invention or to file a provisional or regular patent application on it, that inventor will be entitled to the patent.

Related terms: constructive reduction to practice; interference, defined; Provisional Patent Application (PPA).

reexamination of patent

The U.S. Patent and Trademark Office (PTO) may hold a formal proceeding in which it reexamines an in-force patent to determine whether newly-cited prior art references adversely affect the validity of the patent. A patent may be re-examined any time while it is in-force. The patent owner or anyone else may initiate the reexamination. Upon request, the requester's identity will be kept confidential. (The statute establishing the reexamination process is 35 United States Code, Section 302.)

The patent reexamination process can be useful to patent owners as well as alleged (or would-be) infringers.

EXAMPLE 1: A patent owner discovers infringement and the infringer counters that the patent is invalid in light of certain prior art. The owner decides to refer the prior art in question to the PTO and request a reexamination before filing an infringement lawsuit. If the PTO upholds the claims as drafted, the owner can feel secure about bringing the infringement action, because the results of the reexamination will be admissible in court and the court will almost always honor the PTO's determination.

EXAMPLE 2: A business wants to use an invention covered by an in-force patent that it believes is invalid because of certain prior art. The reexamination process is a relatively inexpensive way for the business to anonymously "test the water" without actually infringing the patent.

The party requesting the reexamination must pay a reexamination fee ($2,520 in October 2000). The requester must also describe the way in which prior art references specifically bear on the validity of the claims contained in the patent.

Upon request for a reexamination, the PTO has three months to decide whether a "substantial new question of patentability has been raised." If not, the requester will be refunded the bulk of the reexamination fee, with the balance retained by the PTO.

If the requester adequately demonstrates why prior art references are relevant, the patent will be reexamined and the claims possibly rejected or amended based on the prior art. Also, the PTO may choose to invite the public into the reexamination process by asking it to submit any known instances of prior art relevant to the reexamination.

If a reexamination finds that the patent claims are still valid, the PTO will issue a Certification of Validity. If it finds that one or more claims are not valid as drafted, the inventor will have an opportunity to redraft the claims to the patent examiner's satisfaction. In the event of such a change, the amended claims will be entitled to the original filing date.

Related terms: in-force patent; nonobviousness, defined; prior art reference.

references

See prior art reference.

regular patent application

See patent application.

reissue patent

To revise the specification or claims of an in-force patent, the patent owner may apply for a reissue patent. If it seeks to broaden the claims, the reissue patent must be applied for within two years of the issue date of the original patent. If issued, the reissue patent takes the place of the original patent and expires when that patent would have.

Reissue patents can be used to correct any significant error in the claims of the original patent, or to narrow or broaden its claims. In fact, reissue patents are relatively rare, because the push and pull of the patent prosecution process tends to make the claims both accurate and as broad as the U.S. Patent and Trademark Office will allow.

Related terms: in-force patent; intervening right; patent application.

repair doctrine

Anyone who is authorized to make, use or sell a patented device is also permitted to repair and replace unpatented components. This right is asserted as an affirmative defense in a patent infringement lawsuit. The defense does not apply to completely rebuilt inventions, unauthorized inventions, or items that are made or sold without authorization of the patent owner.

rejection of patent application

See office action.

Request for Continued Examination

A Request for Continued Examination (RCE) is filed when a patent applicant wishes to continue prosecuting an application that has received a final office action. Filing the RCE with another filing fee effectively removes the final action so that the applicant can submit further amendments, for example, new claims, new arguments, a new declaration or new references.

An RCE must cover the same invention as the parent or basic application and the parent or basic application must be abandoned when a continuation is filed.

When an RCE continuation is filed, the PTO uses the same file jacket and papers as the parent or basic filing. After an RCE is filed, prosecution of the same application simply continues as if there were no final action. The RCE is entitled to the benefit of the filing date of the parent or prior application for purposes of overcoming prior art.

It is also possible to file a continuation of an RCE. In fact, it's theoretically possible to file an unlimited sequence of RCEs or continuation applications. However, an RCE is not an end-run around a previous objection by the PTO. The RCE or continuation will be quickly rejected unless the inventor truly comes up with a different slant on or definition of the invention that was not previously considered by the PTO. When a patent issues on a RCE, the heading of the patent will not indicate that it's based on the RCE.

An RCE must be mailed before the period for response to the final rejection expires or before any extensions expire. The RCE can be mailed on the last day of the period for response.

reverse engineering

"Reverse engineering" is the process of figuring out how a device is built by taking it apart and studying its components.

See also Part 1 (Trade Secret Law): reverse engineering and trade secrets.

search of patentability

See patentability search.

secrecy of patent application

See confidentiality of patent application.

senior party in interference proceedings

The first inventor to file a provisional or regular patent application on an invention is considered the senior party if the PTO declares an interference (when two or more inventors file separate patent applications on the same invention). One's status as the senior party does not necessarily entitle him or her to the patent. This will depend on which inventor was first to conceive of the invention and how diligently that inventor moved to reduce the invention to practice.

Related terms: interference proceeding; junior party in interference proceedings; reduction to practice.

sequence listing

For biotech inventions, the PTO requires an attachment to a patent application that includes a sequence listing of a nucleotide or amino acid sequence. The

Definitions

applicant attaches this information on separate sheets of paper and refers to the sequence listing in the application (*see* PTO Rule 77).

shelving of invention

See anti-shelving clause.

shop rights

An employer has the rights to an irrevocable, non-assignable and non-exclusive, royalty-free license to use an employee's invention if the invention was conceived of and reduced to practice primarily on company time, with company facilities and material. The theory is that because such inventions are developed with the employer's funds or property, the employer should at least be able to use them in the business.

However, the employee still qualifies as the patent owner unless the patent is assigned to the company under an employment agreement, which is common. As patent owner, the employee retains the right to issue non-exclusive licenses to others to use and manufacture the invention in exchange for royalties or other compensation.

Related terms: march-in rights; non-exclusive patent license; patent owner.

shotgun rejection of claims

This slang term refers to the U.S. Patent and Trademark Office (PTO)'s habit of rejecting all claims in its first office action (its first formal response to the application) on the premise that it will deal more seriously with the application if and when the applicant submits amended claims or a more detailed explanation of why the existing claims should be allowed. Although discouraging, a shotgun rejection does not necessarily mean that an applicant should abandon trying to patent the invention. As mentioned, a shotgun rejection has much more to do with general PTO practices than with the merits of a particular patent application.

Related terms: first office action; prosecution of a patent application.

single application rule

See divisional application.

small entity

A for-profit company with 500 or fewer employees, a nonprofit organization, or an independent inventor is referred to by the U.S. Patent and Trademark Office (PTO) as a small entity. The PTO charges small entities half the fees charged large entities for filing a patent application and for issuing and maintaining the patent. A small entity qualifies for these lower fees provided that the company or inventor has not assigned or licensed, or agreed to assign or license, its patent rights to a large entity (a for-profit company with over 500 employees).

Related terms: issue fee; large entity; maintenance fees.

smart money

The colloquial phrase "smart money" is used by patent attorneys to describe the extra damages that can be imposed on defendants found guilty of willful or flagrant infringement. These extra damages—up to three times the actual damages established in court—are awarded to teach the infringers a lesson and make them "smart."

Related terms: infringement action.

software-based inventions

See software patents.

software patents

Patents don't issue on software itself, although they issue on inventions that use innovative software to produce a useful, concrete and tangible result—that is, "software-based" inventions.

When first faced with applications for patents on software-based inventions in the 1950s, the PTO routinely rejected the applications on the grounds that software consists of mathematical algorithms (abstract methods for solving problems not tied to a particular use or tangible structure), which were considered to be unpatentable for the same reason abstract laws of nature are unpatentable.

In the late 1980s, however, the U.S. Patent and Trademark Office began granting patents on inventions that rely heavily on innovative software. Now the PTO issues patents on software if the patent application describes the software in relation to computer hardware and related devices, and limits the software to specific uses.

Software-based inventions that have qualified for patents often involve software that connects to and runs hardware components. For example, consider a device that monitors a patient's heart functions, feeds the raw information into a computer where a program analyzes the information according to a set of algorithms and causes the results of this analysis to be displayed on a monitor in a format that shows whether the person is at risk for a heart attack. While none of the components of this invention would qualify for a patent (the physical items have already been invented and the algorithm itself is unpatentable), the overall

Definitions

invention did qualify for a U.S. patent, even though the software was the key aspect of the invention.

It is also possible to obtain a patent on the process or method used by software as well as on the machine aspect of the invention—that is, the combined software and hardware. For instance, the heart monitor invention described above received a patent on a machine claim (a claim that described the structure which produced the result) as well as a method claim (a claim that described the process by which the structure worked). Other examples of software-based inventions that have received patents are a device that converts sound waves into smooth wave forms for display on an oscilloscope (a rasterizer), and software that moves the cursor on a computer screen.

In a recent case, *State Street Bank and Trust v. Signature* (CAFC 7/23/98), the Court of Appeals for the Federal Circuit has moved even further in the direction of full patentability for software programs. The court ruled that a process carried out by a software program is statutory subject matter if it produces a useful, concrete and tangible result. This ruling seems to indicate that it's no longer necessary to claim structure as part of the invention.

Despite the fact that software-based inventions may qualify for a patent, most do not because they are considered obvious over the prior art, and must therefore be protected in another manner—usually under trade secret or copyright laws.

Virtually all patents that have been obtained on software-based inventions are utility patents, although some design patents have been issued on computer screen icons.

Related terms: algorithms; business methods as statutory subject matter; non-statutory subject matter, *State Street Bank and Trust v. Signature.*

Software Patent Institute

This independent nonprofit corporation, located in Kansas, collects and organizes nonpatented prior art references in the software field. The full address is Software Patent Institute, 9225 Indian Creek Parkway, Suite 1100, Overland Park, KS 66210-2009. 913-451-3355, FAX: 913-451-3361 (http://www.spi.org).

The purpose of the SPI is to facilitate more complete patent searches. Because most software is not patented, a search of the patent database usually produces a small fraction of the prior art in the software field. By collecting as many samples of nonpatented software as possible, SPI hopes to provide patent searchers with a truer picture of the relevant prior art.

Related terms: patent search, computerized; prior art, defined; prior art reference.

specification, defined

The narrative portion of a patent application is called a specification. A specification includes descriptions of:

- the type of invention
- the pertinent prior art (previous developments in the technology utilized in the invention) known to the applicant
- the purpose of the invention
- the invention itself (for example, how it's constructed and what it's made of)
- the operation of the invention (how it works), and
- any accompanying drawings.

As defined by the patent laws, the specification also includes the patent claims and an abstract—a one paragraph summary of the specification. (A sample specification is provided in the Forms & Resources section at the end of this part of the book.)

Essentially, the specification must provide enough information about the invention so that a person having ordinary skill in the art (proficient in the particular area of expertise involved in the invention) could build it without having to be "inventive." Because the specification is where the fullest disclosure of the invention is made, it (rather than the claims) is commonly used to determine whether a later invention has been anticipated by the patent.

Related terms: claims, defined; disclosure requirements for patents.

statement of prior art references

See Information Disclosure Statement.

State Street Bank and Trust v. Signature Financial Group

In this 1998 case, the Court of Appeals for the Federal Circuit made it much easier to obtain a patent on computer software and on methods of doing business. The software invention at issue in this case was designed solely to make financial calculations dealing with advantageous mutual fund investing techniques. In the past, such a program would have been considered to be nothing more than a mathematical algorithm, which does not constitute statutory subject matter. However, in *State Street*, the court ruled that the mathematical algorithms are non-patentable only when they are nothing more than abstract ideas consisting of disembodied concepts that are not useful. In the court's words: "Today we hold that the transformation of data, representing discrete dollar amounts, by a machine through a series of mathematical calculations into a final share price, constitutes a practical application of a mathematical algorithm, formula, or calculation, because it produces a useful, concrete and tangible result—a final share price momentarily fixed for recording and reporting purposes and even accepted and relied upon by regulatory authorities and in subsequent trades."

The court also shed new light on the long-held belief that methods of doing business do not constitute statutory subject matter. The court pointed out that the patent statutes do not specifically exclude business methods from being patentable and that no authoritative case law supported the concept.

statute of limitations, infringement action

In patent law there is no time limit (statute of limitations) for filing a patent infringement lawsuit but monetary damages can only be recovered for infringements committed during the six years prior to filing the lawsuit. For example, if a patent owner sues after 10 years of infringement, the owner cannot recover monetary damages for the first four years of infringement. Despite the fact that there is no law setting a time limit, courts will not permit a patent owner to sue for infringement if the owner has waited an unreasonable time to file the lawsuit (this is the doctrine called "laches"). (35 United States Code, Section 286.)

Related terms: defenses to a patent infringement claim.

statutory bar

A statutory bar is any federal statutory provision that requires the U.S. Patent and Trademark Office or a court to disqualify an invention for a patent. Among the most common types of statutory bars are:

- the rule that prior patents, or other printed publications which describe the invention, may preclude the invention from being considered novel
- the rule that a later invention is precluded from receiving a patent by an earlier invention that contains all of the same elements
- the rule that a patent may not be obtained on an invention if the application has been abandoned by the inventor, or
- the rule that a description in a printed publication, public use or on sale status of the invention more than one year prior to the application filing date precludes a patent from issuing.

Related terms: anticipation; on sale statutory bar; printed publication as statutory bar; prior art reference; public use; swearing behind a prior art reference.

Statutory Invention Registration (SIR)

A patent applicant can abandon an application and prevent anyone else from getting a patent on the underlying invention by in effect putting the invention in the public domain. This is done by converting a patent application to a SIR.

The U.S. Patent and Trademark Office in turn will publish the abstract of the patent included in the original application in the Official Gazette, thereby transforming the invention into a prior art reference effective on the original application's filing date. No patent can issue on the invention unless another inventor has already claimed it in a pending application and is entitled to priority because of an earlier date of conception or reduction to practice.

It is also possible to turn an invention into a prior art reference (thereby placing it in the public domain) by publishing an article on it or by listing it with an invention register, but the effective date of the reference will be the date of publication rather than the filing date of the original application.

Related terms: defensive disclosure; interference proceeding.

statutory subject matter

The U.S. Patent and Trademark Office issues utility patents, design patents and plant patents. To qualify for a utility patent, an invention must fit into at least one of five categories defined in 35 United States Code, Section 101. Qualifications for a design or plant patent are not, however, governed by these statutory categories.

The statutory categories for utility patents are:

- compositions of matter
- manufactures (or articles of manufacture)
- machines (or apparatuses)
- processes (or methods), and
- new and useful improvements of any of the above categories.

Any invention that does not fall within at least one of these categories does not qualify for a utility patent, no matter how novel or nonobvious it may otherwise prove to be. On the other hand, it is not necessary to define exactly which category applies to a particular invention as long as the patent examiner concludes that at least one of them does.

EXAMPLE: A patent application on an automated database invention that answers legal questions can be viewed as claiming a machine (apparatus) or a process (method). Because the invention can fit within one or the other of these categories, it is deemed to be statutory subject matter.

To qualify for a utility patent, an invention must be novel, useful and non-obvious, in addition to fitting within at least one of the five statutory categories. The phrase "statutory subject matter" is often used to refer not only to inventions

Definitions

that fall within one of the five statutory classes, but to those that satisfy these other patent requirements as well.

Related terms: non-statutory subject matter; prosecution of a patent application.

submarine patent

A patent may be deliberately held up in the U.S. Patent and Trademark Office by the applicant while the technology covered by the patent is developed by companies that have no knowledge of the pending application. Then, once the patent issues, it is like a submarine, suddenly emerging from the patent office and forcing the users of the invention to pay hefty license fees. Two changes in patent law have substantially eliminated the possibility of submarine patents. In 1995 the patent laws were amended to limit the duration of patents to 20 years from the date of filing. In 1999, the patent laws were amended to require publication of patent applications within 18 months of filing unless the patent applicant will not be filing the patent application in a foreign country.

Related terms: confidentiality of patent application.

substitute patent application

Inventors sometimes file a new patent application after abandoning an earlier application on the same invention. For example, if an applicant who failed to respond to the U.S. Patent and Trademark Office's first office action within three months refiles a duplicate application, the later application is considered a substitute of the abandoned parent application. The substitute application does not get the benefit of the original filing date, so any prior art that has surfaced in the meantime may operate to anticipate the invention and thus bar the patent from issuing.

Related terms: abandonment of patent; parent application.

supplemental declaration

When claims are broadened or changed in any substantial way in the course of a successful patent prosecution, the applicant must file a supplemental declaration with the U.S. Patent and Trademark Office after receiving a notice of allowance. Under oath, the inventor must:

- specify which claims have been altered in the course of the prosecution, and
- declare that the applicant was the inventor of the subject matter contained in the altered claims, and knows of no prior art that would anticipate the claims as altered.

Related terms: prosecution of a patent application.

swearing behind a prior art reference

Swearing behind a prior art reference is a way of eliminating a prior art reference cited by a patent examiner against an application.

To swear behind a cited prior art reference, the applicant must show that the date his or her invention was conceived of or reduced to practice was before the effective date of the prior art reference. The evidence to establish these facts typically consists of the inventor's testimony under oath and appropriate entries from his or her notebook or disclosure documents that are submitted to the PTO.

If the prior art reference is a publication dated less than one year before the patent application's filing date, a showing that the invention was conceived of prior to the publication, and diligent attempts were made to reduce it to practice, will eliminate the reference as a statutory bar.

EXAMPLE: An article appearing in the November 1999 issue of a leading popular science magazine details an efficient portable photovoltaic cell, able to run various electronic devices. Lou Swift has already conceived of such a cell, and has been busy designing it so that a patent application can be filed. Lou may still be able to obtain a patent if she files a patent application within one year of the article's publication date and shows (swears behind) that she conceived her invention prior to such publication date and was diligently engaged in reducing it to practice.

When a prior art reference is a U.S. patent with a filing date preceding the applicant's filing date and an issue date that is less than one year before the applicant's filing date, a showing that the inventor conceived of the invention prior to the patent's filing date, and thereafter exercised diligence to reduce it to practice, will eliminate the patent acting as a statutory bar to the application.

EXAMPLE: Lou Swift invents a photovoltaic cell, but before she files a patent application she discovers that another inventor has patented the same invention (the patent issued on July 1, 2000). The other patent will be eliminated from consideration if Lou: 1) files her application within one year of the date the patent issued (that is, by July 1, 2001), 2) is able to prove that she conceived of her invention prior to the date the other patent application was filed, and 3) can show that she was diligently attempting to reduce her invention to practice at the time the other patent application was filed.

Related terms: first office action; interference, defined; notebook; prior art reference; reduction to practice; statutory bar.

teach

When a prior publication, invention or patent discusses the elements of, or technology associated with, an invention for which a patent is being sought, it is said to "teach" the invention.

thesis as prior art

A published college or university thesis may count as a prior art reference, even if published in an obscure publication, and thus operate as a statutory bar to a patent if it describes (teaches) the essential characteristics of an invention on which a patent is being sought. This applies to a patent sought by anyone other than the thesis author, and to the thesis author as well if he or she did not file the patent application within one year of the date the thesis was first published.

Because a thesis can count as prior art, a thorough patent search will usually cover listings of theses, as well as prior patents and publications in trade journals.

Related terms: printed publication as statutory bar; prior art reference.

Title 35 of the United States Code

This part of the United States Code (sometimes abbreviated as USC) contains the patent statutes. The entire code can be found in 35 United States Code Annotated (USCA) or 35 United States Code Service, Lawyers Edition (USCS).

transfer of patent or patent application

See assignment of a patent.

transmittal letter for patent application

See patent application.

treaties on international patent protection

See Patent Cooperation Treaty (PCT); Convention application; international patent protection for U.S. inventions.

treble (triple) damages for patent infringement

See infringement action.

tying

See antitrust law (federal) and patents.

unenforceable patent

A patent may be declared unenforceable if the alleged infringer can show that the patent owner has misused the patent. Among the specific types of misuse that can render a patent unenforceable are:

- falsely marking an invention, such as putting a patent number on it that doesn't apply
- illegal or unfair licensing practices
- an extended delay in bringing the infringement lawsuit to the detriment of the defendant (called laches), or
- fraud on the U.S. Patent and Trademark Office (PTO), such as failing to include a pertinent prior art reference in the patent application.

Patents may be declared invalid if a court finds that:
- the PTO didn't discover or properly analyze relevant prior art references that affect the novelty or nonobviousness of the invention (in short, the invention really didn't qualify for a patent)
- the invention doesn't or won't work
- the disclosure of the invention in the patent application contains insufficient information to teach an ordinary person skilled in the art to build the invention
- the patent claims are vague and indefinite
- the patent was issued to the wrong inventor
- antitrust violations occurred, or
- any other facts exist that operate to retroactively invalidate the patent.

Related terms: defenses to a patent infringement claim.

unobviousness

See nonobviousness, defined.

U.S. Patent and Trademark Office (PTO)

An administrative branch of the U.S. Department of Commerce, the U.S. Patent and Trademark Office (http://www.uspto.gov) is charged with the responsibility for overseeing and implementing the federal laws on patents and trademarks. Also known as the PTO, or Patent Office, this agency is responsible for examining, issuing, classifying, and maintaining records of all patents issued by the United States. It also serves as a filing agency for Patent Cooperation Treaty (PCT) applications.

The PTO publishes the Official Gazette (both the patent and trademark versions), a weekly periodical that describes newly issued patents, new regulations and other information of interest to patent practitioners. The PTO also maintains a library in which a complete patent search may be conducted by classification.

Related terms: Patent Cooperation Treaty (PCT).

Definitions

usefulness, required for patents

See utility patents, defined.

utility

See utility patents, defined.

utility model

This provision in Japanese and German law states that inventions that do not qualify for a regular patent may nonetheless receive some protection for a shorter period of time.

utility patents, defined

Patents may issue on inventions that have some type of usefulness (utility), even if the use is humorous, such as a musical condom or a device to hold your big toes together to prevent sunburned inner thighs. However, the invention must work, at least in theory. Thus, a new drug that hasn't been tested or a new chemical for which no use is now known will not receive a patent. Design patents and plant patents, the other two types of patents obtained in the U.S., do not require utility.

Related terms: design patents; plant patents; statutory subject matter.

validity search

A patent search may be conducted after a patent has issued for the purpose of discovering any fact that might be used to invalidate, and thus break, the patent. Generally conducted by the defendant in a patent infringement action, a validity search is often more thorough than the initial patentability search conducted by the inventor prior to filing a patent application, which was used to determine whether the invention was anticipated.

Related terms: defenses to a patent infringement claim; patent search.

working a patent

Actually developing and commercially exploiting the underlying invention covered by a patent is known as working a patent. In many countries outside the U.S., a patent owner's failure to work the patent within a specific period of time may result in the owner's being forced to grant a license (called a compulsory license), at government-set fees, to any party who desires to do so.

Related terms: compulsory licensing of a patent.

World Intellectual Property Organization (WIPO)

See International Bureau of the World Intellectual Property Organization; Patent Cooperation Treaty (PCT).

World Trade Organization (WTO)

This organization was created by the General Agreement on Tariffs and Trade (GATT) for the purpose of enforcing the intellectual property and other trade agreements contained in that treaty.

Related terms: GATT (General Agreement on Tariffs and Trade).

World Wide Web and patent searches

See patent search, computerized.

Definitions

Patent Law

Patent and Trademark Depository Libraries

State	Name of Library	Telephone
Alabama	Auburn University Libraries	205-844-1747
	Birmingham Public Library	205-226-3620
Alaska	Anchorage: Z.J. Loussac Public Library	907-562-7323
Arizona	Tempe: Noble Library, Arizona State Univ.	602-965-7010
Arkansas	Little Rock: Arkansas State Library	501-682-2053
California	Los Angeles Public Library	213-228-7220
	Sacramento: California State Library	916-654-0069
	San Diego Public Library	619-236-5813
	San Francisco Public Library	415-557-4500
	Santa Rosa: Bruce Sawyer Center (not a PTDL, but useful)	707-524-1773
	Sunnyvale Center for Innovation (has APS Image terminals—see Section L1)	408-730-7290
Colorado	Denver Public Library	303-640-6220
Connecticut	Hartford Public Library	860-543-8628
	New Haven Free Public Library	203-946-8130
Delaware	Newark: University of Delaware Library	302-831-2965
D.C.	Washington: Howard University Libraries	202-806-7252
Florida	Fort Lauderdale: Broward County Main Library	305-357-7444
	Miami: Dade Public Library	305-375-2665
	Orlando: Univ.of Central Florida Libraries	407-823-2562
	Tampa: Campus Library, University of South Florida	813-974-2726
Georgia	Atlanta: Price Gilbert Memorial Library, Georgia Institute of Technology	404-894-4508
Hawaii	Honolulu: Hawaii State Public Library System	808-586-3477
Idaho	Moscow: University of Idaho Library	208-885-6235
Illinois	Chicago Public Library	312-747-4450
	Springfield: Illinois State Library	217-782-5659
Indiana	Indianapolis: Marion County Public Library	317-269-1741
	West Lafayette: Purdue University Libraries	317-494-2872
Iowa	Des Moines: State Library of Iowa	515-242-6541
Kansas	Wichita: Ablah Library, Wichita State Univ.	316-689-3155
Kentucky	Louisville Free Public Library	502-574-1611
Louisiana	Baton Rouge: Troy H. Middleton Library, Louisiana State University	504-388-8875
Maine	Orono: Raymond H. Fogler Library, University of Maine	207-581-1678

Patent and Trademark Depository Libraries (continued)

State	Name of Library	Telephone
Maryland	College Park: Engineering and Physical Sciences Library, University of Maryland	301-405-9157
Massachusetts	Amherst: Physical Sciences Library, University of Massachusetts	413-545-1370
	Boston Public Library	617-536-5400 Ext. 265
Michigan	Ann Arbor: Engineering Transportation Library, University of Michigan	734-647-5735
	Big Rapids: Abigail S. Timme Library, Ferris State University	231-592-3602
	Detroit Public Library (has APS Image Terminals—see Section L1)	313-833-3379
Minnesota	Minneapolis Public Library and Information Center	612-630-6120
Mississippi	Jackson: Mississippi Library Commission	601-961-4111
Missouri	Kansas City: Linda Hall Library	816-363-4600
	St. Louis Public Library	314-241-2288 Ext. 390
Montana	Butte: Montana College of Mineral Science & Technology Library	406-496-4281
Nebraska	Lincoln: Engineering Library, University of Nebraska	402-472-3411
Nevada	Las Vegas: Clark County Library	not yet operational
	Reno: University of Nevada-Reno Library	702-784-6500 Ext. 257
New Hampshire	Concord: New Hampshire State Library	603-271-2239
New Jersey	Newark Public Library	973-733-7782
	Piscataway: Library of Science & Medicine, Rutgers University	732-445-2895
New Mexico	Albuquerque: University of New Mexico General Library	505-277-4412
New York	Albany: New York State Library	518-474-5355
	Buffalo and Erie County Public Library	716-858-7101
	New York Public Library (The Research Libraries)	212-592-7000
	Stony Brook: Engineering Library, State University of New York	516-632-7148
North Carolina	Raleigh: D.H. Hill Library, N.C. State U.	919-515-3280
North Dakota	Grand Forks: Chester Fritz Library, University of North Dakota	701-777-4888
Ohio	Akron: Summit County Public Library	330-643-9075
	Cincinnati and Hamilton County, Public Library of	513-369-6971
	Cleveland Public Library	216-623-2870
	Columbus: Ohio State University Libraries	614-292-3022
	Toledo/Lucas County Public Library	419-259-5212

Forms

Patent and Trademark Depository Libraries (continued)

State	Name of Library	Telephone
Oklahoma	Stillwater: Oklahoma State Univ. Library	405-744-7086
Oregon	Portland: Paul L. Boley Law Library, Lewis & Clark College	503-768-6786
Pennsylvania	Philadelphia, The Free Library of	215-686-5331
	Pittsburgh, Carnegie Library of	412-622-3138
	University Park: Pattee Library, Pennsylvania State University	814-865-6369
Puerto Rico	Bayamón: University of Puerto Rico	not yet operational
	Mayaguez General Library, University of Puerto Rico	787-832-4040 Ext. 2022
Rhode Island	Providence Public Library	401-455-8027
South Carolina	Clemson University Libraries	864-656-3024
South Dakota	Rapid City: Devereaux Library, S.D. School of Mines and Technology	605-394-1275
Tennessee	Memphis & Shelby County Public Library and Information Center	901-725-8877
	Nashville: Stevenson Science Library, Vanderbilt University	615-322-2717
Texas	Austin: McKinney Engineering Library, University of Texas at Austin	512-495-4500
	College Station: Sterling C. Evans Library, Texas A & M University	409-845-5745
	Dallas Public Library	214-670-1468
	Houston: The Fondren Library, Rice University	713-348-5483
	Lubbock: Texas Tech University	806-742-2282
	San Antonio Public Library	not yet operational
Utah	Salt Lake City: Marriott Lib., Univ. of Utah	801-581-8394
Vermont	Burlington: Bailey/Howe Library, University of Vermont	802-656-2542
Virginia	Richmond: James Branch Cabell Library, Virginia Commonwealth University	804-828-1104
Washington	Seattle: Engineering Library, University of Washington	206-543-0740
West Virginia	Morgantown: Evansdale Library, West Virginia University	304-293-4695 Ext. 5113
Wisconsin	Madison: Kurt F. Wendt Library, University of Wisconsin	608-262-6845
	Milwaukee Public Library	414-286-3051
Wyoming	Casper: National County Public Library	307-237-4935

Forms

Specification of Sample Patent Application

A-2 KoppleLan. SB

Patent Application of

Lou W. Koppe

for

PAPER-LAMINATED PLIABLE CLOSURE FOR FLEXIBLE BAGS

Background—Field of Invention

This invention relates to plastic tab closures, specifically to such closures which are used for closing the necks of plastic produce bags.

Background—Description of Prior Art

Grocery stores and supermarkets commonly supply consumers with polyethylene bags for holding produce. Such bags are also used by suppliers to provide a resealable container for other items, both edible and inedible.

Originally these bags were sealed by the supplier with staples or by heat. However consumers objected since these were of a rather permanent nature: the bags could be opened only by tearing, thereby damaging them and rendering them impossible to reseal.

Thereafter, inventors created several types of closures to seal plastic bags in such a way as to leave them undamaged after they were opened. U.S. patent 4,292,714 to Walker (1981) discloses a complex clamp which can close the necks of bags without causing damage upon opening; however, these clamps are prohibitively expensive to manufacture. U.S. patent 2,981,990 to Balderree (1961) shows a closure which is of expensive construction, being made of PTFE, and which is not effective unless the bag has a relatively long "neck".

Thus if the bag has been filled almost completely and consequently has a short neck, this closure is useless. Also, being relatively narrow and clumsy, Balderree's closure cannot be easily bent by hand along its longitudinal axis. Finally his closure does not hold well onto the bag, but has a tendency to snap off.

Although twist closures with a wire core are easy to use and inexpensive to manufacture, do not damage the bag upon being removed, and can be used repeatedly, nevertheless they simply do not possess the neat and uniform appearance of a tab closure, they become tattered and unsightly after repeated use, and they do not offer suitable surfaces for the reception of print or labeling. These ties also require much

2

more manipulation to apply and remove.

Several types of thin, flat closures have been proposed—for example, in U.K. patent 883,771 to Britt et al. (1961) and U.S. patents 3,164,250 (1965), 3,417,912 (1968), 3,822,441 (1974), 4,361,935 (1982), and 4,509,231 (1985), all to Paxton. Although inexpensive to manufacture, capable of use with bags having a short neck, and producible in break-off strips, such closures can be used only once if they are made of frangible plastic since they must be bent or twisted when being removed and consequently will fracture upon removal. Thus, to reseal a bag originally sealed with a frangible closure, one must either close its neck with another closure or else close it in makeshift fashion by folding or tying it. My own patent 4,694,542 (1987) describes a closure which is made of flexible plastic and is therefore capable of repeated use without damage to the bag, but nevertheless all the plastic closures heretofore known suffer from a number of disadvantages:

(a) Their manufacture in color requires the use of a compounding facility for the production of the pigmented plastic. Such a facility, which is needed to compound the primary pigments and which generally constitutes a separate production site, requires the presence of very large storage bins for the pigmented raw granules. Also it presents great difficulties with regard to the elimination of the airborne powder which results from the mixing of the primary granules.

(b) If one uses an extruder in the production of a pigmented plastic—especially if one uses only a single extruder—a change from one color to a second requires purging the extruder of the granules having the first color by introducing those of the second color. This process inevitably produces, in sizeable volume, an intermediate product of an undesired color which must be discarded as scrap, thereby resulting in waste of material and time.

(c) The colors of the closures in present use are rather unsaturated. If greater concentrations of pigment were used in order to make the colors more intense, the plastic would become more brittle and the cost of the final product would increase.

(d) The use of pigmented plastic closures does not lend itself to the production of multicolored designs, and it would be very expensive to produce plastic closures in which the plastic is multicolored—for example, in which the plastic has stripes of several colors, or in which the plastic exhibits multicolored designs.

(e) Closures made solely of plastic generally offer poor surfaces for labeling or printing, and the label or print is often easily smudged.

(f) The printing on a plastic surface is often easily erased, thereby allowing the alteration of prices by dishonest consumers.

3

(g) The plastic closures in present use are slippery when handled with wet or greasy fingers.

(h) A closure of the type in present use can be very carefully pried off a bag by a dishonest consumer and then attached to another item without giving any evidence of such removal.

Objects and Advantages

Accordingly, besides the objects and advantages of the flexible closures described in my above patent, several objects and advantages of the present invention are:

(a) to provide a closure which can be produced in a variety of colors without requiring the manufacturer to use a compounding facility for the production of pigments;

(b) to provide a closure whose production allows for a convenient and extremely rapid and economical change of color in the closures that are being produced;

(c) to provide a closure which both is flexible and can be brightly colored;

(d) to provide a closure which can be colored in several colors simultaneously;

(e) to provide a closure which will present a superior surface for the reception of labeling or print;

(f) to provide a closure whose labeling cannot be altered;

(g) to provide a closure which will not be slippery when handled with wet or greasy fingers; and

(h) to provide a closure which will show evidence of having been switched from one item to another by a dishonest consumer—in other words, to provide a closure which makes items tamper-proof.

Further objects and advantages are to provide a closure which can be used easily and conveniently to open and reseal a plastic bag, without damage to the bag, which is simple to use and inexpensive to manufacture, which can be supplied in separate tabs en masse or in break-off links, which can be used with bags having short necks, which can be used repeatedly, and which obviates the need to tie a knot in the neck of the bag or fold the neck under the bag or use a twist closure. Still further objects and advantages will become apparent from a consideration of the ensuing description and drawings.

Drawing Figures

In the drawings, closely related figures have the same number but different alphabetic suffixes.

Forms

4

Figs 1A to 1D show various aspects of a closure supplied with a longitudinal groove and laminated on one side with paper.

Fig 2 shows a closure with no longitudinal groove and with a paper lamination on one side only.

Fig 3 shows a similar closure with one longitudinal groove.

Fig 4 shows a similar closure with a paper lamination on both sides.

Fig 5 shows a similar closure with a paper lamination on one side only, the groove having been formed into the paper as well as into the body of the closure.

Figs 6A to 6K show end views of closures having various combinations of paper laminations, longitudinal grooves, and through-holes.

Figs 7A to 7C show a laminated closure with groove after being bent and after being straightened again.

Figs 8A to 8C show a laminated closure without a groove after being bent and after being straightened again.

Reference Numerals In Drawings

10	base of closure	12	lead-in notch
14	hole	16	gripping points
18	groove	20	paper lamination
22	tear of paper lamination	24	corner
26	longitudinal through-hole	28	neck-down
30	side of base opposite to bend	32	crease

Description—Figs. 1 to 6

A typical embodiment of the closure of the present invention is illustrated in Fig 1A (top view) and Fig 1B (end view). The closure has a thin base **10** of uniform cross section consisting of a flexible sheet of material which can be repeatedly bent and straightened out without fracturing. A layer of paper **20** (Fig 1B) is laminated on one side of base **10**. In the preferred embodiment, the base is a flexible plastic, such as poly-ethylene-tere-phthalate (PET—hyphens here supplied to facilitate pronunciation)—available from Eastman Chemical Co. of Kingsport, TN. However the base can consist of any other material that can be repeatedly bent without fracturing, such as polyethylene, polypropylene, vinyl, nylon, rubber, leather, various impregnated or laminated fibrous materials, various plasticized materials, cardboard, paper, etc.

At one end of the closure is a lead-in notch **12** which terminates in gripping points **16** and leads to a hole **14**. Paper layer **20** adheres to

5

base **10** by virtue either of the extrusion of liquid plastic (which will form the body of the closure) directly onto the paper or the application of heat or adhesive upon the entirety of one side of base **10**. The paper-laminated closure is then punched out. Thus the lamination will have the same shape as the side of the base **10** to which it adheres.

The base of the closure is typically .8 mm to 1.2 mm in thickness, and has overall dimensions roughly from 20 mm x 20 mm (square shape) to 40 mm x 70 mm (oblong shape). The outer four corners **24** of the closure are typically beveled or rounded to avoid snagging and personal injury. Also, when closure tabs are connected side-to-side in a long roll, these bevels or roundings give the roll a series of notches which act as detents or indices for the positioning and conveying of the tabs in a dispensing machine.

A longitudinal groove **18** is formed on one side of base **10** in Fig 1. In other embodiments, there may be two longitudinal grooves—one each side of the base—or there may be no longitudinal groove at all. Grove **18** may be formed by machining, scoring, rolling, or extruding. In the absence of a groove, there may be a longitudinal through-hole **26** (Fig 6L). This through-hole may be formed by placing, in the extrusion path of the closure, a hollow pin for the outlet of air.

Additional embodiments are shown in Figs 2, 3, 4, and 5; in each case the paper lamination is shown partially peeled back. In Fig 2 the closure has only one lamination and no groove; in Fig 3 it has only one lamination and only one groove; in Fig 4 it has two laminations and only one groove; in Fig 5 it has two laminations and one groove, the latter having been rolled into one lamination as well as into the body of the closure.

There are various possibilities with regard to the relative disposition of the sides which are grooved and the sides which are laminated, as illustrated in Fig 6, which presents end views along the longitudinal axis. Fig 6A shows a closure with lamination on one side only and with no groove; Fig 6B shows a closure with laminations on both sides and with no groove; Fig 6C shows a closure with only one lamination and only one groove, both being on the same side; Fig 6D shows a closure with only one lamination and only one groove, both being on the same side and the groove having been rolled into the lamination as well as into the body of the closure; Fig 6E shows a closure with only one lamination and only one groove, the two being on opposite sides; Fig 6F shows a closure with two laminations and only one groove; Fig 6G shows a closure with two laminations and only one groove, the groove having been rolled into one lamination as well as into the body of the closure; Fig 6H shows a closure with only one lamination and with two grooves; Fig 6I shows a closure with only one lamination and

6

with two grooves, one of the grooves having been rolled into the lamination as well as into the body of the closure; Fig 6J shows a closure with two laminations and with two grooves; Fig 6K shows a closure with two laminations and with two grooves, the grooves having been rolled into the laminations as well as into the body of the closure; and Fig 6L shows a closure with two laminations and a longitudinal through-hole.

From the description above, a number of advantages of my paper-laminated closures become evident:

(a) A few rolls of colored paper will contain thousands of square yards of a variety of colors, will obviate the need for liquid pigments or a pigment-compounding plant, and will permit the manufacturer to produce colored closures with transparent, off color, or of left-over plastic, all of which are cheaper than first quality pigmented plastic.

(b) With the use of rolls of colored paper to laminate the closures, one can change colors by simply changing rolls, thus avoiding the need to purge the extruder used to produce the closures.

(c) The use of paper laminate upon an unpigmented, flexible plastic base can provide a bright color without requiring the introduction of pigment into the base and the consequent sacrifice of pliability.

(d) The presence of a paper lamination will permit the display of multicolored designs.

(e) The paper lamination will provide a superior surface for labeling or printing, either by hand or by machine.

(f) Any erasure or alteration of prices by dishonest consumers on the paper-laminated closure will leave a highly visible and permanent mark.

(g) Although closures made solely of plastic are slippery when handled with wet or greasy fingers, the paper laminate on my closures will provide a nonslip surface.

Operation—Figs 1, 6, 7, 8

The manner of using the paper-laminated closure to seal a plastic bag is identical to that for closures in present use. Namely, one first twists the neck of a bag (not shown here but shown in Fig 12 of my above patent) into a narrow, cylindrical configuration. Next, holding the closure so that the plane of its base is generally perpendicular to the axis of the neck and so that lead-in notch 12 is adjacent to the neck, one inserts the twisted neck into the lead-in notch until it is forced past gripping points 16 at the base of the notch and into hole 14.

7

To remove the closure, one first bends it along its horizontal axis (Fig 1C—an end view—and Figs 7 and 8) so that the closure is still in contact with the neck of the bag and so that gripping points **16** roughly point in parallel directions. Then one pulls the closure up or down and away from the neck in a direction generally opposite to that in which the gripping points now point, thus freeing the closure from the bag without damaging the latter. The presence of one or two grooves **18** or a longitudinal through-hole **26** (Fig 6L), either of which acts as a hinge, facilitates this process of bending.

The closure can be used to reseal the original bag or to seal another bag many times; one simply bends it flat again prior to reuse.

As shown in Figs 1C, 7B, and 8B (all end views) when the closure is bent along its longitudinal axis, region **30** of the base will stretch somewhat along the direction perpendicular to the longitudinal axis. (Region 30 is the region which is parallel to this axis and is on the side of the base opposite to the bend.) Therefore, when the closure is flattened again, the base will have elongated in the direction perpendicular to the longitudinal axis. This will cause a necking down **28** (Figs 1D, 7C, and 8C) of the base, as well as either a tell-tale tear **22**, or at least a crease **32** (Figs 7A and 8A) along the axis of bending. Therefore if the closure is attached to a sales item and has print upon its paper lamination, the fact that the closure has been transferred by a dishonest consumer from the first item to another will be made evident by the tear or crease.

Figs 7A and 8A show bent closures with and without grooves, respectively. Figs 7C and 8C show the same closures, respectively, after being flattened out, along their longitudinal axes, paper tear **22** being visible.

Summary, Ramifications, and Scope

Accordingly, the reader will see that the paper-laminated closure of this invention can be used to seal a plastic bag easily and conveniently, can be removed just as easily and without damage to the bag, and can be used to reseal the bag without requiring a new closure. In addition, when a closure has been used to seal a bag and is later bent and removed from the bag so as not to damage the latter, the paper lamination will tear or crease and thus give visible evidence of tampering, without impairing the ability of the closure to reseal the original bag or any other bag. Furthermore, the paper lamination has the additional advantages in that

· it permits the production of closures in a variety of colors without requiring the manufacturer to use a separate facility for the compounding of the powdered or liquid pigments needed in the production of colored closures;

10

· it permits an immediate change in the color of the closure being produced without the need for purging the extruder of old resin;

· it allows the closure to be brightly colored without the need to pigment the base itself and consequently sacrifice the flexibility of the closure; it allows the closure to be multicolored since the paper lamination offers a perfect surface upon which can be printed multi-colored designs;

· it provides a closure with a superior surface upon which one can label or print;

· it provides a closure whose labeling cannot be altered or erased without resulting in tell-tale damage to the paper lamination; and

· it provides a closure which will not be slippery when handled with wet or greasy fingers, the paper itself providing a nonslip surface.

Although the description above contains many specificities, these should not be construed as limiting the scope of the invention but as merely providing illustrations of some of the presently preferred embodiments of this invention. For example, the closure can have other shapes, such as circular, oval, trapezoidal, triangular, etc.; the lead-in notch can have other shapes; the groove can be replaced by a hinge which connects two otherwise unconnected halves, etc.

Thus the scope of the invention should be determined by the appended claims and their legal equivalents, rather than by the examples given.

[CLAIMS FOLLOW, STARTING ON A NEW PAGE]

PAPER-LAMINATED PLIABLE CLOSURE FOR FLEXIBLE BAGS

Abstract: A thin, flat closure for plastic bags and of the type having at one edge a V-shaped notch (**12**): which communicates at its base with a gripping aperture (**14**). The base (**10**) of the closure is made of a flexible material so that it can be repeatedly bent, without fracturing, along an axis aligned with said notch and aperture. In addition, a layer of paper (**20**) is laminated on one or both sides of the closure. The axis of the base may contain one or two grooves (**18**) or a through-hole (**26**), either of which acts as a hinge to facilitate bending.

1/4

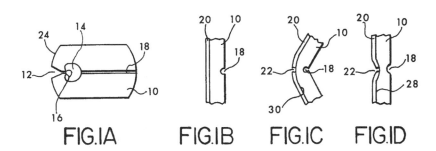

FIG.IA   FIG.IB   FIG.IC   FIG.ID

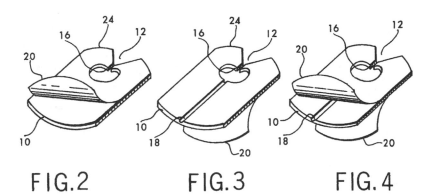

FIG.2   FIG.3   FIG.4

2/4

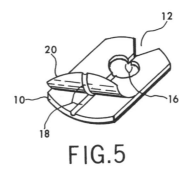

FIG.5

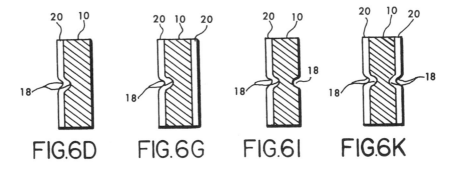

FIG.6D FIG.6G FIG.6I FIG.6K

3/4

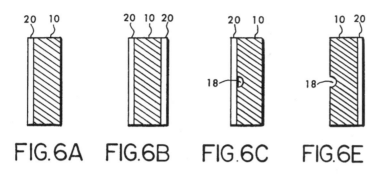

FIG.6A   FIG.6B   FIG.6C   FIG.6E

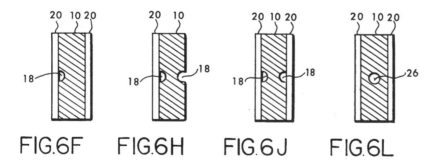

FIG.6F   FIG.6H   FIG.6J   FIG.6L

Forms

4/4

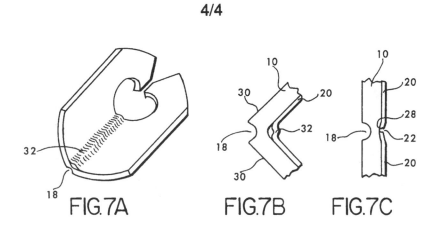

FIG.7A FIG.7B FIG.7C

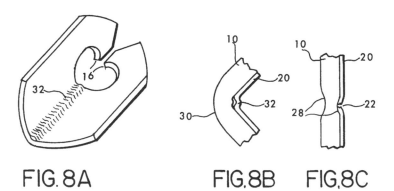

FIG. 8A FIG.8B FIG.8C

Patent Law

PATENT ACT. The selected statutes set out below are all part of a larger statutory scheme known as the Patent Act, found in Title 35 United States Code, Sections 101-376.

§ 101. Inventions patentable

Whoever invents or discovers any new and useful process, machine, manufacture, or composition of matter, or any new and useful improvement thereof, may obtain a patent therefor, subject to the conditions and requirements of this title.

§ 102. Conditions for patentability; novelty and loss of right to patent

A person shall be entitled to a patent unless—

(a) the invention was known or used by others in this country, or patented or described in a printed publication in this or a foreign country, before the invention thereof by the applicant for patent, or

(b) the invention was patented or described in a printed publication in this or a foreign country or in public use or on sale in this country, more than one year prior to the date of the application for patent in the United States, or

(c) he has abandoned the invention, or

(d) the invention was first patented or caused to be patented, or was the subject of an inventor's certificate, by the applicant or his legal representatives or assigns in a foreign country prior to the date of the application for patent in this country on an application for patent or inventor's certificate filed more than twelve months before the filing of the application in the United States, or

(e) the invention was described in a patent granted on an application for patent by another filed in the United States before the invention thereof by the applicant for patent, or on an international application by another who has fulfilled the requirements of paragraphs (1), (2), and (4) of section 371(c) of this title before the invention thereof by the applicant for patent, or

(f) he did not himself invent the subject matter sought to be patented, or

(g) (1) during the course of an interference conducted under section 135 or section 291, another inventor involved therein establishes, to the extent permitted in section 104, that before such person's invention thereof the invention was made by such other inventor and not abandoned, suppressed, or concealed, or (2) before such person's invention thereof, the invention was made in this country by another inventor who had not abandoned, suppressed, or concealed it. In determining priority of invention under this subsection, there shall be considered not only the respective dates of conception and reduction to practice of the invention, but also the reasonable diligence of one who was first to conceive and last to reduce to practice, from a time prior to conception by the other.

§ 103. Conditions for patentability; non-obvious subject matter

This statute sets out the requirement that an invention must be non-obvious to qualify for a patent.

(a) A patent may not be obtained though the invention is not identically disclosed or described as set forth in section 102 of this title, if the differences between the subject matter sought to be patented and the prior art are such that the subject matter as a whole would have been obvious at the time the invention was made to a person having ordinary skill in the art to which said subject matter pertains. Patentability shall not be negatived by the manner in which the invention was made.

(b) (1) Notwithstanding subsection (a), and upon timely election by the applicant for patent to proceed under this subsection, a biotechnological process using or resulting in a composition of matter that is novel under section 102 and nonobvious under subsection (a) of this section shall be considered nonobvious if—

   (A) claims to the process and the composition of matter are contained in either the same application for patent or in separate applications having the same effective filing date; and

   (B) the composition of matter, and the process at the time it was invented, were owned by the same person or subject to an obligation of assignment to the same person.

(2) A patent issued on a process under paragraph (1)—

   (A) shall also contain the claims to the composition of matter used in or made by that process, or

   (B) shall, if such composition of matter is claimed in another patent, be set to expire on the same date as such other patent, notwithstanding section 154.

(3) For purposes of paragraph (1), the term "biotechnological process" means—

   (A) a process of genetically altering or otherwise inducing a single- or multi-celled organism to—

      (i) express an exogenous nucleotide sequence,

      (ii) inhibit, eliminate, augment, or alter expression of an endogenous nucleotide sequence, or

      (iii) express a specific physiological characteristic not naturally associated with said organism;

   (B) cell fusion procedures yielding a cell line that expresses a specific protein, such as a monoclonal antibody; and

   (C) a method of using a product produced by a process defined by subparagraph (A) or (B), or a combination of subparagraphs (A) and (B).

(c) Subject matter developed by another person, which qualifies as prior art only under one or more of subsections (e), (f), and (g) of section 102 of this title, shall not preclude patentability under this section where the subject matter and the claimed invention were, at the time the invention was made, owned by the same person or subject to an obligation of assignment to the same person.

§ 111. Application for patent

This statute addresses several patent application requirements. Specifically, it:

- *requires that an application for a patent must be made or authorized by the inventor*
- *sets out the information that must be contained in a patent application and provisional patent application, and*
- *establishes what constitutes a filing date.*

    (a) In general.—

        (1) Written application. An application for patent shall be made, or authorized to be made, by the inventor, except as otherwise provided in this title, in writing to the Director.

        (2) Contents. Such application shall include—

            (A) a specification as prescribed by section 112 of this title;

            (B) a drawing as prescribed by section 113 of this title; and

            (C) an oath by the applicant as prescribed by section 115 of this title.

        (3) Fee and oath. The application must be accompanied by the fee required by law. The fee and oath may be submitted after the specification and any required drawing are submitted, within such period and under such conditions, including the payment of a surcharge, as may be prescribed by the Director.

        (4) Failure to submit. Upon failure to submit the fee and oath within such prescribed period, the application shall be regarded as abandoned, unless it is shown to the satisfaction of the Director that the delay in submitting the fee and oath was unavoidable or unintentional. The filing date of an application shall be the date on which the specification and any required drawing are received in the Patent and Trademark Office.

    (b) Provisional application.—

        (1) Authorization. A provisional application for patent shall be made or authorized to be made by the inventor, except as otherwise provided in this title, in writing to the Director. Such application shall include—

            (A) a specification as prescribed by the first paragraph of section 112 of this title; and

            (B) a drawing as prescribed by section 113 of this title.

        (2) Claim. A claim, as required by the second through fifth paragraphs of section 112, shall not be required in a provisional application.

        (3) Fee.

            (A) The application must be accompanied by the fee required by law.

            (B) The fee may be submitted after the specification and any required drawing are submitted, within such period and under such conditions, including the payment of a surcharge, as may be prescribed by the Director.

            (C) Upon failure to submit the fee within such prescribed period, the application shall be regarded as abandoned, unless it is shown to the satisfaction of the Director that the delay in submitting the fee was unavoidable or unintentional.

        (4) Filing date. The filing date of a provisional application shall be the date on which the specification and any required drawing are received in the Patent and Trademark Office.

(5) Abandonment. Notwithstanding the absence of a claim, upon timely and as pre-scribed by the Director, a provisional application may be treated as an application filed under subsection (a). Subject to section 119(e)(3) of this title, if no such request is made, the provisional application shall be regarded as abandoned 12 months after the filing date of such application and shall not be subject to revival after such 12-month period.

(6) Other basis for provisional application. Subject to all the conditions in this subsection and section 119(e) of this title, and as prescribed by the Director, an application for patent filed under subsection (a) may be treated as a provisional application for patent.

(7) No right of priority or benefit of earliest filing date. A provisional application shall not be entitled to the right of priority of any other application under section 119 or 365(a) of this title or to the benefit of an earlier filing date in the United States under section 120, 121, or 365(c) of this title.

(8) Applicable provisions. The provisions of this title relating to applications for patent shall apply to provisional applications for patent, except as otherwise provided, and except that provisional applications for patent shall not be subject to sections 115, 131, 135, and 157 of this title.

§ 112. Specification

This statute sets out the detailed requirements for how an invention must be described in a patent application, known as the specification and claims.

The specification shall contain a written description of the invention, and of the manner and process of making and using it, in such full, clear, concise, and exact terms as to enable any person skilled in the art to which it pertains, or with which it is most nearly connected, to make and use the same, and shall set forth the best mode contemplated by the inventor of carrying out his invention.

The specification shall conclude with one or more claims particularly pointing out and distinctly claiming the subject matter which the applicant regards as his invention.

A claim may be written in independent or, if the nature of the case admits, in dependent or multiple dependent form.

Subject to the following paragraph, a claim in dependent form shall contain a reference to a claim previously set forth and then specify a further limitation of the subject matter claimed. A claim in dependent form shall be construed to incorporate by reference all the limitations of the claim to which it refers.

A claim in multiple dependent form shall contain a reference, in the alternative only, to more than one claim previously set forth and then specify a further limitation of the subject matter claimed. A multiple dependent claim shall not serve as a basis for any other multiple dependent claim. A multiple dependent claim shall be construed to incorporate by reference all the limita-tions of the particular claim in relation to which it is being considered.

An element in a claim for a combination may be expressed as a means or step for performing a specified function without the recital of structure, material, or acts in support thereof, and such claim shall be construed to cover the corresponding structure, material, or acts described in the specification and equivalents thereof.

§ 113. Drawings

This statute describes the requirements for submitting a drawing and establishes procedures if the drawing is either not submitted or submitted after the filing date.

The applicant shall furnish a drawing where necessary for the understanding of the subject matter sought to be patented. When the nature of such subject matter admits of illustration by a drawing and the applicant has not furnished such a drawing, the Director may require its submission within a time period of not less than two months from the sending of a notice thereof. Drawings submitted after the filing date of the application may not be used (i) to overcome any insufficiency of the specification due to lack of an enabling disclosure or otherwise inadequate disclosure therein, or (ii) to supplement the original disclosure thereof for the purpose of interpretation of the scope of any claim.

§ 116. Inventors

This statute governs the procedures for filing a patent application when there are two or more inventors.

When an invention is made by two or more persons jointly, they shall apply for patent jointly and each make the required oath, except as otherwise provided in this title. Inventors may apply for a patent jointly even though (1) they did not physically work together or at the same time, (2) each did not make the same type or amount of contribution, or (3) each did not make a contribution to the subject matter of every claim of the patent.

If a joint inventor refuses to join in an application for patent or cannot be found or reached after diligent effort, the application may be made by the other inventor on behalf of himself and the omitted inventor. The Director, on proof of the pertinent facts and after such notice to the omitted inventor as he prescribes, may grant a patent to the inventor making the application, subject to the same rights which the omitted inventor would have had if he had been joined. The omitted inventor may subsequently join in the application.

Whenever through error a person is named in an application for patent as the inventor, or through error an inventor is not named in an application, and such error arose without any deceptive intention on his part, the Director may permit the application to be amended accordingly, under such terms as he prescribes.

§ 118. Filing by other than inventor

This statute explains how to file a patent application when the inventor refuses to cooperate or can't be found.

Whenever an inventor refuses to execute an application for patent, or cannot be found or reached after diligent effort, a person to whom the inventor has assigned or agreed in writing to assign the invention or who otherwise shows sufficient proprietary interest in the matter justifying such action, may make application for patent on behalf of and as agent for the inventor on proof of the pertinent facts and a showing that such action is necessary to preserve the rights of the parties or to prevent irreparable damage; and the Director may grant a patent to such inventor upon such notice to him as the Director deems sufficient, and on compliance with such regulations as he prescribes.

§ 119. Benefit of earlier filing date in foreign country; right of priority

This statute sets out the filing requirements and deadlines in the U.S. if a patent application has previously been filed in another country or the invention has been put into public use or sale, or described in a printed document, in another country.

(a) An application for patent for an invention filed in this country by any person who has, or whose legal representatives or assigns have, previously regularly filed an application for a patent for the same invention in a foreign country which affords similar privileges in the case of applications filed in the United States or to citizens of the United States, or in a WTO member country, shall have the same effect as the same application would have if filed in this country on the date on which the application for patent for the same invention was first filed in such foreign country, if the application in this country is filed within twelve months from the earliest date on which such foreign application was filed; but no patent shall be granted on any application for patent for an invention which had been patented or described in a printed publication in any country more than one year before the date of the actual filing of the application in this country, or which had been in public use or on sale in this country more than one year prior to such filing.

(b) No application for patent shall be entitled to this right of priority unless a claim therefor and a certified copy of the original foreign application, specification and drawings upon which it is based are filed in the Patent and Trademark Office before the patent is granted, or at such time during the pendency of the application as required by the Commissioner not earlier than six months after the filing of the application in this country. Such certification shall be made by the patent office of the foreign country in which filed and show the date of the application and of the filing of the specification and other papers. The Commissioner may require a translation of the papers filed if not in the English language and such other information as he deems necessary.

(c) In like manner and subject to the same conditions and requirements, the right provided in this section may be based upon a subsequent regularly filed application in the same foreign country instead of the first filed foreign application, provided that any foreign application filed prior to such subsequent application has been withdrawn, abandoned, or otherwise disposed of, without having been laid open to public inspection and without leaving any rights outstanding, and has not served, nor thereafter shall serve, as a basis for claiming a right of priority.

(d) Applications for inventors' certificates filed in a foreign country in which applicants have a right to apply, at their discretion, either for a patent or for an inventor's certificate shall be treated in this country in the same manner and have the same effect for purpose of the right of priority under this section as applications for patents, subject to the same conditions and requirements of this section as apply to applications for patents, provided such applicants are entitled to the benefits of the Stockholm Revision of the Paris Convention at the time of such filing.

(e) (1) An application for patent filed under section 111(a) or section 363 of this title for an invention disclosed in the manner provided by the first paragraph of section 112 of this title in a provisional application filed under section 111(b) of this title, by an inventor or inventors named in the provisional application, shall have the same effect, as to such invention, as though filed on the date of the provisional application filed under section 111(b) of this title, if the application for patent filed under section 111(a) or section 363 of this title is filed not later than 12 months after the date on which the provisional application was filed and if it contains or is amended to contain a specific reference to the provisional application.

(2) A provisional application filed under section 111(b) of this title may not be relied upon in any proceeding in the Patent and Trademark Office unless the fee set forth in subparagraph (A) or (C) of section 41(a)(1) of this title has been paid.

(3) If the day that is 12 months after the filing date of a provisional application falls on a Saturday, Sunday, or Federal holiday within the District of Columbia, the period of pendency of the provisional application shall be extended to the next succeeding secular or business day.

(f) Applications for plant breeder's rights filed in a WTO member country (or in a foreign UPOV Contracting Party) shall have the same effect for the purpose of the right of priority

under subsections (a) through (c) of this section as applications for patents, subject to the same conditions and requirements of this section as apply to applications for patents.
(g) As used in this section—
    (1) the term "WTO member country" has the same meaning as the term is defined in section 104(b)(2) of this title; and
    (2) the term "UPOV Contracting Party" means a member of the International Convention for the Protection of New Varieties of Plants.

§ 121. Divisional applications

This statute details the procedure for splitting one patent application into two—while keeping the original filing date—if it turns out that the original application contained at least two separate inventions.

If two or more independent and distinct inventions are claimed in one application, the Director may require the application to be restricted to one of the inventions. If the other invention is made the subject of a divisional application which complies with the requirements of section 120 of this title it shall be entitled to the benefit of the filing date of the original application. A patent issuing on an application with respect to which a requirement for restriction under this section has been made, or on an application filed as a result of such a requirement, shall not be used as a reference either in the Patent and Trademark Office or in the courts against a divisional application or against the original application or any patent issued on either of them, if the divisional application is filed before the issuance of the patent on the other application. If a divisional application is directed solely to subject matter described and claimed in the original application as filed, the Director may dispense with signing and execution by the inventor. The validity of a patent shall not be questioned for failure of the Director to require the application to be restricted to one invention.

§ 122. Confidential status of applications

This statute provides that a patent application shall be kept confidential by the U.S. Patent and Trademark Office.

Applications for patents shall be kept in confidence by the Patent and Trademark Office and no information concerning the same given without authority of the applicant or owner unless necessary to carry out the provisions of any Act of Congress or in such special circumstances as may be determined by the Director.

§ 131. Examination of application

This statute provides that the U.S. Patent and Trademark Office shall issue a patent if the application and invention meet the requirements set by law.

The Director shall cause an examination to be made of the application and the alleged new invention; and if on such examination it appears that the applicant is entitled to a patent under the law, the Director shall issue a patent therefor.

§ 135. Interferences

This statute sets up a procedure within the U.S. Patent and Trademark Office to decide apparent conflicts between a pending patent application and another pending patent application, or between a pending patent application and an in-force patent.

(a) Whenever an application is made for a patent which, in the opinion of the Director, would interfere with any pending application, or with any unexpired patent, an interference may be declared and the Director shall give notice of such declaration to the applicants, or applicant and patentee, as the case may be. The Board of Patent Appeals and Interferences shall determine questions of priority of the inventions and may determine questions of patentability. Any final decision, if adverse to the claim of an applicant, shall constitute the final refusal by the Patent and Trademark Office of the claims involved, and the Director may issue a patent to the applicant who is adjudged the prior inventor. A final judgment adverse to a patentee from which no appeal or other review has been or can be taken or had shall constitute cancellation of the claims involved in the patent and notice of such cancellation shall be endorsed on copies of the patent distributed after such cancellation by the Patent and Trademark Office.

(b) A claim which is the same as, or for the same or substantially the same subject matter as, a claim of an issued patent may not be made in any application unless such a claim is made prior to one year from the date on which the patent was granted.

(c) Any agreement or understanding between parties to an interference, including any collateral agreements referred to therein, made in connection with or in contemplation of the termination of the interference, shall be in writing and a true copy thereof filed in the Patent and Trademark Office before the termination of the interference as between the said parties to the agreement or understanding. If any party filing the same so requests, the copy shall be kept separate from the file of the interference, and made available only to Government agencies on written request, or to any person on a showing of good cause. Failure to file the copy of such agreement or understanding shall render permanently unenforceable such agreement or understanding and any patent of such parties involved in the interference or any patent subsequently issued on any application of such parties so involved. The Director may, however, on a showing of good cause for failure to file within the time prescribed, permit the filing of the agreement or understanding during the six-month period subsequent to the termination of the interference as between the parties to the agreement or understanding.

The Director shall give notice to the parties or their attorneys of record, a reasonable time prior to said termination, of the filing requirement of this section. If the Director gives such notice at a later time, irrespective of the right to file such agreement or understanding within the six-month period on a showing of good cause, the parties may file such agreement or understanding within sixty days of the receipt of such notice.

Any discretionary action of the Director under this subsection shall be reviewable under section 10 of the Administrative Procedure Act.

(d) Parties to a patent interference, within such time as may be specified by the Director by regulation, may determine such contest or any aspect thereof by arbitration. Such arbitration shall be governed by the provisions of title 9 to the extent such title is not inconsistent with this section. The parties shall give notice of any arbitration award to the Director, and such award shall, as between the parties to the arbitration, be dispositive of the issues to which it relates. The arbitration award shall be unenforceable until such notice is given. Nothing in this subsection shall preclude the Director from determining patentability of the invention involved in the interference.

§ 151. Issue of patent

For applications that are allowed by the patent examiner, this statute describes what a patent applicant must do to get a patent issued.

If it appears that applicant is entitled to a patent under the law, a written notice of allowance of the application shall be given or mailed to the applicant. The notice shall specify a sum, constituting the issue fee or a portion thereof, which shall be paid within three months thereafter.

Upon payment of this sum the patent shall issue, but if payment is not timely made, the application shall be regarded as abandoned.

Any remaining balance of the issue fee shall be paid within three months from the sending of a notice thereof and, if not paid, the patent shall lapse at the termination of this three-month period. In calculating the amount of a remaining balance, charges for a page or less may be disregarded.

If any payment required by this section is not timely made, but is submitted with the fee for delayed payment and the delay in payment is shown to have been unavoidable, it may be accepted by the Director as though no abandonment or lapse had ever occurred.

§ 154. Contents and term of patent

This statute establishes the contents of the patent grant, the length of patent protection and authorizes the extension of the patent term under certain conditions.

(a) In general.—

    (1) Contents. Every patent shall contain a short title of the invention and a grant to the patentee, his heirs or assigns, of the right to exclude others from making, using, offering for sale, or selling the invention throughout the United States or importing the invention into the United States, and, if the invention is a process, of the right to exclude others from using, offering for sale or selling throughout the United States, or importing into the United States, products made by that process, referring to the specification for the particulars thereof.

    (2) Term. Subject to the payment of fees under this title, such grant shall be for a term beginning on the date on which the patent issues and ending 20 years from the date on which the application for the patent was filed in the United States or, if the application contains a specific reference to an earlier filed application or applications under section 120, 121, or 365(c) of this title, from the date on which the earliest such application was filed.

    (3) Priority. Priority under section 119, 365(a), or 365(b) of this title shall not be taken into account in determining the term of a patent.

    (4) Specification and drawing. A copy of the specification and drawing shall be annexed to the patent and be a part of such patent.

(b) Adjustment of patent term—

    (1) Patent term guarantees.

        (A) Guarantee of prompt patent and trademark office responses. Subject to the limitations under paragraph (2), if the issue of an original patent is delayed due to the failure of the Patent and Trademark Office to—

            (i) provide at least one of the notifications under section 132 of this title or a notice of allowance under section 151 of this title not later than 14 months after—

                (I) the date on which an application was filed under section 111(a) of this title; or

                (II) the date on which an international application fulfilled the requirements of section 371 of this title;

            (ii) respond to a reply under section 132, or to an appeal taken under section 134, within 4 months after the date on which the reply was filed or the appeal was taken;

            (iii) act on an application within 4 months after the date of a decision by the Board of Patent Appeals and Interferences under section 134 or 135 or a decision by a Federal court under section 141, 145, or 146 in a case in which allowable claims remain in the application; or

   (iv) issue a patent within 4 months after the date on which the issue fee was paid under section 151 and all outstanding requirements were satisfied, the term of the patent shall be extended 1 day for each day after the end of the period specified in clause (i), (ii), (iii), or (iv), as the case may be, until the action described in such clause is taken.

(B) Guarantee of no more than 3-year application pendency. Subject to the limitations under paragraph (2), if the issue of an original patent is delayed due to the failure of the United States Patent and Trademark Office to issue a patent within 3 years after the actual filing date of the application in the United States, not including—

   (i) any time consumed by continued examination of the application requested by the applicant under section 132(b);

   (ii) any time consumed by a proceeding under section 135(a), any time consumed by the imposition of an order under section 181, or any time consumed by appellate review by the Board of Patent Appeals and Interferences or by a Federal court; or

   (iii) any delay in the processing of the application by the United States Patent and Trademark Office requested by the applicant except as permitted by paragraph (3)(C), the term of the patent shall be extended 1 day for each day after the end of that 3-year period until the patent is issued.

(C) Guarantee or adjustments for delays due to interferences, secrecy orders, and appeals. Subject to the limitations under paragraph (2), if the issue of an original patent is delayed due to—

   (i) a proceeding under section 135(a);

   (ii) the imposition of an order under section 181; or

   (iii) appellate review by the Board of Patent Appeals and Interferences or by a Federal court in a case in which the patent was issued under a decision in the review reversing an adverse determination of patentability, the term of the patent shall be extended 1 day for each day of the pendency of the proceeding, order, or review, as the case may be.

(2) Limitations.

(A) In general. To the extent that periods of delay attributable to grounds specified in paragraph (1) overlap, the period of any adjustment granted under this subsection shall not exceed the actual number of days the issuance of the patent was delayed.

(B) Disclaimed term. No patent the term of which has been disclaimed beyond a specified date may be adjusted under this section beyond the expiration date specified in the disclaimer.

(C) Reduction of period of adjustment.

   (i) The period of adjustment of the term of a patent under paragraph (1) shall be reduced by a period equal to the period of time during which the applicant failed to engage in reasonable efforts to conclude prosecution of the application.

   (ii) With respect to adjustments to patent term made under the authority of paragraph (1)(B), an applicant shall be deemed to have failed to engage in reasonable efforts to conclude processing or examination of an application for the cumulative total of any periods of time in excess of 3 months that are taken to respond to a notice from the Office making any rejection, objection, argument, or other request, measuring such 3-month period from the date the notice was given or mailed to the applicant.

(iii) The Director shall prescribe regulations establishing the circumstances that constitute a failure of an applicant to engage in reasonable efforts to conclude processing or examination of an application.

(3) Procedures for patent term adjustment determination.

(A) The Director shall prescribe regulations establishing procedures for the application for and determination of patent term adjustments under this subsection.

(B) Under the procedures established under subparagraph (A), the Director shall—

(i) make a determination of the period of any patent term adjustment under this subsection, and shall transmit a notice of that determination with the written notice of allowance of the application under section 151; and

(ii) provide the applicant one opportunity to request reconsideration of any patent term adjustment determination made by the Director.

(C) The Director shall reinstate all or part of the cumulative period of time of an adjustment under paragraph (2)(C) if the applicant, prior to the issuance of the patent, makes a showing that, in spite of all due care, the applicant was unable to respond within the 3 month period, but in no case shall more than three additional months for each such response beyond the original 3-month period be reinstated.

(D) The Director shall proceed to grant the patent after completion of the Director's determination of a patent term adjustment under the procedures established under this subsection, notwithstanding any appeal taken by the applicant of such determination.

(4) Appeal of patent term adjustment determination.

(A) An applicant dissatisfied with a determination made by the Director under paragraph (3) shall have remedy by a civil action against the Director filed in the United States District Court for the District of Columbia within 180 days after the grant of the patent. Chapter 7 of title 5, United States Code [5 USC §§ 701 et seq.], shall apply to such action. Any final judgment resulting in a change to the period of adjustment of the patent term shall be served on the Director, and the Director shall thereafter alter the term of the patent to reflect such change.

(B) The determination of a patent term adjustment under this subsection shall not be subject to appeal or challenge by a third party prior to the grant of the patent.

§ 157. Statutory invention registration

This statute provides a means for putting an invention into the public domain to preclude anyone else from patenting it.

(a) Notwithstanding any other provision of this title, the Director is authorized to publish a statutory invention registration containing the specification and drawings of a regularly filed application for a patent without examination if the applicant—

(1) meets the requirements of section 112 of this title;

(2) has complied with the requirements for printing, as set forth in regulations of the Director;

(3) waives the right to receive a patent on the invention within such period as may be prescribed by the Director; and

(4) pays application, publication, and other processing fees established by the Director.
    If an interference is declared with respect to such an application, a statutory invention
    registration may not be published unless the issue of priority of invention is finally
    determined in favor of the applicant.

(b) The waiver under subsection (a)(3) of this section by an applicant shall take effect upon
    publication of the statutory invention registration.

(c) A statutory invention registration published pursuant to this section shall have all of the
    attributes specified for patents in this title except those specified in section 183 and sec-
    tions 271 through 289 of this title. A statutory invention registration shall not have any of
    the attributes specified for patents in any other provision of law other than this title. A
    statutory invention registration published pursuant to this section shall give appropriate
    notice to the public, pursuant to regulations which the Director shall issue, of the preced-
    ing provisions of this subsection. The invention with respect to which a statutory inven-
    tion certificate is published is not a patented invention for purposes of section 292 of this
    title.

(d) The Secretary of Commerce shall report to the Congress annually on the use of statutory
    invention registrations. Such report shall include an assessment of the degree to which
    agencies of the Federal Government are making use of the statutory invention registration
    system, the degree to which it aids the management of federally developed technology,
    and an assessment of the cost savings to the Federal Government of the use of such pro-
    cedures.

§ 161. Patents for plants

This statute authorizes the U.S. Patent Office to issue a patent for certain qualifying plants.

Whoever invents or discovers and asexually reproduces any distinct and new variety of plant,
including cultivated sports, mutants, hybrids, and newly found seedlings, other than a
tuberpropagated plant or a plant found in an uncultivated state, may obtain a patent therefor,
subject to the conditions and requirements of this title.

The provisions of this title relating to patents for inventions shall apply to patents for plants,
except as otherwise provided.

§ 171. Patents for designs

*This statute authorizes the U.S. Patent and Trademark Office to issue a patent on certain qualifying
designs.*

Whoever invents any new, original and ornamental design for an article of manufacture may
obtain a patent therefor, subject to the conditions and requirements of this title.

The provisions of this title relating to patents for inventions shall apply to patents for designs,
except as otherwise provided.

§ 203. March-in rights

*This statute establishes a procedure under which a federal agency may obtain the right to develop an
invention that the agency helped to fund.*

(1) With respect to any subject invention in which a small business firm or nonprofit organi-
    zation has acquired title under this chapter, the Federal agency under whose funding
    agreement the subject invention was made shall have the right, in accordance with such
    procedures as are provided in regulations promulgated hereunder to require the contractor,
    an assignee or exclusive licensee of a subject invention to grant a nonexclusive, partially
    exclusive, or exclusive license in any field of use to a responsible applicant or applicants,

upon terms that are reasonable under the circumstances, and if the contractor, assignee, or exclusive licensee refuses such request, to grant such a license itself, if the Federal agency determines that such—

(a) action is necessary because the contractor or assignee has not taken, or is not expected to take within a reasonable time, effective steps to achieve practical application of the subject invention in such field of use;

(b) action is necessary to alleviate health or safety needs which are not reasonably satisfied by the contractor, assignee, or their licensees;

(c) action is necessary to meet requirements for public use specified by Federal regulations and such requirements are not reasonably satisfied by the contractor, assignee, or licensees; or

(d) action is not necessary because the agreement required by section 204 has not been obtained or waived or because a licensee of the exclusive right to use or sell any subject invention in the United States is in breach of its agreement obtained pursuant to section 204.

(2) A determination pursuant to this section or section 202(b)(4) shall not be subject to the Contract Disputes Act (41 U.S.C. § 601 et seq.). An administrative appeals procedure shall be established by regulations promulgated in accordance with section 206. Additionally, any contractor, inventor, assignee, or exclusive licensee adversely affected by a determination under this section may, at any time within sixty days after the determination is issued, file a petition in the United States Claims Court, which shall have jurisdiction to determine the appeal on the record and to affirm, reverse, remand or modify, as appropriate, the determination of the Federal agency. In cases described in paragraphs (a) and (c), the agency's determination shall be held in abeyance pending the exhaustion of appeals or petitions filed under the preceding sentence.

§ 251. Reissue of defective patents

This statute provides a way for the U.S. Patent and Trademark Office to reissue a patent that needs correction without losing the original filing date.

Whenever any patent is, through error without any deceptive intention, deemed wholly or partly inoperative or invalid, by reason of a defective specification or drawing, or by reason of the patentee claiming more or less than he had a right to claim in the patent, the Director shall, on the surrender of such patent and the payment of the fee required by law, reissue the patent for the invention disclosed in the original patent, and in accordance with a new and amended application, for the unexpired part of the term of the original patent. No new matter shall be introduced into the application for reissue.

The Director may issue several reissued patents for distinct and separate parts of the thing patented, upon demand of the applicant, and upon payment of the required fee for a reissue for each of such reissued patents.

The provisions of this title relating to applications for patent shall be applicable to applications for reissue of a patent, except that application for reissue may be made and sworn to by the assignee of the entire interest if the application does not seek to enlarge the scope of the claims of the original patent.

No reissued patent shall be granted enlarging the scope of the claims of the original patent unless applied for within two years from the grant of the original patent.

§ 252. Effect of reissue

This statute maintains the original filing date for a reissue patent, but provides a safe harbor for any activity that didn't infringe the original patent but which may infringe the reissued patent.

Statutes

The surrender of the original patent shall take effect upon the issue of the reissued patent, and every reissued patent shall have the same effect and operation in law, on the trial of actions for causes thereafter arising, as if the same had been originally granted in such amended form, but in so far as the claims of the original and reissued patents are identical, such surrender shall not affect any action then pending nor abate any cause of action then existing, and the reissued patent, to the extent that its claims are identical with the original patent, shall constitute a continuation thereof and have effect continuously from the date of the original patent.

A reissued patent shall not abridge or affect the right of any person or that person's successors in business who, prior to the grant of a reissue, made, purchased, offered to sell, or used within the United States, or imported into the United States, anything patented by the reissued patent, to continue the use of, to offer to sell, or to sell to others to be used, offered for sale, or sold, the specific thing so made, purchased, offered for sale, used, or imported unless the making, using, offering for sale, or selling of such thing infringes a valid claim of the reissued patent which was in the original patent. The court before which such matter is in question may provide for the continued manufacture, use, offer for sale, or sale of the thing made, purchased, offered for sale, used, or imported as specified, or for the manufacture, use, offer for sale, or sale in the United States of which substantial preparation was made before the grant of the reissue, and the court may also provide for the continued practice of any process patented by the reissue that is practiced, or for the practice of which substantial preparation was made, before the grant of the reissue, to the extent and under such terms as the court deems equitable for the protection of investments made or business commenced before the grant of the reissue.

§ 262. Joint owners

This statute authorizes any joint owner to use or sell the patented invention.

In the absence of any agreement to the contrary, each of the joint owners of a patent may make, use, offer to sell, or sell the patented invention within the United States, or import the patented invention into the United States, without the consent of and without accounting to the other owners.

§ 271. Infringement of patent

This statute defines the class of people who may be considered patent infringers and the types of activities that may be considered patent infringement.

(a) Except as otherwise provided in this title, whoever without authority makes, uses or sells any patented invention, within the United States during the term of the patent therefor, infringes the patent.

(b) Whoever actively induces infringement of a patent shall be liable as an infringer.

(c) Whoever sells a component of a patented machine, manufacture, combination or composition, or a material or apparatus for use in practicing a patented process, constituting a material part of the invention, knowing the same to be especially made or especially adapted for use in an infringement of such patent, and not a staple article or commodity of commerce suitable for substantial noninfringing use, shall be liable as a contributory infringer.

(d) No patent owner otherwise entitled to relief for infringement or contributory infringement of a patent shall be denied relief or deemed guilty of misuse or illegal extension of the patent right by reason of his having done one or more of the following: (1) derived revenue from acts which if performed by another without his consent would constitute contributory infringement of the patent; (2) licensed or authorized another to perform acts which if performed without his consent would constitute contributory infringement of the patent; (3) sought to enforce his patent rights against infringement or contributory infringement; (4) refused to license or use any rights to the patent; or (5) conditioned the license of any rights to the patent or the sale of the patented product on the acquisition of a license to rights in another patent or purchase of a separate product, unless, in view of the circumstances, the patent owner has market power in the relevant market for the patent or patented product on which the license or sale is conditioned.

(e)(1) It shall not be an act of infringement to make, use, or sell a patented invention (other than a new animal drug or veterinary biological product as those terms are used in the Federal Food, Drug, and Cosmetic Act and the Act of March 4, 1913, which is primarily manufactured using recombinant DNA, recombinant RNA, hybridoma technology, or other processes involving site specific genetic manipulation techniques) solely for uses reasonably related to the development and submission of information under a Federal law which regulates the manufacture, use, or sale of drugs or veterinary biological products.

(2) It shall be an act of infringement to submit—

(A) an application under section 505(j) of the Federal Food, Drug, and Cosmetic Act or described in section 505(b)(2) of such Act for a drug claimed in a patent or the use of which is claimed in a patent, or

(B) an application under section 512 of such Act or under the Act of March 4, 1913 (21 U.S.C. 151-158) for a drug or veterinary biological product which is not primarily manufactured using recombinant DNA, recombinant RNA, hybridoma technology, or other processes involving site specific genetic manipulation techniques and which is claimed in a patent or the use of which is claimed in a patent,

if the purpose of such submission is to obtain approval under such Act to engage in the commercial manufacture, use, or sale of a drug or veterinary biological product claimed in a patent or the use of which is claimed in a patent before the expiration of such patent.

(3) In any action for patent infringement brought under this section, no injunctive or other relief may be granted which would prohibit the making, using, or selling of a patented invention under paragraph (1).

(4) For an act of infringement described in paragraph (2)—

(A) the court shall order the effective date of any approval of the drug or veterinary biological product involved in the infringement to be a date which is not earlier than the date of the expiration of the patent which has been infringed,

(B) injunctive relief may be granted against an infringer to prevent the commercial manufacture, use, or sale of an approved drug or veterinary biological product, and

(C) damages or other monetary relief may be awarded against an infringer only if there has been commercial manufacture, use, or sale of an approved drug or veterinary biological product.

The remedies prescribed by subparagraphs (A), (B), and (C) are the only remedies which may be granted by a court for an act of infringement described in paragraph (2), except that a court may award attorney fees under section 285.

(f) (1) Whoever without authority supplies or causes to be supplied in or from the United States all or a substantial portion of the components of a patented invention, where such components are uncombined in whole or in part, in such manner as to actively induce the combination of such components outside of the United States in a manner that would infringe the patent if such combination occurred within the United States, shall be liable as an infringer.

(2) Whoever without authority supplies or causes to be supplied in or from the United States any component of a patented invention that is especially made or especially adapted for use in the invention and not a staple article or commodity of commerce suitable for substantial noninfringing use, where such component is uncombined in whole or in part, knowing that such component is so made or adapted and intending that such component will be combined outside of the United States in a manner that would infringe the patent if such combination occurred within the United States, shall be liable as an infringer.

(g) Whoever without authority imports into the United States or sells or uses within the United States a product which is made by a process patented in the United States shall be liable as an infringer, if the importation, sale, or use of the product occurs during the term of such process patent. In an action for infringement of a process patent, no remedy may be granted for infringement on account of the noncommercial use or retail sale of a product unless there is no adequate remedy under this title for infringement on account of the importation or other use or sale of that product. A product which is made by a patented process will, for purposes of this title, not be considered to be so made after—

(1) it is materially changed by subsequent processes; or

(2) it becomes a trivial and nonessential component of another product.

(h) As used in this section, the term "whoever" includes any State, any instrumentality of a State, and any officer or employee of a State or instrumentality of a State acting in his official capacity. Any State, and any such instrumentality, officer, or employee, shall be subject to the provisions of this title in the same manner and to the same extent as any nongovernmental entity.

(i) As used in this section, an "offer for sale" or an "offer to sell" by a person other than the patentee, or any designee of the patentee, is that in which the sale will occur before the expiration of the term of the patent.

§ 282. Presumption of validity; defenses

This statute presumes an in-force patent to be valid, but then describes the types of issues that may be raised to overcome this presumption by a person or organization accused of patent infringement.

A patent shall be presumed valid. Each claim of a patent (whether in independent, dependent, or multiple dependent form) shall be presumed valid independently of the validity of other claims; dependent or multiple dependent claims shall be presumed valid even though dependent upon an invalid claim. The burden of establishing invalidity of a patent or any claim thereof shall rest on the party asserting such invalidity.

The following shall be defenses in any action involving the validity or infringement of a patent and shall be pleaded:

(1) Noninfringement, absence of liability for infringement or unenforceability,

(2) Invalidity of the patent or any claim in suit on any ground specified in part II of this title as a condition for patentability,

(3) Invalidity of the patent or any claim in suit for failure to comply with any requirement of sections 112 or 251 of this title,

(4) Any other fact or act made a defense by this title.

In actions involving the validity or infringement of a patent the party asserting invalidity or noninfringement shall give notice in the pleadings or otherwise in writing to the adverse party at least thirty days before the trial, of the country, number, date, and name of the patentee of any patent, the title, date, and page numbers of any publication to be relied upon as anticipation of the patent in suit or, except in actions in the United States Claims Court, as showing the state of the art, and the name and address of any person who may be relied upon as the prior inventor or as having prior knowledge of or as having previously used or offered for sale the invention of the patent in suit. In the absence of such notice proof of the said matters may not be made at the trial except on such terms as the court requires. Invalidity of the extension of a patent term or any portion thereof under section 156 of this title because of the material failure—

(1) by the applicant for the extension, or

(2) by the Director,

to comply with the requirements of such section shall be a defense in any action involving the infringement of a patent during the period of the extension of its term and shall be pleaded. A due diligence determination under section 156(d)(2) is not subject to review in such an action.

§ 283. Injunction

This statute gives courts the power to order a party to do something or cease from doing something if the order is necessary to enforce a patent owner's rights.

The several courts having jurisdiction of cases under this title may grant injunctions in accordance with the principles of equity to prevent the violation of any right secured by patent, on such terms as the court deems reasonable.

§ 284. Damages

This statute sets out the money damages that a patent owner may recover in court for patent infringement.

Upon finding for the claimant the court shall award the claimant damages adequate to compensate for the infringement, but in no event less than a reasonable royalty for the use made of the invention by the infringer, together with interest and costs as fixed by the court.

When the damages are not found by a jury, the court shall assess them. In either event the court may increase the damages up to three times the amount found or assessed.

The court may receive expert testimony as an aid to the determination of damages or of what royalty would be reasonable under the circumstances.

§ 285. Attorney fees

This statute authorizes the court to award attorney fees.

The court in exceptional cases may award reasonable attorney fees to the prevailing party.

§ 286. Time limitation on damages

This statute establishes the time limit during which damages for infringement can be recovered.

Except as otherwise provided by law, no recovery shall be had for any infringement committed more than six years prior to the filing of the complaint or counterclaim for infringement in the action.

In the case of claims against the United States Government for use of a patented invention, the period before bringing suit, up to six years, between the date of receipt of a written claim for compensation by the department or agency of the Government having authority to settle such claim, and the date of mailing by the Government of a notice to the claimant that his claim has been denied shall not be counted as part of the period referred to in the preceding paragraph.

§ 287. Limitation on damages and other remedies; marking and notice

This statute sets out:

- *a method by which a patent owner may give notice that an invention is patented or that infringement has occurred*

- *the circumstances under which a patent infringer may escape liability for money damages, and*
- *a procedure for dealing with imported goods, if their manufacture may have infringed a process covered by a U.S. patent.*

(a) Patentees, and persons making or selling any patented article for or under them, may give notice to the public that the same is patented, either by fixing thereon the word "patent" or the abbreviation "pat.," together with the number of the patent, or when, from the character of the article, this cannot be done, by fixing to it, or to the package wherein one or more of them is contained, a label containing a like notice. In the event of failure so to mark, no damages shall be recovered by the patentee in any action for infringement, except on proof that the infringer was notified of the infringement and continued to infringe thereafter, in which event damages may be recovered only for infringement occurring after such notice. Filing of an action for infringement shall constitute such notice.

(b) (1) An infringer under section 271(g) shall be subject to all the provisions of this title relating to damages and injunctions except to the extent those remedies are modified by this subsection or section 9006 of the Process Patent Amendments Act of 1988. The modifications of remedies provided in this subsection shall not be available to any person who—

(A) practiced the patented process;

(B) owns or controls, or is owned or controlled by, the person who practiced the patented process; or

(C) had knowledge before the infringement that a patented process was used to make the product the importation, use, or sale of which constitutes the infringement.

(2) No remedies for infringement under section 271(g) of this title shall be available with respect to any product in the possession of, or in transit to, the person subject to liability under such section before that person had notice of infringement with respect to that product. The person subject to liability shall bear the burden of proving any such possession or transit.

(3) (A) In making a determination with respect to the remedy in an action brought for infringement under section 271(g), the court shall consider—

(i) the good faith demonstrated by the defendant with respect to a request for disclosure,

(ii) the good faith demonstrated by the plaintiff with respect to a request for disclosure, and

(iii) the need to restore the exclusive rights secured by the patent.

(B) For purposes of subparagraph (A), the following are evidence of good faith:

(i) a request for disclosure made by the defendant;

(ii) a response within a reasonable time by the person receiving the request for disclosure; and

(iii) the submission of the response by the defendant to the manufacturer, or if the manufacturer is not known, to the supplier, of the product to be purchased by the defendant, together with a request for a written statement that the process claimed in any patent disclosed in the response is not used to produce such product.

The failure to perform any acts described in the preceding sentence is evidence of absence of good faith unless there are mitigating circumstances. Mitigating circumstances include the case in which, due to the nature of the product, the number of sources for the product, or like commercial circumstances, a request for disclosure is not necessary or practicable to avoid infringement.

(4) (A) For purposes of this subsection, a "request for disclosure" means a written request made to a person then engaged in the manufacture of a product to identify all process patents owned by or licensed to that person, as of the time of the request, that the person then reasonably believes could be asserted to be infringed under section 271(g) if that product were imported into, or sold or used in, the United States by an unauthorized person. A request for disclosure is further limited to a request—

   (i) which is made by a person regularly engaged in the United States in the sale of the same type of products as those manufactured by the person to whom the request is directed, or which includes facts showing that the person making the request plans to engage in the sale of such products in the United States;

   (ii) which is made by such person before the person's first importation, use, or sale of units of the product produced by an infringing process and before the person had notice of infringement with respect to the product; and

   (iii) which includes a representation by the person making the request that such person will promptly submit the patents identified pursuant to the request to the manufacturer, or if the manufacturer is not known, to the supplier, of the product to be purchased by the person making the request, and will request from that manufacturer or supplier a written statement that none of the processes claimed in those patents is used in the manufacture of the product.

(B) In the case of a request for disclosure received by a person to whom a patent is licensed, that person shall either identify the patent or promptly notify the licensor of the request for disclosure.

(C) A person who has marked, in the manner prescribed by subsection (a), the number of the process patent on all products made by the patented process which have been sold by that person in the United States before a request for disclosure is received is not required to respond to the request for disclosure. For purposes of the preceding sentence, the term "all products" does not include products made before the effective date of the Process Patent Amendments Act of 1988.

(5) (A) For purposes of this subsection, notice of infringement means actual knowledge, or receipt by a person of a written notification, or a combination thereof, of information sufficient to persuade a reasonable person that it is likely that a product was made by a process patented in the United States.

(B) A written notification from the patent holder charging a person with infringement shall specify the patented process alleged to have been used and the reasons for a good faith belief that such process was used. The patent holder shall include in the notification such information as is reasonably necessary to explain fairly the patent holder's belief, except that the patent holder is not required to disclose any trade secret information.

(C) A person who receives a written notification described in subparagraph (B) or a written response to a request for disclosure described in paragraph (4) shall be deemed to have notice of infringement with respect to any patent referred to in such written notification or response unless that person, absent mitigating circumstances—

    (i) promptly transmits the written notification or response to the manufacturer or, if the manufacturer is not known, to the supplier, of the product purchased or to be purchased by that person; and

    (ii) receives a written statement from the manufacturer or supplier which on its face sets forth a well grounded factual basis for a belief that the identified patents are not infringed.

(D) For purposes of this subsection, a person who obtains a product made by a process patented in the United States in a quantity which is abnormally large in relation to the volume of business of such person or an efficient inventory level shall be rebuttably presumed to have actual knowledge that the product was made by such patented process.

(6) A person who receives a response to a request for disclosure under this subsection shall pay to the person to whom the request was made a reasonable fee to cover actual costs incurred in complying with the request, which may not exceed the cost of a commercially available automated patent search of the matter involved, but in no case more than $500.

(c) (1) With respect to a medical practitioner's performance of a medical activity that constitutes an infringement under section 271(a) or (b) of this title, the provisions of sections 281, 283, 284, and 285 of this title shall not apply against the medical practitioner or against a related health care entity with respect to such medical activity.

(2) For the purposes of this subsection:

(A) the term "medical activity" means the performance of a medical or surgical procedure on a body, but shall not include (i) the use of a patented machine, manufacture, or composition of matter in violation of such patent, (ii) the practice of a patented use of a composition of matter in violation of such patent, or (iii) the practice of a process in violation of a biotechnology patent.

(B) the term "medical practitioner" means any natural person who is licensed by a State to provide the medical activity described in subsection (c)(1) or who is acting under the direction of such person in the performance of the medical activity.

(C) the term "related health care entity" shall mean an entity with which a medical practitioner has a professional affiliation under which the medical practitioner performs the medical activity, including but not limited to a nursing home, hospital, university, medical school, health maintenance organization, group medical practice, or a medical clinic.

(D) the term "professional affiliation" shall mean staff privileges, medical staff membership, employment or contractual relationship, partnership or ownership interest, academic appointment, or other affiliation under which a medical practitioner provides the medical activity on behalf of, or in association with, the health care entity.

(E) the term "body" shall mean a human body, organ or cadaver, or a nonhuman animal used in medical research or instruction directly relating to the treatment of humans.

(F) the term "patented use of a composition of matter" does not include a claim for a method of performing a medical or surgical procedure on a body that recites the use of a composition of matter where the use of that composition of matter does not directly contribute to achievement of the objective of the claimed method.

(G) the term "State" shall mean any state or territory of the United States, the District of Columbia, and the Commonwealth of Puerto Rico.

(3) This subsection does not apply to the activities of any person, or employee or agent of such person (regardless of whether such person is a tax exempt organization under section 501(c) of the Internal Revenue Code [26 USC § 501(c)]), who is engaged in the commercial development, manufacture, sale, importation, or distribution of a machine, manufacture, or composition of matter or the provision of pharmacy or clinical laboratory services (other than clinical laboratory services provided in a physician's office), where such activities are:

(A) directly related to the commercial development, manufacture, sale, importation, or distribution of a machine, manufacture, or composition of matter or the provision of pharmacy or clinical laboratory services (other than clinical laboratory services provided in a physician's office), and

(B) regulated under the Federal Food, Drug, and Cosmetic Act, the Public Health Service Act, or the Clinical Laboratories Improvement Act.

(4) This subsection shall not apply to any patent issued based on an application the earliest effective filing date of which is prior to September 30, 1996.

§ 292. False marking

This statute provides a penalty for marking an unpatented invention with words that erroneously indicate it is patented or has patent pending status, when it is not.

(a) Whoever, without the consent of the patentee, marks upon, or affixes to, or uses in advertising in connection with anything made, used, or sold by him, the name or any imitation of the name of the patentee, the patent number, or the words "patent," "patentee," or the like, with the intent of counterfeiting or imitating the mark of the patentee, or of deceiving the public and inducing them to believe that the thing was made or sold by or with the consent of the patentee; or

Whoever marks upon, or affixes to, or uses in advertising in connection with any unpatented article, the word "patent" or any word or number importing that the same is patented, for the purpose of deceiving the public; or

Whoever marks upon, or affixes to, or uses in advertising in connection with any article, the words "patent applied for," "patent pending," or any word importing that an application for patent has been made, when no application for patent has been made, or if made, is not pending, for the purpose of deceiving the public—

Shall be fined not more than $500 for every such offense.

(b) Any person may sue for the penalty, in which event one-half shall go to the person suing and the other to the use of the United States.

§ 301. Citation of prior art

This statute allows any person to submit to the U.S. Patent and Trademark Office documents (prior art references) that call into question the originality of a patented invention.

Any person at any time may cite to the Office in writing prior art consisting of patents or printed publications which that person believes to have a bearing on the patentability of any claim of a particular patent. If the person explains in writing the pertinency and manner of applying such prior art to at least one claim of the patent, the citation of such prior art and the explanation thereof will become a part of the official file of the patent. At the written request of the person citing the prior art, his or her identity will be excluded from the patent file and kept confidential.

§ 302. Request for reexamination

This statute sets out the procedure for initiating a reexamination by the U.S. Patent and Trademark Office of a previously issued patent.

Any person at any time may file a request for reexamination by the Office of any claim of a patent on the basis of any prior art cited under the provisions of section 301 of this title. The request must be in writing and must be accompanied by payment of a reexamination fee established by the Director pursuant to the provisions of section 41 of this title. The request must set forth the pertinency and manner applying cited prior art to every claim for which reexamination is requested. Unless the requesting person is the owner of the patent, the Director promptly will send a copy of the request to the owner of record of the patent.

§ 303. Determination of issue by Director

This statute sets out the procedure that the U.S. Patent and Trademark Office must follow when deciding whether to reexamine a patent.

(a) Within three months following the filing of a request for reexamination under the provisions of section 302 of this title, the Director will determine whether a substantial new question of patentability affecting any claim of the patent concerned is raised by the request, with or without consideration of other patents or printed publications. On his own initiative, and any time, the Director may determine whether a substantial new question of patentability is raised by patents and publications discovered by him or cited under the provisions of section 301 of this title.

(b) A record of the Director's determination under subsection (a) of this section will be placed in the official file of the patent, and a copy promptly will be given or mailed to the owner of record of the patent and to the person requesting reexamination, if any.

(c) A determination by the Director pursuant to subsection (a) of this section that no substantial new question of patentability has been raised will be final and nonappealable. Upon such a determination, the Director may refund a portion of the reexamination fee required under section 302 of this title.

§ 304. Reexamination order by Director

This statute sets out the procedure to be followed if the U.S. Patent and Trademark Office decides to reexamine a patent.

If, in a determination made under the provisions of subsection 303(a) of this title, the Director finds that a substantial new question of patentability affecting any claim of a patent is raised, the determination will include an order for reexamination of the patent for resolution of the question. The patent owner will be given a reasonable period, not less than two months from the date a copy of the determination is given or mailed to him, within which he may file a statement on such question, including any amendment to his patent and new claim or claims he may wish to propose, for consideration in the reexamination. If the patent owner files such a statement, he promptly will serve a copy of it on the person who has requested reexamination under the provisions of section 302 of this title. Within a period of two months from the date of service, that person may file and have considered in the reexamination a reply to any statement filed by the patent owner. That person promptly will serve on the patent owner a copy of any reply filed.

§ 305. Conduct of reexamination proceedings

This statute describes the procedure to be followed by the U.S. Patent and Trademark Office when reexamining a patent.

After the times for filing the statement and reply provided for by section 304 of this title have expired, reexamination will be conducted according to the procedures established for initial examination under the provisions of sections 132 and 133 of this title. In any reexamination proceeding under this chapter, the patent owner will be permitted to propose any amendment to his patent and a new claim or claims thereto, in order to distinguish the invention as claimed from the prior art cited under the provisions of section 301 of this title, or in response to a decision adverse to the patentability of a claim of a patent. No proposed amended or new claim enlarging the scope of a claim of the patent will be permitted in a reexamination proceeding under this chapter. All reexamination proceedings under this section, including any appeal to the Board of Patent Appeals and Interferences, will be conducted with special dispatch within the Office.

§ 306. Appeal

This statute sets out how a party may appeal an adverse reexamination decision.

The patent owner involved in a reexamination proceeding under this chapter may appeal under the provisions of section 134 of this title, and may seek court review under the provisions of sections 141 to 145 of this title, with respect to any decision adverse to the patentability of any original or proposed amended or new claim of the patent.

§ 307. Certificate of patentability, unpatentability, and claim cancellation

This statute sets out the procedure to be followed by the U.S. Patent and Trademark Office after a decision is made in the reexamination proceeding.

(a) In a reexamination proceeding under this chapter, when the time for appeal has expired or any appeal proceeding has terminated, the Director will issue and publish a certificate canceling any claim of the patent finally determined to be unpatentable, confirming any claim of the patent determined to be patentable, and incorporating in the patent any proposed amended or new claim determined to be patentable.

(b) Any proposed amended or new claim determined to be patentable and incorporated into a patent following a reexamination proceeding will have the same effect as that specified in section 252 of this title for reissued patents on the right of any person who made, purchased, or used anything patented by such proposed amended or new claim, or who made substantial preparation for the same, prior to issuance of a certificate under the provisions of subsection (a) of this section.

Trademark law consists of the legal rules that govern how businesses may:
- identify their products or services in the marketplace to prevent consumer confusion, and
- protect the means they've chosen to identify their products or services against use by competitors.

1. What are trademarks and service marks?

A trademark is a distinctive word, phrase, logo, graphic symbol or other device that is used to identify the source of a product or service and to distinguish a manufacturer's or merchant's products from anyone else's. Some examples are: Ford cars and trucks, IBM computers and Microsoft software. In the trademark context, "distinctive" means unique enough to reasonably serve as an identifier of a product in the marketplace.

A trademark can be more than just a brand name or logo. It can include other non-functional but distinctive aspects of a product or service that tends to promote and distinguish it in the marketplace, such as shapes, letters, numbers, sounds, smells or colors. Titles, character names or other distinctive features of movies, television and radio programs can also serve as trademarks when used to promote a product.

For all practical purposes, a service mark is the same as a trademark—except that trademarks promote products while service marks promote services. Some familiar service marks include: McDonald's (fast food service), Kinko's (photo-copying service), ACLU (legal service), Blockbuster (video rental service), CBS's stylized eye in a circle (television network service), the Olympic Games' multi-colored interlocking circles (international sporting event).

Related terms: certification mark; collective mark; counterfeit mark; deceptive terms as marks; mark, defined; service mark; trademark, defined.

2. What is trade dress?

In addition to a label, logo or other identifying symbol, a product may also come to be identified by its distinctive shape (the Galliano liquor bottle) or packaging (the Kodak film package). Likewise, a service may be identified by its distinctive decor (the decorating motif used by the Banana Republic clothing stores). Collectively, these types of identifying features are commonly termed "trade dress."

Related terms: confusion of consumers; trade dress; unfair competition.

3. What is trademark law?

Broadly, trademark law is concerned with the overlapping and conflicting uses of trademarks, service marks and trade dress by different businesses. More specifically, trademark law determines what happens if a business adopts a logo or product name that either is identical or very similar to a very well-known existing one, or is one that consumers are reasonably likely to confuse with similar names or logos already in use on related products or services.

The basic rules for resolving a dispute over who is entitled to use a trademark, service mark or trade dress in a given context come from decisions by federal and state courts (the common law). These rules usually favor whichever business was first to use the mark or trade dress. A number of additional legal principles used to protect owners against use of their marks or trade dress by others come from U.S. Government statutes known collectively as the Lanham Act.

The Lanham Act also establishes the trademark registration system and provides for judicial remedies in cases of trademark infringement. In addition to the Lanham Act, most states provide for some means of registering trademarks and service marks (but usually not trade dress) with a state agency and allow for remedies in case of infringement.

Finally, federal and state courts have applied their own set of rules to activity deemed "unfair competition," which usually occurs when one business uses another business's name or service mark in a context that is likely to confuse the public. The main goal of an unfair competition lawsuit is to force the second user to modify its use of the name or mark, so that the original business will not lose customers due to confusion.

Trademark law also addresses treaties signed by a number of countries that make it easier to obtain international trademark protection.

Related terms: Inter-American Convention for Trademark and Commercial Protection; international trademark rights; Lanham Act; Madrid Arrangement on International Registration of Trademarks and Madrid Protocol; Paris Convention; prior registration countries; protection of marks under Lanham Act; protection of marks under state law and common law; Trademark Trial and Appeal Board; U.S. Patent and Trademark Office (PTO).

Overview

Overview

4. What kinds of trademarks and service marks receive protection under trademark law?

As a general rule, trademark law confers the most legal protection to names, logos and other marketing devices that are distinctive—that is, memorable because they are creative or out of the ordinary (inherently distinctive), or because over time they have become well known to the public.

Trademarks said to be inherently distinctive typically consist of:

- unique logos or symbols
- words that are made up to be specifically used as a mark ("coined marks"), such as Exxon or Kodak
- words that invoke imaginative images in the context of their usage ("fanciful marks"), such as Double Rainbow ice cream
- words that are surprising or unexpected in the context of their usage ("arbitrary marks"), such as Time Magazine or Diesel for a bookstore, and
- words that cleverly connote qualities about the product or service without literally describing these qualities ("suggestive or evocative marks"), such as Slenderella diet food products or Netscape World Wide Web Browser.

By contrast, marks that consist of common or ordinary words are not considered to be inherently distinctive, absent a showing that consumers recognize them because of their long use. Such weak marks receive less protection under federal or state laws. Typical examples of common or ordinary words are:

- people's names (Pete's Muffins, Smith Graphics)
- geographic terms (Northern Dairy, Central Insect Control), and
- descriptive terms—that is, words that attempt to literally describe the product or its characteristics (Rapid Computers, Clarity Video Monitors, Ice Cold Ice Cream).

As mentioned, it's possible for ordinary marks to become distinctive because they have developed great public recognition through long use and exposure in the marketplace. A mark that has become protectable through exposure or long use is said to have acquired a "secondary meaning." Examples of otherwise common marks that have acquired a secondary meaning and are now considered to be distinctive include Sears (department stores), Ben and Jerry's (ice cream) and Park N Fly (airport parking services).

Related terms: arbitrary mark; coined terms; color used as mark; color used as an element of a mark; composite mark; descriptive mark; distinctive mark; geographic terms as marks; non-profit corporations and trademarks; personal names as marks; phonetic or foreign equivalents for marks; pictures and symbols used as marks; secondary meaning; slogans used as marks; state trademark laws; strong mark; suggestive mark; surnames as marks; trade name; weak mark.

5. What cannot be protected under trademark law?

There are five common situations in which there is no trademark protection. In any of these situations, the intended trademark cannot be registered and the owner has no right to stop others from using a similar name. Generally, when speaking of what *cannot* be protected under trademark law, we are referring to the standards established under the Lanham Act (the federal statute that provides for registration of marks and federal court remedies in case a mark is infringed).

- **nonuse.** Trademark rights are derived from the continued use of a mark in commerce. If there is a significant break in the chain of trademark usage, the owner may lose rights under a principal known as abandonment. Abandonment can occur in many ways, but the most common way is non-use, that is, the mark is no longer used in commerce and there is sufficient evidence that the owner intends to discontinue use of the mark. For example, the owner of a mark for hotel services closed its hotels and failed to use the mark on similar services for a period of thirty years. This was sufficient proof that the owner abandoned the mark. Under the Lanham Act, a trademark is presumed to be abandoned after three years of nonuse. This presumption does not mean that the mark is automatically classified as abandoned after three years of nonuse. It means that the burden of proof shifts to the owner of the mark to prove it is *not* abandoned. The owner must prove an intention to resume commercial use.

- **generics and genericide.** A generic term describes an entire group or class of goods or services. For example, the terms "computer", "eyeglasses" and "eBook" are all generic terms. The public associates these terms with a type of goods, not a specific brand. For example, there are many brands of computers—*Gateway, Dell,* and *Compaq*—but there is no brand of computer known simply as *Computer.* If protection were granted to generics, one company would have a monopoly and could stop all others from using the name of the goods. For example, if only one company could use the term "Jam," any other company would be prevented from using that term with their brand of jam. Consumers are used to seeing a generic term used in conjunction with a trademark (for example, *Avery* labels, or *Hewlett-Packard* printers). From a grammatical point of view, generics are generally nouns, trademarks are generally adjectives and the generic term almost always follows the trademark. On some occasions a company invents a new word for a product (for example *Kleenex* for a tissue). That term may function so successfully as a trademark that the public eventually comes to believe that it *is* the name of the goods, not the trademark. This is what happened with the term "cellophane." This word, originally a registered trademark of the DuPont corporation, became so popular that consumers began to think of cellophane as the generic term for the clear plastic sheets. Other famous terms to move from trademark to generic are "aspirin," "yo-yo," "escalator," "thermos" and "kerosene." The process of moving from trademark to generic is referred to as genericide.

- **confusingly similar marks.** A mark will not be registered or otherwise protected under trademark law if it so resembles another mark currently registered or in use in the United States so as to cause confusion among consumers. This standard, known as "likelihood of confusion," is a foundation of trademark law. Many factors are weighed when considering likelihood of confusion. These factors are derived from the case of *In re: E.I. DuPont DeNemours & Co,* 476 F.2d 1357 (CCPA 1973). However, the most important "confusion factors" are generally the similarity of the marks, similarity of the goods, degree of care exercised by the consumer when purchasing, the intent of the person using the similar mark, and any actual confusion that has occurred.

- **weak marks.** A weak (or descriptive) trademark will not be protected unless the owner can prove that consumers are aware of the mark. There are three types of weak marks: descriptive marks, geographic marks that describe a location and marks that are primarily surnames (last names). When an applicant attempts to register a weak mark, the PTO will permit the applicant to submit proof of distinctiveness or to move the application from the Principal Register to the Supplemental Register. If the applicant fails to prove distinctiveness (known as secondary meaning), the PTO will reject the application. If the applicant disagrees with the PTO decision, the applicant can appeal the decision to the federal district court.

- **functional features.** Trademark law, like copyright law, will not protect functional features. Trademark disputes about this issue (sometimes referred to as functionality) arise in cases involving product shapes or product packaging (sometimes referred to as trade dress). Unfortunately, there is no simple definition for "functional" because this area of law is still evolving. Generally, a functional feature is essential to the usability of a product. That is, the feature is necessary for the item to work. When the feature is not necessary for the item to work, it will be protected under trademark law. For example, the body of an electric guitar can be made in innumerable shapes (as witnessed by oddly-shaped guitars favored by musicians such as Bo Diddley, Kiss and ZZ Top). The design of these guitars may become a trademark because the design is not dictated by the ability of the guitar to function. The design may also be protectible as a design patent.

Related terms: common use of mark; disclaimer of unregistrable material; free words or phrases; generic mark; registrable matter.

6. How is trademark ownership determined?

As a general rule, a mark is owned by the business that is first to use it in a commercial context—that is, the first to attach the mark to a product or use the mark when marketing a product or service. After the first use, the owner may be able to prevent others from using it, or a similar trademark, for their goods and services as long as the owner continues to use the mark in connection with its goods and services.

First use can also be established by filing an intent-to-use (ITU) trademark registration application with the U.S. Patent and Trademark Office. The filing date of this application will be considered the date of first use if the applicant puts the mark into actual use within required time limits (between six months and three years, depending on the reasons for the delay and whether the applicant seeks and pays for extensions), and follows up to obtain an actual registration.

Related terms: assignment of mark; average, reasonably prudent, consumer; competing and non-competing products; geographically separate market; intent-to-use application; licensing of marks; naked license; ownership of mark in the U.S.; registrant; related products and services; senior and junior users of marks; use of mark.

7. What about federal registration of a mark?

Registering a trademark or service mark with the U.S. Patent and Trademark Office (PTO) makes it easier for the owner to protect it against would-be copiers, and puts the rest of the country on notice that the mark is already taken. The registration process involves filling out a simple application, paying an application fee ($325, current in September 2000) and being willing to work with an official of the PTO to correct any errors that he or she finds in the application.

To qualify a mark for registration with the PTO, the mark's owner first must put it into use "in commerce that Congress may regulate." This means the mark must be used on a product or service that crosses state, national or territorial lines or that affects commerce crossing such lines—such as would be the case with a catalog business or a restaurant or motel that caters to interstate or international consumers. If an intent-to-use application is being filed (the applicant intends to use the mark in the near future but hasn't begun using it yet), another document must be filed for a fee once the actual use begins, showing that mark is being used in commerce (as defined above).

Once the PTO receives a trademark registration application, it determines the answers to these questions:

- Does the application have to be amended (because of errors) before it can be examined?
- Is the mark the same as or similar to an existing mark used on similar or related goods or services?
- Is the mark on a list of prohibited or reserved names?
- Is the mark generic—that is, does the mark describe the product or service itself rather than its source?
- Is the mark descriptive—that is , does it consist of words or images that are ordinary or that literally describe one or more aspects of the underlying goods or services?

When the PTO can answer all of these questions in the negative, it will publish the mark in the Official Gazette (a publication of the U.S. Patent and Trademark Office) as being a candidate for registration. Existing trademark and service mark owners may object to the registration by filing an opposition. If this occurs, the PTO will schedule a hearing to resolve the dispute. Even if existing owners don't challenge the registration of the mark at this stage, they may later attack the registration in court if they believe the registered mark infringes one they already own.

If there is no opposition, and use in commerce has been established, the PTO will place the mark on the list of trademarks known as the Principal Register if it is considered distinctive (either inherently or because the applicant has shown that the mark has acquired secondary meaning). Probably the most important benefit of placing a mark on the Principal Register is that anybody who later initiates use of the same or a confusingly similar mark will be presumed by the courts to be a "willful infringer" and therefore liable for large money damages. However, it is still possible to obtain basic protection for a mark from the federal courts under the Lanham Act without prior registration.

If a mark consists of ordinary or descriptive terms (that is, it isn't considered distinctive), it may be placed on a different list of trademarks and service marks known as the Supplemental Register. Placement of a mark on the Supplemental Register produces significantly fewer benefits than those offered by the Principal

Register, but still provides notice of ownership. Also, if the mark remains on the Supplemental Register for five years—that is, the registration isn't cancelled for some reason—and also remains in use during that time, it may then be placed on the Principal Register under the secondary meaning rule (secondary meaning will be presumed).

Related terms: abandonment of mark; Amendment to Allege Use; certificate of registration; commerce; Commissioner of Patents and Trademarks; concurrent registration; constructive notice of mark under Lanham Act; continuous use of mark; duration of federal trademark registration; foreign nationals, registering in U.S.; incontestability status; inter partes proceeding; interference; International Schedule of Classes of Goods and Services; notice of trademark registration; Official Gazette; opposing and cancelling a trademark registration; presumption of ownership; Principal Register; prohibited and reserved marks under Lanham Act; right of publicity; same or similar mark; Sections 8 and 15 Affidavit; Statement of Use; Supplemental Register.

8. How can you tell if a mark proposed for use is already being used by another business?

A "trademark search" is an investigation to discover potential conflicts between a proposed mark and an existing one. Generally done before or at the beginning of a new mark's use, a trademark search reduces the possibility of inadvertently infringing a mark belonging to someone else.

Often, a professional search agency is used to conduct the trademark search—by first checking both federal and state trademark registers for identical or similar marks and then checking journals, telephone books and magazines to see whether the mark is in actual use. It is possible to do a trademark search, without involving a professional, at any of the Patent Depository and Trademark Libraries throughout the country. It is also possible to conduct a preliminary online trademark search to determine if a trademark is distinguishable from other federally registered trademarks. This can be accomplished using the PTO's free trademark databases (http://www. uspto.gov/tmdb/index.html and http://tess.uspto.gov/bin/gate.exe?f=tess&state=vfg9gj.1.1), both of which provide free access to records of federally registered marks or marks that are pending (applications undergoing examination at the PTO). Privately owned fee-based online trademark databases often provide more current PTO trademark information. Below are some private online search companies:

- **Saegis** (http://www.thomson-thomson.com) The most comprehensive trademark searching service, Saegis provides access to all Trademarkscan databases (state, federal and international trademark databases), domain name databases, common law sources on the Internet and access to newly filed United States federal trademark applications. Saegis also provides access to *Dialog* services.

- **Dialog** (http://www.dialog.com) Dialog provides access to Trademarkscan databases, including state and federal registration and some international trademarks. It also provides common law searching of news databases.
- **Micropatent** (http://www.micropatent.com) Micropatent provides access to federal and state trademarks through its MarkSearch Pro and MarkSearch Pro State databases.
- **Corporate Intelligence** (http://www.trademarks.com) Corporate Intelligence provides access to current federal registration information.
- **Trademark Register** (http://www.trademarkregister.com) Trademark register provides access to current federal registration information.
- **Marksonline** (http://www.marksonline.com) Marksonline is a comprehensive trademark link site with listing of state and national trademark offices.
- **LEXIS/NEXIS** (http://www.lexis-nexis.com) LEXIS provides access to federal and state registrations and permits common law searching via NEXIS news services. The PTO utilizes NEXIS for its evaluations of descriptive and generic terms.

Related terms: Internet and trademark searching; Patent and Trademark Depository Library; trademark search.

9. Do mark owners need to provide notice to the public?

Many owners like to put a "TM" (or "SM" for service mark) next to their mark to let the world know that they are claiming ownership of it. There is no legal necessity for providing this type of notice, however, because the use of the mark itself is the act that confers ownership.

The "R" in a circle (®) is a different matter entirely. This notice may not be put on a mark unless it has been registered with the U.S. Patent and Trademark Office. The failure to put the notice on a mark that has been so registered can result in a handicap if it later becomes necessary to file a lawsuit against an infringer of the mark.

Related terms: registered mark; TM; unregistered mark, protection of.

10. How is ownership of a mark enforced?

Whether or not a trademark is federally registered, its owner may go to court to prevent someone else from using it or a confusingly similar mark. Courts will examine such factors as:

Overview

- whether the trademark is being used on competing goods or services (goods or services compete if the sale of one is likely to preclude the sale of the other)
- whether consumers would likely be confused by the dual use of the trademark, and
- whether the trademark is being used in the same part of the country or is being distributed through the same channels.

If the mark is infringing and the mark's owner can prove loss or show that the competitor gained economically as a result of the improper use, the competitor may have to pay the owner damages based on the profit or loss. If the court finds the competitor intentionally copied the owner's trademark, the infringer may have to pay other damages, such as punitive damages, fines or attorney fees. On the other hand, if the trademark's owner has not been damaged, a court has discretion to allow the competitor to also use the mark under very limited circumstances designed to avoid the possibility of consumer confusion.

In addition, under federal and state anti-dilution statutes, an owner may prevent a mark from being used by others (the essence of mark ownership) if:

- the mark is well known, and
- the later use would dilute the mark's strength—that is, impair or tarnish its reputation for quality or render it common through overuse in different contexts (even if it is unlikely that any consumers would be confused by the second use).

Related terms: attorney fees in trademark infringement actions; Bureau of Customs; contributory infringer; damages in trademark infringement cases; defendant's profits; deliberate infringer; dilution of mark; federal trademark registration; infringement action; injunctions against infringement and unfair competition; innocent infringer; loss of mark; palming off; publishers of advertising matter; punitive damages; reverse palming off.

11. If a company has registered its trademark, does it need to register its trademark.com?

If a trademark owner has acquired a federal registration for a mark, there is little to be gained from registering the ".com" version of that mark. For example, if a company sells books under the federally registered mark ReadMe, it is not necessary to federally register its domain name ReadMe.com when the company sells books at its website. Why? The owner of a federally registered trademark can stop others from using the mark for similar goods or services whether they are sold online or off. In addition, the PTO requires that applicants disclaim .com in order to prevent any person from claiming a proprietary right to this generic term.

EXAMPLE: Tom federally registers *Loudness* as a trademark for his line of men's wear. Tom later acquires the domain name Loudness.com to sell his men's wear online. Tom does not need to federally register Loudness.com because his federal registration for *Loudness* permits him to stop others from selling men's wear with a confusingly similar mark either in stores or on the Internet. Similarly, if a competitor registers Loudness.net, Tom's federal registration will permit him to stop the competing domain name use.

A company with a federally registered trademark expanding its product line to include new products can file additional federal registrations for the trademark in these new classes of goods, but there is no reason to register the .com version of the mark. It is only recommended that the .com version of a federally registered trademark be filed if the company is establishing some service unique to its Internet business.

EXAMPLE: Tom federally registers *Loudness* as a trademark for his line of men's wear. Tom later acquires the domain name Loudness.com to sell his men's wear directly to consumers. Tom expands his website to include an interactive shopping guide that allows consumers to order custom-made men's wear. When the user uploads a picture of himself, he sees what he will look like in the men's wear. Tom should federally register Loudness.com because the domain name is now being used as an identifier for shopping services.

12. Trademark resources

If you're interested in protecting your trademark or service mark, you may want to consult these Nolo resources:

- *Trademark: How to Name Your Business Product,* by Kate McGrath and Stephen Elias.
- *Nolo's Quick and Legal Guide to Trademark Registrations,* by Patti Gima and Stephen Elias.

A detailed description of Nolo resources is provided in the Introduction, Section C. (Order information is at the back of this book, or visit http://www.nolo.com.)

The World Wide Web offers convenient access to an enormous amount of trademark materials, including:

- the federal trademark statutes and regulations
- informative articles by trademark experts
- the federal trademark database (for a reasonable fee), and

- recent changes in PTO trademark examination procedures.

Here is a brief list of sites that will either have the information you are looking for or will provide you with links to other sites that do.

Nolo at http://www.nolo.com. Nolo offers self-help information about a wide variety of legal topics, including trademark law (See the Intellectual Property topic in the Legal Encyclopedia, which incidentally includes selected entries from this part of the book).

Findlaw at http://www.findlaw.com. This search engine offers an excellent collection of trademark-related materials on the Web, including trademark statutes, regulations, classification manuals and articles of general interest. Click the intellectual property link in the topics section on the Findlaw homepage and then click trademark in the subcategory section on the intellectual property page.

Marksonline at http://www.marksonline.com. This comprehensive trademark site provides trademark searching services, news, and links as well as domain name information. It's easy to navigate, contains lots of practical information for trademark owners and includes links to state and federal trademark offices.

U.S. Patent and Trademark Office at http://www.uspto.gov. The U.S. Patent and Trademark Office is the place to go for recent policy and statutory changes and transcripts of hearings on various trademark law issues. This site also offers three useful online programs: TESS, TEAS and TARR. TESS is a searchable database of federally registered trademarks, TARR provides information on the status of pending registrations and TEAS (including PrinTEAS and eTEAS) is a system for electronic filing of trademark registrations.

International Trademark Association (INTA) at http://www.inta.org. This non-profit organization of attorneys and corporate professionals provides trademark services, publications and online resources.

Overview

Trademark Law

In this section we provide definitions of the words and phrases commonly used in the world of trademark law. Note that we use the word "mark" to refer broadly to trademarks, service marks, certification marks and collective marks. The term "mark" generally encompasses any means by which a service or product is identified and distinguished from competing products and services, as long as the mark's purpose is to promote the underlying product or service in the market-place. We also use "mark" to refer to trade dress to the extent it is serving the function of a trademark or service mark.

abandonment of mark

An owner's exclusive right to use a trademark or service mark can be lost if the mark is considered to be abandoned. Abandonment commonly occurs when the mark is no longer used in commerce and there is sufficient evidence that the owner intends to discontinue use of the mark.

Under the Lanham Act, a mark registered with the U.S. Patent and Trademark Office is presumed abandoned if it is not used for a continuous period of three years or more. This means that the mark's owner cannot prevent someone else from using the mark unless the owner can convince a court that the mark really wasn't abandoned, despite the lack of use. Acceptable reasons for non-use of a mark are:

- temporary financial difficulty
- bankruptcy proceedings, or
- the need for a product revision.

A company can also prove that a mark is not abandoned by furnishing documents that indicate the company intended to resume use or by the continued existence of customer goodwill. For example, the owners of the *Rambler* trademark (for cars) were able to demonstrate that there were many *Rambler* autos (and related supplies) bearing the mark still in use, signs featuring the trademark were still posted and many consumers still wanted *Rambler* products as evidenced by *Rambler* fan clubs. (*American Motors Corp. v. Action Age, Inc.*178 U.S.P.Q. 377 (TTAB 1973).)

The typical abandonment scenario occurs during registration when an applicant is denied registration because the PTO examiner has found a similar mark. The applicant knows that the similar mark has not been used for many years. It is up to the applicant to demonstrate to the PTO that the other mark has been abandoned because of nonuse. If the applicant can prove abandonment and the owner of the allegedly abandoned mark cannot prove intent to resume, the mark will be considered abandoned and unprotectible. Proving abandonment is often difficult and expensive. It is also affected by a procedure known as Section 8 affidavit, a document that must be filed by the owner in order to demonstrate continued use. The abandonment presumption is located in the definitions section of the Lanham Act. (15 United States Code, Section 1127.) Abandonment of a trademark is different than abandonment of a trademark application. In the latter case, the owner of a mark simply fails to proceed with a trademark application.

Related terms: continuous use of mark; licensing of marks; loss of mark.

Acceptable Description of Goods and Services Manual

When filing an application for federal trademark registration or deciding whether one mark infringes another, it is useful to classify the mark in question according to the kinds of goods or services it is used with. There are 42 classes of goods and services (36 for goods, six for services) that are used by the PTO for this purpose. Because of the limited number of classes, it is often difficult to tell which class a particular good or service fits within. To help this process along, the International Trademark Association has published the Acceptable Description of Goods and Services Manual, an alphabetical listing of hundreds of discrete goods and services with appropriate descriptions and suggested classification numbers. The Manual is available on the PTO's website at http://www.uspto.gov.

affidavit of use

See Sections 8 and 15 Declaration.

Allegation of Use for Intent-to-Use Application, with Declaration

When a trademark application is filed on an intent-to-use basis, the actual registration won't occur until you file a document with the PTO informing it that the mark is now in actual use, and pay an additional fee. The form to use for this purpose is called Allegation of Use for Intent-to-Use Application. The Allegation of Use form may be filed at any time prior to the date the PTO authorizes the publication of the proposed mark, and any time after the PTO issues a Notice of Allowance. It may not be filed between those two dates.

The Allegation of Use form is a combination of two previous forms—the Amendment to Allege Use form, which was used if the mark was placed in actual use before the PTO authorized publication of the mark in the Official Gazette, and the Statement of Use which was used if the mark was placed into actual use after a Notice of Allowance issued.

Amendment to Allege Use

See Allegation of Use for Intent-to-Use Application, with Declaration.

Anticybersquatting Consumer Protection Act

The Anticybersquatting Consumer Protection Act (ACPA) was enacted in order to protect businesses against the increasingly common practice of cybersquatting (15 United States Code, Section 1125(d).) A cybersquatter registers a well-known trademark as a domain name, hoping to later profit by reselling the domain name back to the trademark owner. This new law authorizes a trademark owner to sue an alleged cybersquatter in federal court and obtain a court order transferring the domain name back to the mark's owner. In some cases, the cybersquatter must pay money damages. In order to stop a cybersquatter, the mark's true owner must prove all of the following:

- the domain name registrant had a bad-faith intent to profit from the mark
- the mark was distinctive at the time the domain name was first registered
- the domain name is identical or confusingly similar to the mark, and
- the mark qualifies for protection under federal trademark laws—that is, the mark is distinctive and its owner was the first to use the mark in commerce.

If the person or company who registered the domain name had reasonable grounds to believe that the use of the domain name was fair and lawful, they would avoid a court decision that they acted in bad faith. In other words, if the accused cybersquatter can show a judge that he had reason to register the domain name other than to sell it back to the trademark owner for a profit, then a court will probably allow him to keep the domain name because the name was not acquired in bad faith.

Related terms: cybersquatting; domain names; Internet, effect on trademark law.

anti-dilution statutes

See dilution of mark.

Definitions

Definitions

arbitrary mark

Sometimes a word or phrase used as a mark appears to be arbitrary (random) in the context of its use. Arbitrary marks are generally considered to be memorable because of their very arbitrariness. For example, Penguin (books), Arrow (shirts) and Beefeater (gin) are arbitrary terms in relation to the products they advertise, and therefore stand out because they are original and surprising. These qualities entitle them to the highest degree of trademark protection available.

Related terms: distinctive mark.

assignment of mark

An assignment is a transfer of ownership rights and good will associated with the mark. Assignments are most common when a company is sold. An assignment may also occur as part of a bankruptcy or may be used as a security interest when a business seeks to obtain a loan.

Once the assignment is made, the business buying the trademark rights (the "assignee") becomes the owner, and the seller (the "assignor") has no further ownership interest. On some occasions, an assignment may be transferred back to the original owner if certain conditions are met. The Lanham Act requires the assignment of a mark to be in writing. Assignments should be recorded with the U.S. Patent and Trademark Office, and the new owners can obtain new certificates of registration in their names.

Related terms: certificate of registration; Lanham Act; ownership of mark in the U.S.

attorney fees in trademark infringement actions

The Lanham Act authorizes a court to award attorney fees only in cases of "exceptional" infringement. To qualify as such a case, the defendant must have acted willfully, intentionally or maliciously. This means there must be facts showing that the infringer was fully aware of the infringement and simply hoped to get away with it.

Attorney fees may also be awarded if infringement occurred as a result of a breach of contract or license that itself provides for attorney fees. In these cases, there is no need to show ill will, intent or malice.

Related terms: infringement action; innocent infringer; Lanham Act.

average, reasonably prudent, consumer

In deciding trademark conflicts, courts often try to imagine whether an average, reasonably prudent, consumer would likely be confused by the two marks. This viewpoint is particularly helpful in deciding:

- if an infringed mark is distinctive enough to warrant protection by the court, and
- whether the infringing mark would be likely to mislead or confuse the public.

If a court determines that a hypothetical consumer would be likely to remember the infringed mark because of its distinctiveness and also would be confused by the use of the infringing mark, then infringement may be found.

In a trademark infringement action where consumer confusion is alleged, the parties typically conduct consumer polls to discover the actual views of the "average consumer," and introduce the results of such polls in support of their case.

Related terms: confusion of consumers.

Bureau of Customs

Under the U.S. Customs Act, a trademark owner whose mark is on the Principal Register may record the mark with the U.S. Customs Service. (19 Code of Federal Regulation Part 133, Subparts (A) and (B).) This authorizes customs inspectors to seize any products bearing infringing marks and to contact the mark's owner. If the infringing importer agrees to remove the offending mark, or the mark's owner waives the right to object, the goods will be released. Otherwise, they will be destroyed. As a practical matter, most customs enforcement occurs at the behest of trademark owners who conduct their own investigations and tip off the Bureau of Customs to the arrival of infringing goods.

Related terms: Principal Register; protection of marks under Lanham Act.

cancellation of registration

See opposing and cancelling a trademark registration.

certificate of registration

A certificate of registration is proof that a mark has been registered with the U.S. Patent and Trademark Office (PTO) on the Principal Register of trademarks and service marks. The certificate reproduces the mark and sets out the date of the mark's first use in commerce. In addition, the certificate lists:

- the type of product or service on which the mark is used
- the number and date of registration
- the term of registration
- the date on which the application for registration was received at the PTO, and

- any conditions and limitations that the PTO has imposed on the registration, such as restricting use to a certain marketing area to avoid conflict with another registered mark.

The certificate of registration substantially simplifies the task of obtaining relief from a court if it is necessary to file a trademark infringement lawsuit. Besides proving registration, the certificate will be accepted by a court as proof that the registration is valid and that the registrant owns the mark. The exclusive right to use the mark in commerce on the product or service is also specified in the certificate.

Related terms: ownership of mark in the U.S.; presumption of ownership; protection of marks under Lanham Act.

certification mark

The Lanham Act authorizes organizations (such as educational or marketing groups) to "certify" various characteristics or qualities of products and services manufactured or provided by others. Among the characteristics that this type of mark may cover are regional origin, method of manufacture, product quality and service accuracy. Examples of certification marks are "ASE certified mechanics," "Good Housekeeping Seal of Approval," "Roquefort" (a region in France), "Stilton" cheese (a product from the Stilton locale in England), and "Harris Tweeds" (a special weave from a specific area in Scotland).

EXAMPLE: The Utah Teachers Federation (UTF) endorses the brands of educational computer software it finds especially helpful to students. The educational software producers submit their educational programs to the UTF for analysis and possible endorsement. All programs the UTF endorses carry the legend "Approved by the Utah Teachers Federation," which is a certification mark.

Certification marks must be retained by the persons or groups originating them. Assigning or licensing a certification mark to others destroys any meaning the mark may have had, and constitutes an abandonment of the mark. Certification marks may be registered in the U.S. under the Lanham Act in the same manner as other marks.

Related terms: geographic terms as marks; protection of marks under Lanham Act; trademark, defined.

classes of goods and services

See International Schedule of Classes of Goods and Services.

coined terms

Coined terms are invented words or phrases with no other meaning than to specifically act as a mark to identify a product or service in the marketplace. Coined terms generally are considered strong or distinctive marks, which means the courts will tend to be willing to protect them against unauthorized use. The easiest way to assure protection for a mark is to make up, or "coin," a new word.

A coined term may consist of any combination of letters and/or numerals that are not already in use to identify or distinguish another product or service. Thus, "4711 water" is a coined phrase used as the trademark for a particular brand of cologne. Other common examples of coined terms are Sybex (publisher of computer books), "Kodak" (cameras), "Tylenol" (analgesic), "Maalox" (anti-acid medicine) and "Unix" (computer operating system).

Related terms: distinctive mark; strong mark.

collective mark

A collective mark is a symbol, label, word, phrase or other mark used by members of a group or organization to identify goods members produce or services they render. A common use of collective marks is to show membership in a union, association or other organization. Collective marks are entitled to registration and the same federal protection as other types of marks.

A collective mark differs from a trademark or a service mark in that use of the collective mark is restricted to members of the group. The mark's primary function is to inform the public that specific goods or services come from members of a group, thus distinguishing them from products or services of nonmembers. However, the organization itself, as opposed to its members, cannot use the collective mark on any goods it produces. If the organization itself wants to identify its product, it must use its own trademark or service mark.

EXAMPLE: The letters "ILGWU" on a shirt is a collective mark identifying the shirt as a product of members of the International Ladies Garment Workers

Union and distinguishes it from shirts from those made by nonunion shops. If the ILGWU actually started marketing its own products, however, it could not use the ILGWU collective mark to identify them.

Related terms: protection of marks under Lanham Act.

color used as mark

In 1985, a federal appeals court ruled that a single color—pink—could function as a trademark for fiberglass products. (*In re Owens-Corning Fiberglass Corp.* 774 F.2d 1116 (Fed. Cir. 1985).) This does not preclude every business from using pink, only other makers of fiberglass and related products. In 1995, the U.S. Supreme Court ruled that a single color—green—could function as a trademark for ironing pads. (*Qualitex Company v. Jacobson Prods. Co.*, 514 U.S. 159 (1995).) The Supreme Court held that a single color is registrable if:

- over time, consumers have come to view the color as an identification or the source of the product (rather than the product itself), and
- the color has no function.

EXAMPLE: In the *Qualitex* case, the product in question was a green-gold pad designed for dry cleaning presses. The green-gold color was not associated with dry cleaning pads as such, had no functional purpose, and operated only to identify the pads as originating with Qualitex. Once these facts were established, the court saw no reason why the color couldn't qualify as a trademark as long as it could be shown that consumers relied on the color to identify the source of the pads.

If, on the other hand, a color has a function—for instance, the color blue used to signify a nitrogen content or the color yellow used to signify a type of drug that is always yellow regardless of the manufacturer—it won't qualify as a trademark.

Related terms: color as an element; distinctive mark; trade dress; trademark, defined.

color as an element of a mark

Treating a particular color as a mark in its own right should be distinguished from the thousands of examples where color appears in combination with a graphic design or words to create a distinctive mark. For instance, IBM is often referred to as "big blue" because of the blue color of its famous IBM logo. And McDonald's golden arch is well known not only because of its archness but also because of its color. The red tag associated with Levi's blue jeans is still another example. If registering a mark in which color is claimed as a component, the applicant must submit a written description of the color and indicate where in the mark the color appears.

Related terms: color used as mark.

commerce that Congress may regulate

To qualify for registration and/or protection of a trademark under the Lanham Act, a mark must have first been used "in commerce that Congress may regulate." The Lanham Act defines commerce as business or trade that the federal government, through the U.S. Congress, is authorized by the U.S. Constitution to control. Technically, this means that to qualify for protection under the Lanham Act, a business must do at least one of the following:

- ship a product across state lines, as do most manufacturers, wholesalers and mail order businesses
- ship a product between a state and a territory or a territory and another territory (for instance, between New York and Puerto Rico or between Puerto Rico and the Virgin Islands)
- ship a product between a state or territory and another country (for instance, between California and Hong Kong or between Puerto Rico and Cuba)
- advertise its business outside of its home state
- conduct a service business across state lines, as do most trucking operations and many 900 numbers
- conduct a service business in more than one state (Taco Bell, Chevron, Hilton Hotels) or across international or territorial borders, or
- operate a business that caters to domestic or international travellers, such as a hotel, restaurant, tour guide service or ski resort.

EXAMPLE: Geraldine Smith starts a small business in Vermont that brews a honey wine called "Wine of Geraldyne." She will not be able to register this trademark with the U.S. Patent and Trademark Office unless the mark appears on the product itself and the product crosses state, territorial or international lines in an actual business transaction. Geraldine cannot, however, just send a bottle to Aunt Dinah in South Carolina for the purpose of satisfying the "commerce" requirement. The commerce must be genuine.

The reason for the "commerce" requirement is that Congress only has power under the commerce clause of the Constitution to regulate U.S. businesses to the extent they engage in interstate, interterritorial or international activity. Thus, the Lanham Act (the statute governing trademark registration) can only affect marks

Definitions

in commerce as defined here. Because Congress has no power under the commerce clause to affect marks used in only one state, the regulation of such marks is up to the individual states.

As a general rule, the PTO doesn't question a registration applicant's assertion that a mark is being used in "commerce," which means the issue of commerce will arise only if the validity of the registration is called into question in an opposition or cancellation proceeding or in an infringement lawsuit. Also, as more businesses do commerce on the Internet, which by definition crosses state, territorial and international boundaries, commerce will become even less of an issue in the future than it is now.

Related terms: Lanham Act; state trademark laws; use of mark.

commercial name

See trade name.

Commissioner for Trademarks

The Commissioner for Trademarks is the title of the person who manages the trademark division of the U.S. Patent and Trademark Office. The previous title for this position was the Assistant Commissioner for Trademarks.

Related terms: Director of the U.S. Patent and Trademark Office; U.S. Patent and Trademark Office.

Community Trademark

Effective April 1, 1996, the European Union started accepting applications for a community trademark that would be good in 15 EU countries. To qualify for registration, the proposed mark must be acceptable in all 15 countries. Applications are to be submitted to the Office for Harmonization of the Internal Market in Alicante, Spain. For more information on the Community Trademark, visit the website at http://oami.eu.int.

competing and non-competing products

When the sale of one product might preclude the sale of another product, the products are said to be competing. For instance, if one company sells a car, it obviously competes with another company's ability to sell a similar car, but it may also compete with the sales of pickup trucks or motorcycles.

Products are non-competing when consumers could reasonably purchase both items—that is, the purchase of one is not at the expense of the other. For example, perfume does not compete with long haul trailer trucks.

If the marks used on two competing products or services are similar enough to potentially confuse consumers, the owner of the mark found to be infringed upon may sometimes be awarded money damages measured by the amount of profits the other mark's owner earned as a result of the infringement (called defendant's profits). The owner may also be entitled to prevent future infringing use of the mark by the infringing party.

When goods are found to be not competing but are related enough to warrant a finding of potential consumer confusion (for example, they are distributed in the same channels to the same consumer base), the mark's owner can collect any actual damages, and also prevent the other party from using the mark in the future. However, defendant's profits are generally not awarded in this situation because the infringer by definition did not earn its profits at the expense of the mark's owner.

Related terms: infringement action; related products and services.

composite mark

Marks that consist of several words are called composite or hybrid marks. The strength of a composite mark depends on the effect of the whole mark, not just its individual terms. That is, every term in the mark may be ordinary, and yet the whole may be distinctive. For example, the slogan "Don't Leave Home Without It" is a composite mark owned by American Express. Each term is ordinary, but the whole creates a distinctive and therefore protectible mark. No other financial or travel business can use this phrase, although all of the individual terms are available for use without restriction.

When registering a composite mark with the U.S. Patent and Trademark Office, the applicant is usually required to disclaim ownership of the unregistrable parts in order to register the mark as a whole. This may mean that each individual term in the mark is disclaimed, even while ownership in the entire mark is asserted.

Definitions

Related terms: disclaimer of unregistrable material.

concurrent registration

In some circumstances, two or more owners of identical or similar marks may be allowed to register their marks with the U.S. Patent and Trademark Office (PTO). This can happen if:

- both marks were in use in commerce before either owner applied for registration, and
- the likelihood of consumer confusion is slight, either because the products or services to which the marks will be connected are not closely related or because they will be distributed in entirely different markets.

When allowing concurrent registrations, the PTO may specify marketing and use limitations on each of the marks to preclude consumer confusion. For example, the PTO may restrict the use of one mark to ten western states and allow the use of the other mark in the rest of the states. Or the use of the respective marks may be restricted to their original products or services.

Related terms: competing and non-competing products; interference; related products and services.

confusion of customers

In order to stop trademark infringement, the senior user—the first business to adopt and use a particular mark in connection with its goods or services—must prove likelihood of confusion. When determining likelihood of confusion, courts use several factors derived from a 1961 Supreme Court case. (*Polaroid Corp. v. Polarad Elecs. Corp.* 287 F.2d 492 (2d Cir. 1961).) These factors, sometimes known as the "Polaroid factors," may vary slightly as federal courts apply them throughout the country. The factors are intended as a guide, and not all factors may be particularly helpful in any given case.

- **strength of the senior user's mark**—the stronger or more distinctive the senior user's mark, the more likely the confusion
- **similarity of the marks**—the more similarity between the two marks, the more likely the confusion
- **similarity of the products or services**—the more that the senior and junior user's goods or services are related, the more likely the confusion
- **likelihood that the senior user will bridge the gap**—if it is probable that the senior user will expand into the junior user's product area, the more likely there will be confusion
- **the junior user's intent in adopting the mark**—if the junior user adopted the mark in bad faith, confusion is more likely

- **evidence of actual confusion**—proof of consumer confusion is not required but it is powerful evidence
- **sophistication of the buyers**—the less sophisticated the purchaser, the more likely the confusion, and
- **quality of the junior user's products or services**—in some cases, the lesser the quality of the junior users goods, the more harm is likely from consumer confusion.

constructive notice of mark under Lanham Act

When a mark is placed on the federal Principal Register, the law assumes that all other mark users anywhere in the U.S. will know that someone else owns that registered mark. This means that even if a second user has no actual knowledge of the registered mark, such knowledge will be implied because the Principal Register is a public record, available for inspection.

This constructive (assumed) notice precludes anyone else's legal use of the mark anywhere in the U.S., unless such use began before the registration. Assuming the mark's owner affixed proper notice of registration to the mark (usually an "R" in a circle—®), the constructive notice also means the trademark owner qualifies to recover large (treble) damages and perhaps attorney fees.

The courts will generally refuse to find infringement if the marks in question are used in geographically separate markets. However, if the owner of a registered mark later chooses to expand into a market in which the infringing mark is being used, the infringer will have to give up the mark, unless its use predated the registration. As a result, it is always wise to do a trademark search before selecting a new mark to make sure the mark is available.

EXAMPLE 1: A California comedy group puts together a satirical revue about lawyers called Lawbotics and performs it in a number of Western states. The California group successfully registers "Lawbotics" as a service mark under the Lanham Act. Anti-lawyer jokes are popular everywhere, and a group of Vermont comedians, never having heard of the California revue, uses the same name for its act and starts packing them in along the Eastern seaboard. Because the California show was registered under the Lanham Act before the Vermont group used the mark, the Vermonters have infringed the California group's service mark. Also, because registration provides "constructive notice" of prior ownership, the Vermont group will be considered a deliberate infringer if the matter gets to court, even if it was unaware of the prior use. However, the matter will probably only get to court if the California Lawbotics act gets bookings anywhere near the Eastern seaboard.

Definitions

EXAMPLE 2: Assume the same facts, but this time the Vermont Lawbotics group produces a CD-ROM that is nationally distributed. The California group could move against the infringement. California Lawbotics would be entitled to collect damages for willful infringement because the mark on the CD-ROM would now be in use in California, creating a high likelihood of consumer confusion.

Related terms: geographically separate market; infringement action; Principal Register.

continuous use of mark

A mark that is continuously used for five years after placement on the federal Principal Register may qualify as "incontestable." That means that the mark may no longer be challenged by another user on the ground that it is too weak (ordinary) to warrant legal protection. Any showing of a substantial interruption in the use of the mark during the five-year period may, however, prevent the mark from becoming incontestable.

Related terms: duration of federal trademark registration; incontestability status.

contributory infringer

Like a criminal accomplice, a contributory infringer is a party who furthers or encourages the infringing activity of another. For example, a store that sells records carrying an infringing mark is considered a contributory infringer, as is the wholesale distributor of the records and any other person or business whose actions contribute to the infringement.

Contributory infringers are not liable for damages or defendant's profits as long as they were innocent (they didn't know about the infringement), but they may be enjoined (barred) from any further contributory activity. Thus, the record store owner might have to stop selling the infringing records unless the offending mark were removed. But if a contributory infringer knows of the infringement, he or she can be held liable on the same basis and in the same amount as the principal infringer.

Related terms: infringement action; innocent infringer; publishers of advertising matter.

counterfeit

Counterfeiting is the act of making or selling lookalike goods or services bearing fake trademarks, for example, a business deliberately duplicates the *Adidas* trademark on shoes. Likelihood of confusion is self-evident in counterfeiting because the counterfeiter's primary purpose is to confuse or dupe consumers. Even when a buyer knows that the product is a fake, the business is still liable for counterfeiting because the product can still be used to deceive others.

Counterfeiting is not limited to consumer products such as watches and handbags. A website that copied the Playboy Bunny logo for adult sex subscription services was assessed $10,000 for trademark counterfeiting. (*Playboy Enterprises Inc. v. Universal Tel-A-Talk Inc.*, 1999 U.S. Dist LEXIS 6124 (E.D. Pa. 1999).)

The remedies for trademark counterfeiting under the Lanham Act are much harsher than for traditional trademark infringement and only apply if the counterfeiter duplicated the trademark on the goods or services for which the trademark was federally registered. For example, it is not counterfeiting to put the *Gucci* mark on automobile seat covers as these are not goods for which Gucci has a registered trademark.

An offer to sell counterfeit products can also trigger liability as a counterfeiter. For example, an individual offered to sell counterfeit jeans and provided a sample to an undercover police officer. Proof of actual production or sale of the jeans was not necessary to prove counterfeiting.

Related terms: confusion of consumers; related products and services; same or similar mark.

Customs, Bureau of

See Bureau of Customs.

cyber-squatting

The practice that's come to be known as cybersquatting originated at a time when most businesses were not savvy about the commercial opportunities on the World Wide Web. Some entrepreneurial souls registered the names of well-known companies as domain names with the intent of selling the names back to the companies when they finally realized the economic potential of the Internet. Panasonic, Fry's Electronics, Hertz and Avon were among the early victims of cybersquatters. Opportunities for cybersquatters are rapidly diminishing, because businesses now know the importance of registering domain names and because there are two legal mechanisms of wresting the name from the cybersquatter.

A victim of cybersquatting in the U.S. can now sue under the provisions of the Anticybersquatting Consumer Protection Act (ACPA) or can fight the cybersquatter using an international arbitration system created by the Internet Corporation of Assigned Names and Numbers (ICANN). The ACPA defines cybersquatting as registering, trafficking in, or using a domain name with the intent to profit in bad faith from the goodwill of a trademark belonging to someone else. The ICANN arbitration system is considered by trademark experts to be faster and less expensive than suing under the ACPA and the procedure does not require an attorney. For information on the ICANN policy, visit the organization's website at http://www.icann.org.

Related terms: Anticybersquatting Consumer Protection Act; dilution of mark; domain name; Internet, effect on trademark law.

damages in trademark infringement cases

As a general rule, when a mark's owner proves that the mark has been infringed, a court will order the infringer to compensate the owner for actual losses caused by the infringement (for instance, lost profits from lost sales or loss of good will) and also order that the infringement cease.

If the infringed mark was federally registered and the owner provided proper notice of registration when using the mark (that is, "®" or "Reg. U.S. Pat. Off."), a court is also authorized under the Lanham Act to award the owner:

- treble damages—that is, up to three times the actual money damages suffered as a result of the infringement (37 United States Code, Section 1117)
- defendant's profits—the profits made by the defendant from the infringing activity (usually only awarded if infringement was deliberate on products or services that compete in the marketplace), and
- attorney fees, in clear-cut cases of deliberate infringement.

The court may not, however, award the owner of the infringed mark defendant's profits and money damages on the same lost sales.

Related terms: deliberate infringer; federal trademark registration; infringement action; trademark, defined.

deceptive terms as marks

Any mark that is deceptive, misleading or just plain false is not entitled to protection under the Lanham Act or under most state law trademark protection statutes. For example, a trademark that suggests chocolate in a product that contains no chocolate is deceptive and so not protectible as a valid mark. Like-wise, any mark that uses the word "champagne" would be considered deceptive unless the product originated in the Champagne region of France. For this reason, domestic "champagnes" are usually referred to as "sparkling wines."

Related terms: geographic terms as marks; prohibited and reserved marks under Lanham Act.

defendant's profits

Profits earned by a defendant as a result of infringing a mark may be awarded to the owner of a mark federally registered under the Lanham Act if:

- the owner placed proper notice of registration next to the mark (that is, "®" or "Reg. U.S. Pat. Off.")
- the infringement was deliberate rather than innocent, and
- the underlying goods or services competed with each other in the market-place.

Awarding defendant's profits to the injured party prevents an infringer from realizing any gain from infringement.

To recover defendant's profits, the owner only needs to prove the amount the defendant earned from the sales of the goods or services. Then, the defendant is given the opportunity to establish his or her costs (for instance, cost of production, sales attributable to other factors, and so on) and deduct them from the gross sales amount to arrive at the amount of profits.

Related terms: competing and non-competing products; damages in trademark infringement cases; related products and services.

deliberate infringer (or willful infringer)

Anyone who uses a mark with actual or constructive notice that the mark is owned by someone else is called a deliberate infringer. Deliberate infringers are generally liable for the harm their infringement causes to the mark's rightful owner, as well as for profits that they made from their infringing activity. In addition, deliberate infringers may be liable for treble (triple) damages if the infringement was flagrantly willful.

As a general rule, an infringement will be deemed deliberate if it begins after the mark in question has been federally registered, because the infringer is deemed to have notice of the existing mark.

Related terms: constructive notice of mark under Lanham Act; contributory infringer; innocent infringer.

descriptive mark

A descriptive mark is one that describes the type or characteristics of the product or service to which it's attached. Examples are: "Beer Nuts," "Chap Stick," "FashionKnit," "Bufferin," "Tender Vittles" and "Rich 'n Chips." In each of these examples, the names focus more on describing some aspect of the product than on distinguishing it from others in the public's mind.

Descriptive marks are considered ordinary and therefore weak. Weak marks do not merit much judicial protection because a mark that describes the characteristics of a product or service does not effectively distinguish it from similar products or services offered by others. Protecting descriptive marks does not fulfill the primary purpose of the trademark laws, which is to protect marks that operate as indicators of origin. Also, the law doesn't want to grant a trademark owner the exclusive use of words and phrases that are in common use as descriptive adjectives, because that would limit others' legitimate need to use such a word in their advertising and which do not have secondary meaning do not. A descriptive mark will only be protected under trademark law if it achieves secondary meaning—that is, it becomes distinctive because consumers associate the mark with specific goods or services.

Marks that are judged to be descriptive and which do not have secondary meaning do not qualify for placement on the Principal Register under the Lanham Act. Instead, they are placed on a list called the Supplemental Register, which offers much less protection than the Principal Register. After a descriptive mark has been in continuous use for five years, however, it can be moved to the Principal Register under the theory that it has developed secondary meaning: it has become a well known identifier of a product or service through public exposure. At that point, a descriptive mark does act to distinguish certain products or services from others.

If a descriptive mark is mistakenly placed on the Principal Register by the U.S. Patent and Trademark Office, another party may challenge the mark's validity up until the time the mark becomes incontestable (five years on the Principal Register). Once incontestability occurs, the mark is immune from a challenge on the ground that it is descriptive.

Related terms: incontestability status; secondary meaning; Supplemental Register.

dilution of mark

Dilution means the lessening of the capacity of a famous mark to identify and distinguish goods or services, regardless of the presence or absence of:

- competition between the owner of the famous mark and other parties, or
- likelihood of confusion, mistake, or deception (15 United States Code, Section 1527).

Dilution is therefore different than trademark infringement because trademark infringement always involves a probability of customer confusion whereas dilution can occur even if customers wouldn't be misled. For example, if Fred starts selling a line of sex aids named "Microsoft," no consumer is likely to associate Fred's products with the original Microsoft. However, because Microsoft has become such a strong and famous mark, the use of the word on sex aids would definitely trivialize the original Microsoft mark (dilute its strength by tarnishing its reputation for quality or blurring its distinctiveness).

Until 1996 there was no federal law against trademark dilution. And only about half the states provided some recourse—usually an injunction against further use of the mark. In January 1996, however, the Federal Trademark Dilution Act of 1995 was signed into law (15 United States Code §1125(c); see statutes at the end of this part). As with the state statutes, this new federal law applies only to famous marks, and provides primarily for injunctive relief (a court order requiring the infringing party to stop using the mark). However, if the famous mark's owner can prove the infringer "willfully intended to trade on the owner's reputation or to cause dilution of the famous mark," the court has discretion to award the owner attorney's fees and defendant's profits as well as actual damages.

While it is still possible to sue for dilution under a state statute, most actions to stop dilution are now brought under the new federal law. One exception to this is when use of the famous mark also tarnishes its reputation. For example, in the Microsoft sex aid example, the association of "Microsoft" with sex aids may fairly be said to detract from the dignity of the Microsoft mark (there is little room for humor in the commercial world). Under state statutes, an action may be brought for tarnishment as well as dilution, whereas the federal act does not speak to tarnishment at all, although many observers believe that the courts will interpret the statute to include it as a basis for relief.

Related terms: famous marks.

Director of the U.S. Patent and Trademark Office

This is the title of the person who runs the U.S. Patent and Trademark Office, a branch of the U.S. Department of Commerce. The full title is actually: Undersecretary of Commerce for Intellectual Property and Director of the U.S. Patent and Trademark Office. Prior to 2000 the title for this position was the Commissioner of Patents and Trademarks.

Related terms: Commissioner for Trademarks; U.S. Patent and Trademark Office.

disclaimer of unregistrable material

Often a trademark will consist of a distinctive word (for instance "Nolo") in combination with one more unprotectible terms (such as the ".com" in Nolo.com). Or the entire mark may consist of unprotectible terms that taken together are distinctive because of how the terms are combined.

When owners of these types of marks seek to register them with the PTO, the PTO will normally require the applicants to "disclaim" (agree to give up any claim to) ownership of the unprotectible terms, even though the mark itself would be registered. Thus, Nolo had to disclaim ".com" and the owner of "Snappy Salsa" probably would have to disclaim Salsa. These disclaimers make it clear that other businesses are free to use the disclaimed terms, as long as they don't use them in a way that would conflict with the distinctive aspects of the registered mark.

Related terms: composite mark; geographic terms as marks; protection of marks under Lanham Act.

disparaging mark

See prohibited and reserved marks under Lanham Act.

distinctive mark

A mark that is unusual in the context of its use—and therefore memorable—is considered distinctive. Some marks are created to be distinctive and typically consist of terms that are arbitrary (Target Stores), fanciful (Midas Muffler), suggestive (Jaguar cars) or coined (Reebok shoes). In addition, mundane or common marks—typically peoples' names, geographic designators and descriptive terms—can become distinctive if they become well known over time (such as Microsoft Windows).

Distinctive marks excel in distinguishing their products or services from competing ones, which qualifies them for maximum judicial protection under state and federal laws. Because of this protection, distinctive marks are considered to be legally stronger than are marks considered common or ordinary, because they describe the product's qualities (descriptive marks), use the owner's name or are in wide-spread use for the particular product or service (in common use).

For example, any mark using the term "Kodak" would be considered infringing, since "Kodak" is a very strong mark, and has no meaning other than as a mark. On the other hand, a mark with a common term like "data" will probably not infringe on another use of "data," since that word is already in wide use among large numbers of high-tech businesses.

A mark must be distinctive to qualify for placement on the Principal Register under the Lanham Act. A descriptive mark will only be protected under trademark law if it achieves secondary meaning—that is, it becomes distinctive because consumers associate the mark with specific goods or services.

Related terms: arbitrary mark; coined terms; descriptive mark; dilution of mark; generic mark; Principal Register; secondary meaning; strong mark; suggestive mark.

domain names

How do customers find businesses on the World Wide Web part of the Internet? Every business on the Web has what's called a domain name. The domain name is a unique "address" that computers understand, and so if you enter a particular

Examples of Distinctive Marks

Below is a chart showing examples of the different categories of distinctive trademarks. Look at it carefully to see if these distinctions make sense to you.

Suggestive	Fanciful/Arbitrary	Coined
Verbatim computer discs	Jellibeans skating rink	Barbasol shaving lotion
Suave shampoo	Penguin books	Curel hand lotion
Accuride tires	Ajax cleanser	Reebok shoes
Glacier ice	Domino sugar	Exxon oil
Greyhound bus	Apple computers	Nyquil cold medicine
Coppertone tanning lotion	Nova TV series	Amtrak trains
Roach Motel insect trap	Banana Republic clothes	Kodak film
Wearever cookware	Beefeater gin	Blistex lip balm
Maternally Yours clothes	Arrow shirts	Maalox antacid
Esprit clothes	Hang Ten clothes	Tylenol pain reliever
Q-tips	Hard Rock Cafe	Actifed antihistamine
7-Eleven stores	Camel cigarettes	
Liquid Paper	Ivory soap	
Chicken of the Sea tuna	Double Rainbow Ice Cream	
Wrangler jeans	The Icing apparel	
L.A. Gear shoes	Tea Rose flour	
Cachet clothes	Guess? jeans	
Brim Coffee		

Reprinted with permission from *Trademark: How to Name Your Business and Product*, by Kate McGrath and Stephen Elias (Nolo).

Definitions

domain name in a Web browser, the computer will know what to do: it links your computer with the website (business location) connected with the domain name you entered.

Most World Wide Web business addresses consist of two main sections. Consider this Web address: http://www.nolo.com. The first section (http://www) tells the computer that it is looking for a site on the World Wide Web. You will find this section in virtually every Web address. The second section (nolo.com) is the domain name. The domain name itself consists of two parts. The ".com" portion is termed a top level domain name (TLD) while the "nolo" section is termed a second level domain name (SLD).

The reason the .com part is called a top-level domain is that the World Wide Web has been organized, for the purpose of U.S. participants, into five broad categories:

- com (for commercial groups)
- edu (for educational institutions)
- gov (for governmental institutions)
- org (for non-profit organizations), and
- net (for interactive discussion groups).

The reason the Nolo part is called a second-level domain is that the name denotes one of the approximately 2 million unique identifiers that is part of the .com top-level domain. The fact that all businesses in the U.S. who want to do business on the Web have had to operate under one domain, the .com domain, has given rise to enormous trademark-related problems. To reduce the pressure placed on existing top level domain names, an International Ad Hoc Committee created by the Internet Society has come up with a plan to add new TLDs:

- firm (for businesses or firms)
- store (for businesses selling goods)
- arts (for entities emphasizing cultural and entertainment activities)
- info (for sites offering information services) and
- nom (for sites supported by individuals.)

Some of these new top-level domain names are expected to be available for assignment in 2001.

Because each domain name must unique—so that all the computers attached to the Internet can find it—it is impossible for two different businesses to have the same domain name. If, when Nolo applied for its Web address, another business had already grabbed Nolo as its second-level domain name, Nolo would have had to come up with something at least a little different.

The easiest way is to check if a domain name is available is at one of the dozens of online companies that have been approved to register domain names. A listing of these registrars can be accessed at either the InterNIC site (http://www.internic.net) or at the ICANN site (http://www.icann.org). ICANN is the organization that oversees the process of approving domain name registrars. Every registrar provides a searching system to determine if a domain name is available. Type in the domain name choice and the registrar will determine if it is available.

In addition to determining whether a domain name is available, it is possible to locate information about the owner of the domain name. A simple way to check ownership is to use http://www.whois.net. Type in the domain name, and the website provides the contact information supplied by the domain name registrant.

Beware that some registrants, especially those acting in bad faith, may supply false information about domain name ownership and in these cases, there's not much that can be done to track down the domain name holder. This lack of information should not stop those pursuing a cybersquatter—a speculator who is holding a domain name for ransom. There are ways to wrestle a domain name from a bad faith registrant even if the identity or location of the cybersquatter is unknown.

Keep in mind that even if a company owns a federally registered trademark, someone else may still have the right to own the domain name. For example, many different companies have federally registered the trademark *Executive* for different goods or services. All of these companies may want http://www.executive.com but the first one to purchase it—in this case, Executive Software—is the one that acquired the domain name.

When registering a domain name, a company should be sure that nobody else is using it as a trademark for similar goods and services. If another business is selling similar goods or services with a similar name, the use of the domain name can be terminated under trademark law principles.

EXAMPLE: Jim's catalog company, Ahab, has been selling ocean-themed artwork and merchandise since 1980. Jim has registered the Ahab trademark with the PTO. Bob registers the domain name ahab.com and uses it to sell artwork depicting whales. Jim can stop Bob's use of the domain name, ahab.com. If Bob were using ahab.com to sell Ahab-brand educational software, Jim could not stop Bob's use of the domain name.

Definitions

Registration of a domain name can be accomplished at any of the approved domain name registrars. A complete list is provided at both InterNIC (http://www.internic.net) or ICANN (http://www.icann.org). An applicant completes the online domain name registration form indicating basic contact information (name, telephone number and address). The fee is usually $35 per year, although some registrars offer lower rates. The whole procedure takes a matter of minutes and the domain name registrant is notified by email of the domain name ownership, which is effective immediately.

Payment of the annual fee for a domain name only grants ownership of an address on the Internet; it doesn't establish a website presence. In order to use it in conjunction with a website, a business must establish a web hosting arrangement with an ISP (Internet Service Provider), usually for a fee of approximately $20 per month. The business must also construct and upload a website and coordinate the reassignment of the domain name from the domain name registrar to the ISP. Usually an ISP will assist the company through the process. Domain name registration grants exclusive title to the domain name owner, who can stop others from using it with the following exceptions:

- **Failure to pay annual domain name fees**. Domain name ownership, unlike trademark ownership, must be renewed either every year or every two years (depending on the initial arrangement with the registrar). Failure to pay fees will result in cancellation of the domain name ownership and it may eventually be sold to another buyer.
- **The domain name registrant is a cybersquatter.** If a domain name is registered in bad faith, for example for the purpose of selling it back to a company with the same name, the domain name can be taken away under federal law or under international arbitration rules for domain name owners.
- **The domain name infringes a trademark.** If a domain name is likely to confuse consumers because it is similar to another trademark, the domain name use may be terminated. For example, if a company registered adoobie.com for the purposes of selling software, it's very likely that the Adobe company, makers of graphics software, would be able to stop the use.
- **The domain name dilutes a famous trademark.** If a domain name dilutes the power of a famous trademark, the owner of the famous mark can sue under federal laws to stop the continued use. Dilution refers to the fact that the domain name is being used for commercial

purposes and it blurs or tarnishes the reputation of a famous trademark. For example, if a company registered guccigoo.com for the purpose of selling baby diapers, the owners of the Gucci trademark could stop the use of the domain name under dilution principles.

Related terms: Anticybersquatting Consumer Protection Act; cybersquatting; dilution of mark; Internet, effect on trademark law.

duration of federal trademark registration

Once a trademark or service mark is placed on the Principal Register, the owner receives a certificate of registration good for an initial term of ten years (20 years if the registration occurred before 11/16/89).

Although the initial registration is good for a ten-year (or 20-year) period, the registration may lapse unless the registrant files a sworn statement within six years of the filing date (the "Sections 8 and 15 Affidavit") that the mark is either still in use in commerce or that the mark is not in use for legitimate reasons that do not constitute abandonment.

The original registration may be renewed indefinitely for additional ten-year periods if the owner timely files the required renewal applications (called a Section 9 Affidavit) with the U.S. Patent and Trademark Office. Failure to renew a registration does not void all rights to the mark; however, unless it is re-registered, the mark's owner will not have the benefits of federal registration, such as the presumed nationwide notice and the presumption of validity.

> **EXAMPLE:** Andramae Associates, Inc., registers a service mark for her graphics design business on May 1, 1995. The registration is good for ten years, or until May 1, 2005. To keep the registration in force, Andramae must file a Sections 8 and 15 Affidavit between November 1, 2000 (five years and six months after her registration date), and May 1, 2001 (the expiration of the six year period), and she must renew it decennially (for example, between November 1, 2005 and April 30, 2006, and again between November 1, 2015 and April 30, 2016). By continuing to renew the mark in this manner, Andramae can keep it on the Principal Register indefinitely.

Related terms: incontestability status; Sections 8 and 15 Affidavit; Supplemental Register.

e-TEAS

This program, found on the United States Patent and Trademark Office Website (http://www.uspto.gov), allows you to file a trademark application online. A companion program, PrinTEAS, also found on the same site, lets you fill in the

Definitions

application online, but you have to print it out, sign it and send it in by regular mail. Both online programs are free and come with instructions provided by the USPTO.

exclusive right to use mark

See ownership of mark in the U.S.

fair use of trademarks

As a general rule, the owner of a trademark has the exclusive right to use the trademark in a commercial context. However, under a principle known as trademark fair use, another business can use a trademark as a descriptive term. For example, the maker of an electric dishwasher may describe the *joy* of clean dishes without infringing the trademark, *Joy,* for dishwashing liquid. A company promoting toothpaste may state that it is the *choice* of *dentists* without infringing the trademark, *Dentist's Choice.* The fair use defense is set forth in the Lanham Act. (15 United States Code, Section 1115(b)(4).)

The following uses, although technically not trademark fair use, are often lumped under the same label by courts and attorneys:

- comparative advertising
- journalistic accounts of the owner of the mark or the goods or services identified by the mark, and
- parodies involving the mark.

What all of these uses have in common is that the public is not being led to believe that the non-owner is the source of the goods or services identified by the mark. In other words, fair use of a mark is possible when no customer confusion is likely to result from the use.

Related terms: free speech and trademarks.

false advertising

A business that makes misleading advertising statements about its products or another company's products can be sued in federal court under section 43(a) of the federal Lanham Act. (15 United States Code, Section 1125(a).) It is not necessary to have a federally registered trademark to make a claim under section 43(a). All that is required is that a business has made false or misleading statements as to its own product or another's, and there is actual deception or at least a tendency to deceive a substantial portion of the intended audience and the advertised goods traveled in interstate commerce. The deception must be material, that is, it is likely to influence purchasing decisions and there must be likelihood of injury to another company in terms of declining sales or loss of goodwill. In other words, if the false advertising has no impact on purchasers, goodwill or sales, then the claim will be dismissed.

For purposes of section 43(a), advertising is more than traditional print and television advertisements; it is any commercial speech intended to influence consumers and disseminated to the relevant purchasing public. "Commercial speech" refers to statements generally made for the purposes of promoting a business or trade; not editorial or informational speech protected under free speech principles. For example, it is not commercial speech to make statements about a product in a newspaper article.

Deceptive advertising is generally categorized as either statements that are simply untrue (or "false on their face") or statements that are accurate but deceptive. An example of a statement that is false on its face would be falsely claiming that a motor oil additive will increase mileage. An example of a statement that is accurate but deceptive would be that a motor oil additive protects against engine corrosion, but failing to mention that the protection is for boat engines and not automobile engines. In cases of accurate but deceptive claims, a court must examine evidence, for example to determine if a company's test results have been distorted or exaggerated.

Related terms: unfair competition; unregistered mark, protection of.

famous mark

Under federal law and most state laws, only owners of famous marks can claim dilution. Examples of famous marks include: the NBA logo of a silhouetted basketball player; *Saks Fifth Avenue* for retail stores; *Hyatt* for hotel services; and *Godzilla* for entertainment services.

Proving a mark is famous requires more evidence than commonly used to show trademark strength and distinctiveness. Courts demand proof that the mark has been heavily advertised or has had widespread acceptance within its channels of trade. Whether a mark is famous depends on several factors, including the distinctiveness of the mark; the duration and extent of use of the mark; the duration and extent of advertising and publicity of the mark; the geographical extent of the trading area in which the mark is used; the channels of trade for the goods or services with which the mark is used; the degree of recognition of the mark in both parties' trading areas and channels of trade; the nature and extent of use of the same or similar marks by third parties; and whether the senior user's mark is registered.

Related terms: dilution.

fanciful words and phrases

See distinctive mark.

Federal Trademark Dilution Act of 1995

See dilution of mark.

federal trademark registration

The U.S. Patent and Trademark Office (PTO) maintains two lists of registered trademarks and service marks:

- the Principal Register, and
- the Supplemental Register.

The Principal Register is reserved for distinctive marks and marks that have become distinctive through acquiring secondary meaning. There are many benefits to having a mark on the Principal Register rather than the Supplemental Register. Chief among these are:

- potential competitors will be assumed to know that the marks are off-limits, and
- the mark can achieve incontestability status if it remains on the Principal Register for five years.

The Supplemental Register is for marks that are not yet distinctive and do not merit the same protection as Principal Register marks. However, registration on the Supplemental Register allows placement of the trademark registration symbol (®) on the mark, which is likely to scare away most potential copiers.

Federal registration of a mark entails all of the following:

1. The mark must be used in commerce (used across state, national or territorial lines or used in a way that affects interstate, inter-territorial or international commerce).
2. A registration application, a Statement of Use or an Application Alleging Use (if an intent-to-use application was previously filed) must be filed with the PTO.
3. If the mark qualifies for the Principal Register, it will be published in the Official Gazette by the PTO.
4. If another party claims ownership of the mark in a pending application, the PTO may declare that an interference exists and schedule a hearing. Similarly, an interested party may file an opposition to the registration after publication in the Official Gazette, and the owner may have to refute or reply to the opposition.
5. If there is no interference or opposition, the PTO will issue a certificate of registration on either the Principal Register or the Supplemental Register.

Definitions

Once a mark is registered, the trademark registration symbol "(®)" or "Reg. U.S. Pat. Off." should always appear next to the mark whenever it is used. Without this designation, it may be harder to collect damages if a federal court lawsuit is occasioned by an infringement of the mark.

Applications for federal registration of trademarks and information on procedures for registration may be downloaded from the PTO website (http://www.uspto.gov) or by writing to:

Commissioner for Trademarks
U.S. Department of Commerce
Washington, DC 20231
PTO information line: 703-557-4636.

Related terms: constructive notice of mark under Lanham Act; Principal Register; protection of marks under Lanham Act; Supplemental Register; trademark search.

first to file countries

See prior registration countries.

first to register

See ownership of mark in the U.S.

first to use mark in U.S.

See ownership of mark in the U.S.

flags as marks

See prohibited and reserved marks under Lanham Act.

foreign language equivalent terms

See phonetic or foreign language equivalents for marks.

foreign nationals, registering in U.S.

A citizen, permanent resident or business of another country is entitled to federally register a mark in the U.S. if the other country affords reciprocal trademark rights to U.S. citizens, and if the mark meets U.S. requirements for registration.

Registration of a mark by a foreign national in the U.S. may be accomplished if:

- the mark has been placed in use in interstate, inter-territorial, or international commerce in the U.S.
- the mark has been registered within the last six months in another country with which the U.S. has a reciprocal treaty, or
- the mark has been the subject of an intent-to-use application filed in the U.S.

Definitions

If the basis for registration in the U.S. is a previous registration in another country, the date of filing in the other country establishes the filing date in the U.S. as well.

A foreign national who registers a mark in the U.S. but lives abroad must designate a U.S. representative to receive notices and official communications from the U.S. Patent and Trademark Office.

Related terms: Inter-American Convention for Trademark and Commercial Protection; international trademark rights; Paris Convention.

franchising, service marks

See naked license.

free speech and trademark law

Trademark law does not prohibit the use of another company's trademark for purposes of commentary or criticism. For example, the owner of a newsletter can write an article critical of Microsoft and use the Microsoft logo. Two factors may convert such commentary and criticism into a lawsuit based on trademark infringement or dilution: the newsletter is offering goods and services as part of its criticism, or the newsletter is likely to confuse readers as to whether Microsoft is a sponsor of the newsletter. In addition, if the newsletter is making false statements regarding Microsoft, this may trigger additional claims including product disparagement, false advertising and trade libel.

However, if it is clear that the use does not confuse consumers and is not being used deceptively, courts will permit use of trademarks for purposes of commentary. In one case, a disgruntled former customer of the Bally Health Club created a website featuring the company's logo over which appeared the word "sucks," and included a statement that the site was "Unauthorized." A court permitted this use because the site had distinguished itself from the legitimate Bally site by prominent use of disclaimers and the site was not offering competing goods or services. (*Bally Total Fitness Holding Corp. v. Faber*, 29 F. Supp. 2d 1161 (C.D. Cal. 1998).)

The *Bally* case triggered widespread registration of "sucks" domain names (despite the fact that the defendant had not registered ballysucks.com). Disgruntled consumers of other companies registered domain names such as nikesucks.com, toysrussucks.com, waltmartsucks.com and cadillacsucks. In some cases, companies have successfully stopped the use of these "sucks" domain names either because they were determined to be in violation of the law or because the domain name owner refused to respond to the legal action. Keep in mind when using trademarks under free speech principles: even though there is right of free speech, this doesn't prevent a trademark owner from filing lawsuit. The economics of litigation often silence company critics despite their free speech rights.

In addition to these rights, trademark law permits the use of trademarks for comparative advertising and for descriptive purposes.

Related terms: fair use.

generic mark

Words or symbols commonly used to describe an entire type of product or service rather than to distinguish one product or service from another are known as generic. Generic marks never receive protection because such terms cannot fulfill the function of a mark, which is to distinguish specific goods or services from competing ones. Therefore they belong in the public domain rather than to an exclusive owner.

> **EXAMPLE:** "Raisin bran" is a generic phrase that describes a kind of cereal; it defines the product itself rather than its source. Several different cereal manufacturers produce raisin bran, each of which is identified by its own mark—for instance, Post Raisin Bran, Kellogg's Raisin Bran, Skinner's Raisin Bran. While each of these manufacturer's marks is entitled to protection, the words "raisin bran" are not.

Some protectible marks may lose their protection by becoming generic. "Genericide" occurs when a mark is used widely and indiscriminately to refer to a type of product or service, rather than the service or product of one company. For example, "escalator" was originally a protected trademark used to designate the moving stairs manufactured by a specific company. Eventually, the word became synonymous with the very idea of moving stairs and thus lost its protection. Other examples of marks that have become generic are lite beer, softsoap and cola.

How can a company keep a mark from becoming generic? To begin, most companies need not worry about this issue, since very few products or services are successful enough to produce a generic mark. But for those that are, the Xerox campaign is instructive. The "Xerox" mark was in danger of becoming generic because it was so commonly used to describe photocopiers, the process of photocopying and the result. To counter this threatened genericide, the Xerox Corporation has spent millions of advertising dollars advising the public that Xerox is in fact a registered mark, should only be used as a proper adjective in connection with a noun (for instance, Xerox brand photocopier), and should not be used as a verb (that is, to xerox something) or as a general noun indicating

Definitions

the result of the photocopying process (a xerox). If anyone challenges the Xerox Corporation's right to the exclusive use of the word "Xerox" on the ground that it has become generic, Xerox may prevail if it can show that people understood these advertisements, and continued to consider the term "Xerox" as a brand, rather than generic, name.

Related terms: common use of mark; loss of trademark; unfair competition.

geographic terms as marks

Trademark laws will not protect a mark that uses a geographic term descriptively unless the mark as a whole has become distinctive (closely identified with the particular product in the minds of consumers) through the secondary meaning rule.

Marks that use geographic words such as "American," "Texan," "Antarctica" and "Nationwide" are generally not eligible for protection. However, "American," as in "American Airlines," "Nationwide," as in "Nationwide Move-it-yourself" and "Atlantic," as in "Atlantic Magazine" are all examples of geographic terms that have become distinctive by use over time.

A fanciful use of a geographic term, for a business not located in the named area, may be protectible if it does not cause consumers to mistakenly assume the product came from that place. For example, L.A. Gear evokes a certain style, the name is memorable and people buy the goods not caring where they actually come from. However, a geographic mark becomes deceptive—and therefore not protectible—when it falsely suggests a place of origin and the consumer purchases the item based on the apparent origin of the goods (for example, Texan picante sauce that is made in St. Louis).

Terms that are not primarily geographical in nature (do not refer to defined locations) may be used and protected as marks if they are distinctive in the context of their use or gain a secondary meaning through extended exposure in the marketplace. Examples of such words are Southern (Comfort) whisky, Metropolitan (life insurance) and Globe (realty).

Geographical terms are also acceptable in certification marks and the owners of such marks are entitled to full protection under the Lanham Act.

Related terms: disclaimer of unregistrable material; prohibited and reserved marks under Lanham Act; secondary meaning.

geographically separate market

When goods or services coming from different sources are sold geographically far enough away from each other to preclude consumers from getting confused, they are said to be in geographically separate markets. In general, using the same or similar marks in geographically separate markets does not constitute infringement.

Related terms: constructive notice of mark under Lanham Act; infringement action; ownership of mark in the U.S.

good will, sale of

See assignment of mark.

hybrid mark

See composite mark.

immoral marks

See prohibited and reserved marks under Lanham Act.

incontestability status

When a mark has been in continuous use for five years after being placed on the Principal Register, it may be classified as incontestable, or immune from legal challenge. (37 United States Code, Section 1065.) The business seeking to make its mark incontestable must show that:

- no final legal decision has issued against the mark owner's claim
- no challenge to the owner's claim is pending
- a Sections 8 and 15 Declaration describing the mark's use was filed on a timely basis, and
- the mark is not and has not become generic.

In essence, achieving "incontestability status" conclusively establishes owner-ship of the mark for the uses specified in the Sections 8 and 15 Declaration that is filed between the fifth and sixth year after the mark was placed on the Principal Register.

Whether a mark is incontestable usually arises in a lawsuit for infringement where the party being sued attempts to defend by challenging the validity of the plaintiff's mark. If the plaintiff can establish that the mark is incontestable, the mark will be presumed valid unless the defendant can establish one or more incontestability defenses. The fact that there are a number of these defenses adds up to the fact that the term "incontestable" really means "somewhat difficult to contest."

Incontestability status may be challenged on any of the following grounds:

- the registration or the incontestable right to use the mark was obtained by fraud

- the registrant has abandoned the mark
- the mark is used to misrepresent the source of its goods or services (for instance, use of the mark involves palming off)
- the infringing mark is an individual's name used in his or her own business, or is otherwise prohibited or reserved under the Lanham Act
- the infringing mark was used in commerce first—before the incontestable mark's registration
- the infringing mark was registered first, or
- the mark is being used to violate the antitrust laws of the United States.

Even though an incontestable mark can still be challenged on these grounds, it is safe from attack on the otherwise common ground that it lacks distinctiveness. Thus, when Park N Fly, Inc., sued Dollar Park and Fly, Inc., for trademark infringement, the U.S. Supreme Court ruled that because the Park N Fly mark had obtained incontestability status, Dollar Park and Fly, Inc., could not allege as a defense that its rival's mark is actually descriptive.

Related terms: federal trademark registration; infringement action; loss of mark.

infringement action

A party who claims to own a mark (the plaintiff) may file a lawsuit against another user of the same or similar mark (the defendant) to prevent further use of the mark and collect money damages for the wrongful use. An infringement action may be brought in state court or in federal court, if the mark in question is protected under the Lanham Act, which applies to both registered and unregistered marks that are used in commerce that Congress may regulate.

The success of an infringement action normally turns on whether the defendant's use causes a likelihood of confusion and so weakens the value of the plaintiff's mark. A mark need not be identical to one already in use to infringe upon the owner's rights. If the proposed mark is similar enough to the earlier mark to risk confusing the average consumer, its use may constitute infringement if the services or goods on which the two marks are used are related to each other—that is, they share the same market.

The extent of damages awarded in an infringement action will usually depend on whether the infringement was willful and on the actual amount of harm that the plaintiff can prove.

Related terms: confusion of consumers; constructive notice of mark under Lanham Act; incontestability status; injunctions against infringement and unfair competition; opposing and cancelling a trademark registration; trade dress; unfair competition.

injunctions against infringement and unfair competition

The winner in an infringement lawsuit can obtain an injunction—a court order that prevents further infringing activity or unfair competition. The state and federal laws of trademarks, service marks and unfair competition authorize courts to require or prohibit any action or inaction necessary to protect the owner of a mark from economic harm.

Because lawsuits often take years to resolve, the courts have power to issue interim injunctions. Promptly upon filing the case, the plaintiff may be able to obtain a temporary restraining order if the judge is convinced that irreparable injury is occurring. A few weeks later, the court will hold a formal hearing and, if it appears that the plaintiff is likely to prevail when the case is finally decided, the court will issue a preliminary injunction that will last until the case is tried.

If, after a trial, a court finds that infringement or unfair competition has occurred, it will issue a permanent injunction ordering the defendant to stop using the infringing mark. In addition, the defendant may be required to destroy items or labels carrying the offending mark if necessary to prevent further use of the mark. In some cases, especially if the defendant was an innocent infringer, the court may allow some continued use of the mark in a particular locality, but bar it in other parts of the country.

The courts have broad powers ("equity" powers) to fashion their injunctions to obtain justice under varying circumstances. If necessary, an injunction that addresses the parties in a case may be enforced against other parties as well.

Related terms: infringement action.

injury to business reputation

See dilution of mark.

innocent infringer

An infringer who didn't know that he or she was infringing a mark is termed an innocent infringer. When an infringer is considered innocent, the owner of the infringed mark will usually be able to prevent future infringements but will not be able to collect money damages or defendant's profits. In some cases, the owner may not even be able to prevent the innocent infringer from continuing to use the mark, at least in a limited geographical area that doesn't create the risk of consumer confusion.

If a mark has been federally registered on the Principal Register before an infringement of the mark begins, the infringer cannot claim innocence. This is because the registration provides notice that the mark is already owned by

Definitions

someone else, and the infringer could have discovered this fact by doing a trademark search. However, If registration occurs after the infringing activity begins, the infringer may still be able to claim innocence until he or she actually learns of the registration.

Related terms: contributory infringer; infringement action; injunctions against infringement and unfair competition.

intent-to-use application

The Lanham Act permits a mark not yet put into commercial use to be reserved for later registration by filing an intent-to-use (ITU) application with the U.S. Patent and Trademark Office (PTO). The initial reservation is for six months from the date the PTO approved the mark (which may be six months to a year after you file your application) and can be extended for up to five additional six-month periods for good cause. The date of the original ITU application serves as the priority date in case of conflict, regardless of when the use actually begins, as long as the applicant completes the registration process.

Actual registration will occur once the owner begins to use the mark in commerce and files an Allegation of Use for Intent-to-Use Application informing the PTO of that fact. Without the timely filing of one of these forms, or a purchase of an extension, the ITU application will lapse.

The initial intent-to-use application costs the same as an actual use application ($325 as of September 2000), plus an additional $150 for each additional six-month extension and $100 to file the Statement of Use—when you finally start using it in commerce.

Related terms: Amendment to Allege Use; Principal Register; Statement of Use.

Inter-American Convention for Trademark and Commercial Protection

This treaty provides reciprocal trademark rights between the U.S. and a number of Latin American nations that are not signatories to the Paris Convention. These countries are: Brazil, Colombia, Cuba, the Dominican Republic, Guatemala, Haiti, Honduras, Nicaragua, Panama, Paraguay and Peru.

Related terms: international trademark rights; Paris Convention.

inter partes proceeding

This type of an administrative hearing is conducted by the Trademark Trial and Appeal Board to resolve:

- conflicts between pending applications (called interferences)
- the merits of opposition and cancellation petitions, and

- disputes over decisions of the Commissioner of Patents and Trademarks about applications for registration under the Lanham Act.

Related terms: interference; opposing and cancelling a trademark registration.

interference

When two or more marks awaiting registration in the U.S. Patent and Trademark Office (PTO) appear to overlap or conflict with each other, an "interference" is said to exist and the applicants are informed of this fact. Any applicant may then request that the PTO set up an interference hearing to decide who should be the registered owner. Interference hearings tend to be expensive, lengthy, and rare. Most often, applicants facing an interference will simply withdraw their application and devise a new mark, which is then made the subject of a new application.

When an interference hearing is held, the PTO uses a set of rules developed by the courts over the years to decide which applicant is entitled to the registration. The rules are based on such variables as:

- who was first to use the mark anywhere
- who was first to use the mark in commerce
- who was first to file the registration application, and
- if the first filer is not also the first user, whether the first filer knew or should have known of the previous use.

Related terms: inter partes proceeding; ownership of mark in the U.S.

International Convention for the Protection of Industrial Property of 1883

See Paris Convention.

International Schedule of Classes of Goods and Services

All marks that are federally registered are classified by the U.S. Patent and Trademark Office according to a master list called the International Schedule of Classes of Goods and Services (used by virtually all countries). Classification allows marks to be efficiently stored and retrieved according to the class assigned to such product or service.

Because a mark's meaning is inseparable from the product or service to which it is attached, all registered marks must be classified by the category of goods or services it identifies. Because many marks naturally fall into two or more categories, simultaneous registration in different classes is permitted, with an extra fee for each extra class.

If a mark has been registered for use on one type of product or service, and the mark's owner wants to use it on a type of product or service that falls in a different class, the mark must be registered anew.

Definitions

EXAMPLE: Sweets Inc., a candy manufacturer, attaches the trademark "TummyYummy Candies" to its line of chocolate candies. Later on, Sweets decides to enter the fresh fruit juice market. If it wants to use the trademark "TummyYummy Fruit Juice," it should obtain a new registration, since fruit juice and candy are in different classes.

Related terms: federal trademark registration; protection of marks under Lanham Act; trademark, defined.

See the accompanying chart for a listing of the International Schedule of Classes of Goods and Services.

international trademark rights

Trademark rights in each country depend solely on the trademark laws of that country; there is no set of international laws. Mark owners must start anew to establish rights to a mark in every new country they enter for commercial purposes, a concept known as "territoriality." In other words, previous use or registration in other countries is generally irrelevant.

In the U.S., first use often decides who owns a mark. Most other countries, however, award ownership to whoever is the first to register a mark (although use on the same or related goods usually must follow within a reasonable time). As a result, if the seller of wood patio furniture under the mark "Sueno" wants to expand to a first-to-register country, it will have to pick a new mark if "Sueno" is already registered in that country. This is true even if the U.S. seller was first to use the mark and even if the company that registered that mark in the other country does not currently make related goods. This "registration" system often allows people to anticipate international marketing trends, and to register the rights to valuable marks before another company thinks to do so.

The territoriality rule has an important exception: countries that have established treaty rights among themselves, like the U.S. and Syria, may permit nationals of other treaty countries to establish their right to a mark based on prior use or registration in their own country alone. In the U.S., the Lanham Act allows nationals of the Paris Convention countries to register their marks in the U.S. based on registration in their native country without alleging use here first (if they allege a bona fide intention to use the mark in the U.S. within a reasonable time).

Other treaties, like the Madrid Arrangement on International Registration of Trademarks and the Madrid Protocol, use an international bureau, the World Intellectual Property Organization (WIPO) as a central registration office for

International Schedule of Classes of Goods and Services

Goods

1. Chemical products used in industry, science, photography, agriculture, horticulture, forestry; artificial and synthetic resins; plastics in the form of powders, liquids or pastes, for industrial use; manures (natural and artificial); fire extinguishing compositions; tempering substances and chemical preparations for soldering; chemical substances for preserving foodstuffs; tanning substances; adhesive substances used in industry.

2. Paints, varnishes, lacquers; preservatives against rust and against deterioration of wood; colouring matters, dyestuffs; mordants; natural resins; metals in foil and powder form for painters and decorators.

3. Bleaching preparations and other substances for laundry use; cleaning, polishing, scouring and abrasive preparations; soaps; perfumery, essential oils, cosmetics, hair lotions; dentifrices.

4. Industrial oils and greases (other than oils and fats and essential oils); lubricants; dust laying and absorbing compositions; fuels (including motor spirit) and illuminants; candles, tapers, night lights and wicks.

5. Pharmaceutical, veterinary, and sanitary substances; infants' and invalids' foods; plasters, material for bandaging; material for stopping teeth, dental wax, disinfectants; preparations for killing weeds and destroying vermin.

6. Unwrought and partly wrought common metals and their alloys; anchors, anvils, bells, rolled and cast building materials; rails and other metallic materials for railway tracks; chains (except driving chains for vehicles); cables and wires (nonelectric); locksmiths' work; metallic pipes and tubes; safes and cash boxes; steel balls; horseshoes; nails and screws; other goods in nonprecious metal not included in other classes; ores.

7. Machines and machine tools; motors (except for land vehicles); machine couplings and belting (except for land vehicles); large size agricultural implements; incubators.

8. Hand tools and instruments; cutlery, forks, and spoons; side arms.

9. Scientific, nautical, surveying and electrical apparatus and instruments (including wireless), photographic, cinematographic, optical, weighing, measuring, signalling, checking (supervision), life-saving and teaching apparatus and instruments; coin or counterfreed apparatus; talking machines; cash registers; calculating machines; fire extinguishing apparatus.

10. Surgical, medical, dental, and veterinary instruments and apparatus (including artificial limbs, eyes, and teeth).

International Schedule of Classes of Goods and Services (con't)

11. Installations for lighting, heating, steam generating, cooking, refrigerating, drying, ventilating, water supply, and sanitary purposes.

12. Vehicles; apparatus for locomotion by land, air, or water.

13. Firearms; ammunition and projectiles; explosive substances; fireworks.

14. Precious metals and their alloys and goods in precious metals or coated therewith (except cutlery, forks and spoons); jewelry, precious stones, horological and other chronometric instruments.

15. Musical instruments (other than talking machines and wireless apparatus).

16. Paper and paper articles, cardboard and cardboard articles; printed matter, newspaper and periodicals, books; bookbinding material; photographs; stationery, adhesive materials (stationery); artists' materials; paint brushes; typewriters and office requisites (other than furniture); instructional and teaching material (other than apparatus); playing cards; printers' type and cliches (stereotype).

17. Gutta percha, india rubber, balata and substitutes, articles made from these substances and not included in other classes; plastics in the form of sheets, blocks and rods, being for use in manufacture; materials for packing, stopping or insulating; asbestos, mica and their products; hose pipes (nonmetallic).

18. Leather and imitations of leather, and articles made from these materials and not included in other classes; skins, hides; trunks and travelling bags; umbrellas, parasols and walking sticks; whips, harness and saddlery.

19. Building materials, natural and artificial stone, cement, lime, mortar, plaster and gravel; pipes of earthenware or cement; roadmaking materials; asphalt, pitch and bitumen; portable buildings; stone monuments; chimney pots.

20. Furniture, mirrors, picture frames; articles (not included in other classes) of wood, cork, reeds, cane, wicker, horn, bone, ivory, whalebone, shell, amber, mother-of-pearl, meerschaum, celluloid, substitutes for all these materials, or of plastics.

21. Small domestic utensils and containers (not of precious metals, or coated therewith); combs and sponges; brushes (other than paint brushes); brushmaking materials; instruments and material for cleaning purposes, steel wool; unworked or semi-worked glass (excluding glass used in building); glassware, procelain and earthenware, not included in other classes.

22. Ropes, string, nets, tents, awnings, tarpaulins, sails, sacks; padding and stuffing materials (hair, kapok, feathers, seaweed, etc.); raw fibrous textile materials.

International Schedule of Classes of Goods and Services (con't)

23. Yarns, threads.
24. Tissues (piece goods); bed and table covers; textile articles not included in other classes.
25. Clothing, including boots, shoes and slippers.
26. Lace and embroidery, ribands and braid; buttons, press buttons, hooks and eyes, pins and needles; artificial flowers.
27. Carpets, rugs, mats and matting; linoleums and other materials for covering existing floors; wall hangings (nontextile).
28. Games and playthings; gymnastic and sporting articles (except clothing); ornaments and decorations for Christmas trees.
29. Meats, fish, poultry and game; meat extracts; preserved, dried and cooked fruits and vegetables; jellies, jams; eggs, milk and other dairy products; edible oils and fats; preserves, pickles.
30. Coffee, tea, cocoa, sugar, rice, tapioca, sago, coffee substitutes; flour, and preparations made from cereals; bread, biscuits, cakes, pastry and confectionary, ices; honey, treacle; yeast, baking powder; salt, mustard, pepper, vinegar, sauces, spices; ice.
31. Agricultural, horticultural and forestry products and grains not included in other classes; living animals; fresh fruits and vegetables; seeds; live plants and flowers; foodstuffs for animals, malt.
32. Beer, ale and porter; mineral and aerated waters and other nonalcoholic drinks; syrups and other preparations for making beverages.
33. Wines, spirits and liqueurs.
34. Tobacco, raw or manufactured; smokers' articles; matches.

Services

35. Advertising and business.
36. Insurance and financial.
37. Construction and repair.
38. Communication.
39. Transportation and storage.
40. Material treatment.
41. Education and entertainment.
42. Miscellaneous.

trademarks in use in the member countries. Each country still can accept or reject any mark registered with WIPO, so the fact that a mark is registered with WIPO does not mean that it will be given protection by any particular country. Rather, the list is primarily for informational purposes. The U.S. has not yet signed the Madrid treaties, but all members of the European Community have, plus 16 other countries.

One other exception to the territoriality rule concerns marks that have such international fame that they act as marks even without use in the U.S. Such marks (like Maxim's in Paris, or Wimbledon in England) have developed enough trademark recognition, even without use or registration in the U.S., to prevent another's use of the same mark.

Related terms: foreign nationals, registering in U.S.; Inter-American Convention for Trademark and Commercial Protection; Madrid Arrangement on International Registration of Trademarks and Madrid Protocol; Paris Convention; phonetic or foreign equivalents for marks; prior registration countries.

Internet domain names

See domain names.

Internet, effect on trademark law

The legal relationship between trademarks and domain names has created considerable confusion and has not been completely sorted out. A few more years of lawsuits and new laws will probably make it clearer. Two things are certain:

- registration of a domain name does not automatically create trademark rights, and
- a trademark owner can sue a domain name owner who is likely to confuse consumers or who dilutes a famous trademark.

Domain name registration, by itself, does not permit the registrant to stop another business from using the name for its business or product. For example, if Sam acquires the domain name greatgrammar.com, that does not mean Sam can stop others from using Great Grammar for services or products online or off. It only means that Sam has the right to use that specific Internet address.

A domain name will function as a trademark only if it is used in connection with the sale of goods or services and consumers associate the name with the Internet business. When that happens, the domain name owner can stop others from using a similar name.

Consider Amazon.com, a domain name that functions as a trademark because consumers associate the name with a certain company and its services. Amazon.com achieved trademark status because the company was the first to use this distinctive name for online retail sales and the name has been promoted to consumers through advertising and sales. If another company sold books on the Internet or off, under the name Amazon, the owners of Amazon.com could sue under trademark law to stop the use.

In short, to be protectible as a trademark, a domain name must be distinctive or must achieve distinction through consumer awareness and the owner must be the first to use the name in connection with certain services or products.

A domain name owner can run into problems if the domain name legally conflicts with an existing trademark. For example, if a company launched a website with the domain name Xon.com to sell automobile accessories, that company could be stopped from using the name by the owners of the Exxon trademark. That's because Exxon has the right to stop lookalike and soundalike business names that are likely to confuse consumers of a wide range of auto products.

Whether a domain name would legally conflict with an existing trademark depends on which was first put into actual use and whether the existing mark is famous or use of the domain name would confuse customers regarding the existing mark. The legal standards used in these conflicts are no different than other trademark disputes.

Related terms: Anticybersquatting Consumer Protection Act; confusion of customers; dilution of mark; domain name.

Lanham Act

The main federal statute that governs trademarks, service marks and unfair competition is the Lanham Act, passed in 1946 (and amended repeatedly since).

The Lanham Act covers such matters as: 1) when owners of marks may be entitled to federal judicial protection against infringement of a mark by others; 2) the types of remedies for infringement that the federal courts are authorized to provide, such as injunctive relief, money damages and defendant's profits; 3) procedures for registering marks with the U.S. Patent and Trademark Office (on the Principal Register or Supplemental Register); 4) guidelines for when trademarks become incontestable; and 5) remedies for activity that constitutes unfair competition. Selected sections of the Lanham Act are included at the end of this part.

Related terms: commerce; protection of marks under Lanham Act; unfair competition; unregistered mark, protection of; use of mark.

licensing of marks

The owner of a mark (licensor) gives a "license" when the owner authorizes another party (licensee) in writing to use the mark for commercial purposes. Such written licenses must be very carefully drafted to provide control over the use of the mark, because the unfettered use of a mark by another party can harm the mark's value as a reliable identifier of a particular product or service. In an extreme case, allowing someone to use a mark without adequate restriction and supervision may result in the mark being considered abandoned.

Related terms: abandonment of mark; assignment of mark; naked license; ownership of mark in the U.S.

likelihood of confusion

See confusion of consumers.

loss of mark

Ownership of an otherwise valid trademark may be lost in several situations. This occurs when a mark is deliberately abandoned (non-use), when it becomes the generic term for the goods (genericide), when it is used improperly (in violation of antitrust laws), or when an unfavorable decision is made in a cancellation or interference proceeding (which passes the mark's ownership to another party).

Related terms: abandonment of mark; generic mark; interference; opposing and cancelling a trademark registration.

Madrid Arrangement on International Registration of Trademarks and Madrid Protocol

Under these international treaties, trademark owners in the member nations may submit their national trademark registrations to the International Bureau of the World Intellectual Property Organization (WIPO) for registration. The mark may then be protected in all member countries on the same basis as a national trademark. The U.S. is not a member of the Madrid treaties.

Each member country has one year from the date of international registration to reject the mark for coverage in that country. If the year passes without such rejection, however, and the mark is used for five years after the international registration, it is valid for an additional 15 years, and longer if it is renewed on a timely basis.

Related terms: international trademark rights.

mark, defined

This book uses "mark" to refer broadly to:

- trademarks

- service marks
- certification marks
- collective marks, and
- trade dress (when used as a trademark or service mark).

The term "mark" generally encompasses any means that a business uses to identify or distinguish its product or service from competitors in the marketplace. Features of the mark must be nonfunctional and may include symbols, shapes, designs, logos, phrases, colors, tunes and smells.

Related terms: trademark, defined.

mark dilution

See dilution of mark.

meta tag

A meta tag is programming code used in the creation of a website. Meta tags do not affect the appearance of a website and are not visible when you look at a Web page, but they provide information regarding the content of the site. Meta tags are used primarily by search engines that wade through the programming code and text of each page. When a search engine finds a search term in a meta tag, it indexes the Web page and displays it in the search results. In other words, meta tags have a direct effect on the frequency with which a search engine will find a website.

Even though an Internet user never sees this code, meta tags have been the subject of trademark lawsuits because companies have used them to divert or confuse consumers. Instead of using terms that properly describe the site, some programmers substitute the business names of competing companies. For example, a rival shoe manufacturer may bury the meta tag "Nike" in its Web page to Web surfers searching for Nike products. In the case of the website selling handmade watches, the meta tag might include "Rolex, Swatch, Bulova, Cartier." One company went so far as to copy and use all of the meta tags at a rival site. This kind of deceptive use of another company's trademark in a meta tag is a form of trademark infringement when it confuses consumers. One judge described the practice as similar to a shop owner posting a sign with another company's trademark in front of its shop. (*Brookfield Communications v. West Coast Entertainment,* 174 F.3d 1036 (9th Cir. 1999).)

There are some instances when the use of another company's trademark is permitted in a meta tag. For example, it is permissible to use another company's trademark as a meta tag if it is used only to describe the goods or services of a company, or their geographic origin. This is permitted under trademark law as a "fair use." In one case, former Playmate Terri Welles created a website and used Playboy and Playmate in her site's meta tags. This use of Playboy's trademarks was permitted because Ms. Welles was using the terms to describe herself and to properly index the pages. In addition, the court was influenced by the fact that most of the free Web pages at the site included a disclaimer at the bottom: "This site is neither endorsed, nor sponsored by, nor affiliated with Playboy Enterprises, Inc. PLAYBOY, PLAYMATE OF THE YEAR and PLAYMATE OF THE MONTH are registered trademarks of Playboy Enterprises, Inc." (*Playboy Enterprises, Inc. v. Welles*, 7 F. Supp. 2d 1098 (Cal. S.D. 1998).)

Related terms: fair use; free speech and trademarks.

misuse of mark

See loss of mark.

money damages for mark infringement

See damages in trademark infringement cases.

naked license

An owner of a mark gives another party a "naked license" when he or she allows the party to use it without adequate safeguards or restrictions. In some situations, especially those involving franchise operations, the grant of a naked license can result in the abandonment of the mark. This occurs when the mark is used on goods and services of varying quality so that it no longer identifies and distinguishes specific products and services from competing ones, and does not indicate a particular level of quality attached to some product or service.

Related terms: abandonment of mark; licensing of marks.

names as marks

Names that are primarily surnames (last names) are considered weak and cannot be listed on the Principal Register unless they acquire a secondary meaning (for example, Heinz, Macy's, Miller). First names and nicknames, unless very unusual or memorable as a mark but not as a name, need to acquire secondary meaning by becoming very well known over time before others can be stopped from using them.

EXAMPLE: "Henry's" is a mark used to advertise the Henry Weinhart's line of beers. Over time, "Henry's" has become associated in the public's mind with the underlying product and therefore has taken on a secondary meaning. If Henry Clark came along and used his first name to advertise his line of beers, the Henry Weinhart company could probably successfully sue him for infringement of its "Henry's" mark.

Related terms: prohibited and reserved marks under Lanham Act; secondary meaning; surnames as marks.

non-competing goods

See competing and non-competing products.

nonprofit corporations and trademarks

A nonprofit corporation is entitled to the same protection as a for-profit entity for its trademarks and service marks.

Related terms: protection of marks under Lanham Act; state trademark laws; trade name.

notice of trademark registration

To denote that a mark is registered with the U.S. Patent and Trademark Office (PTO) under the Lanham Act, a symbol must be placed next to the mark. The most commonly used symbol in the U.S. is an "R" in a circle "(®)" but "Reg. U.S. Pat. Off." is equally valid. Both symbols indicate that the mark is registered with the PTO on either the Principal Register or the Supplemental Register (a list of marks that didn't qualify for the Principal Register because they lacked distinctiveness).

If a mark owner systematically does not use one of these symbols to identify a registered mark when using it to promote a product or service, the owner cannot collect treble damages or defendant's profits for an infringement, unless he or she can show that the infringer actually knew the mark was registered.

> **EXAMPLE:** While searching for a name for his new computer game, Phil Hacker sees an advertisement in the newspaper for a new database manager called "Sorcerer's Apprentice." No notice of registration appears in the advertisement, so Phil concludes the mark is probably not registered and proceeds to use the name as a trademark for his program. The mark had in fact been registered. While the owners of the mark "Sorcerer's Apprentice" could sue Phil for infringement, they won't be able to collect treble damages, defendant's profits or attorney fees unless they can show that they generally did accompany the mark with a proper notice of registration, and that the absence of a notice on the advertis°ement was an oversight.

Related terms: constructive notice of mark under Lanham Act; damages in trademark infringement cases.

Official Gazette

As part of the application process for placing a mark on the Principal Register, the U.S. Patent and Trademark Office (PTO) publishes the mark in a newspaper called the Official Gazette (OG).

The OG contains lists of marks proposed for registration on the Principal Register, together with examples of their designs, to give other mark owners notice of the impending registrations. If any other mark owners believe the new mark would infringe on or dilute theirs, they can file an opposition to protest the registration.

If no one objects to the mark's registration within 30 days of the publication date, the PTO will register the mark. If, however, any interested person files a timely opposition to the registration, the PTO will schedule an administrative (inter partes) hearing to resolve the dispute.

Related terms: opposing and cancelling a trademark registration; Principal Register; U.S. Patent and Trademark Office (PTO).

opposing and cancelling a trademark registration

Under the Lanham Act, any party who may be damaged by the actual or proposed registration of a mark is entitled to challenge the registration. If the mark has been published for proposed registration on the Principal Register, the party—usually the owner of a competing mark—can oppose the registration. The opposition must be in writing and be filed within 30 days of the proposed mark's publication in the Official Gazette. The U.S. Patent and Trademark Office (PTO) may grant extensions of the 30-day period upon written request.

If the mark has already been placed on the Principal Register, the party may petition the PTO for cancellation of the registration. (15 United States Code, Section 1064.) A cancellation petition may be filed:

- within five years from the date the mark is published in the Official Gazette
- any time, if the mark becomes generic, is abandoned or its use becomes fraudulent in some way, or
- any time, if the mark is a certification mark and it is being misused (for instance, the registrant no longer exercises control or the registrant begins to manufacture goods subject to the certification).

Marks proposed for placement on the Supplemental Register are not published for opposition. If a party believes that a mark's placement on the Supplemental Register may cause it harm, the party may file an application with the PTO to have the registration cancelled. (15 United States Code, Section 1092.)

When a petition for opposition or cancellation is filed, or the PTO declares an interference, an inter partes proceeding to resolve the dispute will be scheduled before the Trademark Trial and Appeal Board. (15 United States Code, Section 1067.) At the conclusion of this hearing, the Patent and Trademark Commissioner may:

- refuse to register the opposed mark (in an opposition case)
- cancel the registration of a mark or place restrictions on its use (in a cancellation case)
- refuse to register any mark, or some or all of several marks (in an interference case)
- register the opposed mark or marks of persons who are found to be entitled to ownership, or
- order concurrent registration of marks along with conditions or restrictions on their use designed to prevent consumer confusion in the marketplace.

The PTO will cancel a mark on its own—without anyone asking for it—if the mark's owner fails to timely file a Section 8 and Declaration showing that the mark is still in use. Because this form must be filed between the fifth and sixth years following the initial registration, and because the PTO doesn't send a reminder, the registrations of many marks are cancelled for this reason. And because the PTO also doesn't send notice of the cancellation, many trademark owners continue to use their marks in the belief that they are registered, when they're not.

The fact that a mark's registration is cancelled in no way affects the right of the mark's owner to challenge other users of the mark on the basis of first use. But as long as the mark remains unregistered, the owner will not be entitled to the benefits of registration should a trademark infringement suit become necessary.

Related terms: federal trademark registration; interference; ownership of mark in the U.S.

ownership, presumption of

See presumption of ownership.

ownership of mark, international

See international trademark rights.

ownership of mark in the U.S.

In the U.S., ownership of a mark generally comes from first use. Use of a distinctive mark on goods or services in the marketplace is sufficient to establish ownership in that mark unless:

- someone else is already using the same or similar mark on related goods or services, or
- an intent-to-use (ITU) application has been filed for the mark.

If, however, a business that is first to use a mark does not federally register it, and a second business uses the mark in a geographically separate market (which means no consumer confusion is likely), it is possible for both businesses to concurrently own the mark.

As mentioned, ownership of a mark may arise from the filing of an ITU registration application, before a mark goes into use. The ownership vests (becomes effective) when the mark is put in use and the application process is complete, but ownership will begin on the date the ITU application was filed.

Whether derived from actual use or from the ITU application, ownership of a mark confers an exclusive right to use that mark in a certain way and in a certain place.

Ownership rights may last forever, unless the mark is abandoned or becomes generic. The fact that a mark is not registered or that a registration is cancelled or not renewed does not affect the basic ownership of the mark, which is primarily based on use. However, additional remedies provided by federal registration will not be available to the owner of an unregistered mark if an infringement occurs.

Although the exclusive right to use the mark initially exists in the geographic area where the mark is being used, if someone uses the same or similar mark in the U.S., the scope of this right depends on the following factors:

- Which mark was first used anywhere in the United States?
- Which mark was first subject to a registration application under the Lanham Act on the basis of actual use or an intent to use the mark in the future?
- Was the first registrant under the Lanham Act the junior user or the senior user?
- If the first registrant under the Lanham Act was the junior user, did that party know of the mark's prior use by the senior user?
- Is there geographical proximity between areas in which two conflicting marks are used?
- Are the types of products or services to which the marks are attached related or unrelated?
- Is confusion of consumers likely to result from the use of the two marks?

EXAMPLE 1: Malou markets her marshmallow cookies, "Malou's Marvelous Mallows," in California only. Because there is no interstate use, Malou is only entitled to register her mark under her state's trademark laws. Lou, who lives in Colorado, decides to market cookies exclusively in Colorado under the name of "Lou's Marvy Mallows." Although Lou's mark is confusingly similar to that used by Malou, Malou probably would have no recourse as long as Lou's mark was confined to the Colorado market (there would be no likelihood of consumer confusion).

EXAMPLE 2: Suppose now that Malou markets cookies only on the West Coast while Lou markets his cookies only in the East. Even if Malou federally registered her mark before Lou started using his mark, Malou will not be able to force Lou to stop using his mark unless she can show a likelihood of consumer confusion as a result of the two uses. But since Malou is the national owner of the mark, if Malou later decides to start marketing her product in the East, Lou could be forced to stop using his mark.

EXAMPLE 3: Using the same facts, with a last wrinkle, if Lou federally registers before Malou and Lou does not know of Malou's prior use of the mark, Lou will become entitled to exclusive use on a national basis except where Malou is already marketing. If Lou does know of Malou's prior use or if Malou objects to the registration, however, his registration may be deemed fraudulent and set aside.

These priorities can be somewhat complicated and obviously depend greatly on the facts of each case. We only discuss them to provide the reader with a general idea of the parameters.

Trademark law as it exists today developed at a time when geography played an important role in resolving trademark conflicts. If the same trademark was used by different businesses in different parts of the country, there was no likelihood of customer confusion and therefore no need for intervention by a court unless and until one of the users expanded into the other user's territory. As more and more businesses start to do commerce on the World Wide Web, however, this concept of territory is becoming less and less important as more and more businesses buy and sell goods and services on the Internet. Although most businesses are still local in the sense that they aren't franchises or chain stores, doing business on the World Wide Web automatically extends a business's marketing activity to all parts of the country and world simultaneously.

The more important information becomes to our society, the greater the chance that users of the same mark anywhere in the country or world will be offering goods and services that will compete in that new territory called cyberspace. And this competition will put the marks in competition, a state of affairs that can only lead to trademark infringement issues.

Related terms: assignment of mark; infringement action; Internet, effect on trademark law; licensing of marks; protection of marks under Lanham Act.

Definitions

Definitions

palming off

A person engages in palming off (also called "passing off") when he or she intentionally causes one product or service to be confused with another for commercial gain. Examples of palming off include:

- substituting one product for another—for instance, representing a computer as having one kind of microprocessor when it has another, or
- deliberately infringing a mark belonging to another—for instance, using "IBN" as a mark on a new computer line.

Although the phrase "palming off" is appropriate only in situations where there is an intent to confuse, it is sometimes used colloquially to designate any infringement where there is a likelihood of confusion, even where the infringer may not have intended it.

Related terms: confusion of consumers; infringement action; innocent infringer; reverse palming off.

Paris Convention

The primary treaty regulating trademark relations between the U.S. and other countries is called the Paris Convention. The Paris Convention provides that each signatory country will give members of other signatory countries the same protections regarding marks and unfair competition that it affords its own nationals.

Related terms: foreign nationals, registering in U.S.; international trademark rights.

passing off

See palming off.

Patent and Trademark Depository Library

See trademark search.

phonetic or foreign equivalents for marks

In trademark law, a word that sounds the same as another mark, or one that means the same in another language, will normally be treated similarly. If a word or phrase is descriptive or generic (ineligible for protection), simply misspelling or translating it will not make it distinctive (that is, eligible for protection.)

> **EXAMPLE:** If DateTime is too descriptive for a singles dating service, then Dayttyme won't work either. Or, if GoodTimes is considered too descriptive for a party-catering service, then using the French equivalent BonTemps will not help.

Related terms: composite mark; generic mark; international trademark rights.

pictures and symbols used as marks

Pictures and symbols may be protectible as marks if they are distinctive rather than descriptive. For example, the Quaker man on Quaker Oats cereals is a strong, distinctive pictorial mark. Similarly, the apple on Apple computer products is very distinctive and non-descriptive. A generic illustration such as the no-smoking symbol—a diagonal bar through a burning cigarette within a circle —would be barred from trademark use for an anti-smoking product or service.

Related terms: descriptive mark; secondary meaning; trademark, defined.

presidents' names and likenesses as marks

See prohibited and reserved marks under Lanham Act.

presumption of ownership

If an infringement suit is filed, a court will assume that the owner who is listed on a certificate of registration on the Principal Register is the owner of a mark. This presumption means that the owner does not have to present further evidence to support the ownership claim unless the defendant offers evidence to the contrary. In that event, the certificate holder will need to introduce evidence to back up the ownership claim.

The presumption of ownership is not available for marks on the Supplemental Register (a list of marks that didn't qualify for the Principal Register because they lacked distinctiveness).

Related terms: certificate of registration; infringement action.

Principal Register

The Principal Register is the list on which distinctive trademarks and service marks approved for federal registration are placed. To qualify for placement on the Principal Register, the mark must be distinctive and:

- It must not infringe another mark that is already registered.
- It cannot include certain types of pictures, words and symbols—the U.S. flag; other federal and local governmental insignias; names of living persons without their consent; names or likenesses of dead U.S. Presidents without their widows' consent; words or symbols that disparage living or

dead persons, institutions, beliefs or national symbols; or marks that are judged immoral, deceptive or scandalous.

- It cannot consist primarily of surnames or of deceptive geographical names.

Benefits of placement on the Principal Register include all of the following:

- It provides official notice to all would-be copiers that the mark is in use on particular goods or services, and that someone claims ownership of the mark for that use.
- It gives the owner the right to file an infringement action in federal court.
- It creates a presumption, in the event of litigation, that the registrant owns the mark, requiring the other party to challenge the registrant's ownership. (Placing the burden of proof on the challenger can often make the difference between winning and losing a lawsuit.)
- It gives the owner the right to seek an award of treble damages, defendant's profits and attorney fees.
- It gives the owner the right to register in countries that afford reciprocal rights to the U.S.
- It confers on the owner the right to exclusive use of the mark in all parts of the U.S., except where a senior unregistered user may have already been using the mark at the time of registration.
- After the mark is on the Principal Register for five years, it gives the mark's owner the right to file for incontestability status. If granted, incontestability status prevents a challenger from challenging the registrant's ownership on the basis that the registered mark lacks sufficient distinctiveness to warrant protection.

Related terms: incontestability status; opposing and cancelling a trademark registration; prohibited and reserved marks under Lanham Act; protection of marks under Lanham Act; Supplemental Register.

prinTEAS *See* eTEAS.

prior registration countries

Most countries determine ownership of a mark by who registers first, instead of who uses it first. These are called prior registration countries (or first to file countries) to distinguish them from countries that base trademark rights on first use, such as the U.S. However, since the U.S. has permitted the filing of intent-to-use applications, the line between the U.S. and first to file countries has become somewhat blurred.

Related terms: international trademark rights.

profits

See defendant's profits.

prohibited and reserved marks under Lanham Act

Under the Lanham Act, certain marks may be refused federal registration. (15 United States Code, Section 1052.) These are:

- marks that comprise "immoral," "deceptive" or "scandalous" matter. For example, a mark resembling a sex organ would be considered immoral; a mark suggesting miracle properties in a product that are not substantiated would be deceptive; and a mark showing a mutilated corpse would be scandalous.
- marks that disparage or falsely suggest a connection with persons (living or dead), institutions, beliefs or national symbols.

EXAMPLE: A mark that showed Clara Barton clad only in Red Cross-decorated bikini would constitute a disparagement of a person, of an institution (the Red Cross), and, if she were wearing the bikini while embracing Uncle Sam, of a national symbol. A baseball insignia with Babe Ruth's face would falsely suggest a connection with Babe Ruth unless authorized by his heirs.

- marks comprising the flag or coat of arms or other insignia of the United States, or of any state or municipality, or of any foreign nation, or any simulation of these items.
- marks that consist of or comprise a name, portrait or signature identifying a particular living individual (except with his or her written consent), or the name, signature or portrait of a deceased President of the United States during the life of his widow, if any, except with the written consent of the widow.
- marks that so resemble marks previously registered with the U.S. Patent and Trademark Office that their use is likely to cause confusion or mistake, or to deceive consumers.
- marks that are merely descriptive, are primarily surnames, geographical names or terms that describe the qualities or characteristics of the product or service. This last category of marks may be placed on the Supplemental Register until they have become well known enough to qualify as distinctive under the secondary meaning rule.

In addition to these prohibitions, certain organizations, such as the Boy Scouts and the U.S. Olympic Committee, have the exclusive right to use their marks and symbols mandated by statute. Similarly, the use of the character and name "Smokey the Bear" is reserved to the Department of the Interior.

Related terms: Principal Register; Supplemental Register.

protection of marks under Lanham Act

The degree of protection offered to a mark under the Lanham Act (the federal statute that addresses trademark protection) depends on many variables, such as:

- whether the mark is listed on the Principal Register or the Supplemental Register
- the length of time the registration has been in effect
- whether the registrant is the senior user or the junior user, and
- whether the infringer had either actual knowledge or constructive knowledge of the registrant's mark.

Protection under the Lanham Act varies in scope and effectiveness. The owner of a registered mark can prevent others from later using a similar mark if such use would likely confuse the average, reasonably prudent, consumer as to the source of the product or service.

In addition, owners of such marks can prevent persons in other countries from using the same or a similar mark on their goods or services anywhere in the U.S. where consumer confusion is likely to result. On the other hand, the owner of a registered mark may have to accept another's use of the same or similar mark in a specific marketing area where the mark has already been in use by the other party.

Although state and federal statutes and court decisions offer unregistered marks some local protection against mark infringement, this protection is greatly expanded if the mark is federally registered under the Lanham Act. For example, by federally registering a mark that's in use in two or three states, its owner may reserve the rest of the country for the trademark, except in places where the same or similar mark is already in use.

Some provisions of the Lanham Act are available to unregistered trademarks. For example, Section 43(a) of the Lanham Act protects against unfair competition. It makes anyone liable to another business that suffers damages as a result of its use of a false designation of origin, a false description or a misleading mark, word, symbol or name on any goods or services in commerce, in a way that is likely to cause confusion. This is the section most often used when a plaintiff claims that its trade name, unregistered mark or trade dress has been misappropriated.

Related terms: constructive notice of mark under Lanham Act; incontestability status; infringement action; ownership of mark in the U.S.; Principal Register; Supplemental Register; unfair competition.

protection of marks under state law and common law

See state trademark laws.

PTO

See U.S. Patent and Trademark Office (PTO).

public domain

See generic mark.

publication of mark in Official Gazette

See Official Gazette.

publishers of advertising matter

If an infringement of a mark occurs in advertising copy carried in a magazine, newspaper or other periodical, and the publisher has not been made aware of the infringement, the Lanham Act exempts the publisher from liability for money damages or profits. (15 United States Code, Section 1114.)

A court may bar (enjoin) the publication from any future advertising copy carrying the infringing mark unless the effect of the injunction would be to delay the normal publication, delivery or distribution of a scheduled issue. Such a compromise is needed to prevent the injunction from harming the innocent publisher.

If a publisher engages in infringing activity after becoming aware of the infringement, it can be treated like any other deliberate infringer.

Related terms: contributory infringer; false advertising.

Definitions

puffery

When advertising claims are so broad that consumers do not take them seriously, they are referred to as "puffery" and they do not give rise to claims of false advertising. For example, grand and immeasurable statements such as "world's greatest detergent" or "the best hamburger in the world" are considered as puffery. Consumers understand that these claims are generalities intended to "puff up" a product. However, if the statement is capable of being measured or the puffery is related to specific attributes, the statement may be subject to false advertising claims.

Related terms: false advertising.

punitive damages

In trademark infringement lawsuits, the Lanham Act bars a court from awarding punitive damages—civil damages that are intended to punish a wrongdoer and serve as an example to future potential wrongdoers. The Lanham Act does, however, authorize treble (triple) damages in instances of egregious and intentional infringement. Also, unfair competition and related laws of many states provide for either punitive or treble damages. Therefore, in an effort to qualify for more generous damages, it is common to charge an alleged infringer with violations of both the Lanham Act and any applicable state laws.

Related terms: damages in trademark infringement cases; state trademark laws; unfair competition.

reasonably prudent consumer

See average, reasonably prudent, consumer.

"Reg. U.S. Pat. Off." or "®"

See notice of trademark registration.

registered mark

Technically, any trademark, service mark, certification mark or collective mark that is placed on a state or federal list of protected marks is considered registered. Registered marks are usually entitled to a higher degree of protection than unregistered marks. However, under Section 43(a) of the Lanham Act, unregistered marks used in commerce receive protection comparable to that provided marks placed on the federal Principal Register.

Because state laws usually provide a mark much less protection than does the Lanham Act, the phrase "registered mark" commonly is understood as applying only to federally registered marks—that is, marks placed on the Principal Register.

Related terms: commerce; Principal Register; Supplemental Register; unregistered mark, protection of.

registered with the U.S. Patent and Trademark Office

See protection of marks under Lanham Act.

registrable matter

Under the Lanham Act, certain parts of a mark may meet the standards for registration while others do not. The parts that do are called registrable matter; those that don't are disclaimed as unregistrable.

Related terms: disclaimer of unregistrable material; Principal Register; protection of marks under Lanham Act.

registrant

A registrant is any person or business who registers a mark under the Lanham Act or under state registration laws. The registrant is also usually the owner at the time of registration.

Related terms: registered mark.

related products and services

Deciding whether goods or services are related is a key determination in trademark conflicts and in deciding whether a mark qualifies for federal registration. This is because the extent to which goods or services are related will determine whether marks used on them are likely to confuse consumers if the marks are the same or very similar to one another.

How closely related goods or services are considered to be depends on many factors, the most important of which are:

- the international product/service categories (international classes) to which the goods and services belong. If they are in the same class, they will be presumed to be related and the U.S. Patent and Trademark Office (PTO) will not register the second mark.
- whether the goods and services pass through related marketing channels. For example, if goods are sold in similar outlets, marketed in similar media, placed near each other in stores, and generally considered similar by the consumer, they will be considered related.

The courts have developed a number of additional criteria to determine when one product or service is related to another, which are used in infringement cases. These are:

- the likelihood that the goods or services of one business will be mistaken for those of the other
- the likelihood that one business will expand its activities so that its goods or services will compete with those of another business

Definitions

- the extent to which the goods or services of businesses have common purchasers or users
- the market relationship, if any, between the goods produced, or the services provided, by the two businesses
- the degree of distinctiveness of the mark in question when compared to a competing mark
- the degree of attention usually given to trademarks or service marks in the purchase of goods or services of the type provided by the two businesses
- the length of time during which the allegedly infringing business has used the designation, and
- the intent of the allegedly infringing business in adopting and using the mark in question.

When products or services are considered to be totally unrelated, the courts will generally find that use of the same or similar mark does not constitute infringement. On the other hand, if the products or services are found to be related, infringement may be found to exist, assuming the other requirements for infringement are also present.

Whether a product or service is considered related or unrelated depends on the exact facts of the case, how the criteria listed above are weighed in light of the facts, and the subjective perceptions of the judge, based on the evidence, as to whether the average consumer might be confused by the use of the same or similar marks on different products or services. In short, there is no firm dividing line between marks that are ruled to be related and those that are not.

EXAMPLE: Ethereal Fragrance Company produces a line of perfumes with the distinctive registered trademark "Ekbara Scents," which it markets primarily to boutiques in Western states. One day, Ruben Santiago of Portland, Oregon, opens a small printing company specializing in business cards; he calls his product "Ekbara Cards" and markets the cards to small businesses in the Portland area. Ethereal claims infringement and Santiago denies its assertion. The courts could use the following analysis: "Purchasers of business cards will not likely think they come from a fragrance company. In addition, neither business is likely to begin competing with the other. The purchasers of the two products, as well as the distribution channels, are different; there is no relationship between the functions of the two goods; consumers give little attention to the origin of business cards; there is no indication that Ruben Santiago intended to take advantage of Ethereal's reputation; and length of use is not a factor. Therefore, the uses are unrelated and there is no infringement. The fact that

Ethereal has a very strong mark is simply not enough to overcome all the other factors." On the other hand, if Ruben created a line of scented greeting cards and marketed them under the Ekbara mark to boutiques as well as card shops, he may be held liable for infringement.

Although the use of the same or a similar mark might not result in a finding of infringement under the "related/unrelated" analysis, this does not mean that the alleged infringer may continue to use the mark. Even though no infringement is found, the court may rule that the use of the allegedly infringing mark constitutes dilution of the original mark and restrict further use of the mark on that ground. However, the dilution rule only applies if the original mark is famous.

Related terms: competing and non-competing products; dilution of mark; ownership of mark in the U.S.

renewal of registration

See duration of federal trademark registration.

reservation system for acquiring ownership of mark

See intent-to-use application; international trademark rights.

reverse confusion

In traditional trademark infringement cases, the second user of a trademark confuses consumers into believing that they are buying goods from the first user. However, it is possible that through massive advertising, a second user may create the impression that it is actually the first to use a trademark and that the real senior user is the infringer. This is known as reverse confusion.

EXAMPLE: Big O Tires, a mid-sized regional tire distributor, began marketing a bias-belted tire under the unregistered mark BigFoot in early 1974. The tire giant Goodyear decided to market a radial tire under the BigFoot mark in late 1974. The larger company pumped millions of dollars into its advertising effort, which overlapped Big O's advertising effort to some extent. As a result, the public began coming to Big O asking for Goodyear's tire. Angry and disappointed, consumers suspected Big O of stealing the idea from Goodyear. But in fact Goodyear had become aware of Big O's prior use of the same mark midway into its marketing plans, and had unsuccessfully negotiated to buy the mark from them. Nevertheless, they continued to use the mark. Under a theory of reverse confusion, Big O was awarded a judgment of $4.7 million dollars. (*Big O Tire Dealers, Inc. v. Goodyear Tire & Rubber Co.*, 408 F. Supp. 1219 (D. Col. 1976) *affirmed* 561 F.2d 1365 (10th Cir. 1977).)

Definitions

The *Big O* case introduced the theory of reverse confusion, a form of unfair competition, to trademark law. Goodyear competed unfairly because it intentionally undertook conduct with its trademark that deceived the public into thinking badly of a competitor. The traditional likelihood of confusion factors are used in a reverse confusion dispute. The only difference is that the court focuses on the strength of the junior user's mark rather than the senior user's. That's because the essence of reverse confusion is that the senior user's mark may be less well known than that of the powerful junior user.

Related terms: confusion of customers; unfair competition.

reverse palming off

Palming off occurs when goods are marketed in a way that makes people think they are really manufactured by someone else; to do this, an infringer usually uses the true trademark on substitute goods. Reverse palming off, on the other hand, occurs when a non-infringing label is placed on someone else's goods and the goods are then sold under the non-infringing name.

> **EXAMPLE:** Joe Kane buys 500 pairs of Levis (manufactured by Levi Strauss), rips the labels off them, puts his own designer jean label on them, and sells them for twice as much as the going price for Levis.

Either way, the public is being deceived and the owner of the original goods or mark may file a lawsuit under Section 43(a) of the Lanham Act to prevent this type of activity and recover damages caused by it.

Related terms: palming off.

right of publicity

The right of publicity is the right of a person to prevent the use of their name or persona for commercial purposes. Although the right of publicity is commonly associated with celebrities, every person, regardless of how famous, has a right to prevent unauthorized use of their name or image to sell products. The right extends beyond the commercial use of a person's name or image and includes the use of any personal element that implies an individual's endorsement of a product, provided that the public can identify the individual based upon the use.

For example, the right of publicity extends to a performer's identifiable voice. For this reason, courts have ruled that vocal performances that sounded like singers Tom Waits or Bette Midler could not be used to sell products. In many states, the right of publicity survives death and can be exercised by the person's estate. Because the right of publicity can trigger a claim of false endorsement or false advertising, these claims are sometimes brought under unfair competition laws, such as Section 43(a) of the Lanham Act. (15 United States Code, Section 1125(a).)

Related terms: false advertising; infringement action; unfair competition.

same or similar mark

Any mark that is enough like another mark in appearance or meaning to lead the average, reasonably prudent, consumer to confuse the two under the circumstances is considered the "same or similar." Whether any mark is deemed the same as or similar to another mark is necessarily decided on a case-by-case basis.

Related terms: confusion of consumers; counterfeit mark; infringement action.

secondary meaning

Marks that are not distinctive when they are first used can become so in the minds of the consuming public over time and through long, widespread use and/or intensive advertising. This distinctiveness arises from the fact that the mark has acquired a secondary meaning as a mark that transcends the literal meaning of its words.

> **EXAMPLE:** The mark "Dollar a Day" initially just described a service—car rentals for a dollar a day. However, over time, and with the help of an advertising campaign and virtually exclusive use of the phrase by the firm, the phrase lost its descriptive literal meaning and instead stood for a specific car rental service.

If the owner of a non-distinctive mark can show (usually through consumer polls) that the mark has acquired a secondary meaning, the mark will qualify for placement on the Principal Register. Even without such a showing, a mark that is kept in continuous and exclusive use by its owner for five years will be presumed to have acquired such secondary meaning and will qualify for registration on the Principal Register as a distinctive mark.

Related terms: descriptive mark; distinctive mark; Principal Register; Supplemental Register.

secondary register

See Supplemental Register.

Section 8 Declaration

Sometime during the fifth year after federal registration, the trademark owner must file a Declaration Of Use Of A Mark declaring the continued use of the mark (or an explanation as to the special circumstances for any period of non-use). The declaration must also be filed at the time of trademark renewal. The requirements for the declaration are set forth in Section 8 of the Lanham Act. (15 United States Code, Section 1058.) The fee must be enclosed along with a specimen of the mark as it is currently used for each class of goods or services. In lieu of the specimen, the trademark owner may recite facts as to the sales or advertising that demonstrate that the mark is in use.

If the owner fails to timely file the Section 8 Declaration, federal trademark rights will be canceled. There are no extensions for filing the declaration. The only way to reclaim federal trademark rights is to file a new application for registration. In the event that the mark has been assigned to a new owner since registration, the Section 8 Declaration is filed by the current owner and the change in ownership should be reflected by the current owner filing a copy of the assignment with the PTO. When the Section 8 Declaration is filed for the first time (between the fifth and sixth years of registration) it is usually combined with a Section 15 Declaration. Forms for the Section 8, Section 15 and combined Sections 8 & 15 Declaration can be downloaded from the PTO website (http://www.uspto.gov).

Related terms: Section 15 Declaration.

Section 15 Declaration

After five years of consecutive use from the date of federal registration, the mark may be declared incontestable. An incontestable mark is immune from challenge except if it has become the generic term for the goods, abandoned for nonuse or the registration was acquired under fraudulent conditions. In order to achieve incontestability, a Declaration Of Incontestability must be filed containing the requirements as provided in Section 15 of the Lanham Act. (15 United States Code, Section1065.)

A Section 15 Declaration is not necessary for maintaining ownership or rights under trademark law and the failure to file the declaration does not result in the loss of any rights. However, the filing of the Section 15 Declaration is recommended because it expands trademark rights by making it more difficult to challenge the mark. A Section 15 Declaration form can be downloaded from the PTO website. The Section 8 Declaration and Section 15 Declaration can be combined into one declaration and a copy of this combined declaration can be downloaded from the PTO website.

Related terms: Section 8 Declaration.

Section 43(a)

See false advertising; unfair competition; unregistered mark, protection of.

selling goods or services with infringing marks

See contributory infringer.

senior and junior users of marks

When a dispute exists over the ownership of a mark, the person (or entity) who first used the mark is called the senior user and the second person or entity to use the mark is termed the junior user. Although the senior user will usually be found to be the owner of the disputed mark, this is not always so. For example, if the junior user did not know about the senior user, and is first to register the mark under the Lanham Act or under state laws, the junior user may still be able to use the mark in areas other than where the senior user's mark is being used.

Related terms: infringement action; ownership of mark in the U.S.

service mark

A service mark promotes a service in the same way as a trademark promotes a product. Examples of services and their marks are Jack-in-the-Box (prepares and sells food), Blue Cross (sells health insurance), Berkeley Repertory Theatre (produces live plays), the Cirque de Soleil (produces a circus) and Greyhound (transports people by bus).

In the U.S., the rules for determining when and how service marks qualify for protection are the same as the rules applicable to trademarks. This means that when you read this book or other sources of information on trademarks, every time you read "trademark" (or "mark") in relation to a product, you can substitute the words "service mark" and "service" instead. One exception to this general rule is that some states will register trademarks but refuse to register service marks.

Note that a service mark is different from a trade name. A service mark is the name under which the service is promoted; a trade name is the name of the business that does the promoting. McDonald's Corp. (trade name) prepares and sells food under the service mark McDonald's, and sells one specific product under the trademark Big Mac. Especially for small businesses, the service mark and trade name are often the same words, but used in different contexts. For instance, Universal Auto Repair is both the name of a business (it appears on the company checks, invoices and stationery) and the name that appears on the sign designed to bring consumers into the shop (that is, a service mark).

Some countries, like the United Kingdom, do not protect service marks at all.

Definitions

Related terms: trade name; trademark, defined.

similar marks, use of

See ownership of mark in the U.S.; same or similar mark.

slogans used as marks

Advertising slogans that function as marks may be protected as marks. To qualify as protectible marks, slogans must be either:

- inherently distinctive and creative, or
- have developed enough secondary meaning to immediately call a product or service to mind.

The more mundane a slogan is, the more secondary meaning the owner will need to show to obtain protection from imitators. For example, the owners of Excedrin had to prove that "Extra Strength Pain Reliever" had developed a strong secondary meaning.

Related terms: composite mark; secondary meaning; strong mark.

state trademark laws

In addition to the federal Lanham Act, all states have laws under which marks may be registered and receive judicial protection should infringement occur. State trademark protections are, like federal law, based on use. However, unlike federal law, no state offers registration on an intent-to-use basis; use of a mark must always precede its state registration. Registering with the state does not give a mark owner significantly greater rights, but it does offer notice to potential infringers who bother to search the registration list, and in a few states may provide litigation benefits (for instance, attorney fees, presumptions of validity of the ownership claim, punitive damages).

Generally, marks used only within a state are limited to invoking state law protections, while marks used in two or more states (interstate), or across territorial or international boundaries, may use both national and state trademark laws. Simultaneously registering under both state and federal systems is a way to provide notice to both local and national competitors of claims of ownership of a mark. It also provides a choice of remedies and courts in which to sue. Also, because the laws of many states provide for punitive damages in situations where the Lanham Act does not, it is common for an infringement action to claim violations of both federal and state trademark statutes.

In addition to trademark infringement laws, most states have laws prohibiting unfair competition (business practices that confuse or deceive the consumer public). Often the facts that prove infringement of a mark will also prove unfair competition, thus most states offer at least two theories under which a business's mark will be protected.

Although the federal Lanham Act has generally replaced state law as the most important source of protection for marks on goods and services that move between states or across territorial or national borders, the state systems are still the only source of trademark or service mark protection for those businesses, nonprofit organizations, craftspersons, dance and artist groups, theater companies and restaurants that only operate on a local basis.

Finally, a number of states offer protection against dilution of a famous mark. This protects against the use of a famous mark in a context where consumers aren't likely to be confused but the use is likely to detract from the distinctiveness of the mark. Since the Federal Trademark Dilution Act was signed into law in January 1996, these state statutes are expected to diminish in importance.

A listing of state trademark agencies is provided in the Forms & Resources section at the end of this part of the book.

Related terms: dilution of mark; presumption of ownership; protection of marks under Lanham Act; unfair competition.

Statement of Use

See Allegation of Use for Intent-to-Use Application, with Declaration.

strong mark

A mark that effectively identifies the origin of a product or service rather than its characteristics is a strong (good) mark and a court can protect it from most or all uses by others. For example, the word "Cobalt" as a mark for a music recording label would be strong. As a word that means a metal and a blue color, its use on music is original and in no way descriptive. Thus it is distinctive and highly protectible. As a general rule, strong marks are made up of terms that are:

- arbitrary (Owl Ice Co. or Diesel, a Bookstore)
- coined (Rackafrax Wax)
- fanciful (Pea in a Pod Maternity Clothes), or
- suggestive (ShadeTree Restaurant).

Only strong marks are entitled to be listed on the federal Principal Register; however, even unregistered strong marks are entitled to wide protections. Courts can enjoin (prevent) almost any infringing use of a strong mark. The test is whether the allegedly infringing use is likely to cause consumer confusion. The stronger the mark, the greater the likelihood that its use by another will confuse consumers. Because a strong mark stands out as the mark of a particular service or product, any imitation of it would be confusing.

Descriptive marks are weak but they can make strong by advertising and consumer awareness (secondary meaning). The weaker the mark, the more reluctant a court will be to find it has been infringed, and the less protection it will receive.

Related terms: distinctive mark; Principal Register; related products and services; secondary meaning; weak mark.

suggestive mark

A suggestive mark is a lesser cousin of the family of distinctive marks, which also includes coined, arbitrary and fanciful marks. Suggestive marks qualify for the federal Principal Register, but are not as strong as their cousins. They escape being descriptive, however, because they suggest interesting qualities or concepts about a product or service, rather than directly describing it. Examples of suggestive marks are "Roach Motel" insect traps and "Accuride" tires.

Whether a mark is descriptive or suggestive is a highly subjective determination depending on how a consumer (or a judge) perceives the word in relation to the product or service. For example, the mark "Enduring" can be descriptive on lipstick, suggestive on a photographic service, and arbitrary/fanciful on ice cream.

As a general rule, the more brain power it takes to see the descriptive qualities underlying a suggestive mark, the greater the protection it will receive.

Related terms: descriptive mark; distinctive mark.

Supplemental Register

The federal Supplemental Register is a secondary list maintained by the U.S. Patent and Trademark Office for trademarks and service marks that do not qualify for the Principal Register. Any name or symbol may be placed on the Supplemental Register as long as it is in actual use in commerce that Congress may regulate and can in some way distinguish the applicant's goods or services from others.

Descriptive, surname and geographical term marks all qualify for the Supplemental Register. Generic terms do not qualify, since by definition a generic term calls to mind a type of product rather than a specific product. For instance, "Blue Jeans" means any pants made of blue denim, rather than a specific manufacturer's jeans. Marks that are barred from the Principal Register for reasons other than sheer descriptiveness are also barred from the Supplemental Register.

It is often difficult to prove infringement of a mark listed on the Supplemental Register, because such registration is an admission by the mark's owner that the mark is insufficiently distinctive to be placed on the Principal Register. Neither

Definitions

trademark nor unfair competition laws protect marks in any significant way unless consumer confusion is likely to result. Consumers are not likely to be confused by dual uses of any marks unless they are well-known or memorable—in other words, distinctive. As a result, marks on the Supplemental Register do not receive all the protections given to those on the Principal Register. Specifically, placement on the Supplemental Register does not:

- provide constructive notice of ownership or a presumption of ownership in the event of infringement litigation
- support a later claim of incontestability status
- imply the right to exclusive use of the mark, or
- allow the mark's owner to request exclusion of imports by the Bureau of Customs.

On the other hand, supplemental registration does offer some benefits such as:

- the right to use the circled "®" or "Reg. U.S. Pat. Off." abbreviation to discourage would-be infringers
- the ability to register the mark in countries that offer reciprocal trademark rights, and
- the right to obtain injunctive relief, money damages, treble damages and defendant's profits, in the unlikely event that the mark owner should win an infringement action (assuming that the mark bore the proper notice of registration).

An applicant should always apply for the Principal Register first. If rejected, an applicant can then apply for the Supplemental Register.

Related terms: commerce that Congress may regulate; prohibited and reserved marks under Lanham Act; unfair competition.

surnames as marks

The use of surnames (family names) is sometimes a controversial issue because some business owners believe they have an inalienable right to use their own name as a trademark. They are surprised to find they cannot register their name or that someone else has preempted the field. For example, anyone with the family name McDonald or Denny would not be able to obtain a trademark for restaurant services.

A mark that is primarily a surname does not qualify for placement on the Principal Register under the Lanham Act unless the name has become well-known as a mark through advertising or long use—that is, until it acquires a secondary meaning. Until then, surname marks can only be listed on the Supplemental Register. To register a mark that consists primarily of the surname of a living person (assuming the mark has acquired secondary meaning), the mark owner must have the namesake's written permission to register the mark.

Surnames are treated this way because theoretically everyone should be able to use his or her own name to promote their own business or product. In practice, however, as soon as someone establishes secondary meaning for a surname, it becomes off-limits for all uses that might cause consumer confusion. Del Monte, Disney, Spiegel and Johnson & Johnson's are just a few of the hundreds of surnames that have become effective marks over time.

A trademark is "primarily a surname" if the public would initially recognize it as a surname. However, a mark that is part surname and part distinctive mark may be registrable if the mark as a whole is distinctive, or if the surname is disclaimed as unregistrable material.

For example, two names may be combined (*Smith and Wesson*) or perhaps a name used with a design may be registrable. The reason for this is that when a surname is used with other matter, the "other matter" can affect public perception diminishing (or perhaps reinforcing) the impact of the surname. If a surname has a dictionary meaning (that is, it also functions as a word), it is treated like any other trademark. For example, *King* and *Bird* both have significance other than as a family name.

Whether registered or not, if a name mark has become well known, even a person with the same name may not be able to use that name as a mark. Courts do, however, sometimes permit two conflicting uses of the same surname with modifications to try to minimize consumer confusion. For instance, If McGuffy's bar faces a crosstown competitor by the same name, the second McGuffy may be forced to use a modifier, such as McGuffy's Cross-Town Bar.

A person who obviously tries to capitalize on his own name to take advantage of an identical famous mark (for example, Fred Ford opens Ford's Muffler Service) can be forced to give up all use of that name.

Related terms: composite mark; dilution of mark; disclaimer of unregistrable material; personal names as marks; right of publicity; Supplemental Register.

symbols and pictures as marks

See pictures and symbols used as marks; prohibited and reserved marks under Lanham Act.

TM

Although only marks that are federally registered can use the "®" symbol, any business that uses a mark can place the "™" symbol after it to publicly claim ownership of the mark. The "™" mark has no legal significance other than to notify the public that the mark owner views the words, design and/or symbol as a protectible trademark. It also may serve as evidence against a claim of innocent infringement by a junior user, and thus enhance the possibility of collecting damages.

Related terms: damages in trademark infringement cases; infringement action.

trade dress

Trade dress consists of all the various elements that are used to promote a product or service. For a product, trade dress may be the packaging, attendant displays and even the configuration of the product itself. For a service, it may be the decor or environment in which a service is provided—for example the distinctive decor of the Hard Rock Café restaurant chain.

As with other types of trademarks, trade dress can be registered with the PTO, and receive protection from the federal courts.

To receive protection:

- the trade dress must be inherently distinctive, unless it has acquired secondary meaning, and
- the junior use must cause a likelihood of consumer confusion.

For trade dress to be considered inherently distinctive, one court has required that it "must be unusual and memorable, conceptually separable from the product and likely to serve primarily as a designator of origin of the product." (*Duraco Products Inc. v. Joy Plastic Enterprises Ltd.,* 40 F.3d 1431 (3d Cir. 1994).)

The U.S. Supreme Court found that a Mexican restaurant chain's décor could be considered inherently distinctive because, in addition to murals and bright colored pottery, the chain also uses a specific indoor and outdoor decor based upon neon colored border stripes (primarily pink), distinctive outdoor umbrellas and a novel buffet style of service. (*Two Pesos, Inc. v. Taco Cabana, Inc.,* 505 U.S. 763 (1992).) However, the Supreme Court ruled that product designs such as the appearance of a line of children's clothing are not inherently distinctive and can only be protected if they acquire distinctiveness through sales or advertising. (*Wal-Mart Stores, Inc. v. Samara Brothers, Inc.,* 120 S. Ct. 1339, 146 L. Ed. 2d 182 (2000).)

Functional aspects of trade dress cannot be protected under trademark law. Only designs, shapes or other aspects of the product that were created strictly to promote the product or service are protectible trade dress.

EXAMPLE: Many liqueur bottles have a unique shape designed for advertising rather than for any particular function. The tall, tapered shape of the bottle

Definitions

used for Galliano is not necessary to hold the product, but helps to identify it and is therefore protectible as trade dress.

The trade dress aspect of packaging may be protected if a showing can be made that the average consumer would likely be confused as to product origin if another product is allowed to appear in similar dress. Legal protection is provided under the Lanham Act provisions relating to registered and unregistered marks.

Related terms: confusion of consumers; Lanham Act; trademark, defined; unfair competition; *WalMart v. Samara.*

trade name

Trade names are used to identify both nonprofit and for-profit business entities, whereas marks are used to identify products and services produced by such entities. Under the Lanham Act, a trade name is the name of any commercial firm, association, corporation, company or other organization capable of suing and being sued in a court of law.

Trade names cannot be registered under the trademark and service mark provisions of the Lanham Act. However, they are entitled to protection under the unfair competition provision of the Lanham Act. (15 United States Code, Section 1125.) They are also protected under state unfair competition statutes and court decisions, if the public is likely to be confused by the use of the same or a similar name.

Companies frequently use their trade names as trademarks or service marks for their products and services—that is, as designators of origin in their advertising and on the products. For instance, Apple Computer Corporation uses the trade name "Apple" as a trademark, and the McDonald's fast food chain uses "McDonald's" as a service mark. In these situations, the trade name may be registered in its capacity as a mark, and may receive additional protection under the Lanham Act's provisions applicable to infringement of marks.

Related terms: confusion of consumers; service mark; trademark, defined; unfair competition.

trademark, defined

Manufacturers and merchants use trademarks for the sole purpose of distinguishing their products from those of others in the marketplace, not for any functional purpose. A trademark usually consists of a word, phrase, logo or other graphic symbol. Examples of trademarks are Honda (automobiles), Post (cereals), Hewlett-Packard (computer equipment) and Quicken (software). A trademark is not limited to a brand name or logo. It can also consist of a distinctive shape, letters, numbers, package design, sound, smell, color or other aspects of a product that tend to promote it. Titles, character names or other distinctive features of movies, television, video games and radio programs can serve as trademarks when used to promote a product.

Many people use the term "trademark law" to refer broadly to all the laws that cover how businesses distinguish their products and services from those of others. This includes subjects like trade names, trade dress, commercial misappropriation, unfair competition, unfair business practices and palming off. The above definition, however, focuses on the narrower meaning of "trademark" as a product identifier.

Related terms: federal trademark registration; International Schedule of Classes of Goods and Services; service mark; trade dress.

trademark dilution
See dilution of mark.

trademark infringement action
See infringement action.

trademark owner
See ownership of mark in the U.S.

trademark protection
See protection of marks under Lanham Act; state trademark laws.

trademark search
A trademark search is an investigation to discover any potential conflicts between a proposed mark and an existing one. Preferably done before a proposed new mark is used, a trademark search reduces the possibility of inadvertently infringing a mark belonging to someone else.

Trademark searches are extremely important. If a chosen mark is already owned and/or registered by someone else, the proposed mark may have to be replaced. Obviously, no one wants to discover that a new mark infringes another mark and must be changed after time and expense have been put into marketing, advertising and implementing usage of the mark. In addition, if the earlier mark was registered under the Lanham Act prior to an infringing use, the infringing mark's owner may have to pay the mark's rightful owner any profits earned from the infringing use (defendant's profits).

Although the most thorough trademark searches are accomplished by professional search firms such as Thomson & Thomson, it is also possible to conduct a preliminary online trademark search to determine if a trademark is distinguishable from other federally registered trademarks. This can be accomplished using the PTO's free trademark databases, http://www.uspto.gov/tmdb/index.html and http://tess.uspto.gov/bin/gate.exe?f=tess&state=vfg9gj.1.1, both of which provide free access to records of federally registered marks or marks that are pending (applications undergoing examination at the PTO). Privately owned fee-based online trademark databases often provide more current PTO trademark information. Below are some private online search companies:

- **Saegis** (http://www.thomson-thomson.com) Saegis is the most comprehensive trademark searching service and provides access to all Trademarkscan databases (state, federal and international trademark databases), domain name databases, common law sources on the Internet and access to newly filed United States federal trademark applications. Saegis also provides access to *Dialog* services.
- **Dialog** (http://www.dialog.com) Dialog provides access to *Trademarkscan* databases including state and federal registration and some international trademarks and provides common law searching of news databases.
- **Micropatent** (http://www.micropatent.com) Micropatent provides access to federal and state trademarks through its *MarkSearch Pro* and *MarkSearch Pro State* databases.
- **Corporate Intelligence** (http://www.trademarks.com) Corporate Intelligence provides access to current federal registration information.
- **Trademark Register** (http://www.trademarkregister.com) Trademark Register provides access to current federal registration information.
- **Marks on Line** (http://www.marksonline.com) MarksonLine is a comprehensive trademark link site providing access to federal registration information and a listing of state and international trademark offices.
- **LEXIS/NEXIS** (http://www.lexis-nexis.com) LEXIS provides access to federal and state registrations and permits common law searching via NEXIS news services. The PTO utilizes NEXIS for its evaluations of descriptive and generic terms.

It's also a good idea to check the World Wide Web for a possible conflict with existing domain names as well as names of firms already doing business there. The report issued by the searcher notes all uses of identical or similar marks and the products or services on which they are used.

If the search fails to disclose use of the same or similar mark by anyone in a related business, the mark owner can feel free to use it and register it federally (if used in commerce), or with the state (if only used within one state).

Related terms: damages in trademark infringement cases; federal trademark registration; Internet domain names.

Trademark Trial and Appeal Board

An administrative arm of the U.S. Patent and Trademark Office, this body hears and decides disputes involving the registrability of, or conflicts between, marks. The Trademark Trial and Appeal Board consists of the Trademark Commissioner, the Deputy Commissioner, Assistant Commissioners and members appointed by the Trademark Commissioner.

Related terms: opposing and cancelling a trademark registration; U.S. Patent and Trademark Office (PTO).

unfair competition

Unfair competition is the legal umbrella that governs any commercial activity that tends to confuse, mislead or deceive the public about the sale of products or services. Such diverse activities as trademark infringement, trade name infringement, simulation of trade dress and packaging, palming off, false advertising, false designation of origin and theft of trade secrets all constitute unfair competition. Once a court defines any given activity as "unfair competition," it generally is authorized to enjoin (judicially prevent) further activity from occurring, and to award money damages.

Although most unfair competition law in the U.S. has been fashioned by legislatures and courts at the state level, Section 43(a) of the Lanham Act provides remedies for a broad range of activity generally described as unfair competition.

EXAMPLE: For two years, Henry Landberry has run a stand on a popular North Carolina beach selling "Landberry's Homemade Cherry Cider." One day, Paul Landberry (no relation), decides to establish a "Landberry's Homemade Peach Nectar" stand at the other end of the same beach, hoping to cash in on Henry's success. Even though Henry cannot register his mark (because it is primarily a surname that has not yet acquired secondary meaning), he can go to court to get Paul ordered (enjoined) to cease using the Landberry name

Definitions

because its use deceives consumers into thinking both products come from the same source. Henry can use the North Carolina unfair business practices act to do this, and possibly the unfair competition provision in Section 43(a) of the Lanham Act, if his service affects commerce that crosses state, territorial or international boundaries (for instance, assume the beach is famous and visited by people from all over the world).

State unfair competition laws provide judicial relief in situations where a mark or trade name has been copied or simulated, but where federal or state trademark infringement laws don't apply. Also, in most cases where trademark or service mark infringement is alleged, unfair competition claims are also raised as an alternative basis for judicial relief, in part because state law may offer the successful plaintiff the chance to get more money in the form of damages.

Related terms: false advertising; loss of mark; secondary meaning; unregistered mark, protection of.

unregistered mark, protection of

Unregistered distinctive marks are entitled under the Lanham Act to nearly as much protection from infringement as are registered ones. Federal registration does, however, make it easier to prove infringement and recover significant damages; thus strong marks are usually registered.

The federal unfair competition statute, Section 43(a) of the Lanham Act (15 United States Code, Section 1125), is the main mechanism for protecting unregistered marks and trade names in interstate commerce. It prohibits two basic types of commercial activity (which are, in most cases, also treated as unfair competition under state laws):

- the use of a mark or label to designate falsely the origin of any product or service, and
- the description of a product or service in false terms (that is, false advertising).

If the products or services carrying the false designation or description were used in interstate commerce, anyone who engages in such activity may be sued in federal court by a person or business who can prove resulting economic injury.

This type of unfair competition suit for infringement of unregistered marks is not technically a trademark infringement action due to the lack of registration. Such an action does, however, enable the owner of an unregistered mark to use the federal courts to stop the use of a similar mark that is likely to lead to consumer confusion. But the plaintiffs in such an action do not get some of the litigation benefits of federal registration, such as presumption of ownership, constructive notice and incontestability. They are, however, entitled to recover triple damages and possibly attorneys' fees in case of a willful infringement.

Related terms: false advertising; Lanham Act; registered mark; unfair competition.

unregistrable material

See disclaimer of unregistrable material.

unrelated goods and services

See related products and services.

U.S. Patent and Trademark Office (PTO)

The PTO is the federal governmental wing of the U.S. Department of Commerce that governs trademark registration. As a practical matter, the PTO determines the initial degree of protection that a mark is likely to receive in the courts. If registration of a mark is disputed, the Trademark Trial and Appeal Board, an arm of the PTO, will hold hearings to resolve the dispute.

Related terms: federal trademark registration; Official Gazette.

use it or lose it

See abandonment of mark.

use of mark

The term "use" has a special meaning when it comes to protection and registration under the Lanham Act. As a general rule, "use" means that the mark has been, is being or will be actually utilized in the marketplace to identify goods and services. This doesn't mean that the product or service actually has to be sold, as long as it is offered to the public under the mark in question.

A mark is being used for a service if the service is being marketed under the mark and the service can be legitimately delivered upon request by a consumer.

A mark is used for goods if the mark is place on the goods or on labels or tags attached to them, and the goods are shipped to a store for resale. However, sales made only for the purpose of getting a mark in use don't count.

Related terms: commerce; service mark; trademark, defined.

Wal-Mart Stores, Inc. v. Samara Brothers, Inc.

In *Wal-Mart Stores, Inc. v. Samara Brothers, Inc.*, 120 S. Ct. 1339, 146 L. Ed. 2d 182 (2000), the Supreme Court ruled that product designs, like colors, are not inherently distinctive. Samara created a line of children's clothing that featured one-piece seersucker outfits decorated with appliques of hearts, flowers, fruits, and the like. Wal-Mart authorized another clothing company to copy Samara's designs and then sold the knock-offs at a lower price than that offered by Samara. Samara sued Wal-Mart and a district court ordered Wal-Mart to pay Samara $1.6 million. The Supreme Court eventually overruled that decision, holding that the designs were not protected under trademark law because they were not distinctive. The result is that no matter how creative and clever a product design is made, it will only be protected under trademark law if the owner can demonstrate secondary meaning—that the public associates that product design with one source.

Related terms: trade dress.

weak mark

Trademark protection is based around a "strength" classification system. Strong trademarks are distinctive and are protectible. Weak trademarks are not distinctive. Weak marks cannot be registered or protected unless the trademark owner pumps up the mark with consumer awareness or "secondary meaning".

As a general rule, the more that the mark describes the goods or services (for example, *Shake 'n Bake*), the weaker or less distinguishable the mark. In some cases, if a mark is so descriptive that it is indistinguishable from the goods or service (for example, *Light Beer* for a beer low in calories) then it may be generic or too weak to ever obtain protection.

There are three common types of weak marks: descriptive marks that merely describe the nature, quality, characteristics, ingredients or origin of a product or service; geographic marks that describe the origin or location of the goods or services; and family names (surnames) that are used as trademarks. All weak marks are capable of becoming strong if secondary meaning can be demonstrated.

Related terms: descriptive mark; generic mark; geographic terms as marks; surnames as marks.

words in common use

See common use of mark; weak mark.

willful infringer

See deliberate infringer.

World Intellectual Property Organization (WIPO)

See international trademark rights.

World Wide Web and trademarks

See Internet, effect on trademark law.

Trademark Law

State Trademark Agencies and Statutes

A complete listing of state trademark office websites is provided at http://www. marksonline.com.

ALABAMA

Ala. Code § 8-12-6 to 8-12-19 (1984)
Secretary of State
Lands & Trademark Division
Room 528, State Office Building
Montgomery, AL 36130-7701
205-242-7200

ALASKA

Alaska Stat. 45.50.101 et seq.
Department of Commerce and
Economic Development
Corporations Section
P.O. Box D
Juneau, AK 99811
907-465-2530

ARIZONA

Ariz. Rev. Stat. 44-1441 et seq.
Office of Secretary of State
1700 W. Washington St.
Phoenix, AZ 85007
602-542-6187

ARKANSAS

Ark. Code A. §§ 4-71-101 thru 4-71-114
Secretary of State
State Capitol
Little Rock, AR 72201-1094
501-682-3405
FAX 501-682-3481

CALIFORNIA

Cal. Bus. & Prof. Code § 14200 et seq.
Secretary of State
Attn: Trademark Unit
State of California
1230 "J" Street
Sacramento, CA 95814
916-445-4984

COLORADO

Colo. Rev. Stat. §§ 7-70-102 to 7-70-113
Colorado Secretary of State
Corporations Office
1560 Broadway, Suite 200
Denver, CO 80202
303-894-2200

CONNECTICUT

Conn. Gen. Stats, 621a §§ 35-11a et seq.
and 622a §§ 35-18a et seq.
Secretary of State
Division of Corporations, UCC
& Trademarks
Attn: Trademarks
State of Connecticut
30 Trinity St.
Hartford, CT 06106
203-566-1721

DELAWARE

6 Del. C. § 3301 et seq.
State of Delaware
Department of State
Division of Corporations
Attn: Trademark Filings
Townsend Building
P.O. Box 898
Dover, DE 19903
302-739-3073

FLORIDA

Fla. Stat. ch. 495.011 et seq.
Corporation Records Bureau
Division of Corporations
Department of State
P.O. Box 6327
Tallahassee, FL 32301
904-488-9000

State Trademark Agencies and Statutes (continued)

GEORGIA

O.C.G.A. §§ 10-1-440 et seq.
Office of Secretary of State
State of Georgia
306 W. Floyd Towers
2 MLK Drive
Atlanta, GA 30334
404-656-2817

HAWAII

Hawaii Revised Stats. § 482 et seq.
Department of Commerce and
Consumer Affairs
Business Registration Division
1010 Richards St.
Honolulu, HA 96813
808-586-2727

IDAHO

Idaho Code §§ 48-501 et seq. (1979)
Secretary of State
Room 203
Statehouse
Boise, ID 83720
208-334-2300
FAX 208-334-2300

ILLINOIS

Ill. Rev. Stat. 1987, ch. 140, §§ 8-22
Illinois Secretary of State
The Index Dept., Trademark Division
111 E. Monroe
Springfield, IL 62756
217-524-0400

INDIANA

Indiana Code § 24-2-1-1 et seq.
Secretary of State of Indiana
Trademark Division
Rm 155, State House
Indianapolis, IN 46204
317-232-6540

IOWA

Iowa Code ch. 548
Secretary of State
Corporate Division, Hoover Bldg.
Des Moines, IA 50319
(515) 281-5204

KANSAS

K.S.A. § 81-111 et seq.
Secretary of State
Statehouse Bldg., Room 235N
Topeka, KS 66612
913-296-2034

KENTUCKY

K.R.S. 365.560 to 365.625
Office of Kentucky Secretary of State
Frankfort, KY 40601
502-564-2848

LOUISIANA

La. Rev. Stat. Ann. 51:211 et seq.
Secretary of State, Corporation Division
P.O. Box 94125
Baton Rouge, LA 70804-9125
504-925-4704

MAINE

10 M.R.S.A. § 1521-1532
State of Maine
Department of State
Division of Public Administration
State House Station 101
Augusta, ME 04333
207-287-3676

MARYLAND

Md. Ann. Code Art. 41, §§ 3-101 thru 3-114
Secretary of State
State House
Annapolis, MD 21404
410-974-5531

Forms

State Trademark Agencies and Statutes (continued)

MASSACHUSETTS

Mass. Laws Ann., Ch. 110 B, § 1-16.
Office of Secretary of State
Trademark Division
Rm. 1711
One Ashburton Place
Boston, MA 02108
617-727-8329

MICHIGAN

Mich. Compiled Laws §§ 429.31 et seq.
Michigan Department of Commerce
Corporations and Securities Bureau
Corporation Division
P.O. Box 30054
Lansing, MI 48909
517-334-6206

MINNESOTA

M.S.A. §§ 333.001-333.54
Secretary of State of Minnesota
Corporations Division
180 State Office Bldg.
St. Paul, MN 55155
612-296-9215

MISSISSIPPI

Miss. Code Ann., § 75-25-1 (1971)
Office of Secretary of State
P.O. Box 1350
Jackson, MS 39215
601-359-1350
FAX 601-359-1350

MISSOURI

Missouri Rev. Stat. 1978 §§ 417.005 et seq.
Office of Secretary of State
Attn: Trademark Division
P.O. Box 778
Jefferson City, MO 65101
314-751-4756

MONTANA

Mont. Code Ann., §§ 30-13-301 et seq. (1985)
Office of Secretary of State
Montana State Capitol
Helena, MT 59620
406-444-3665
FAX 406-444-3976

NEBRASKA

N.R.S. 1943, ch. 87 §§ 87.101 et seq.
Secretary of State, State Capitol Bldg.
Lincoln, NE 68509
402-471-4079

NEVADA

Nev. Rev. Stat. 600.240 et seq.
Secretary of State of Nevada
Capitol Complex
Carson City, NV 89710
702-687-5203

NEW HAMPSHIRE

RSA 350-A
Corporation Division
Office of Secretary of State
State House Annex
Concord, NH 03301
603-271-3244

NEW JERSEY

N. J. Stat. § 56:3-13.1 thru 56:3-13-15
Secretary of State
State House, CN-300
West State Street
Trenton, NJ 08625
609-984-1900

NEW MEXICO

N.M.S.A. 57-3-1 thru 57-3-14
Secretary of State
Capitol Bldg., Rm. 400
Santa Fe, NM 87503
505-827-3600

State Trademark Agencies and Statutes (continued)

NEW YORK

N. Y. Gen. Bus. Law § 360 et seq.
Secretary of State
Department of State
Miscellaneous Records
162 Washington Avenue
Albany, NY 12231
518-474-4770

NORTH CAROLINA

N.C.G.S. § 80-1 et seq.
Trademark Division
Office of Secretary of State
300 N. Salisbury Street
Raleigh, NC 27611
919-733-4161

NORTH DAKOTA

N.D.C.C., ch. 47-22
Secretary of State
State Capitol
Bismark, ND 58505
701-224-2900
FAX 701-328-2992

OHIO

ORC, ch. 1329.54 thru 1329.68
Secretary of State
Corporations Department
30 E. Broad St., 14th Floor
Columbus, OH 43215-0418
614-466-3910

OKLAHOMA

78 Okla. St. Ann. § 21 thru 34
Office of the Secretary of State
State of Oklahoma
101 State Capitol Bldg.
Oklahoma City, OK 73105
405-521-3911

OREGON

ORS 647.005 thru 647.105(i) and 647.115
Director, Corporation Division
Office of Secretary of State
158 12th Street N.E.
Salem, OR 97310-0210
503-986-2200

PENNSYLVANIA

54 Pa. Cons. Stat. Ann. § 1101-1126
Department of State
(Purdon 1987 Supp.)
Corporation Bureau
308 North Office Bldg.
Harrisburg, PA 17120
717-787-1997

PUERTO RICO

Title 10, Laws of P. R. Ann. § 191-195
Secretary of State of Puerto Rico
P.O. Box 3271
San Juan, PR 00904
809-722-2121, Ext. 337

RHODE ISLAND

R. I. Gen. Laws §§ 6-2-1 thru 6-2-18
Secretary of State
The Trademarks Division
100 No. Main St.
Providence, RI 02903
401-277-2340

SOUTH CAROLINA

S. C. Code Ann. § 39-15-120 et seq.
Office of Secretary of State
P.O. Box 11350
Columbia, SC 29211
803-734-2158

Forms

State Trademark Agencies and Statutes (continued)

SOUTH DAKOTA

SDCL ch 37-6
Secretary of State
State Capitol Bldg.
500 East Capitol
Pierre, SD 57501
605-773-4845

TENNESSEE

Tenn. Code Ann. § 47-25-501 et seq.
Secretary of State
Suite 500
James K. Polk Bldg.
Nashville, TN 37219
615-741-0531

TEXAS

Tex. Bus. & Com. Code § 16.01 thru 16.28
Secretary of State
Corporations Section, Trademark Office
Box 13697, Capitol Station
Austin, TX 78711-3697
512-463-5586

UTAH

U.C.A. 70-3-1 et seq.
Division of Corporations
& Commercial Code
Heber M. Wells Bldg.
160 E. 300 South St
Salt Lake City, UT 84111
801-530-6955

VIRGINIA

Va. Code § 59.1-77 et seq.
State Corp. Commission
Division of Securities and Retail Franchises
1220 Bank Street
Richmond, VA 23209
804-371-9733

VERMONT

§ 9 V.S.A. §§ 2521 thru 2532
Vermont Secretary of State
Corporations Division
Redstone Bldg., 26 Terrace St.
Mail: State Office Bldg.
Montpelier, VT 05602-2199
802-828-2386

WASHINGTON

R.C.W. 19.77.010 et seq.
Corporations Division
Office of Secretary of State
Republic Building—2nd Floor
505 E. Union St
Olympia, WA 98504
206-753-7120

WEST VIRGINIA

*W. Va. Code § 47-2-1- et seq. and
  § 47-3-1 et seq.*
Secretary of State
Corporations Division
State Capitol
Charleston, WV 25305
304-558-8000

WISCONSIN

Wisconsin Stat. § 132.01 et seq.
Secretary of State
Trademark Records
P.O. Box 7848
Madison, WI 53707
608-266-5653

WYOMING

W.S. §§ 40-1-101 et seq.
Office of Secretary of State
Corporation Division
Capitol Bldg.
Cheyenne, WY 82002
307-777-7378

Forms

Sample PrinTeas Application Based on Use in Commerce
(Two Classes) (Page 1)

PTO Form 1478 (Rev 9/98)
OMB Control #0651-0009 (Exp. 08/31/2001)

Trademark/Service Mark Application

* To the Commissioner for Trademarks *

\<DOCUMENT INFORMATION\>
\<TRADEMARK/SERVICEMARK APPLICATION\>
\<VERSION 1.22\>

\<APPLICANT INFORMATION\>
\<NAME\>   Pinstripes, Inc.
\<STREET\>   100 Main Street
\<CITY\>   Anytown
\<STATE\>   MO
\<COUNTRY\>   USA
\<ZIP/POSTAL CODE\>   12345

\<APPLICANT ENTITY INFORMATION\>
\<CORPORATION: STATE/COUNTRY OF INCORPORATION\>   Missouri

\<TRADEMARK/SERVICEMARK INFORMATION\>
\<MARK\>
\<TYPED FORM\>   No
~ Applicant requests registration of the above-identified trademark/service mark in the United States Patent and Trademark Office on the Principal Register established by the Act of July 5, 1946 (15 U.S.C. §1051 et seq., as amended). ~

\<BASIS FOR FILING AND GOODS/SERVICES INFORMATION\>
\<USE IN COMMERCE: SECTION 1(a)\>   Yes
~ Applicant is using or is using through a related company the mark in commerce on or in connection with the below-identified goods/services. (15 U.S.C. §1051(a), as amended.). Applicant attaches one SPECIMEN for each class showing the mark as used in commerce on or in connection with any item in the class of listed goods and/or services. ~
\<SPECIMEN DESCRIPTION\>   Issue of Magazine
\<INTERNATIONAL CLASS NUMBER\>   016
\<LISTING OF GOODS AND/OR SERVICES\>   Magazines in the field of business management
\<FIRST USE ANYWHERE DATE\>   01/15/1992
\<FIRST USE IN COMMERCE DATE\>   01/15/1992

\<BASIS FOR FILING AND GOODS/SERVICES INFORMATION\>
\<USE IN COMMERCE: SECTION 1(a)\>   Yes
~ Applicant is using or is using through a related company the mark in commerce on

Forms

Sample PrinTeas Application Based on Use in Commerce
(Two Classes) (Page 2)

or in connection with the below-identified goods/services. (15 U.S.C. §1051(a), as amended.). Applicant attaches one SPECIMEN for each class showing the mark as used in commerce on or in connection with any item in the class of listed goods and/or services. ~

<SPECIMEN DESCRIPTION>   Advertisement of services
<INTERNATIONAL CLASS NUMBER>   035
<LISTING OF GOODS AND/OR SERVICES>   Business management consulting services
<FIRST USE ANYWHERE DATE>   08/27/1990
<FIRST USE IN COMMERCE DATE>   08/27/1990

<FEE INFORMATION>
<TOTAL FEES PAID>   650
<NUMBER OF CLASSES PAID>   2
<NUMBER OF CLASSES>   2

<LAW OFFICE INFORMATION>
<E-MAIL ADDRESS FOR CORRESPONDENCE>   N/A

<SIGNATURE AND OTHER INFORMATION>
~ **PTO-Application Declaration**: The undersigned, being hereby warned that willful false statements and the like so made are punishable by fine or imprisonment, or both, under 18 U.S.C. §1001, and that such willful false statements may jeopardize the validity of the application or any resulting registration, declares that he/she is properly authorized to execute this application on behalf of the applicant; he/she believes the applicant to be the owner of the trademark/service mark sought to be registered, or, if the application is being filed under 15 U.S.C. §1051(b), he/she believes applicant to be entitled to use such mark in commerce; to the best of his/her knowledge and belief no other person, firm, corporation, or association has the right to use the mark in commerce, either in the identical form thereof or in such near resemblance thereto as to be likely, when used on or in connection with the goods/services of such other person, to cause confusion, or to cause mistake, or to deceive; and that all statements made of his/her own knowledge are true; and that all statements made on information and belief are believed to be true. ~

<SIGNATURE>_____ * please sign here*

<DATE>   _____
<NAME>   Andrew Luther
<TITLE>   President

Sample PrinTEAS Application Based on Intent to Use in Commerce (One Class) (Page 1)

PTO Form 1478 (Rev 9/98)
OMB Control #0651-0009 (Exp. 08/31/2001)

Trademark/Service Mark Application

* To the Commissioner for Trademarks *

<DOCUMENT INFORMATION>
<TRADEMARK/SERVICEMARK APPLICATION>
<VERSION 1.22>

<APPLICANT INFORMATION>
<NAME>   A-OK Software Development Group
<STREET>   100 Main Street
<CITY>   Anytown USA
<STATE>   MO
<COUNTRY>   USA
<ZIP/POSTAL CODE>   12345

<APPLICANT ENTITY INFORMATION>
<PARTNERSHIP: STATE/COUNTRY UNDER WHICH ORGANIZED>   Missouri
<NAME(S) OF GENERAL PARTNER(S) & CITIZENSHIP/INCORPORATION>   Mary Baker, USA
Jane Witlow, USA Harry Parker, USA

<TRADEMARK/SERVICEMARK INFORMATION>
<MARK>   THEORYTEC
<TYPED FORM>   Yes
~ Applicant requests registration of the above-identified trademark/service mark in the United
States Patent and Trademark Office on the Principal Register established by the Act of July 5,
1946 (15 U.S.C. §1051 et seq., as amended). ~

<BASIS FOR FILING AND GOODS/SERVICES INFORMATION>
<INTENT TO USE: SECTION 1(b)>   Yes
~ Applicant has a bona fide intention to use or use through a related company the mark in
commerce on or in connection with the below-identified goods/services. (15 U.S.C. §1051(b), as
amended.) ~
<INTERNATIONAL CLASS NUMBER>   009
<LISTING OF GOODS AND/OR SERVICES>   Computer software for analyzing sales statistics for retail
stores

<FEE INFORMATION>
<TOTAL FEES PAID>   325
<NUMBER OF CLASSES PAID>   1
<NUMBER OF CLASSES>   1

<LAW OFFICE INFORMATION>
<E-MAIL ADDRESS FOR CORRESPONDENCE>   N/A

<SIGNATURE AND OTHER INFORMATION>
~ **PTO-Application Declaration**: The undersigned, being hereby warned that willful false
statements and the like so made are punishable by fine or imprisonment, or both, under 18

Forms

Sample PrinTEAS Application Based on Intent to Use in Commerce (One Class) (Page 2)

U.S.C. §1001, and that such willful false statements may jeopardize the validity of the application or any resulting registration, declares that he/she is properly authorized to execute this application on behalf of the applicant; he/she believes the applicant to be the owner of the trademark/service mark sought to be registered, or, if the application is being filed under 15 U.S.C. §1051(b), he/she believes applicant to be entitled to use such mark in commerce; to the best of his/her knowledge and belief no other person, firm, corporation, or association has the right to use the mark in commerce, either in the identical form thereof or in such near resemblance thereto as to be likely, when used on or in connection with the goods/services of such other person, to cause confusion, or to cause mistake, or to deceive; and that all statements made of his/her own knowledge are true; and that all statements made on information and belief are believed to be true. ~

<SIGNATURE>_____ * please sign here*

<DATE>   _____
<NAME>   Mary Baker
<TITLE>   General Partner

Forms

Sample Drawing–PrinTEAS

Drawing Page
Date/Time Stamp: Monday, 09-18-2000 18:06:38 EDT

Applicant:
A-OK Software Development Group
100 Main Street
Anytown USA , MO 12345
USA
Date of First Use Anywhere: Intent-To-Use (Section 1(b))
Date of First Use In Commerce: Intent-To-Use (Section 1(b))

Goods and Services:
Computer software for analyzing sales statistics for retail stores

Mark:

THEORYTEC

Sample Drawing–Special Form
8 1/2" x 11" (21.6 cm x 27.9 cm)

APPLICANT'S NAME: Pinstripes Inc.

APPLICANT'S ADDRESS: 100 Main Street, Anytown, MO 12345

GOODS AND SERVICES: Magazines in the field of business
management; business management
consulting services

FIRST USE: Magazines (Class 16) January 15, 1992
Consulting (Class 35) August 27, 1990

FIRST USE IN COMMERCE: Magazines (Class 16) January 15, 1992
Consulting (Class 35) August 27, 1990

DESIGN: A zebra

Sample Specimens for Goods
(Label affixed to computer disc)

Forms

Sample Specimen for Services (Advertisement)

If better business management solutions are what you're after, then think of Pinstripes for consulting. We'll come wherever you are to offer a wide range of consulting services for diverse industries, including high-tech fields. You'll like the results, as well as our competitive price.

The more you get to know us, the more you'll realize that we're a best choice for consulting that can make a big difference. Call or write us.

Pinstripes, Inc.
(123) 456-7890
100 Main St. Anytown, MO 12345

Sample Specimen for Services
(Business card showing mark <u>and</u> reference to service)

BUSINESS MANAGEMENT CONSULTANTS

John Doe, *President*

100 Main Street
Anytown, MO 12345 U.S.A.
(123) 456-7890

Sample Specimen for Goods (Issue of Magazine)

April — May 1992 $2.00

PINSTRIPES

"The Magazine for the Business Professional"

IN THIS ISSUE

- Managing business in tough times.

- The need for quality in everything redefines priorities.

- Managing turned inside out.

- Employee ideas can really count.

- Our business report on Washington, D.C.

- Working together to create new markets and new jobs.

- In business to stay.

- Investing feature: future outlook on futures.

- "Pinstripes forever" (our humor column).

Trademark Law

The Lanham Act. The selected statutes set out below are all part of a larger statutory scheme known as the Lanham Act, found in Title 15 United States Code, Sections 1051-1127. Definitions of commonly used terms in the Lanham Act are at the end of this section, in § 1127.

§ 1051. (§ 1) Registration of trademarks

This statute describes the procedure for getting a mark placed on the principal trademark register.

(a) Trademarks used in commerce

(1) The owner of a trademark used in commerce may request registration of its trademark on the principal register hereby established by paying the prescribed fee and filing in the Patent and Trademark Office an application and a verified statement, in such form as may be prescribed by the Director, and such number of specimens or facsimiles of the mark as used as may be required by the Director.

(2) The application shall include specification of the applicant's domicile and citizenship, the date of the applicant's first use of the mark, the date of the applicant's first use of the mark in commerce, the goods in connection with which the mark is used, and a drawing of the mark.

(3) The statement shall be verified by the applicant and specify that—

(A) the person making the verification believes that he or she, or the juristic person in whose behalf he or she makes the verification, to be the owner of the mark sought to be registered;

(B) to the best of the verifier's knowledge and belief, the facts recited in the application are accurate;

(C) the mark is in use in commerce; and

(D) to the best of the verifier's knowledge and belief, no other person has the right to use such mark in commerce either in the identical form thereof or in such near resemblance thereto as to be likely, when used on or in connection with the goods of such other person, to cause confusion, or to cause mistake, or to deceive, except that, in the case of every application claiming concurrent use, the applicant shall—

(i) state exceptions to the claim of exclusive use; and

(ii) shall specify, to the extent of the verifier's knowledge—
    (I) any concurrent use by others;
    (II) the goods on or in connection with which and the areas in which each concurrent use exists;
    (III) the periods of each use; and
    (IV) the goods and area for which the applicant desires registration.

(4) The applicant shall comply with such rules or regulations as may be prescribed by the Director. The Director shall promulgate rules prescribing the requirements for the application and for obtaining a filing date herein.

(b) Trademarks intended for use in commerce

(1) A person who has a bona fide intention, under circumstances showing the good faith of such person, to use a trademark in commerce may request registration of its trademark on the principal register hereby established by paying the prescribed fee and filing in the Patent and Trademark Office an application and a verified statement, in such form as may be prescribed by the Director.

(2) The application shall include specification of the applicant's domicile and citizenship, the goods in connection with which the applicant has a bona fide intention to use the mark, and a drawing of the mark.

(3) The statement shall be verified by the applicant and specify—
    (A) that the person making the verification believes that he or she, or the juristic person in whose behalf he or she makes the verification, to be entitled to use the mark in commerce;
    (B) the applicant's bona fide intention to use the mark in commerce;
    (C) that, to the best of the verifier's knowledge and belief, the facts recited in the application are accurate; and
    (D) that, to the best of the verifier's knowledge and belief, no other person has the right to use such mark in commerce either in the identical form thereof or in such near resemblance thereto as to be likely, when used on or in connection with the goods of such other person, to cause confusion, or to cause mistake, or to deceive.

    Except for applications filed pursuant to section 44 [15 USC § 1126], no mark shall be registered until the applicant has met the requirements of subsections (c) and (d) of this section.

(4) The applicant shall comply with such rules or regulations as may be prescribed by the Director. The Director shall promulgate rules prescribing the requirements for the application and for obtaining a filing date herein.

(c) Amendment of application under subsection (b) to conform to requirements under subsection (a)

At any time during examination of an application filed under subsection (b), an applicant who has made use of the mark in commerce may claim the benefits of such use for purposes of this Act, by amending his or her application to bring it into conformity with the requirements of subsection (a).

(d) Verified statement that trademark is used in commerce.

(1) Within six months after the date on which the notice of allowance with respect to a mark is issued under section 13(b)(2) 15 USC § 1063(b)(2)] to an applicant under subsection (b) of this section, the applicant shall file in the Patent and Trademark Office, together with such number of specimens or facsimiles of the mark as used in commerce as may be required by the Director and payment of the prescribed fee, a verified statement that the

mark is in use in commerce and specifying the date of the applicant's first use of the mark in commerce and,[,] those goods or services specified in the notice of allowance on or in connection with which the mark is used in commerce. Subject to examination and acceptance of the statement of use, the mark shall be registered in the Patent and Trademark Office, a certificate of registration shall be issued for those goods or services recited in the statement of use for which the mark is entitled to registration, and notice of registration shall be published in the Official Gazette of the Patent and Trademark Office. Such examination may include an examination of the factors set forth in subsections (a) through (e) of section 2 [15 USC § 1052]. The notice of registration shall specify the goods or services for which the mark is registered.

(2) The Director shall extend, for one additional 6-month period, the time for filing the statement of use under paragraph (1), upon written request of the applicant before the expiration of the 6-month period provided in paragraph (1). In addition to an extension under the preceding sentence, the Director may, upon a showing of good cause by the applicant, further extend the time for filing the statement of use under paragraph (1) for periods aggregating not more than 24 months, pursuant to written request of the applicant made before the expiration of the last extension granted under this paragraph. Any request for an extension under this paragraph shall be accompanied by a verified statement that the applicant has a continued bona fide intention to use the mark in commerce and specifying those goods or services identified in the notice of allowance on or in connection with which the applicant has a continued bona fide intention to use the mark in commerce. Any request for an extension under this paragraph shall be accompanied by payment of the prescribed fee. The Director shall issue regulations setting forth guidelines for determining what constitutes good cause for purposes of this paragraph.

(3) The Director shall notify any applicant who files a statement of use of the acceptance or refusal thereof and, if the statement of use is refused, the reasons for the refusal. An applicant may amend the statement of use.

(4) The failure to timely file a verified statement of use under paragraph (1) or an extension request under paragraph (2) shall result in abandonment of the application, unless it can be shown to the satisfaction of the Director that the delay in responding was unintentional, in which case the time for filing may be extended, but for a period not to exceed the period specified in paragraphs (1) and (2) for filing a statement of use.

(e) Designation of resident for service of process and notices.

If the applicant is not domiciled in the United States he shall designate by a written document filed in the Patent and Trademark Office the name and address of some person resident in the United States on whom may be served notices or process in proceedings affecting the mark. Such notices or process may be served upon the person so designated by leaving with him or mailing to him a copy thereof at the address specified in the last designation so filed. If the person so designated cannot be found at the address given in the last designation, such notice or process may be served upon the Director.

§ 1052. (§ 2) Trademarks registrable on principal register; concurrent registration

This statute describes the specific requirements for a mark to be eligible for placement on the principal register. Namely, the statute:

- *requires that a mark be distinctive*
- *sets out the factors that may be used to disqualify a distinctive mark from placement on the principal register*

- *authorizes concurrent registration for marks that are the same or similar to one another if no customer confusion is likely to result*
- *authorizes registration of a mark on the basis of secondary meaning, and*
- *allows the trademark Director to presume secondary meaning if the mark has been in substantially exclusive and continuous use for five years prior to the date of application for registration on the principal register.*

No trademark by which the goods of the applicant may be distinguished from the goods of others shall be refused registration on the principal register on account of its nature unless it—

(a) Consists of or comprises immoral, deceptive, or scandalous matter; or matter which may disparage or falsely suggest a connection with persons, living or dead, institutions, beliefs, or national symbols, or bring them into contempt, or disrepute; or a geographical indication which, when used on or in connection with wines or spirits, identifies a place other than the origin of the goods and is first used on or in connection with wines or spirits by the applicant on or after one year after the date on which the WTO Agreement (as defined in section 2(9) of the Uruguay Round Agreements Act [19 USC § 3501(9)]) enters into force with respect to the United States.

(b) Consists of or comprises the flag or coat of arms or other insignia of the United States, or of any State or municipality, or of any foreign nation, or any simulation thereof.

(c) Consists of or comprises a name, portrait, or signature identifying a particular living individual except by his written consent, or the name, signature, or portrait of a deceased President of the United States during the life of his widow, if any, except by the written consent of the widow.

(d) Consists of or comprises a mark which so resembles a mark registered in the Patent and Trademark Office, or a mark or trade name previously used in the United States by another and not abandoned, as to be likely, when used on or in connection with the goods of the applicant, to cause confusion, or to cause mistake, or to deceive: *Provided,* That if the Director determines that confusion, mistake, or deception is not likely to result from the continued use by more than one person of the same or similar marks under conditions and limitations as to the mode or place of use of the marks or the goods on or in connection with which such marks are used, concurrent registrations may be issued to such persons when they have become entitled to use such marks as a result of their concurrent lawful use in commerce prior to (1) the earliest of the filing dates of the applications pending or of any registration issued under this chapter; (2) July 5, 1947, in the case of registrations previously issued under the Act of March 3, 1881, or February 20, 1905, and continuing in full force and effect on that date; or (3) July 5, 1947, in the case of applications filed under the Act of February 20, 1905, and registered after July 5, 1947. Use prior to the filing date of any pending application or a registration shall not be required when the owner of such application or registration consents to the grant of a concurrent registration to the applicant. Concurrent registrations may also be issued by the Director when a court of competent jurisdiction has finally determined that more than one person is entitled to use the same or similar marks in commerce. In issuing concurrent registrations, the Director shall prescribe conditions and limitations as to the mode or place of use of the mark or the goods on or in connection with which such mark is registered to the respective persons.

(e) Consists of a mark which (1) when used on or in connection with the goods of the applicant is merely descriptive or deceptively misdescriptive of them, (2) when used on or in connection with the goods of the applicant is primarily geographically descriptive of them, except as indications of regional origin may be registrable under section 4 [15 USC § 1054], (3) when used on or in connection with the goods of the applicant is primarily geographically deceptively misdescriptive of them, (4) is primarily merely a surname, or (5) comprises any matter that, as a whole, is functional.

(f) Except as expressly excluded in subsections (a), (b), (c), (d), (e)(3), and (e)(5) of this section, nothing herein shall prevent the registration of a mark used by the applicant which has become distinctive of the applicant's goods in commerce. The Director may accept as prima facie evidence that the mark has become distinctive, as used on or in connection with the applicant's goods in commerce, proof of substantially exclusive and continuous use thereof as a mark by the applicant in commerce for the five years before the date on which the claim of distinctiveness is made. Nothing in this section shall prevent the registration of a mark which, when used on or in connection with the goods of the applicant, is primarily geographically deceptively misdescriptive of them, and which became distinctive of the applicant's goods in commerce before the date of the enactment of the North American Free Trade Agreement Implementation Act [enacted Dec. 8, 1993].

A mark which when used would cause dilution under section 43(c) [15 USC § 1125(c)] may be refused registration only pursuant to a proceeding brought under section 13 [15 USC § 1063]. A registration for a mark which when used would cause dilution under section 43(c) [15 USC §1125(c)] may be canceled pursuant to a proceeding brought under either section 14 [15 USC §1064] or section 24 [15 USC §1092].

§ 1053. (§ 3) Service marks registrable

This statute applies those laws governing registration and protection of trademarks to service marks.

Subject to the provisions relating to the registration of trademarks, so far as they are applicable, service marks shall be registrable, in the same manner and with the same effect as are trademarks, and when registered they shall be entitled to the protection provided in this chapter in the case of trademarks. Applications and procedure under this section shall conform as nearly as practicable to those prescribed for the registration of trademarks.

§ 1056. (§ 6) Disclaimer of unregistrable matter

This statute governs when an applicant for trademark registration may be required by the PTO to give up any ownership claims to certain words or other components of the mark as a condition of registration. Section b states that any disclaimer of a component will not prevent the applicant from later applying for a mark on the disclaimed material under the secondary meaning rule.

(a) Compulsory and voluntary disclaimers

The Director may require the applicant to disclaim an unregistrable component of a mark otherwise registrable. An applicant may voluntarily disclaim a component of a mark sought to be registered.

(b) Prejudice of rights

No disclaimer, including those made under subsection (e) of section 1057 of this title shall prejudice or affect the applicant's or registrant's rights then existing or thereafter arising in the disclaimed matter, or his right of registration on another application if the disclaimed matter be or shall have become distinctive of his goods or services.

§ 1057. (§ 7) Certificates of registration

This statute addresses the following:
  * *describes the certificate that is issued when a mark is placed on the principal register*

- *provides that the certificate shall be considered proof of ownership if ownership later becomes an issue, and*
- *provides that the date of the trademark application shall be considered proof of the date of first use for the purpose of any dispute about ownership, provided that the mark is subsequently placed on the principal register.*
- *Sections d–h of § 1057 which govern such issues as the issuance to assignee, surrender, cancellation, or amendment of the application by registrant and the use of copies of Patent and Trademark Office records as evidence*

(a) Issuance and form

Certificates of registration of marks registered upon the principal register shall be issued in the name of the United States of America, under the seal of the Patent and Trademark Office, and shall be signed by the Director or have his signature placed thereon, and a record thereof shall be kept in the Patent and Trademark Office. The registration shall reproduce the mark, and state that the mark is registered on the principal register under this chapter, the date of the first use of the mark, the date of the first use of the mark in commerce, the particular goods or services for which it is registered, the number and date of the registration, the term thereof, the date on which the application for registration was received in the Patent and Trademark Office, and any conditions and limitations that may be imposed in the registration.

(b) Certificate as prima facie evidence

A certificate of registration of a mark upon the principal register provided by this chapter shall be prima facie evidence of the validity of the registered mark and of the registration of the mark, of the registrant's ownership of the mark, and of the registrant's exclusive right to use the registered mark in commerce on or in connection with the goods or services specified in the certificate, subject to any conditions or limitations stated in the certificate.

(c) Application to register mark considered constructive use

Contingent on the registration of a mark on the principal register provided by this chapter, the filing of the application to register such mark shall constitute constructive use of the mark, conferring a right of priority, nationwide in effect, on or in connection with the goods or services specified in the registration against any other person except for a person whose mark has not been abandoned and who, prior to such filing—

(1) has used the mark;

(2) has filed an application to register the mark which is pending or has resulted in registration of the mark; or

(3) has filed a foreign application to register the mark on the basis of which he or she has acquired a right of priority, and timely files an application under section 1126(d) of this title to register the mark which is pending or has resulted in registration of the mark.

(d) Issuance to assignee

A certificate of registration of a mark may be issued to the assignee or the applicant, but the assignment must first be recorded in the Patent and Trademark Office. In case of change of ownership the Director shall, at the request of the owner and upon a proper showing and the payment of the prescribed fee, issue to such assignee a new certificate of registration of the said mark in the name of such assignee, and for the unexpired part of original period.

§ 1058. (§ 8) Duration of registration

This statute sets the trademark registration period for ten years, subject to renewal, provided that an affidavit is filed between the fifth and sixth year of use showing that the mark is still in use or that good reasons exist for its nonuse.

(a) Each registration shall remain in force for 10 years, except that the registration of any mark shall be canceled by the Director for failure to comply with the provisions of subsection (b) of this section, upon the expiration of the following time periods, as applicable:

   (1) For registrations issued pursuant to the provisions of this Act, at the end of 6 years following the date of registration.

   (2) For registrations published under the provisions of section 12(c) [15 USCS §1062(c)], at the end of 6 years following the date of publication under such section.

   (3) For all registrations, at the end of each successive 10-year period following the date of registration.

(b) During the 1-year period immediately preceding the end of the applicable time period set forth in subsection (a), the owner of the registration shall pay the prescribed fee and file in the Patent and Trademark Office—

   (1) an affidavit setting forth those goods or services recited in the registration on or in connection with which the mark is in use in commerce and such number of specimens or facsimiles showing current use of the mark as may be required by the Director; or

   (2) an affidavit setting forth those goods or services recited in the registration on or in connection with which the mark is not in use in commerce and showing that any such nonuse is due to special circumstances which excuse such nonuse and is not due to any intention to abandon the mark.

(c) (1) The owner of the registration may make the submissions required under this section within a grace period of 6 months after the end of the applicable time period set forth in subsection (a). Such submission is required to be accompanied by a surcharge prescribed by the Director.

   (2) If any submission filed under this section is deficient, the deficiency may be corrected after the statutory time period and within the time prescribed after notification of the deficiency. Such submission is required to be accompanied by a surcharge prescribed by the Director.

(d) Special notice of the requirement for affidavits under this section shall be attached to each certificate of registration and notice of publication under section 12(c) [15 USCS § 1062(c)].

(e) The Director shall notify any owner who files 1 of the affidavits required by this section of the Director's acceptance or refusal thereof and, in the case of a refusal, the reasons therefor.

(f) If the registrant is not domiciled in the United States, the registrant shall designate by a written document filed in the Patent and Trademark Office the name and address of some person resident in the United States on whom may be served notices or process in proceedings affecting the mark. Such notices or process may be served upon the person so designated by leaving with that person or mailing to that person a copy thereof at the address specified in the last designation so filed. If the person so designated cannot be found at the address given in the last designation, such notice or process may be served upon the Director.

§ 1059. (§ 9) Renewal of registration

This statute sets out the procedure for renewing a trademark registration.

(a) Period of renewal; time for renewal

Subject to the provisions of section 8 [15 USCS § 1058], each registration may be renewed for periods of 10 years at the end of each successive 10-year period following the date of registration upon payment of the prescribed fee and the filing of a written application, in such form as may be prescribed by the Director. Such application may be made at any time within 1 year before the end of each successive 10-year period for which the registration was issued or renewed, or it may be made within a grace period of 6 months after the end of each successive 10-year period, upon payment of a fee and surcharge prescribed therefor. If any application filed under this section is deficient, the deficiency may be corrected within the time prescribed after notification of the deficiency, upon payment of a surcharge prescribed therefor.

(b) Notification of refusal of renewal

If the Director refuses to renew the registration, the Director shall notify the registrant of the Director's refusal and the reasons therefor.

(c) Registrant for renewal not domiciled in the United States

If the registrant is not domiciled in the United States, the registrant shall designate by a written document filed in the Patent and Trademark Office the name and address of some person resident in the United States on whom may be served notices or process in proceedings affecting the mark. Such notices or process may be served upon the person so designated by leaving with that person or mailing to that person a copy thereof at the address specified in the last designation so filed. If the person so designated cannot be found at the address given in the last designation, such notice or process may be served upon the Director.

§ 1060. (§ 10) Assignment of mark; execution; recording; purchaser without notice

This statute sets out the conditions under which a mark that has been, or is to be, registered may be sold (assigned) to another party.

(a) A registered mark or a mark for which an application to register has been filed shall be assignable with the good will of the business in which the mark is used, or with that part of the good will of the business connected with the use of and symbolized by the mark. Notwithstanding the preceding sentence, no application to register a mark under section 1(b) [15 USCS §1051(b)] shall be assignable prior to the filing of an amendment under section 1(c) [15 USCS §1051(c)] to bring the application into conformity with section 1(a) [15 USCS §1051(a)] or the filing of the verified statement of use under section 1(d) [15 USCS §1051(d)], except for an assignment to a successor to the business of the applicant, or portion thereof, to which the mark pertains, if that business is ongoing and existing. In any assignment authorized by this section, it shall not be necessary to include the good will of the business connected with the use of and symbolized by any other mark used in the business or by the name or style under which the business is conducted. Assignments shall be by instruments in writing duly executed. Acknowledgment shall be prima facie evidence of the execution of an assignment, and when the prescribed information reporting the assignment is recorded in the Patent and Trademark Office, the record shall be prima facie evidence of execution. An assignment shall be void against any subsequent purchaser for valuable consideration without notice, unless the prescribed information reporting the assignment is recorded in the Patent and Trademark Office within 3 months after the date of the subsequent purchase or prior to the subsequent purchase. The Patent and Trademark Office shall maintain a record of information on assignments, in such form as may be prescribed by the Director.

(b) An assignee not domiciled in the United States shall designate by a written document filed in the Patent and Trademark Office the name and address of some person resident in the United States on whom may be served notices or process in proceedings affecting the mark. Such notices or process may be served upon the person so designated by leaving with that person or mailing to that person a copy thereof at the address specified in the last designation so filed. If the person so designated cannot be found at the address given in the last designation, such notice or process may be served upon the Director.

§ 1062. (§ 12) Publication

This statute provides for the publication of a mark for public comment after the PTO has determined that it otherwise qualifies for placement on the principal register. It also sets up a reapplication procedure to be followed if the published mark is found not to be entitled to registration (because of information received as a result of the publication).

(a) Examination and publication

Upon the filing of an application for registration and payment of the prescribed fee, the Director shall refer the application to the examiner in charge of the registration of marks, who shall cause an examination to be made and, if on such examination it shall appear that the applicant is entitled to registration, or would be entitled to registration upon the acceptance of the statement of use required by section 1051(d) of this title, the Director shall cause the mark to be published in the Official Gazette of the Patent and Trademark Office: *Provided,* That in the case of an applicant claiming concurrent use, or in the case of an application to be placed in an interference as provided for in section 1066 of this title, the mark, if otherwise registrable, may be published subject to the determination of the rights of the parties to such proceedings.

(b) Refusal of registration; amendment of application; abandonment

If the applicant is found not entitled to registration, the examiner shall advise the applicant thereof and of the reasons therefor. The applicant shall have a period of six months in which to reply or amend his application, which shall then be re-examined. This procedure may be repeated until (1) the examiner finally refuses registration of the mark or (2) the applicant fails for a period of six months to reply or amend or appeal, whereupon the application shall be deemed to have been abandoned, unless it can be shown to the satisfaction of the Director that the delay in responding was unavoidable, whereupon such time may be extended.

(c) Republication of marks registered under prior acts

A registrant of a mark registered under the provisions of the Act of March 3, 1881, or the Act of February 20, 1905, may, at any time prior to the expiration of the registration thereof, upon the payment of the prescribed fee file with the Director an affidavit setting forth those goods stated in the registration on which said mark is in use in commerce and that the registrant claims the benefits of this chapter for said mark. The Director shall publish notice thereof with a reproduction of said mark in the Official Gazette, and notify the registrant of such publication and of the requirement for the affidavit of use or nonuse as provided for in subsection (b) of section 1058 of this title. Marks published under this subsection shall not be subject to the provisions of section 1063 of this title.

§ 1063. (§ 13) Opposition to registration

This statute sets out the procedure to be followed if a person or organization believes that a mark published for comment should not be registered.

(a) Any person who believes that he would be damaged by the registration of a mark upon the principal register may, upon payment of the prescribed fee, file an opposition in the

Patent and Trademark Office, stating the grounds therefor, within thirty days after the publication under subsection (a) of section 1062 of this title of the mark sought to be registered. Upon written request prior to the expiration of the thirty-day period, the time for filing opposition shall be extended for an additional thirty days, and further extensions of time for filing opposition may be granted by the Director for good cause when requested prior to the expiration of an extension. The Director shall notify the applicant of each extension of the time for filing opposition. An opposition may be amended under such conditions as may be prescribed by the Director.

(b) Unless registration is successfully opposed—

　(1) a mark entitled to registration on the principal register based on an application filed under section 1051(a) or pursuant to section 1126 of this title shall be registered in the Patent and Trademark Office, a certificate of registration shall be issued, and notice of the registration shall be published in the Official Gazette of the Patent and Trademark Office; or

　(2) a notice of allowance shall be issued to the applicant if the applicant applied for registration under section 1051(b) of this title.

§ 1064. (§ 14) Cancellation of registration

This statute explains when a mark registration may be canceled, and specifically defines when a certification mark may be canceled and when a mark may be canceled on the ground that it has become generic.

A petition to cancel a registration of a mark, stating the grounds relied upon, may, upon payment of the prescribed fee, be filed as follows by any person who believes that he is or will be damaged by the registration of a mark on the principal register established by this chapter, or under the Act of March 3, 1881, or the Act of February 20, 1905:

(1) Within five years from the date of the registration of the mark under this chapter.

(2) Within five years from the date of publication under section 1062(c) of this title of a mark registered under the Act of March 3, 1881, or the Act of February 20, 1905.

(3) At any time if the registered mark becomes the generic name for the goods or services, or a portion thereof, for which it is registered, or has been abandoned, or its registration was obtained fraudulently or contrary to the provisions of section 1054 of this title or of subsection (a), (b), or (c) of section 1052 of this title for a registration under this chapter, or contrary to similar prohibitory provisions of such prior Acts for a registration under such Acts, or if the registered mark is being used by, or with the permission of, the registrant so as to misrepresent the source of the goods or services on or in connection with which the mark is used. If the registered mark becomes the generic name for less than all of the goods or services for which it is registered, a petition to cancel the registration for only those goods or services may be filed. A registered mark shall not be deemed to be the generic name of goods or services solely because such mark is also used as a name of or to identify a unique product or service. The primary significance of the registered mark to the relevant public rather than purchaser motivation shall be the test for determining whether the registered mark has become the generic name of goods or services on or in connection with which it has been used.

(4) At any time if the mark is registered under the Act of March 3, 1881, or the Act of February 20, 1905, and has not been published under the provisions of subsection (c) of section 1062 of this title.

(5) At any time in the case of a certification mark on the ground that the registrant (A) does not control, or is not able legitimately to exercise control over, the use of such mark, or (B) engages in the production or marketing of any goods or services to which the certification mark is applied, or (C) permits the use of the certification mark for purposes other than to certify, or (D) discriminately refuses to certify or to continue to certify the goods or services of any person who maintains the standards or conditions which such mark certifies: *Provided*, That the Federal Trade Commission may apply to cancel on the grounds specified in paragraphs (3) and (5) of this section any mark registered on the principal register established by this chapter, and the prescribed fee shall not be required.

§ 1065. (§ 15) Incontestability of right to use mark under certain conditions

This statute defines the reasons that may be used to attack the validity of a mark that has been in continuous use for at least five years after its registration. Unless one of these reasons is present, the statute provides that the mark shall be considered incontestable.

Except on a ground for which application to cancel may be filed at any time under paragraphs (3) and (5) of section 1064 of this title, and except to the extent, if any, to which the use of a mark registered on the principal register infringes a valid right acquired under the law of any State or Territory by use of a mark or trade name continuing from a date prior to the date of registration under this chapter of such registered mark, the right of the registrant to use such registered mark in commerce for the goods or services on or in connection with which such registered mark has been in continuous use for five consecutive years subsequent to the date of such registration and is still in use in commerce, shall be incontestable: *Provided,* That—

(1) there has been no final decision adverse to registrant's claim of ownership of such mark for such goods or services, or to registrant's right to register the same or to keep the same on the register; and

(2) there is no proceeding involving said rights pending in the Patent and Trademark Office or in a court and not finally disposed of; and

(3) an affidavit is filed with the Director within one year after the expiration of any such five-year period setting forth those goods or services stated in the registration on or in connection with which such mark has been in continuous use for such five consecutive years and is still in use in commerce, and the other matters specified in paragraphs (1) and (2) of this section; and

(4) no incontestable right shall be acquired in a mark which is the generic name for the goods or services or a portion thereof, for which it is registered.

Subject to the conditions above specified in this section, the incontestable right with reference to a mark registered under this chapter shall apply to a mark registered under the Act of March 3, 1881, or the Act of February 20, 1905, upon the filing of the required affidavit with the Director within one year after the expiration of any period of five consecutive years after the date of publication of a mark under the provisions of subsection (c) of section 1062 of this title.

The Director shall notify any registrant who files the above-prescribed affidavit of the filing thereof.

§ 1072. (§ 22) Registration as constructive notice of claim of ownership

This statute provides that registration of a mark on the principal register is the equivalent of giving notice to all later users that ownership of the mark is claimed by the registrant.

Registration of a mark on the principal register provided by this chapter or under the Act of March 3, 1881, or the Act of February 20, 1905, shall be constructive notice of the registrant's claim of ownership thereof.

§ 1091. (§ 23) Supplemental register

Comment: This statute establishes a supplemental register for the purpose of registering marks that are insufficiently distinctive to warrant placement on the principal register. In addition, it sets out the procedures for applying to have a mark placed on the supplemental register.

(a) Marks registrable

In addition to the principal register, the Director shall keep a continuation of the register provided in paragraph (b) of section 1 of the Act of March 19, 1920, entitled "An Act to give effect to certain provisions of the convention for the protection of trademarks and commercial names, made and signed in the city of Buenos Aires, in the Argentine Republic, August 20, 1910, and for other purposes," to be called the supplemental register. All marks capable of distinguishing applicant's goods or services and not registrable on the principal register provided in this chapter, except those declared to be unregistrable under subsections (a), (b), (c), (d), and (e)(3) of section 1052 of this title, which are in lawful use in commerce by the owner, thereof, on or in connection with any goods or services may be registered on the supplemental register upon the payment of the prescribed fee and compliance with the provisions of subsections (a) and (e) of section 1051 of this title so far as they are applicable. Nothing in this section shall prevent the registration on the supplemental register of a mark, capable of distinguishing the applicant's goods or services and not registrable on the principal register under this chapter, that is declared to be unregistrable under section 1052(e)(3) of this title, if such mark has been in lawful use in commerce with any goods or services, since before the date of enactment of the North American Treaty Implementation Act (12/8/1993).

(b) Application and proceeding for registration

Upon the filing of an application for registration on the supplemental register and payment of the prescribed fee the Director shall refer the application to the examiner in charge of the registration of marks, who shall cause an examination to be made and if on such examination it shall appear that the applicant is entitled to registration, the registration shall be granted. If the applicant is found not entitled to registration the provisions of subsection (b) of section 1062 of this title shall apply.

(c) Nature of mark

For the purposes of registration on the supplemental register, a mark may consist of any trademark, symbol, label, package, configuration of goods, name, word, slogan, phrase, surname, geographical name, numeral, or device or any combination of any of the foregoing, but such mark must be capable of distinguishing the applicant's goods or services.

§ 1092. (§ 24) Publication; not subject to opposition; cancellation

This statute establishes a procedure for canceling the registration of a mark on the supplemental register.

Marks for the supplemental register shall not be published for or be subject to opposition, but shall be published on registration in the Official Gazette of the Patent and Trademark Office. Whenever any person believes that he is or will be damaged by the registration of a mark on this register he may at any time, upon payment of the prescribed fee and the filing of a petition stating the ground therefor, apply to the Director to cancel such registration. The Director shall refer such application to the Trademark Trial and Appeal Board which shall give notice thereof to the registrant. If it is found after a hearing before the Board that the registrant is not entitled to registration thereof, or that the mark has been abandoned, the registration shall be canceled by the Director. However, no final judgment shall be entered in favor of an applicant under section 1051(b) of this title before the mark is registered, if such applicant cannot prevail without establishing constructive use pursuant to section 1057(c) of this title.

§ 1111. (§ 29) Notice of registration; display with mark; recovery of profits and damages in infringement suit

This statute authorizes a trademark owner to use the trademark registration symbol (®) in conjunction with a mark when the mark has been placed on either the principal or the supplemental trademark register. It also requires use of that symbol as a condition of receiving certain types of damages in a trademark infringement lawsuit.

Notwithstanding the provisions of section 1072 of this title, a registrant of a mark registered in the Patent and Trademark Office, may give notice that his mark is registered by displaying with the mark the words "Registered in U.S. Patent and Trademark Office" or "Reg. U.S. Pat. & Tm. Off." or the letter R enclosed within a circle, thus ®; and in any suit for infringement under this chapter by such a registrant failing to give such notice of registration, no profits and no damages shall be recovered under the provisions of this chapter unless the defendant had actual notice of the registration.

§ 1112. (§ 30) Classification of goods and services; registration in plurality of classes

This statute allows the PTO to accept the registration of a mark in more than one class, but requires that an extra fee be paid for each additional class.

The Director may establish a classification of goods and services, for convenience of Patent and Trademark Office administration, but not to limit or extend the applicant's or registrant's rights. The applicant may apply to register a mark for any or all of the goods and services on or in connection with which he or she is using or has a bona fide intention to use the mark in commerce: *Provided*, That if the Director by regulation permits the filing of an application for the registration of a mark for goods or services which fall within a plurality of classes, a fee equaling the sum of the fees for filing an application in each class shall be paid, and the Director may issue a single certificate of registration for such mark.

§ 1114. (§ 32) Remedies; infringement; innocent infringement by printers and publishers

This statute defines infringement of a registered mark as well as some of the federal remedies available to the owner of a registered or unregistered mark that has been infringed. Additional remedies are outlined in § 1117. In addition, the statute explains when printer and publisher of infringing material may escape liability.

(1) Any person who shall, without the consent of the registrant—
   (a) use in commerce any reproduction, counterfeit, copy, or colorable imitation of a registered mark in connection with the sale, offering for sale, distribution, or advertising of any goods or services on or in connection with which such use is likely to cause confusion, or to cause mistake, or to deceive; or
   (b) reproduce, counterfeit, copy, or colorably imitate a registered mark and apply such reproduction, counterfeit, copy, or colorable imitation to labels, signs, prints, packages, wrappers, receptacles or advertisements intended to be used in commerce upon or in connection with the sale, offering for sale, distribution, or advertising of goods or services on or in connection with which such use is likely to cause confusion, or to cause mistake, or to deceive
   shall be liable in a civil action by the registrant for the remedies hereinafter provided. Under subsection (b) of this section, the registrant shall not be entitled to recover profits or damages unless the acts have been committed with knowledge that such imitation is intended to be used to cause confusion, or to cause mistake, or to deceive. As used in this subsection, the term "any person" includes any State, any instrumen-

tality of a State, and any officer or employee of a State or instrumentality of a State acting in his or her official capacity. Any State, and any such instrumentality, officer, or employee, shall be subject to the provisions of this Act in the same manner and to the same extent as any nongovernmental entity.

(2) Notwithstanding any other provision of this chapter, the remedies given to the owner of a right infringed under this chapter or to a person bringing an action under section 1125(a) of this title shall be limited as follows:

(a) Where an infringer or violator is engaged solely in the business of printing the mark or violating matter for others and establishes that he or she was an innocent infringer or innocent violator, the owner of the right infringed or person bringing the action under section 1125(a) of this title shall be entitled as against such infringer or violator only to an injunction against future printing.

(b) Where the infringement or violation complained of is contained in or is part of paid advertising matter in a newspaper, magazine, or other similar periodical or in an electronic communication as defined in section 2510(12) of Title 18, the remedies of the owner of the right infringed or person bringing the action under section 1125(a) of this title as against the publisher or distributor of such newspaper, magazine, or other similar periodical or electronic communication shall be limited to an injunction against the presentation of such advertising matter in future issues of such newspapers, magazines, or other similar periodicals or in future transmissions of such electronic communications. The limitations of this subparagraph shall apply only to innocent infringers and innocent violators.

(c) Injunctive relief shall not be available to the owner of the right infringed or person bringing the action under section 1125(a) of this title with respect to an issue of a newspaper, magazine, or other similar periodical or an electronic communication containing infringing matter or violating matter where restraining the dissemination of such infringing matter or violating matter in any particular issue of such periodical or in an electronic communication would delay the delivery of such issue of transmission of such electronic communication after the regular time for such delivery or transmission, and such delay would be due to the method by which publication and distribution of such periodical or transmission of such electronic communication is customarily conducted in accordance with sound business practice, and not due to any method or device adopted to evade this section or to prevent or delay the issuance of an injunction or restraining order with respect to such infringing matter or violating matter.

(d) (i) (I) A domain name registrar, a domain name registry, or other domain name registration authority that takes any action described under clause (ii) affecting a domain name shall not be liable for monetary relief or, except as provided in subclause (II), for injunctive relief, to any person for such action, regardless of whether the domain name is finally determined to infringe or dilute the mark.

(II) A domain name registrar, domain name registry, or other domain name registration authority described in subclause (I) may be subject to injunctive relief only if such registrar, registry, or other registration authority has—

(aa) not expeditiously deposited with a court, in which an action has been filed regarding the disposition of the domain name, documents sufficient for the court to establish the court's control and authority regarding the disposition of the registration and use of the domain name;

   (bb) transferred, suspended, or otherwise modified the domain name during the pendency of the action, except upon order of the court; or

   (cc) willfully failed to comply with any such court order.

  (ii) An action referred to under clause (i)(I) is any action of refusing to register, removing from registration, transferring, temporarily disabling, or permanently canceling a domain name—

   (I) in compliance with a court order under section 43(d) [<=5> 15 USCS @ 1125(d)]; or

   (II) in the implementation of a reasonable policy by such registrar, registry, or authority prohibiting the registration of a domain name that is identical to, confusingly similar to, or dilutive of another's mark.

  (iii) A domain name registrar, a domain name registry, or other domain name registration authority shall not be liable for damages under this section for the registration or maintenance of a domain name for another absent a showing of bad faith intent to profit from such registration or maintenance of the domain name.

  (iv) If a registrar, registry, or other registration authority takes an action described under clause (ii) based on a knowing and material misrepresentation by any other person that a domain name is identical to, confusingly similar to, or dilutive of a mark, the person making the knowing and material misrepresentation shall be liable for any damages, including costs and attorney's fees, incurred by the domain name registrant as a result of such action. The court may also grant injunctive relief to the domain name registrant, including the reactivation of the domain name or the transfer of the domain name to the domain name registrant.

  (v) A domain name registrant whose domain name has been suspended, disabled, or transferred under a policy described under clause (ii)(II) may, upon notice to the mark owner, file a civil action to establish that the registration or use of the domain name by such registrant is not unlawful under this Act. The court may grant injunctive relief to the domain name registrant, including the reactivation of the domain name or transfer of the domain name to the domain name registrant.

 (e) As used in this paragraph—

  (i) the term "violator" means a person who violates section 1125(a) of this title; and

  (ii) the term "violating matter" means matter that is the subject of a violation under section 1125(a) of this title.

§ 1115. (§ 33) Registration on principal register as evidence of exclusive right to use mark; defenses

This statute provides that placement of a mark on the principal register creates a presumption that the mark is valid and that the mark's owner has a national exclusive right to use it. It also identifies possible defenses to a claim by the mark's owner that the mark is incontestable and that the registration is therefore conclusive evidence of the mark's validity.

(a) Evidentiary value; defenses

Any registration issued under the Act of March 3, 1881, or the Act of February 20, 1905, or of a mark registered on the principal register provided by this chapter and owned by a party to an action shall be admissible in evidence and shall be prima facie evidence of the validity of the registered mark and of the registration of the mark, of the registrant's ownership of the mark, and of the registrant's exclusive right to use the registered mark in commerce on or in connection with the goods or services specified in the registration subject to any conditions or limitations stated therein, but shall not preclude another person from proving any legal or equitable defense or defect, including those set forth in subsection (b) of this section, which might have been asserted if such mark had not been registered.

(b) Incontestability defenses

To the extent that the right to use the registered mark has become incontestable under section 1065 of this title, the registration shall be conclusive evidence of the validity of the registered mark and of the registration of the mark, of the registrant's ownership of the mark, and of the registrant's exclusive right to use the registered mark in commerce. Such conclusive evidence shall relate to the exclusive right to use the mark on or in connection with the goods or services specified in the affidavit filed under the provisions of section 1065 of this title, or in the renewal application filed under the provisions of section 1059 of this title if the goods or services specified in the renewal are fewer in number, subject to any conditions or limitations in the registration or in such affidavit or renewal application. Such conclusive evidence of the right to use the registered mark shall be subject to proof of infringement as defined in section 1114 of this title, and shall be subject to the following defenses or defects:

(1) That the registration or the incontestable right to use the mark was obtained fraudulently; or

(2) That the mark has been abandoned by the registrant; or

(3) That the registered mark is being used, by or with the permission of the registrant or a person in privity with the registrant, so as to misrepresent the source of the goods or services on or in connection with which the mark is used; or

(4) That the use of the name, term, or device charged to be an infringement is a use, otherwise than as a mark, of the party's individual name in his own business, or of the individual name of anyone in privity with such party, or of a term or device which is descriptive of and used fairly and in good faith only to describe the goods or services of such party, or their geographic origin; or

(5) That the mark whose use by a party is charged as an infringement was adopted without knowledge of the registrant's prior use and has been continuously used by such party or those in privity with him from a date prior to (A) the date of the constructive use of the mark established pursuant to section 1057(c) of this title, (B) the registration of the mark under this Act if the application for registration is filed before the effective date of the Trademark Law Revision Act of 1988, or (C) publication of the registered mark under subsection (c) of section 1062 of this title: *Provided, however,* That this defense or defect shall apply only for the area in which such continuous prior use is proved; or

(6) That the mark whose use is charged as an infringement was registered and used prior to the registration under this chapter or publication under subsection (c) of section 1062 of this title of the registered mark of the registrant, and not abandoned: *Provided, however,* That this defense or defect shall apply only for the area in which the mark was used prior to such registration or such publication of the registrant's mark; or

(7) That the mark has been or is being used to violate the antitrust laws of the United States; or

(8) That the mark is functional; or

(9) That equitable principles, including laches, estoppel, and acquiescence, are applicable.

§ 1117. (§ 35) Recovery for violation of rights

This statute sets out the types of money damages that the owner of a registered or unregistered mark is entitled to recover in a trademark infringement lawsuit and provides for attorney fees to be awarded in exceptional cases.

(a) Profits, damages and costs; attorney fees

When a violation of any right of the registrant of a mark registered in the Patent and Trademark Office, or a violation under section 1125(a) of this title, shall have been established in any civil action arising under this chapter, the plaintiff shall be entitled, subject to the provisions of sections 1111 and 1114 of this title, and subject to the principles of equity, to recover (1) defendant's profits, (2) any damages sustained by the plaintiff, and (3) the costs of the action. The court shall assess such profits and damages or cause the same to be assessed under its direction. In assessing profits the plaintiff shall be required to prove defendant's sales only; defendant must prove all elements of cost or deduction claimed. In assessing damages the court may enter judgment, according to the circumstances of the case, for any sum above the amount found as actual damages, not exceeding three times such amount. If the court shall find that the amount of the recovery based on profits is either inadequate or excessive the court may in its discretion enter judgment for such sum as the court shall find to be just, according to the circumstances of the case. Such sum in either of the above circumstances shall constitute compensation and not a penalty. The court in exceptional cases may award reasonable attorney fees to the prevailing party.

(b) Treble damages for use of counterfeit mark

In assessing damages under subsection (a), the court shall, unless the court finds extenuating circumstances, enter judgment for three times such profits or damages, whichever is greater, together with a reasonable attorney's fee, in the case of any violation of section 1114(1)(a) of this title or section 380 of Title 36 that consists of intentionally using a mark or designation, knowing such mark or designation is a counterfeit mark (as defined in section 1116(d) of this title), in connection with the sale, offering for sale, or distribution of goods or services. In such cases, the court may in its discretion award prejudgment interest on such amount at an annual interest rate established under section 6621 of Title 26, commencing on the date of the service of the claimant's pleadings setting forth the claim for such entry and ending on the date such entry is made, or for such shorter time as the court deems appropriate.

(c) Statutory damages for use of counterfeit

In a case involving the use of a counterfeit mark (as defined in section 1116(d)) in connection with the sale, offering for sale, or distribution of goods or services, the plaintiff may elect, at any time before final judgment is rendered by the trial court, to recover, instead of actual damages and profits under subsection (a), an award of statutory damages for any such use in connection with the sale, offering for sale, or distribution of goods or services in the amount of—

(1) not less than $ 500 or more than $ 100,000 per counterfeit mark per type of goods or services sold, offered for sale, or distributed, as the court considers just; or

(2) if the court finds that the use of the counterfeit mark was willful, not more than $ 1,000,000 per counterfeit mark per type of goods or services sold, offered for sale, or distributed, as the court considers just.

(d) Statutory damages for cybersquatting

In a case involving a violation of section 1125(d)(1), the plaintiff may elect, at any time before final judgment is rendered by the trial court, to recover, instead of actual damages and profits, an award of statutory damages in the amount of not less than $ 1,000 and not more than $ 100,000 per domain name, as the court considers just.

§1118. (§ 36) Destruction of infringing articles

This statute authorizes the destruction of goods that carry a trademark which has been found by a court to be infringing on another mark.

In any action arising under this chapter, in which a violation of any right of the registrant of a mark registered in the Patent and Trademark Office, or a violation under section 1125(a) of this title, shall have been established, the court may order that all labels, signs, prints, packages, wrappers, receptacles, and advertisements in the possession of the defendant, bearing the registered mark or, in the case of a violation of section 1125(a) of this title, the word, term, name, symbol, device, combination thereof, designation, description, or representation that is the subject of the violation, or any reproduction, counterfeit, copy, or colorable imitation thereof, and all plates, molds, matrices, and other means of making the same, shall be delivered up and destroyed. The party seeking an order under this section for destruction of articles seized under section 1116(d) of this title shall give ten days' notice to the United States attorney for the judicial district in which such order is sought (unless good cause is shown for lesser notice) and such United States attorney may, if such destruction may affect evidence of an offense against the United States, seek a hearing on such destruction or participate in any hearing otherwise to be held with respect to such destruction.

§ 1125. (§ 43) False designations of origin and false descriptions forbidden

This statute authorizes a trademark owner to obtain damages in a federal court lawsuit for infringement of an unregistered mark and other activities such as dilution, false advertising and palming off which are all commonly considered to be unfair competition.

(a) (1) Any person who, on or in connection with any goods or services, or any container for goods, uses in commerce any word, term, name, symbol, or device, or any combination thereof, or any false designation of origin, false or misleading description of fact, or false or misleading representation of fact, which—

(A) is likely to cause confusion, or to cause mistake, or to deceive as to the affiliation, connection, or association of such person with another person, or as to the origin, sponsorship, or approval of his or her goods, services, or commercial activities by another person, or

(B) in commercial advertising or promotion, misrepresents the nature, characteristics, qualities, or geographic origin of his or her or another person's goods, services, or commercial activities,

shall be liable in a civil action by any person who believes that he or she is or is likely to be damaged by such act.

(2) As used in this subsection, the term "any person" includes any State, instrumentality of a State or employee of a State or instrumentality of a State acting in his or her official capacity. Any State, and any such instrumentality, officer, or employee, shall be subject to the provisions of this chapter in the same manner and to the same extent as any nongovernmental entity.

(b) Any goods marked or labeled in contravention of the provisions of this section shall not be imported into the United States or admitted to entry at any customhouse of the United States. The owner, importer, or consignee of goods refused entry at any customhouse under this section may have any recourse by protest or appeal that is given under the customs revenue laws or may have the remedy given by this chapter in cases involving goods refused entry or seized.

(c) (1) The owner of a famous mark shall be entitled, subject to the principles of equity and upon such terms as the court deems reasonable, to an injunction against another person's commercial use in commerce of a mark or trade name, if such use begins after the mark has become famous and causes dilution of the distinctive quality of the mark, and to obtain such other relief as is provided in this subsection. In determining whether a mark is distinctive and famous, a court may consider factors such as, but not limited to—

- (A) the degree of inherent or acquired distinctiveness of the mark;
- (B) the duration and extent of use of the mark in connection with the goods or services with which the mark is used;
- (C) the duration and extent of advertising and publicity of the mark;
- (D) the geographical extent of the trading area in which the mark is used;
- (E) the channels of trade for the goods or services with which the mark is used;
- (F) the degree of recognition of the mark in the trading areas and channels of trade used by the mark's owner and the person against whom the injunction is sought;
- (G) the nature and extent of use of the same or similar marks by third parties; and
- (H) whether the mark was registered under the Act of March 3, 1881, or the Act of February 20, 1905, or on the principal register.

(2) In an action brought under this subsection, the owner of the famous mark shall be entitled only to injunctive relief unless the person against whom the injunction is sought willfully intended to trade on the owner's reputation or to cause dilution of the famous mark. If such willful intent is proven, the owner of the famous mark shall also be entitled to the remedies set forth in sections 35(a) and 36, subject to the discretion of the court and the principles of equity.

(3) The ownership by a person of a valid registration under the Act of March 3, 1881, or the Act of February 20, 1905, or on the principal register shall be a complete bar to an action against that person, with respect to that mark, that is brought by another person under the common law or a statute of a State and that seeks to prevent dilution of the distinctiveness of a mark, label, or form of advertisement.

(4) The following shall not be actionable under this section:
- (A) Fair use of a famous mark by another person in comparative commercial advertising or promotion to identify the competing goods or services of the owner of the famous mark.
- (B) Noncommercial use of a mark.
- (C) All forms of news reporting and news commentary.

(d) Cyberpiracy prevention.

(1) (A) A person shall be liable in a civil action by the owner of a mark, including a personal name which is protected as a mark under this section, if, without regard to the goods or services of the parties, that person—
- (i) has a bad faith intent to profit from that mark, including a personal name which is protected as a mark under this section; and
- (ii) registers, traffics in, or uses a domain name that—
  - (I) in the case of a mark that is distinctive at the time of registration of the domain name, is identical or confusingly similar to that mark;
  - (II) in the case of a famous mark that is famous at the time of registration of the domain name, is identical or confusingly similar to or dilutive of that mark; or
  - (III) is a trademark, word, or name protected by reason of section 706 of title <=3> 18, United States Code, or section 220506 of title 36, United States Code.

(B) (i) In determining whether a person has a bad faith intent described under subparagraph (A), a court may consider factors such as, but not limited to—

(I) the trademark or other intellectual property rights of the person, if any, in the domain name;

(II) the extent to which the domain name consists of the legal name of the person or a name that is otherwise commonly used to identify that person;

(III) the person's prior use, if any, of the domain name in connection with the bona fide offering of any goods or services;

(IV) the person's bona fide noncommercial or fair use of the mark in a site accessible under the domain name;

(V) the person's intent to divert consumers from the mark owner's online location to a site accessible under the domain name that could harm the goodwill represented by the mark, either for commercial gain or with the intent to tarnish or disparage the mark, by creating a likelihood of confusion as to the source, sponsorship, affiliation, or endorsement of the site;

(VI) the person's offer to transfer, sell, or otherwise assign the domain name to the mark owner or any third party for financial gain without having used, or having an intent to use, the domain name in the bona fide offering of any goods or services, or the person's prior conduct indicating a pattern of such conduct;

(VII) the person's provision of material and misleading false contact information when applying for the registration of the domain name, the person's intentional failure to maintain accurate contact information, or the person's prior conduct indicating a pattern of such conduct;

(VIII) the person's registration or acquisition of multiple domain names which the person knows are identical or confusingly similar to marks of others that are distinctive at the time of registration of such domain names, or dilutive of famous marks of others that are famous at the time of registration of such domain names, without regard to the goods or services of the parties; and

(IX) the extent to which the mark incorporated in the person's domain name registration is or is not distinctive and famous within the meaning of subsection (c)(1) of section 43 [subsec. (c)(1) of this section].

(ii) Bad faith intent described under subparagraph (A) shall not be found in any case in which the court determines that the person believed and had reasonable grounds to believe that the use of the domain name was a fair use or otherwise lawful.

(C) In any civil action involving the registration, trafficking, or use of a domain name under this paragraph, a court may order the forfeiture or cancellation of the domain name or the transfer of the domain name to the owner of the mark.

(D) A person shall be liable for using a domain name under subparagraph (A) only if that person is the domain name registrant or that registrant's authorized licensee.

(E) As used in this paragraph, the term "traffics in" refers to transactions that include, but are not limited to, sales, purchases, loans, pledges, licenses, exchanges of currency, and any other transfer for consideration or receipt in exchange for consideration.

(2) (A) The owner of a mark may file an in rem civil action against a domain name in the judicial district in which the domain name registrar, domain name registry, or other domain name authority that registered or assigned the domain name is located if—

(i) the domain name violates any right of the owner of a mark registered in the Patent and Trademark Office, or protected under subsection (a) or (c); and

(ii) the court finds that the owner—

(I) is not able to obtain in personam jurisdiction over a person who would have been a defendant in a civil action under paragraph (1); or

(II) through due diligence was not able to find a person who would have been a defendant in a civil action under paragraph (1) by—

(aa) sending a notice of the alleged violation and intent to proceed under this paragraph to the registrant of the domain name at the postal and email address provided by the registrant to the registrar; and

(bb) publishing notice of the action as the court may direct promptly after filing the action.

(B) The actions under subparagraph (A)(ii) shall constitute service of process.

(C) In an in rem action under this paragraph, a domain name shall be deemed to have its situs in the judicial district in which—

(i) the domain name registrar, registry, or other domain name authority that registered or assigned the domain name is located; or

(ii) documents sufficient to establish control and authority regarding the disposition of the registration and use of the domain name are deposited with the court.

(D) (i) The remedies in an in rem action under this paragraph shall be limited to a court order for the forfeiture or cancellation of the domain name or the transfer of the domain name to the owner of the mark. Upon receipt of written notification of a filed, stamped copy of a complaint filed by the owner of a mark in a United States district court under this paragraph, the domain name registrar, domain name registry, or other domain name authority shall—

(I) expeditiously deposit with the court documents sufficient to establish the court's control and authority regarding the disposition of the registration and use of the domain name to the court; and

(II) not transfer, suspend, or otherwise modify the domain name during the pendency of the action, except upon order of the court.

(ii) The domain name registrar or registry or other domain name authority shall not be liable for injunctive or monetary relief under this paragraph except in the case of bad faith or reckless disregard, which includes a willful failure to comply with any such court order.

(3) The civil action established under paragraph (1) and the in rem action established under paragraph (2), and any remedy available under either such action, shall be in addition to any other civil action or remedy otherwise applicable.

(4) The in rem jurisdiction established under paragraph (2) shall be in addition to any other jurisdiction that otherwise exists, whether in rem or in personam.

Statutes

§ 1127. (§ 45) Construction and definitions; intent of chapter

This statute provides definitions of certain terms used throughout the Lanham Act.

In the construction of this chapter, unless the contrary is plainly apparent from the context—

The United States includes and embraces all territory which is under its jurisdiction and control.

The word "commerce" means all commerce which may lawfully be regulated by Congress.

The term "principal register" refers to the register provided for by sections 1051 to 1072 of this title, and the term "supplemental register" refers to the register provided for by sections 1091 to 1096 of this title.

The term "person" and any other word or term used to designate the applicant or other entitled to a benefit or privilege or rendered liable under the provisions of this chapter includes a juristic person as well as a natural person. The term "juristic person" includes a firm, corporation, union, association, or other organization capable of suing and being sued in a court of law. The term "person" also includes any State, any instrumentality of a State, and any officer or employee of a State or instrumentality of a State acting in his or her official capacity. Any State, and any such instrumentality, officer, or employee, shall be subject to the provisions of this Act in the same manner and to the same extent as any nongovernmental entity.

The terms "applicant" and "registrant" embrace the legal representatives, predecessors, successors and assigns of such applicant or registrant.

The term "Director" means the Director of Patents and Trademarks.

The term "related company" means any person whose use of a mark is controlled by the owner of the mark with respect to the nature and quality of the goods or services on or in connection with which the mark is used.

The terms "trade name" and "commercial name" mean any name used by a person to identify his or her business or vocation.

The term "trademark" includes any word, name, symbol, or device, or any combination thereof—

(1) used by a person, or

(2) which a person has a bona fide intention to use in commerce and applies to register on the principal register established by this chapter,

to identify and distinguish his or her goods, including a unique product, from those manufactured or sold by others and to indicate the source or the goods, even if that source is unknown. The term "service mark" means any word, name, symbol, or device, or any combination thereof—

(1) used by a person, or

(2) which a person has a bona fide intention to use in commerce and applies to register on the principal register established by this chapter,

to identify and distinguish the services of one person, including a unique service, from the services of others and to indicate the source of the services, even if that source is unknown. Titles, character names, and other distinctive features of radio or television programs may be registered as service marks notwithstanding that they, or the programs, may advertise the goods of the sponsor.

The term "certification mark" means any word, name, symbol, or device, or any combination thereof—

(1) used by a person other than its owner, or

(2) which its owner has a bona fide intention to permit a person other than the owner to use in commerce and files an application to register on the principal register established by this chapter,

to certify regional or other origin, material, mode of manufacture, quality, accuracy, or other characteristics of such person's goods or services or that the work or labor on the goods or services was performed by members of a union or other organization.

The term "collective mark" means a trademark or service mark—

(1) used by the members of a cooperative, an association, or other collective group or organization, or

(2) which such cooperative, association, or other collective group or organization has a bona fide intention to use in commerce and applies to register on the principal register established by this chapter, and includes marks indicating membership in a union, an association, or other organization.

The term "mark" includes any trademark, service mark, collective mark, or certification mark.

The term "use in commerce" means the bona fide use of a mark in the ordinary course of trade, and not made merely to reserve a right in a mark. For purposes of this chapter, a mark shall be deemed to be in use in commerce—

(1) on goods when—

(A) it is placed in any manner on the goods or their containers or the displays associated therewith or on the tags or labels affixed thereto, or if the nature of the goods makes such placement impracticable, then on documents associated with the goods or their sale, and

(B) the goods are sold or transported in commerce, and

(2) on services when it is used or displayed in the sale or advertising of services and the services are rendered in commerce, or the services are rendered in more than one State or in the United States and a foreign country and the person rendering the services is engaged in commerce in connection with the services.

A mark shall be deemed to be "abandoned" when either of the following occurs:

(1) When its use has been discontinued with intent not to resume such use. Intent not to resume may be inferred from circumstances. Nonuse for three consecutive years shall be prima facie evidence of abandonment. "Use" of a mark means the bona fide use of that mark made in the ordinary course of trade, and not made merely to reserve a right in a mark.

(2) When any course of conduct of the owner, including acts of omission as well as commission, causes the mark to become the generic name for the goods or services on or in connection with which it is used or otherwise to lose its significance as a mark. Purchaser motivation shall not be a test for determining abandonment under this paragraph.

The term "dilution" means the lessening of the capacity of a famous mark to identify and distinguish goods or services, regardless of the presence or absence of—

(1) competition between the owner of the famous mark and other parties, or

(2) likelihood of confusion, mistake, or deception.

The term "colorable imitation" includes any mark which so resembles a registered mark as to be likely to cause confusion or mistake or to deceive.

The term "registered mark" means a mark registered in the United States Patent and Trademark Office under this chapter or under the Act of March 3, 1881, or the Act of February 20, 1905, or the Act of March 19, 1920. The phrase "marks registered in the Patent and Trademark Office" means registered marks.

The term "Act of March 3, 1881," "Act of February 20, 1905," or "Act of March 19, 1920," means the respective Act as amended.

A "counterfeit" is a spurious mark which is identical with, or substantially indistinguishable from, a registered mark.

The term "domain name" means any alphanumeric designation which is registered with or assigned by any domain name registrar, domain name registry, or other domain name registration authority as part of an electronic address on the Internet.

The term "Internet" has the meaning given that term in section 230(f)(1) of the Communications Act of 1934.

Words used in the singular include the plural and vice versa.

The intent of this chapter is to regulate commerce within the control of Congress by making actionable the deceptive and misleading use of marks in such commerce; to protect registered marks used in such commerce from interference by State, or territorial legislation; to protect persons engaged in such commerce against unfair competition; to prevent fraud and deception in such commerce by the use of reproductions, copies, counterfeits, or colorable imitations of registered marks; and to provide rights and remedies stipulated by treaties and conventions respecting trademarks, trade names, and unfair competition entered into between the United States and foreign nations.

●

CATALOG

...more from nolo

		PRICE	CODE

BUSINESS

		PRICE	CODE
	Avoid Employee Lawsuits (Quick & Legal Series)	$24.95	AVEL
⊙	The CA Nonprofit Corporation Kit (Binder w/CD-ROM)	$49.95	CNP
▣	Consultant & Independent Contractor Agreements (Book w/Disk—PC)	$24.95	CICA
▣	The Corporate Minutes Book (Book w/Disk—PC)	$69.95	CORMI
	The Employer's Legal Handbook	$39.95	EMPL
	Firing Without Fear (Quick & Legal Series)	$29.95	FEAR
▣	Form Your Own Limited Liability Company (Book w/Disk—PC)	$44.95	LIAB
▣	Hiring Independent Contractors: The Employer's Legal Guide (Book w/Disk—PC)	$34.95	HICI
▣	How to Create a Buy-Sell Agreement & Control the Destiny of your Small Business (Book w/Disk—PC)	$49.95	BSAG
▣	How to Form a California Professional Corporation (Book w/Disk—PC)	$49.95	PROF
▣	How to Form a Nonprofit Corporation (Book w/Disk —PC)—National Edition	$44.95	NNP
⊙	How to Form a Nonprofit Corporation in California (Book w/CD-ROM)	$44.95	NON
▣	How to Form Your Own California Corporation (Binder w/Disk—PC)	$39.95	CACI
▣	How to Form Your Own California Corporation (Book w/Disk—PC)	$39.95	CCOR
▣	How to Form Your Own New York Corporation (Book w/Disk—PC)	$39.95	NYCO
⊙	How to Form Your Own Texas Corporation (Book w/CD-ROM)	$39.95	TCOR
	How to Write a Business Plan	$29.95	SBS
	The Independent Paralegal's Handbook	$29.95	PARA
	Leasing Space for Your Small Business	$34.95	LESP
	Legal Guide for Starting & Running a Small Business, Vol. 1	$29.95	RUNS
▣	Legal Guide for Starting & Running a Small Business, Vol. 2: Legal Forms (Book w/Disk—PC)	$29.95	RUNS2
	Marketing Without Advertising	$22.00	MWAD
▣	Music Law (Book w/Disk—PC)	$29.95	ML
	Nolo's California Quick Corp (Quick & Legal Series)	$19.95	QINC
	Nolo's Guide to Social Security Disability	$29.95	QSS
	Nolo's Quick LLC (Quick & Legal Series)	$24.95	LLCQ
⊙	Open Your California Business in 24 Hours (Book w/CD-ROM)	$24.95	OPEN
▣	The Partnership Book: How to Write a Partnership Agreement (Book w/Disk—PC)	$39.95	PART
	Sexual Harassment on the Job	$24.95	HARS
	Starting & Running a Successful Newsletter or Magazine	$29.95	MAG
	Tax Savvy for Small Business	$34.95	SAVVY
	Wage Slave No More: Law & Taxes for the Self-Employed	$24.95	WAGE
▣	Your Limited Liability Company: An Operating Manual (Book w/Disk—PC)	$49.95	LOP
	Your Rights in the Workplace	$29.95	YRW

CONSUMER

	PRICE	CODE
Fed Up with the Legal System: What's Wrong & How to Fix It	$9.95	LEG
How to Win Your Personal Injury Claim	$29.95	PICL
Nolo's Everyday Law Book	$24.95	EVL
Nolo's Pocket Guide to California Law	$15.95	CLAW
Trouble-Free Travel...And What to Do When Things Go Wrong	$14.95	TRAV

ESTATE PLANNING & PROBATE

	PRICE	CODE
8 Ways to Avoid Probate (Quick & Legal Series)	$16.95	PRO8
9 Ways to Avoid Estate Taxes (Quick & Legal Series)	$24.95	ESTX
Estate Planning Basics (Quick & Legal Series)	$18.95	ESPN
How to Probate an Estate in California	$39.95	PAE

▣ Book with disk   ⊙ Book with CD-ROM

	PRICE	CODE
...ur Own Living Trust (Book w/CD-ROM)	$34.95	LITR
...w Form Kit: Wills	$24.95	KWL
...ll Book (Book w/Disk—PC)	$34.95	SWIL
...lan Your Estate	$39.95	NEST
Quick & Legal Will Book (Quick & Legal Series)	$21.95	QUIC

FAMILY MATTERS

	PRICE	CODE
Child Custody: Building Parenting Agreements That Work	$29.95	CUST
Child Support in California: Go to Court to Get More or Pay Less (Quick & Legal Series)	$24.95	CHLD
The Complete IEP Guide	$24.95	IEP
Divorce & Money: How to Make the Best Financial Decisions During Divorce	$34.95	DIMO
Do Your Own Divorce in Oregon	$29.95	ODIV
Get a Life: You Don't Need a Million to Retire Well	$24.95	LIFE
The Guardianship Book for California	$34.95	GB
⦿ How to Adopt Your Stepchild in California (Book w/CD-ROM)	$34.95	ADOP
A Legal Guide for Lesbian and Gay Couples	$25.95	LG
⦿ The Living Together Kit (Book w/CD-ROM)	$34.95	LTK
Nolo's Pocket Guide to Family Law	$14.95	FLD
Using Divorce Mediation: Save Your Money & Your Sanity	$21.95	UDMD

GOING TO COURT

	PRICE	CODE
Beat Your Ticket: Go To Court and Win! (National Edition)	$19.95	BEYT
The Criminal Law Handbook: Know Your Rights, Survive the System	$29.95	KYR
Everybody's Guide to Small Claims Court (National Edition)	$18.95	NSCC
Everybody's Guide to Small Claims Court in California	$24.95	CSCC
Fight Your Ticket ... and Win! (California Edition)	$24.95	FYT
How to Change Your Name in California	$34.95	NAME
How to Collect When You Win a Lawsuit (California Edition)	$29.95	JUDG
How to Mediate Your Dispute	$18.95	MEDI
How to Seal Your Juvenile & Criminal Records (California Edition)	$34.95	CRIM
Mad at Your Lawyer	$21.95	MAD
Nolo's Deposition Handbook	$29.95	DEP
Represent Yourself in Court: How to Prepare & Try a Winning Case	$29.95	RYC

HOMEOWNERS, LANDLORDS & TENANTS

	PRICE	CODE
California Tenants' Rights	$24.95	CTEN
▣ Contractors' and Homeowners' Guide to Mechanics' Liens (Book w/Disk—PC)—California Edition	$39.95	MIEN
The Deeds Book (California Edition)	$24.95	DEED
Dog Law	$14.95	DOG
⦿ Every Landlord's Legal Guide (National Edition, Book w/CD-ROM)	$44.95	ELLI
Every Tenant's Legal Guide	$26.95	EVTEN
For Sale by Owner in California	$29.95	FSBO
How to Buy a House in California	$29.95	BHCA
The Landlord's Law Book, Vol. 1: Rights & Responsibilities (California Edition)	$44.95	LBRT
⦿ The California Landlord's Law Book, Vol. 2: Evictions (Book w/CD-ROM)	$44.95	LBEV
Leases & Rental Agreements (Quick & Legal Series)	$24.95	LEAR
Neighbor Law: Fences, Trees, Boundaries & Noise	$24.95	NEI
⦿ The New York Landlord's Law Book (Book w/CD-ROM)	$39.95	NYLL
Renters' Rights (National Edition—Quick & Legal Series)	$19.95	RENT
Stop Foreclosure Now in California	$34.95	CLOS

HUMOR

	PRICE	CODE
29 Reasons Not to Go to Law School	$12.95	29R
Poetic Justice	$9.95	PJ

IMMIGRATION

	PRICE	CODE
How to Get a Green Card	$29.95	GRN
U.S. Immigration Made Easy	$44.95	IMEZ

▣ Book with disk　　⦿ Book with CD-ROM

	PRICE	CODE

MONEY MATTERS

	Title	Price	Code
▣	101 Law Forms for Personal Use (Quick & Legal Series, Book w/Disk—PC)	$29.95	SPOT
	Bankruptcy: Is It the Right Solution to Your Debt Problems? (Quick & Legal Series)	$19.95	BRS
	Chapter 13 Bankruptcy: Repay Your Debts	$29.95	CH13
▣	Credit Repair (Quick & Legal Series, Book w/Disk—PC)	$18.95	CREP
▣	The Financial Power of Attorney Workbook (Book w/Disk—PC)	$29.95	FINPOA
	How to File for Chapter 7 Bankruptcy	$29.95	HFB
	IRAs, 401(k)s & Other Retirement Plans: Taking Your Money Out	$24.95	RET
	Money Troubles: Legal Strategies to Cope With Your Debts	$24.95	MT
	Nolo's Law Form Kit: Personal Bankruptcy	$16.95	KBNK
	Stand Up to the IRS	$29.95	SIRS
	Surviving an IRS Tax Audit (Quick & Legal Series)	$24.95	SAUD
	Take Control of Your Student Loan Debt	$24.95	SLOAN

PATENTS AND COPYRIGHTS

	Title	Price	Code
◉	The Copyright Handbook: How to Protect and Use Written Works (Book w/CD-ROM)	$34.95	COHA
	Copyright Your Software	$24.95	CYS
	Domain Names	$24.95	DOM
▣	Getting Permission: How to License and Clear Copyrighted Materials Online and Off (Book w/Disk—PC)	$34.95	RIPER
	How to Make Patent Drawings Yourself	$29.95	DRAW
	The Inventor's Notebook	$34.95	INOT
	Nolo's Patents for Beginners (Quick & Legal Series)	$29.95	QPAT
▣	License Your Invention (Book w/Disk—PC)	$39.95	LICE
	Patent, Copyright & Trademark	$29.95	PCTM
	Patent It Yourself	$49.95	PAT
	Patent Searching Made Easy	$29.95	PATSE
	The Public Domain	$34.95	PUBL
◉	Software Development: A Legal Guide (Book w/ CD-ROM)	$44.95	SFT
	Trademark: Legal Care for Your Business and Product Name	$39.95	TRD
	The Trademark Registration Kit (Quick & Legal Series)	$19.95	TREG

RESEARCH & REFERENCE

Title	Price	Code
Legal Research: How to Find & Understand the Law	$34.95	LRES

SENIORS

Title	Price	Code
Beat the Nursing Home Trap: A Consumer's Guide to Assisted Living and Long-Term Care	$21.95	ELD
The Conservatorship Book for California	$44.95	CNSV
Social Security, Medicare & Pensions	$24.95	SOA

SOFTWARE

Call or check our website at www.nolo.comfor special discounts on Software!

	Title	Price	Code
◉	LeaseWriter CD—Windows/Macintosh	$129.95	LWD1
◉	Living Trust Maker CD—Windows/Macintosh	$89.95	LTD3
◉	LLC Maker—Windows	$89.95	LLPC
◉	Patent It Yourself CD—Windows	$229.95	PPC12
◉	Personal RecordKeeper 5.0 CD—Windows/Macintosh	$59.95	RKD5
◉	Small Business Pro 4 CD—Windows/Macintosh	$89.95	SBCD4
◉	WillMaker 8.0 CD—Windows	$69.95	WP8

▣ Book with disk   ◉ Book with CD-ROM

Order Form

Name

Address

City

State, Zip

Daytime Phone

E-mail

Item Code	Quantity	Item	Unit Price	Total Price

Method of payment

☐ Check ☐ VISA ☐ MasterCard
☐ Discover Card ☐ American Express

Subtotal	
Add your local sales tax (California only)	
Shipping: RUSH $8, Basic $3.95 (See below)	
"I bought 3, Ship it to me FREE!"(Ground shipping only)	
TOTAL	

Account Number

Expiration Date

Signature

Shipping and Handling

Rush Delivery-Only $8

We'll ship any order to any street address in the U.S. by UPS 2nd Day Air* for only $8!

* Order by noon Pacific Time and get your order in 2 business days. Orders placed after noon Pacific Time will arrive in 3 business days. P.O. boxes and S.F. Bay Area use basic shipping. Alaska and Hawaii use 2nd Day Air or Priority Mail.

Basic Shipping—$3.95

Use for P.O. Boxes, Northern California and Ground Service.

Allow 1-2 weeks for delivery. U.S. addresses only.

For faster service, use your credit card and our toll-free numbers

Order 24 hours a day

Online	www.nolo.com
Phone	1-800-992-6656
Fax	1-800-645-0895
Mail	Nolo.com
	950 Parker St.
	Berkeley, CA 94710

Visit us online at
www.nolo.com

Take 2 minutes & Give us your 2 cents

Your comments make a big difference in the development and revision of Nolo books and software. Please take a few minutes and register your Nolo product—and your comments—with us. Not only will your input make a difference, you'll receive special offers available only to registered owners of Nolo products on our newest books and software. Register now by:

PHONE
1-800-992-6656

FAX
1-800-645-0895

EMAIL
cs@nolo.com

or **MAIL** us
this registration card

REMEMBER:
Little publishers have big ears. We really listen to you.

fold here

REGISTRATION CARD

NAME		DATE	
ADDRESS			
CITY		STATE	ZIP
PHONE		E-MAIL	

WHERE DID YOU HEAR ABOUT THIS PRODUCT?

WHERE DID YOU PURCHASE THIS PRODUCT?

DID YOU CONSULT A LAWYER? (PLEASE CIRCLE ONE)   YES   NO   NOT APPLICABLE

DID YOU FIND THIS BOOK HELPFUL?   (VERY)   5   4   3   2   1   (NOT AT ALL)

COMMENTS

WAS IT EASY TO USE?   (VERY EASY)   5   4   3   2   1   (VERY DIFFICULT)

DO YOU OWN A COMPUTER? IF SO, WHICH FORMAT? (PLEASE CIRCLE ONE)   WINDOWS   DOS   MAC

❑ If you do not wish to receive mailings from these companies, please check this box.

❑ You can quote me in future Nolo.com promotional materials. Daytime phone number _____.

PCTM 4.0

NOLO IN THE NEWS

"Nolo helps lay people perform legal tasks without the aid—or fees—of lawyers."

—USA TODAY

Nolo books are ..."written in plain language, free of legal mumbo jumbo, and spiced with witty personal observations."

—ASSOCIATED PRESS

"...Nolo publications...guide people simply through the how, when, where and why of law."

—WASHINGTON POST

"Increasingly, people who are not lawyers are performing tasks usually regarded as legal work... And consumers, using books like Nolo's, do routine legal work themselves."

—NEW YORK TIMES

"...All of [Nolo's] books are easy-to-understand, are updated regularly, provide pull-out forms...and are often quite moving in their sense of compassion for the struggles of the lay reader."

—SAN FRANCISCO CHRONICLE

fold here

- -

nolo
950 Parker Street
Berkeley, CA 94710-9867

Attn: PCTM 4.0